DISABILITY DISCRIMINATION IN EMPLOYMENT

SPENCER KEEN

RICHARD OULTON

OXFORD
UNIVERSITY PRESS

OXFORD
UNIVERSITY PRESS

Great Clarendon Street, Oxford OX2 6DP
Oxford University Press is a department of the University of Oxford.
It furthers the University's objective of excellence in research, scholarship,
and education by publishing worldwide in

Oxford New York

Auckland Cape Town Dar es Salaam Hong Kong Karachi
Kuala Lumpur Madrid Melbourne Mexico City Nairobi
New Delhi Shanghai Taipei Toronto

With offices in

Argentina Austria Brazil Chile Czech Republic France Greece
Guatemala Hungary Italy Japan Poland Portugal Singapore
South Korea Switzerland Thailand Turkey Ukraine Vietnam

Published in the United States
by Oxford University Press Inc., New York

First published 2009

British Library Cataloguing in Publication Data
Data available

Library of Congress Cataloging in Publication Data
Data available

Typeset by Cepha Imaging Private Ltd, Bangalore, India
Printed by the
MPG Books Group
in the UK

ISBN 978-0-19-923227-7

1 3 5 7 9 10 8 6 4 2

PREFACE

Writing this book has felt a little like trying to catch leaves in the autumn. As the winds of change have continued to gust through this area of the law, it seems as though Spencer and I have been standing under the tree for a very long time indeed.

We are eternally grateful to our families, Joey, Theo and Romey, and Jane and Hattie, for their love, support and endless cups of tea whilst we did so; and to Dennis for leaving the manuscript intact.

We have tried to explain the law as it stood as at 1 January 2009. All future developments will be posted on a regular basis on our website, www.disability-discrimination.com.

Richard Oulton & Spencer Keen
5 Essex Court
Temple
London EC4Y 9AH

CONTENTS

1

INTRODUCTION

A. Introduction

1.01 It is an undeniable fact that disabled people in this country are at a serious disadvantage in the employment field. Although the rate of employment of disabled people has risen from 38 per cent ten years ago to 48 per cent today, a disabled person is still two and a half times more likely to be out of work than a non-disabled person.[1] Those with mental health problems and learning disabilities are particularly badly affected.[2] It is also an undeniable fact that many disabled workers in this country are the victims of discrimination. Disturbingly, statistics show that claims of disability discrimination in employment are on the rise.[3]

[1] See the Government's consultation paper 'Framework for a Fairer Future–The Equality Bill' presented to Parliament in June 2008.

[2] Statistics taken from the UK's Office for National Statistics Labour Force Survey, Sept-Dec 2006, show employment rates of only 21 per cent and 26 per cent respectively for these two categories.

[3] ACAS statistics show an increase in cases of disability discrimination in which it was involved from 3,654 in 2006/2007 to 3,850 in 2007/2008. These figures are significantly higher than cases of race discrimination for the same periods.

1.02 The aim of this book is to provide a detailed explanation of the laws which have been passed in an attempt to prevent such discrimination. In particular, it is intended to be of practical assistance to those dealing with disability-related issues in the workplace on a day-to-day basis, and to those involved in bringing or defending claims of disability discrimination in employment tribunals.

1.03 The law on disability discrimination in employment forms part of a wide framework of laws designed to promote equality in society generally, and it is constantly evolving. This introductory chapter will briefly explain how the law has developed to date, and will consider the impact of EC law which has been of particular significance in the development of equality legislation in this country. Finally, it will consider the Government's proposal to combine all the existing equality laws into one consolidated statute, and assess how this is likely to affect the existing law relating to disability discrimination in employment.

B. Legislative History

1. Disability Discrimination Act 1995

1.04 Discrimination against disabled people in employment was first made unlawful in the UK by Part II of the Disability Discrimination Act 1995 (throughout this book 'the DDA 1995') which came into force on 2 December 1996.[4] At that stage, equality laws outlawing discrimination on the grounds of race or sex had already been in existence for the last 20 years.[5] However, the introduction of a law designed to achieve equality for disabled people required a different approach. Any attempt to provide equality of opportunity in the workplace for disabled people had to confront head-on the fact that a disabled person might well be disadvantaged by his disability. In those circumstances, unlike sex or race, a like-for-like comparison for the purposes of identifying whether there had been any less favourable treatment would clearly have been inappropriate.

1.05 The DDA 1995 attempted to address this difficulty in two ways. First, it introduced a new definition of 'disabled person' in which functionality was the key issue. Disability was to be defined by the extent to which a person's ability to carry out normal day-to-day activities was impaired.[6] Second, the DDA 1995 introduced two innovative measures designed to ensure that disabled people were not disadvantaged

[4] See Disability Discrimination Act 1995 (Commencement No.1) Order SI 1995/3330. There had been previous legislation: The Disabled Persons (Employment) Act 1944, which was designed to integrate disabled servicemen back into employment after the war, but it was only enforceable as a criminal sanction and it proved to be ineffective. There was not a single prosecution under it.

[5] Sex Discrimination Act 1975 and Race Relations Act 1976.

[6] It therefore adopted a medical as opposed to a social model of disability. See Chapter 2.

in the workplace because of their disability: the duty to make reasonable adjustments, and disability-related discrimination.

The duty to make reasonable adjustments imposes a positive duty on employers to make *reasonable adjustments* to their working practices and/or premises in order to eliminate any disadvantages caused to disabled employees as a result of them. A failure to comply with that duty constitutes discrimination.[7] Disability-related discrimination provides that an employer discriminates against a disabled person if he treats him less favourably for a reason *related to* his disability than he treats, or would treat, someone to whom that reason does not or would not apply. This clearly has a wider potential reach than less favourable treatment *on the ground of* disability. Although, unlike the other equality statutes, the DDA 1995 contains no express provisions covering indirect discrimination, the clear intention of Parliament was that this form of discrimination would cover not only situations of direct discrimination but indirect discrimination as well.[8] **1.06**

Since its inception, the DDA 1995 has been subject to a number of major amendments. One unfortunate consequence of this is that its section numbers have changed over the years, and it now has a rather clumsy structure. For example, the meaning of discrimination which was originally contained in s 5 has been renumbered s 3A; and the duty to make reasonable adjustments, which was commonly referred to as a section 6 duty (its original section), has now been renumbered s 4A. Practitioners must be alert to this when reading older cases. The principle amendments are summarised below. **1.07**

2. The Disability Discrimation Act (Amendment) Regulations 2003[9]

The 2003 Regulations were passed in order to ensure that the UK complied with its obligations under a major piece of secondary EC legislation, the Framework Directive for Equal Treatment in Employment and Occupation dated 27 November 2000 ('the Framework Directive').[10] **1.08**

The purpose of the Framework Directive is to lay down a general framework for combating discrimination on the grounds of religion or belief, disability, age or sexual orientation as regards employment and occupation, with a view to putting into effect in the Member States the principle of equal treatment.[11] **1.09**

---

[7] See Chapter 4.

[8] See *Clark v Novacold* [1999] IRLR 318, CA at para 65. However, the scope of this form of discrimination has been dramatically reduced by the decision of the House of Lords in *London Borough of Lewisham v Malcolm* [2008] UKHL 43; [2008] 4 All ER 525. See Chapter 5.

[9] SI 2003/1673. These regulations are referred to throughout this book as the 2003 Regulations.

[10] (2000/78/EC).

[11] Article 1.

1.10 The following provisions of the Framework Directive are of particular importance:

(i) Article 2 provides that the 'principle of equal treatment' shall mean that there shall be no direct or indirect discrimination whatsoever on any of the grounds referred to in Article 1. It goes on to define what is meant by direct and indirect discrimination, and to provide that harassment shall be deemed to be a form of discrimination.

(ii) Article 3 sets out the scope of the Framework Directive, making it clear that it is to apply not just to employees, but also to the self-employed and those in any occupation; vocational training; and membership of organizations of workers or employers.

(iii) Article 5 contains provisions relating to the reasonable accommodation to be provided for persons with disabilities (this translates into the duty to make reasonable adjustments under the DDA 1995).

(iv) Article 10 contains provisions relating to the burden of proof. It requires member states to take such measures as are necessary to ensure that, where claimants establish facts from which it may be presumed that there has been direct or indirect discrimination, it shall be for the respondent to prove that there has been no breach of the principle of equal treatment.

(v) Article 11 contains provisions requiring member states to introduce measures protecting employees against victimization.

1.11 As noted above, the 2003 Regulations were passed in order to comply with the Framework Directive. They came into force on 1 October 2004 and take effect by making, inter alia, the following amendments to the DDA 1995:

(i) A new section prohibiting direct discrimination (s 3A(5));
(ii) New sections defining and prohibiting harassment (s 3B and s 4(3));
(iii) Removal of the defence of justification where an employer has failed to comply with a duty to make reasonable adjustments;
(iv) Removal of the small employer exemption which had applied, thereby extending the protection of the DDA 1995 to all employees;
(v) Extension of the protection afforded by the DDA 1995 to a wide range of workers, not just employees (s 4B–s 15C);
(vi) A new section providing for the burden of proof to be reversed if the complainant has made out a prima facie case of discrimination (s 17A (1C));
(vii) A new section extending the protection of the provisions relating to victimization to those who are not themselves disabled (s 55(5)).

3. Disability Discrimination Act 2005

Further amendments were made by the Disability Discrimination Act 2005 ('DDA 2005'). In particular, new provisions covering discrimination beyond the employment field were added. Amendments relevant to disability discrimination in employment are as follows: **1.12**

(i) The removal of the requirement that an impairment resulting from or consisting of a mental illness could only qualify as a mental impairment, for the purposes of the statutory definition of disability, if the illness was a clinically well-recognised illness;

(ii) A change to the law so that people who have been diagnosed with cancer, HIV infection, or multiple sclerosis are deemed to be disabled from the point of diagnosis;

(iii) The introduction of a new public equality duty imposed on public authorities to take steps to encourage and promote the equal treatment of disabled people.

Public Equality Duty

DDA 1995, s 49A, inserted by DDA 2005, s 3, provides that every public authority, when carrying out its functions, must have regard to: **1.13**

(a) the need to eliminate discrimination that is unlawful under this Act;
(b) the need to eliminate harassment of disabled persons that is related to their disabilities;
(c) the need to promote equality of opportunity between disabled persons and other persons;
(d) the need to take steps to take account of disabled persons' disabilities, even where that involves treating disabled persons more favourably than other persons;
(e) the need to promote positive attitudes towards disabled persons; and
(f) the need to encourage participation by disabled persons in public life.

This general duty is without prejudice to any obligation of a public authority to comply with any other provisions of the DDA 1995.[12] Similar amendments have been made to the SDA 1975 and to the RRA 1976 introducing public equality duties in respect of sex and race discrimination. **1.14**

'Public authority' is defined to include any person, certain of whose functions are functions of a public nature.[13] Thus the expression includes not only core public authorities such as government departments, local authorities, the police and the **1.15**

[12] DDA 1995, s 49A(2).
[13] DDA 1995, s 49B(1)(a).

armed forces, but also private bodies which exercise some functions of a public nature. The extension of the public equality duty to these private bodies reflects the fact that some traditionally governmental tasks, such as the running of prisons, are now commonly undertaken by the private sector. Where a public body exercises both public and non-public functions, it will only be a 'public authority' for the purposes of the public equality duty when it is exercising its public functions.[14]

1.16 The purpose of the public equality duty is to ensure that public authorities are pro-active in promoting equality of opportunity for disabled people and in eliminating unlawful discrimination. To that end, certain public authorities are now required to publish a Disability Equality Scheme, showing how they intend to fulfil their public equality duty, and explaining their methods for assessing the impact of their policies and practices on equality for disabled people.[15]

1.17 A breach of the public equality duty is not actionable by individuals in the tribunal. It may, however, be subject to judicial review. In addition, any such breach may lead to enforcement proceedings instituted by the Commission for Human Rights and Equality.[16]

4. The Equality Act 2006

The Commission for Equality and Human Rights

1.18 The Equality Act 2006 forms part of the government's drive towards a single equality statute. It created a single equality commission called the Commission for Equality and Human Rights ('CEHR') which replaced the Disability Rights Commission ('DRC')[17], the Equal Opportunities Commission ('EOP') and the Commission for Racial Equality ('CRE'), and took over the work of all three. In addition, the CEHR assumed new duties and powers in respect of the new areas of discrimination on the grounds of religion, belief, sexual orientation, and age.

1.19 The general duty of the CEHR is set out in Equality Act 2006, s 3. It is to encourage and support the development of a society in which:

(a) people's ability to achieve their potential is not limited by prejudice or discrimination;
(b) there is respect for and protection of each individual's human rights;
(c) there is respect for the dignity and worth of each individual;
(d) each individual has an equal opportunity to participate in society;

---

14 DDA 1995, s 49B(2). *Aston Cantlow PCC v Wallbank* [2004] 1 AC 546; [2003] 3WLR 283, HL, per Lord Nicholls.

15 See the Disability Discrimination (Public Authorities) (Statutory Duties) Regulations 2005.

16 For the role of the CEHR, see paras 1.18–1.24 below.

17 The DRC has now been dissolved.

(e) there is mutual respect between groups based on an understanding and valuing of diversity and on shared respect for equality and human rights.

A specific duty in relation to disabled people follows in Equality Act 2006, s 8. This provides that, in promoting equality of opportunity between disabled persons and others, the CEHR may, in particular, promote the favourable treatment of disabled persons.[18] **1.20**

Codes of Practice

Equality Act 2006, s 14 provides that the CEHR may issue codes of practice in order to provide guidance on complying with the DDA 1995 and in order to promote equality of opportunity. It has yet to do so. Practitioners should therefore still refer to the code of practice on employment and occupation which was produced by the DRC and which came into effect on 1 October 2004 ('The Code of Practice 2004'). Although the DRC has now been dissolved, due to the transitional provisions of the Equality Act 2006, the Code of Practice 2004 remains in force.[19] **1.21**

The Code of Practice 2004 is an important document for two reasons. First, it provides invaluable guidance for those dealing with disability issues in the workplace. Second, it is admissible in evidence in both civil and criminal proceedings. Although a breach of the Code of Practice 2004 does not of itself give rise to any liability, it shall be taken into account by a court or tribunal in any case in which it appears to the court or tribunal to be relevant.[20] **1.22**

Legal Assistance

The CEHR may assist an individual who is or may become party to legal proceedings if: **1.23**

(a) the proceedings relate or may relate (wholly or partly) to a provision of the equality enactments; and
(b) the individual alleges that he has been the victim of behaviour contrary to a provision of the equality enactments.[21]

Although the Equality Act 2006 does not provide any guidance as to when the CEHR will use its power to provide legal assistance, the criteria used by the DRC are likely to remain relevant: **1.24**

(a) the case raises a question of principle;
(b) it is unreasonable to expect the claimant to deal with the case unaided (because of its complexity, the claimant's position in relation to another party or for some other reason);

18 Equality Act 2006, s 8(3).
19 See Equality Act 2006, s 42.
20 Equality Act 2006, s 15.
21 Equality Act 2006, s 28(1).

(c) there is some other special consideration which makes it appropriate for assistance to be provided.

C. European Community Law

1.25 As the legislative history set out above clearly demonstrates, European Community ('EC') law has played a major role in the development of equality legislation in this country. Although a detailed explanation of the workings of EC law is beyond the scope of this book, it is essential that practitioners have a broad understanding of how it operates. A brief summary is therefore given below.

1. Sources of EC law

1.26 EC law has applied to the UK ever since it joined the EC on 1 January 1973. By becoming a member state of the EC, the UK recognized the supremacy of EC law over its own national legal system. See European Communities Act 1972, s 2(1) which provides that any rights or obligations created under the EC Treaty are to be given legal effect in the UK.

1.27 The principal sources of EC law are as follows:

(a) The Treaty of Rome 1957 which established the EC in the first place, as variously amended over the years ('the EC Treaty');[22]
(b) EC legislation;
(c) Decisions of the European Court of Justice ('ECJ').

EC Legislation: Regulations and Directives

1.28 EC legislation takes the form of regulations and directives. Regulations are directly applicable in member states and do not need to be implemented by national legislation.[23] Directives, on the other hand, are instructions issued to member states to pass laws in order to bring their national legislation into conformity with EC law.[24] The directive will stipulate a date by which the member state must take action to implement it (typically three years).

---

[22] The provision of the EC Treaty which is of direct relevance to equality legislation is Article 13 which confers power on the European Council to take appropriate action to combat discrimination based on sex, racial or ethnic origin, religion or belief, disability, age, or sexual orientation.

[23] No relevant regulations relating to equality laws have been passed and the practitioner need not concern himself further with this form of legislation.

[24] See, for example, the Framework Directive which led to the introduction of the 2003 Regulations discussed in paras 1.08–1.11 above.

The ECJ

The ECJ is the court of the EC and sits in Luxembourg. It is assisted by an Advocate General who issues an opinion on the issues to be decided after the ECJ has heard argument from the parties involved. The ECJ then issues its decision. Decisions of the ECJ are binding on UK courts and tribunals which are obliged to determine questions of EC law in accordance with the decisions of the ECJ.[25] National courts and tribunals can refer questions to the ECJ for a preliminary issue.[26] **1.29**

2. Effect of EC law

Where UK legislation has been passed in order to comply with EC law, an individual can of course have recourse to that UK legislation in order to enforce any right conferred by it. There is no need to look further. Difficulties only arise where no national legislation has been passed in order to comply with an EC law; or where national legislation is implemented but it is ineffective to comply, in whole or in part, with the EC law which it was seeking to apply. **1.30**

Doctrine of direct effect

In certain circumstances, this lacuna is filled by the doctrine of direct effect which means that the EC legislation in question can be enforced by the individual without any (or any fully effective) implementing national legislation. Such directly effective rights can be provided by a provision in the EC Treaty itself, or by the regulations or directives made under it. **1.31**

Directly effective rights operate in one of two ways. First, they may have vertical effect. In this case, the provision in question creates rights which an individual can only enforce against the state. Alternatively, they may create rights with horizontal effect, in which case they create rights which an individual can enforce against other individuals. In any case, therefore, in which an individual wishes to rely on EC legislation, two questions arise: **1.32**

(a) Is the particular piece of EC legislation in question directly effective? If so,
(b) Is it enforceable against another individual, or only against the state?

A provision of the EC Treaty will only have direct effect if certain conditions are satisfied. In short, the provision must be clear and precise; unconditional; and must not require any positive action by member states. Where the provision in **1.33**

[25] See European Communities Act 1972, s 2(1).

[26] This procedure was used by the tribunal at first instance in the case of *Coleman v Attridge Law* [2007] IRLR 951, EAT. The question it referred was whether the Framework Directive covered associative discrimination. See paras 1.37–1.38.

question is capable of conferring rights on an individual and satisfies the above requirements, it may be both vertically and horizontally effective.[27]

1.34 The position with regard to directives is less clear. Although the test for determining whether a directive has direct vertical effect is the same as the test for a provision of the EC Treaty set out above, doubt has been cast on the proposition that a directive could have direct horizontal effect. See *Marshall v Southampton and South West Hampshire Area Health Authority (Teaching)*,[28] in which the ECJ held that, since directives were binding on member states, there was no justification for them having horizontal effect.

1.35 However, in the case of *Mangold v Helm*,[29] the ECJ held that, in pursuance of the general principle of equality enshrined in EC law, courts could be required to give horizontal direct effect to a directive in order to set aside incompatible domestic legislation. In the subsequent case of *Bartsch*,[30] the ECJ concluded that a directive could have horizontal direct effect where proceedings fell within the scope of community law. A provision fell within the scope of community law when a national law purported to implement EC law. Once this occurred, 'the general principle of equality ... could indeed be invoked horizontally, operating through directive 2000/78 without the need for any other element bringing the employment relationship within the scope of community law.'[31]

Indirect effect

1.36 Courts and tribunals are required to give a purposive interpretation to national law, insofar as it is possible to do so, in order to make it accord with the wording and purpose of any relevant EC directive.[32] This interpretative principle means that a claimant can very often achieve his purpose indirectly, even if a directive is not directly effective.

1.37 The House of Lords has shown itself willing to go to surprising lengths in order to give full effect to an EC directive. In *Litster v Forth Dry Dock and Engineering Co Ltd*,[33] it was prepared to read additional words into the Transfer of Undertakings (Protection of Employment) Regulations 1981 in order to make them fully compliant with the Acquired Rights Directive.[34] The creative

---

27 *Defrenne v Sabena* [1976] ICR 547.

28 [1986] ICR 335, ECJ.

29 [2006] IRLR 143, ECJ.

30 *Bartsch v Bosch und Siemens Hausgerate (BSH) Altersfursorge Gmbh* C-427/06.

31 See paras 69–76 and 87 of opinion.

32 *Marleasing SA v La Commercial Internacionale de Alimentacion SA*: C-106/89 [1992] 1 CMLR 305.

33 [1989] ICR 341, HL.

34 EC Council Directive 77/187.

ingenuity of the courts is set to be tested again as a result of the decision of the ECJ in *Coleman v Attridge Law*[35] holding that the Framework Directive protects people who, although not themselves disabled, nevertheless suffer direct discrimination and/or harassment in employment because they are associated with a disabled person ('associative discrimination').

In anticipation of the decision of the ECJ, the EAT has already reached the view that the relevant sections of DDA 1995 can be construed so as to cover associative discrimination. Given that the sections defining direct discrimination and harassment are expressly worded so as to refer to *the disabled person's* disability, and not to anyone else's, this is a startling conclusion. It seems clear that the DDA 1995 cannot be read in that way as currently drafted. However, as noted above, the courts can and will, if necessary, read additional words into a statute in order to give proper effect to an EC directive. It remains to be seen how that power will be exercised in this case. **1.38**

D. The Future: The Equality Bill

1. Overview

The government made a commitment in its 2005 general election manifesto to introduce an Equality Act during the course of this parliament in order to modernize and simplify equality legislation.[36] Work towards that goal is ongoing. A discrimination law review was launched and its findings resulted in a consultation paper on proposals for the Equality Bill.[37] In July 2008, the government published its response to that consultation. **1.39**

In summary, the government remains committed to introducing an Equality Act which will simplify and strengthen the existing law. Its main proposals are as follows: **1.40**

(a) A new equality duty on public bodies which will bring together the three existing public sector equality duties for race, disability, and gender and extend them to gender reassignment, age, sexual orientation, and religion and belief;
(b) New powers to end age discrimination by those providing goods, facilities, and services;

---

[35] C-303/06

[36] There are currently nine major pieces of discrimination legislation and around 100 statutory instruments setting out connected rules and regulations.

[37] 'A Framework for Fairness: Proposals for a Single Equality Bill for Great Britain' published in June 2007.

(c) New powers requiring public bodies to report on inequalities in gender pay, ethnic minority employment, and disability employment;
(d) An extension of positive action enabling employers to take into account under-representation of disadvantaged groups when selecting between two equally qualified candidates;
(e) New enforcement powers allowing tribunals to make wider recommendations in discrimination cases;
(f) New measures simplifying the definitions in the RRA 1975 and standardizing the definition of indirect discrimination;
(g) New proposals streamlining and strengthening the law for transsexual people, pregnant women, and new mothers, disabled people, and members of private clubs.

2. Specific proposals for disability discrimination

1.41 A number of specific proposals have been made for disability discrimination. Most of them relate to discrimination in areas other than employment, namely the provision of goods, facilities and services; public functions; private clubs; and premises. In many cases, the proposed amendments are designed to bring the law in those areas into line with the law in employment. For example, it is proposed that:

(a) The separate definitions of discrimination which currently exist for goods, facilities and services etc should all be replaced with a single definition based on that relating to employment;

(b) The provision currently allowing a failure to make a reasonable adjustment for service providers etc to be justified should be removed to bring it into line with the employment provisions;

(c) A single threshold for the point at which the duty to make a reasonable adjustment is triggered should be established, based on the employment provision which is triggered when 'substantial disadvantage' is caused;

(d) The reverse burden of proof provisions which apply in employment cases should be extended to cover the provision of goods, services and facilities, and education.

1.42 The above proposals will therefore not affect the existing law relating to disability discrimination in employment. However, the following proposals will have a direct bearing on the subject matter of this book.

1.43 First, it is proposed that the various justification defences which are contained within different parts of DDA 1995 should all be replaced with a single 'objective justification' test, which would require that the conduct in question should be 'a proportionate means of achieving a legitimate aim.' That test would therefore replace the only existing justification defence currently found in Part II of DDA 1995, namely that relating to disability-related discrimination. The current provision states that less favourable treatment of a disabled person for a reason related to the disabled person's disability is justified if, but only if, the reason for it is both material to the circumstances of the particular case and substantial. Although this proposed amendment does represent a significant change, it is unlikely to pose any great problems of interpretation, since the new wording is that already found in relation to indirect discrimination in the other equality statutes.

Second, it is proposed that the list of capacities, one of which must be affected if a person is to satisfy the statutory definition of disability under the DDA 1995, should be removed.[38] This is a welcome development. The requirement to demonstrate that a capacity has been affected created some confusion, and evidence suggested that it was an unnecessary extra barrier put in the way of disabled people. In particular, it was commonly found that people with mental health conditions and people with short-term but recurrent conditions experienced difficulties in showing how their impairment impacted on one or more of the capacities. However, the government stopped short of adopting a proposal suggested by the Disability Rights Commission recommending the removal of the requirement that a person's impairment must be long-term in order to satisfy the statutory definition of disability. **1.44**

Finally, there are two problem areas which do not currently form part of the Government's proposals but which it will certainly have to address in the near future. The first is the issue of associative discrimination discussed at paras 1.37–1.38 above. As a result of the ECJ decision in *Coleman v Attridge Law*, as presently worded, the DDA 1995 clearly fails to implement the Framework Directive in this area. The Government has already stated that it 'will look at areas where decisions may be influenced by the outcome of the ECJ judgment on Coleman.'[39] It has also now launched an inquiry in order to evaluate the effectiveness of current equality legislation in the context of the Equality Bill. One particular issue which it will be seeking to address is how to improve protection for carers in the light of the decision in the Coleman case.[40] **1.45**

The second problem area which the Government will have to consider is how it should respond to the decision of the House of Lords in *London Borough of* **1.46**

---

38 See chapter 2 at para 2.6.

39 The Equality Bill – Government response to the Consultation July 2008. Note that one of the questions which the Government is looking into is how disability fits into a single Equality Act. Is it having second thoughts about the wisdom of this proposal?

40 Work and Pensions Committee Press Notice dated 23 October 2008.

Lewisham v Malcolm.[41] A consideration of this issue is also to form part of the inquiry referred to in the previous paragraph. In view of the fact that the scope of disability-related discrimination has been radically reduced by virtue of this decision, it would appear to be strongly arguable that the DDA 1995 is now in breach of the Framework Directive in this area as well.[42] New legislation in this area is urgently required.

41 [2008] UKHL 43; [2008] 4 All ER 525. For a full discussion of this case, see Chapter 5.

42 In particular, Article 2 of the Framework Directive outlawing any direct or indirect discrimination whatsoever on any of the stated grounds. See para 1.10 above.

2

THE MEANING OF 'DISABILITY'

A. Introduction

The DDA 1995 makes it unlawful to discriminate against disabled persons in the employment field. The term 'disabled person' is given a special statutory meaning which reflects a medical and not a social model of disability. Unless a claimant can prove that he is a 'disabled person' within the meaning of the statutory definition, he will not be able to bring a claim under the DDA 1995, however legitimate his **2.01** complaints may be. It follows that references to 'disability' in the context of other legislation are not relevant in determining whether someone is a disabled person under the DDA 1995 and should be disregarded. Thus, for example, the fact that the claimant has been awarded disability living allowance by a Social Security Appeals Tribunal is not determinative of the issue of disability for the purposes of the DDA 1995.[1] Nor is the fact that the claimant has been compulsorily admitted for treatment under the Mental Health Act 1983.[2]

B. The Statutory Definition

1. The Meaning of 'Disability' and 'Disabled Person'

2.02 DDA 1995, s 1 provides as follows:

> (1) Subject to the provisions of Schedule 1, a person has a disability for the purposes of this Act if he has a physical or mental impairment which has a substantial and long-term adverse effect on his ability to carry out normal day-to-day activities.
> (2) In this Act, 'disabled person' means a person who has a disability.

2.03 The words of the section therefore require a tribunal to ask itself four questions:

(a) Does the claimant have an impairment which is either mental or physical?
(b) Does the impairment have an adverse effect on the claimant's ability to carry out normal day-to-day activities?
(c) Is the adverse effect upon the claimant's ability substantial?
(d) Is the adverse effect upon the claimant's ability long-term?[3]

2.04 This basic definition is supplemented by the provisions of DDA 1995, sch 1 which further define what is meant by 'long-term effects' and 'normal day-to-day activities'.

2.05 DDA 1995, sch 1, para 2 provides that the effect of an impairment is only a long-term effect if:

(a) it has lasted at least 12 months;
(b) the period for which it lasts is likely to be at least 12 months; or
(c) it is likely to last for the rest of the life of the person affected.

---

1 *Hill v Clacton Family Trust Ltd* [2005] EWCA Civ 1456.
2 *McDougall v Richmond Adult Community College* [2007] ICR 1567, [2007] IRLR 771, EAT.
3 As formulated in *Goodwin v The Patent Office* [1999] ICR 302, [1999] IRLR 4, EAT.

2.06 DDA 1995, sch 1, para 4 provides that an impairment is to be taken to affect the ability of the person concerned to carry out normal day-to-day activities only if it affects one of the following:

(a) mobility;
(b) manual dexterity;
(c) physical co-ordination;
(d) continence;
(e) ability to lift, carry or otherwise move everyday objects;
(f) speech, hearing or eyesight;
(g) memory or ability to concentrate, learn or understand; or
(h) perception of the risk of physical danger.[4]

2.07 DDA 1995, sch 1 also contains provisions dealing with severe disfigurements, the effect of medical treatment, persons deemed to be disabled, and progressive conditions. The component parts of the statutory definition set out above and the supplementary provisions of DDA 1995, sch 1 will all be addressed in detail later in this chapter.

2. Past Disability

2.08 DDA 1995, s 2 provides that the provisions of DDA 1995, Parts 1 and 2 apply in relation to a person who *has had* a disability as they apply in relation to a person who *has* that disability. This is an important safeguard—those with a history of disability are just as vulnerable to discrimination by employers, perhaps, as those who are currently disabled. Take, for example, the job applicant who has repeatedly had to miss work in the past because of a depressive illness from which he has now recovered. If he is turned down for the new job because of his attendance record, he will be able to claim that he has been discriminated against because of his past disability.

2.09 Modifications are made to the statutory definition by DDA 1995, sch 2 which provides that, in the case of a past disability, the effect of an impairment is a long-term effect if it has in fact lasted for at least 12 months. If the impairment ceases to have a substantial adverse effect (within 12 months) it is to be treated as continuing to have that effect if that effect recurs.[5] The question whether a person had a disability at a particular time in the past ('the relevant time') is determined as if the provisions of the DDA 1995 were in force at the relevant time, even if that time was before the DDA 1995 came into force.[6]

---

[4] One of the changes proposed by the government for inclusion in the forthcoming Equality Bill is to remove the list of capacities from the definition of disability.

[5] DDA 1995, s 2 and sch 2, para 5. For a case in which these provisions were relied on, see *British Gas Trading Limited v Scott* UKEAT/0322/07, [2008] All ER (D) 135, EAT.

[6] DDA 1995, s 2(4) and s 2(5).

2.10 In other words, a person who had a disability at a time before the DDA 1995 came into force but from which he is now recovered, can still bring a complaint of disability discrimination if he is discriminated against now. He would still have to show, however, that his past disability would have satisfied the statutory definition if it had been in force at the time. There is one exception to this. People who were on the register of disabled persons maintained under the Disabled Persons (Employment) Act 1944, s 6 at the time when the employment provisions of the DDA 1995 came into force, are treated as having a disability in the past, regardless of whether the person otherwise met the statutory definition of a disabled person contained in the DDA 1995.[7]

3. The Statutory Guidance

2.11 In some cases, it may be difficult to determine whether or not the claimant satisfies the statutory definition of disability. To cater for such cases, statutory guidance has been issued about matters to be taken into account in determining whether a person is a disabled person, particularly with regard to determining:

(a) whether an impairment has a substantial adverse effect on a person's ability to carry out normal day-to-day activities; and
(b) whether such an impairment has a long-term effect.[8]

2.12 This statutory guidance was originally contained in a document entitled Guidance on Matters to be taken into Account in Determining Questions Relating to the Definition of Disability, which was issued and came into force on 31 July 1996. That guidance has now been replaced by a revised document with the same title which came into force on 1 May 2006. The original guidance was revoked on the same day, but it (and not the revised guidance) will continue to apply in relation to any claim arising out of an act of discrimination occurring before 1 May 2006. The revised guidance will apply in relation to acts of discrimination occurring after that date. In the remainder of this chapter, the original guidance will be referred to as the 1996 Guidance, and the revised guidance will be referred to as the 2006 Guidance. Collectively, the 1996 Guidance and the 2006 Guidance will be referred to as the statutory guidance.

2.13 The statutory guidance (particularly the 2006 Guidance) is essential reading for anyone advising in this area for two reasons. First, DDA 1995, s 3(3) provides that an adjudicating body determining whether an impairment has a substantial and long-term adverse effect on a person's ability to carry out normal day-to-day

[7] DDA 1995, sch 1, para 7.
[8] The statutory guidance is issued by the Secretary of State pursuant to powers conferred by DDA 1995, s 3.

activities, *shall* take into account any guidance which appears to it to be relevant. In an employment context, an adjudicating body means the employment tribunal. The use of the word 'shall' makes it clear that this is a mandatory requirement. The tribunal must take into account any guidance which appears to it to be relevant, and is open to criticism if it fails to do so.[9]

Second, the 2006 Guidance has been rewritten in the light of judicial interpretation of the various elements of the definition of disability, both at EAT and Court of Appeal level. It is a much lengthier document than its predecessor. Although it does not impose any legal obligations in itself, and although it expressly disclaims any suggestion that it is an authoritative statement of the law, the fact remains that the guidance it gives is, in part at least, based upon what judges have had to say about the meaning of disability within the context of the DDA 1995. **2.14**

4. The Disability Discrimination (Meaning of Disability) Regulations 1996

These regulations were passed pursuant to powers contained in DDA 1995, sch 1, para 1(2). They provide that certain addictions and other personality disorders and conditions are not to be treated as amounting to impairments, regardless of whether they would otherwise satisfy the statutory definition. These are dealt with in section G of this chapter. **2.15**

C. Physical or Mental Impairment

1. Meaning of 'Impairment'

The word 'impairment' is not defined in the DDA 1995. Although we are told that the word should be given its ordinary meaning,[10] it is a word more easily and intuitively understood, perhaps, than defined. It has been described by the EAT as meaning 'some damage, defect, disorder or disease compared with a person having a full set of physical and mental equipment in normal condition.'[11] A dictionary meaning would include the condition of being unable to perform (or of being unable to perform as well) as a consequence of physical or mental unfitness. **2.16**

[9] *Goodwin v The Patent Office* [1999] ICR 302, EAT. This does not mean, of course, that the tribunal is obliged to take statements made in the statutory guidance at face value. If a statement or opinion expressed in the statutory guidance is inconsistent with the DDA 1995, it should be not be followed. See *Spence v Intype Libra Ltd* [2007] All ER (D) 261, EAT, per Elias J at para 28.

[10] The 2006 Guidance, para A3, repeating the observation made by Mummery LJ in *McNicol v Balfour Beatty Rail Maintenance Ltd* [2002] IRLR 711, CA.

[11] *Rugamer v Sony Music Entertainment UK Ltd* [2001] IRLR 644, EAT, at para 34.

At the heart of the definition is the sense that the person impaired is, somehow, 'worse off'.[12]

2.17 The 2006 Guidance states that the question whether a person is disabled for the purposes of the DDA 1995 is determined by reference to the *effect* that an impairment has on that person's ability to carry out normal day-to-day activities.[13] That observation is clearly correct (what matters is the effect of an impairment on someone's functionality, not the nature of the impairment itself) and it takes on board the interpretations made by case law in this area—it was not in the 1996 Guidance. However, the statutory definition does still require the claimant to have something which can be described as a physical or mental impairment, and the first task of the person seeking to prove disability for the purposes of the DDA 1995 is to identify the impairment in question. The adverse effects must spring from something.

2.18 In a case in which it held that the concept of sickness was different from the concept of disability, such that a Spanish worker dismissed solely on account of sickness was not protected by the prohibition against discrimination on grounds of disability under the Framework Directive, the ECJ has tentatively confirmed that a distinction is to be drawn between an impairment and its effects:

> Disabled people are people with serious functional limitations (disabilities) due to physical, psychological or mental afflictions. From this two conclusions can be drawn:
>
> the cause of the limitations must be a health problem or physiological abnormality which is of a long-term or permanent nature;
>
> the health problem as cause of the functional limitation should in principle be distinguished from that limitation.[14]

2.19 The claimant must, therefore, identify an impairment (the 'health problem' referred to in *Chacon*). It is not sufficient simply to point to the effects of the impairment. However, any attempt to define further what constitutes an impairment becomes a circular exercise because an impairment is defined by the DDA 1995 purely by reference to its effects. An impairment amounts to a disability if it is sufficiently serious in terms of its effects to qualify as one. The Court of Appeal has described attempts to define further the concept of 'impairment' as ambitious and unnecessary.[15]

2.20 Whilst acknowledging that it is not possible to provide an exhaustive list of conditions that qualify as impairments for the purposes of the DDA 1995, the 2006

---

12 It is derived from the Latin word 'peior' meaning 'worse'.

13 The 2006 Guidance, para A4.

14 *Chacon Navas v Eurest Colectividades SA* [2006] IRLR 706, ECJ at paras 76–77.

15 *McNicol v Balfour Beatty Rail Maintenance Ltd* [2002] IRLR 711, CA, at para 19.

Guidance notes that a disability can arise from a wide range of impairments which can be:

(i) sensory impairments, such as those affecting sight or hearing;
(ii) impairments with fluctuating or recurring effects such as rheumatoid arthritis, myalgic encephalitis (ME)/chronic fatigue syndrome (CFS), fibromyalgia, depression, and epilepsy;
(iii) progressive, such as motor neurone disease, muscular dystrophy, forms of dementia, and lupus (SLE);
(iv) organ-specific, including respiratory conditions, such as asthma, and cardiovascular diseases, including thrombosis, stroke and heart disease;
(v) developmental, such as autistic spectrum disorders (ASD), dyslexia and dyspraxia;
(vi) learning difficulties;
(vii) mental health conditions and mental illnesses, such as depression, schizophrenia, eating disorders, bipolar affective disorders, obsessive compulsive disorders, as well as personality disorders and some self-harming behaviour;
(viii) produced by injury to the body or brain.[16]

2. Physical Impairment

Where the claimant is suffering from a physical impairment, there will generally be little difficulty in identifying the impairment in question. However, this is not always as straightforward as it sounds. The problem stems from the fact that the word 'impairment' is apt to cover both cause and effect; both the underlying impairment, and the physical manifestations of that impairment. The distinction between the two is not always clear. As can be seen in the extract quoted in the preceding paragraph, the 2006 Guidance tends to use the word 'condition' as a synonym for 'impairment' when trying to describe the underlying cause, but this is not a word used in the statutory definition.[17] **2.21**

As noted in the 2006 Guidance, there may be adverse effects which are both physical and mental in nature. Furthermore, effects of a mainly physical nature may stem from an underlying mental impairment, and vice versa.[18] Care needs to **2.22**

---

[16] The 2006 Guidance, para A6.

[17] DDA 1995, sch 1 para 1 provides that regulations may make provision, for the purposes of the DDA 1995, for conditions of a prescribed description to be treated as amounting to impairments, or as not amounting to impairments, and that such regulations may make provision as to the meaning of 'condition' for the purposes of those regulations. However, no such regulations have been made and 'condition' remains undefined. See paras 2.17–2.19.

[18] The 2006 Guidance, para A7.

be taken with classifying the impairment correctly. If a claimant bases his claim on a physical impairment, and the evidence shows that he is in fact suffering from a mental impairment, the claim will fail.

2.23 That is what happened in two cases[19] in which the EAT heard appeals together because they both involved functional overlay, an expression used to describe the situation where physical symptoms are exaggerated or felt as a result of someone's mental condition. No conscious or deliberate simulation of symptoms is involved, but equally there is no physical or organic cause for symptoms, or symptoms of that degree of intensity, to be felt. In short, there is a mental cause for a physical effect.

2.24 Mr Rugamer was an engineer who claimed that he had a physical injury to his shoulder which prevented him lifting and moving equipment. Mr McNicol was a trackman who claimed that he had suffered a compression injury to his spine as a result of an accident at work which he said had left him quite severely disabled. Both claimed to be a disabled person by reason of a physical impairment alone. However, their claims were not supported by the medical evidence, with the tribunal finding in Mr Rugamer's case that the physical effects of his injuries were no longer present at the relevant time, and in Mr McNicol's case that he had no physical impairment of any significance which would result in symptoms of the kind about which he had given evidence.

2.25 Although the medical evidence in each case suggested that the claimant's problems might have been caused by functional overlay, neither claimant claimed to have a mental impairment, and neither put forward any psychiatric evidence establishing the presence of a mental illness. In those circumstances, the tribunals ruled that they could not claim to be disabled within the meaning of the DDA 1995. They did not have a physical impairment and they did not claim to have a mental impairment.

2.26 The EAT dismissed appeals from these decisions, ruling that 'the difficult dividing line between physical and mental impairment has in our judgment to depend not on whether a physical or mental function or activity is affected (a physical impairment may affect mental activities as well as physical ones, and vice versa) but rather on whether the nature of the impairment itself is physical, or mental'.[20] In other words, the EAT concentrated on cause rather than effect in determining whether the claimants could be said to be suffering from an impairment.

---

19 *Rugamer v Sony Music Entertainment UK Ltd; McNicol v Balfour Beatty Rail Maintenance Ltd* [2002] ICR 381, [2001] IRLR 644, EAT.

20 Ibid para 34, per Mr Commissioner Howell QC. Note that the claimants could have avoided this result if they had pleaded their cases in the alternative.

A different approach was taken in *College of Ripon & York St John v Hobbs*[21] where the EAT concentrated more on effect than cause in upholding the tribunal's finding that a college lecturer was disabled within the meaning of the statutory definition, despite the fact that the medical expert who examined her had concluded that there was no organic disease process causing the symptoms which she described, and despite the fact that she did not claim to have a mental impairment. **2.27**

The EAT held that the tribunal was entitled to conclude that the claimant had a physical impairment within the meaning of the definition and dismissed the college's appeal. The expert's finding that the claimant's disability was not organic did not necessarily exclude a finding of physical impairment within the DDA 1995. The EAT concluded: **2.28**

> Nor does anything in the Act or the Guidance expressly require that the primary task of the ascertainment of the presence or absence of physical impairment has to, or is likely to, involve any distinctions, scrupulously to be observed, between an underlying fault, shortcoming or defect of or in the body on the one hand and evidence of the manifestations or effects thereof on the other...

There is an inconsistency of approach between the two cases, and it is tempting to suggest that the outcome was different because Dr Hobbs's case was a more deserving one. There was no doubt about the existence of her physical symptoms; the difficulty arose from the attempt to ascertain what caused them. On the other hand, the tribunal expressed doubt about the credibility of Mr McNicol—video evidence secretly taken of him was described as entirely inconsistent with the allegations of disability which he was making. **2.29**

However, it is now clear that the approach in *Hobbs* is to be preferred and that tribunals should concentrate on effect rather than cause when determining whether a claimant can be said to have an impairment. When Mr McNicol's case went to the Court of Appeal, Mummery LJ expressly approved the observations made by the EAT in *Hobbs*, and said this: **2.30**

> It is left to the good sense of the tribunal to make a decision in each case on whether the evidence available establishes that the applicant has a physical or mental impairment with the stated effects. Such a decision can and should be made without substituting for the statutory language a different word or form of words in an ambitious and unnecessary attempt to describe or to define the concept of 'impairment'. The essential question in each case is whether, on sensible interpretation of the relevant evidence, including the expert medical evidence and reasonable inferences which can be made from all the evidence, the applicant can fairly be described as having a physical or mental impairment. The ordinary meaning of the statutory language and

21 [2002] IRLR 185, EAT.

of the Guidance issued by the Secretary of State under s 3(1) is sufficiently clear to enable the tribunal to answer the question on the basis of the evidence.[22]

2.31 In any case where uncertainty exists as to the nature of the underlying impairment causing the symptoms in question, (such as, for example, in cases of ME/chronic fatigue syndrome), the obvious practical solution to the problem is to plead the impairment in the alternative, that is, either physical or mental.

3. Mental Impairment

Mental Illness

2.32 In the DDA 1995 as originally enacted, sch 1 para 1 provided that 'mental impairment' included an impairment resulting from, or consisting of, a mental illness *only* if the illness was a clinically well-recognized illness. That requirement was removed by the DDA 2005 with effect from 5 December 2005.

2.33 That amendment to the DDA 1995 removes an unnecessary hurdle put in the path of claimants with mental illnesses. Those suffering from a mental impairment which either results from, or consists of, a mental illness no longer have to prove that the illness is clinically well-recognized. As a result, the three routes suggested by the EAT in an early case for proving that a mental illness was clinically well-recognized can now be disregarded.[23]

2.34 However, a claimant who has a mental impairment *including one resulting from a mental illness* will still need to meet the requirements of the statutory definition, in order to demonstrate that he has a disability under the DDA 1995.[24] Whether the mental impairment results from, or actually consists of, a mental illness, a claimant will still have to prove that the mental impairment has a substantial and long-term adverse effect on his ability to carry out normal day-to-day activities.

2.35 In practice, this means that, in most cases of mental illness, claimants will still have to rely on medical evidence to help prove their case. Even if the illness is not a clinically well-recognized one, what exactly is it? What is the mental impairment in question? Whether it is cause or effect, a mental impairment must still

---

22 *McNicol v Balfour Beatty Rail Maintenance Ltd* [2002]IRLR 711, CA, at para 19. See also the observations of the Court of Session in *Millar v Inland Revenue Commissioners* [2006] IRLR 112, where it was pointed out that physical impairment could be established without reference to causation, and, in particular, without reference to any form of 'illness'. See, however, *Chacon Navas v Eurest Coliectividades SA* [2006] IRLR 711 discussed at paras 2.18–2.19.

23 *Morgan v Staffordshire University* [2002] IRLR 190, EAT at para 9, suggesting that, in order to qualify as clinically well-recognized, the illness would have to be specifically mentioned in the World Health Organisation's International Classification of Diseases; some other such classification of very wide professional acceptance; or proof by other means of a medical illness recognized by a respected body of medical opinion.

24 The 2006 Guidance, Part 2, para A9.

be identified. What is the prognosis? How long will the impairment last? Will it be long-term? As noted in *Morgan*, in mental illness cases, the existence or not of a mental impairment is very much a matter for qualified and informed medical opinion. Even if a consultant psychiatrist's report is not needed, there will normally have to be evidence from the claimant's GP, at the very least, if disability is an issue.[25]

Other Mental Impairments

It is not necessary to have a mental illness to suffer from a mental impairment. One only has to think of those with learning difficulties or specific conditions such as dyslexia. No one, presumably, would describe those as mental illnesses. It also seems obvious that such conditions always fell within the ambit of the statutory definition. When the DDA 1995 said that mental impairment was to include mental illnesses (but only if they were clinically well-recognized) it was surely implicit in that wording that it did not thereby mean to exclude all other mental impairments. On the contrary, the wording assumes the existence of mental impairments which do not constitute mental illnesses. **2.36**

Whilst this construction was recognized by Lindsay J in *Morgan*, he was strangely sceptical about the possibility that there could be a state recognisable as mental impairment which neither resulted from, nor consisted, of mental illness: **2.37**

> If, as a matter of medical opinion and possibility, there may exist a state recognisable as mental impairment yet which neither results from nor consists of a mental illness, then such state could be accepted as a mental impairment within the Act because the statutory definition is inclusive only, rather than purporting to exclude anything not expressly described by it. This fourth category is likely to be rarely if ever invoked and could be expected to require substantial and very specific medical evidence to support its existence.[26]

That view is clearly too limited, and was held to be so by the EAT in a case in which the claimant's disability consisted of severe reading and writing difficulties.[27] He relied on a report from a chartered psychologist which concluded that he had generalized learning difficulties causing a cognitive, or mental, impairment which had been present since birth and would remain the same throughout his life. However, a tribunal found that he was not disabled. Directing itself in accordance with the decision of the EAT in *Morgan*, a tribunal dismissed his claim because the psychologist, whose report he relied on, was not a medical practitioner. **2.38**

25 *Morgan v Staffordshire University* [2002] IRLR 190, EAT, at para 20.
26 Ibid para 9.
27 *Dunham v Ashford Windows* [2005] IRLR 608, EAT.

2.39 The EAT allowed the claimant's appeal. It accepted that a tribunal, hearing a mental impairment case based on learning difficulties, should look for expert evidence of an identified condition. However, it held that the tribunal had erred in rejecting the claimant's expert evidence on the grounds that the claimant's expert was a psychologist and not a qualified medical practitioner. In a case of learning difficulties, there was no reason why the essential evidence which establishes the nature of the claimant's condition should not be provided by a suitably qualified psychologist. What is important is that there should be evidence from a suitably qualified expert who can speak, on the basis of their experience and expertise, as to the relevant condition.[28]

D. Ability to Carry out Normal Day-to-day Activities

1. List of Capacities[29]

2.40 As noted earlier in this chapter at paragraph 2.06, the DDA 1995 states that an impairment is to be taken to affect the ability of the person concerned to carry out normal day-to-day activities *only* if it affects one of a number of capacities.[30] Those capacities are listed below. Examples of cases relating to each of the capacities are also listed in the footnotes for ease of reference.

mobility;[31]
manual dexterity;[32]
physical co-ordination;[33]
continence;[34]
ability to lift, carry or otherwise move everyday objects;[35]

---

28 As a result, the reservations expressed by Lindsay J about this category of mental impairment referred to in para 2.37 above should be disregarded.

29 So labelled in the 2006 Guidance, Part 2, para D1.

30 DDA 1995, sch 1, para 4(1).

31 *College of Ripon & York St John v Hobbs* [2002] IRLR 185, EAT; *Archibald v Fife Council* [2004] UKHL 32, [2004] ICR 954, [2004] IRLR 651, HL.

32 *Vicary v British Telecommunications plc* [1999] IRLR, EAT; *Ekpe v Commissioner of Police of the Metropolis* [2001] ICR 1084, [2001] IRLR 605, EAT; *Collins v Royal National Theatre Board Ltd* [2004] EWCA Civ 144, [2004] IRLR 395, CA; *Baynton v Saurus General Engineers Ltd* [2000] ICR 375, [1999] IRLR 604, EAT.

33 *Leonard v Southern Derbyshire Chamber of Commerce* [2001] IRLR 19, EAT.

34 *Kirton v Tetrosyl Ltd* [2003] EWCA Civ 619, [2003] IRLR 353, CA; *McConnachie v D C Thomson & Co Ltd* EATS/0015/05.

35 *Smith v Churchill Stairlifts plc* [2005] EWCA 1220, [2006] ICR 524, [2006] IRLR 41, CA; *Vicary v British Telecommunications plc* [1999] IRLR 680, EAT.

speech,[36] hearing[37] or eyesight;[38]
memory or ability to concentrate, learn or understand;[39]
perception of the risk of physical danger.[40]

This is a curiously restrictive list. It does not include, for example, a sense of smell or touch; stamina; disruption of normal sleep patterns; loss of appetite; loss of interest or pleasure; or loss of self-confidence. It might be thought that an impairment which had an adverse effect on any of those might well affect a person's ability to carry out normal day-to-day activities. Indeed, many of the above are common symptoms of clinical depression. However, the list is exhaustive and the requirement for the claimant to be affected in one of the listed ways is mandatory. The task for the adviser, then, is to identify which one (or more) of the capacities listed is affected by the impairment in question. If it does not affect any of them, the statutory definition is not met, however substantial or long-term the particular adverse effect of the impairment on other capacities might be. One of the changes which the government proposes to make in the Equality Bill is to remove the list of capacities from the definition of disability.[41] **2.41**

The list of capacities will, however, be given a wide interpretation. In *Hewett v Motorola Ltd*,[42] the claimant had autism, in the form of Asperger's Syndrome. The tribunal acknowledged that his condition had an adverse effect on his ability to participate in human interaction, social relationships and communication, but held that he did not satisfy the statutory definition of a disabled person because these were not included in the list of capacities. The EAT allowed the claimant's appeal, ruling that ability to 'understand' is not limited simply to an ability to understand information, knowledge or instructions. The EAT said that a broad approach to the concept of 'understanding' should be taken. The tribunal's approach to the concept failed to acknowledge that someone who has difficulty in understanding normal social interaction among people, and/or the subtleties of human non-factual communication, can be regarded as having their understanding affected.[43] **2.42**

36 *Southampton City College v Randall* [2006] IRLR 24, EAT.

37 *Taylor v OCS Group Ltd* [2006] EWCA Civ 702, [2006] IRLR 613, CA.

38 *Nottinghamshire County Council v Meikle* [2004] EWCA Civ 859, [2005] ICR 1, [2004] IRLR 703, CA; *Williams v J Walter Thompson Group Ltd* [2005] EWCA Civ 133, [2005] IRLR 376, CA; *Kirker v British Sugar plc* [1998] IRLR 624, EAT.

39 *Hewett v Motorola Ltd* [2004] IRLR 545, EAT; *Dunham v Ashford Windows* [2006] IRLR 608, EAT; *Paterson v Commissioner of Police of the Metropolis* [2007] IRLR 763, EAT.

40 *Goodwin v The Patent Office* [1999] ICR 302, [1999] IRLR 4.

41 See the White Paper Framework for a Fairer Future – The Equality Bill published in June 2008.

42 [2004] IRLR 545, EAT.

43 Ibid at para 24.

2.43 That ruling has now been incorporated into the 2006 Guidance, which states that the list of capacities should be looked at in a broad sense. Furthermore, it states that the list of capacities should be applied equally to both physical and mental impairments, noting that a person with a mental impairment may also have difficulties carrying out activities that involve mobility or other 'physical' skills, and that people with a physical impairment may also have effects that involve mental processes such as the ability to concentrate (for example, as a result of pain or fatigue).[44]

2. Adverse Effect

2.44 The impairment in question must have an adverse effect on the ability of the person concerned to carry out normal day-to-day activities. As emphasized in the early case of *Goodwin v Patent Office*[45] in which the EAT gave guidance on the proper approach to the question whether a person has a disability in disability discrimination cases, what the DDA 1995 is concerned with is the adverse effect which an impairment has on the person's *ability* to carry out activities. The fact that a person can, in fact, carry out activities does not mean that his ability to carry them out has not been impaired. A person may still be able to cook, but only with the greatest difficulty. In order to constitute an adverse effect, it is not the doing of the acts which is the focus of attention, but rather the ability to do the acts. That point should always be borne in mind when considering whether an impairment has had an adverse effect on a claimant's ability to carry out normal day-to-day activities.

3. Meaning of 'Normal Day-to-day Activities'

2.45 The first and obvious question which arises in considering whether an impairment has an effect on normal day-to-day activities is: normal for whom? Normal for the claimant, or normal for people in general? The starting point in answering this question is the 2006 Guidance, which states that:

> The term 'normal day-to-day activities' is not intended to include activities which are normal only for a particular person, or a small group of people. In deciding whether an activity is a normal day-to-day activity, account should be taken of how far it is normal for a large number of people, and carried out by people on a daily or frequent and fairly regular basis. In this context, 'normal' should be given its ordinary, everyday meaning.[46]

---

44 The 2006 Guidance, Part 2, paras D2 and D19.

45 [1999] IRLR 4, EAT.

46 The 2006 Guidance, Part 2, para D5.

2.46 It is not relevant to enquire whether the activity is normal for *most* people. In *Ekpe v Commissioner of Police of the Metropolis*,[47] a tribunal had decided that Mrs Ekpe's inability to put rollers in her hair or to apply make-up other than with her left hand were not normal day-to-day activities, because they were activities carried out almost exclusively by women (and were thus not normal for most people). Although the tribunal's decision did accord with the 1996 Guidance which was still in force at the time,[48] the EAT described this reasoning as plainly wrong, saying that:

> The logic would exclude anything done by women rather than men, or vice versa, as not being normal. What would strike the person in the street as entirely normal behaviour—doing up the zip on her dress, for a woman; shaving, for a man—would not be classed as a normal day-to-day activity.[49]

2.47 The same point is made by the early case of *Vicary v British Telecommunications plc*,[50] another striking example of the mistake of defining a normal day-to-day activity by reference to whether most people do it. This reasoning led a tribunal to conclude that the doing of DIY tasks, filing nails, tonging hair, ironing, shaking quilts, grooming animals, polishing furniture, knitting and sewing, and cutting with scissors were not normal day-to-day activities, since it could not be said that these activities were carried out by most people on a daily or frequent and fairly regular basis. The EAT described this decision as perverse.

2.48 The most helpful way, perhaps, of considering what is meant by normal in this context is to contrast it with what is abnormal. As stated in *Ekpe*: 'The antithesis for the purposes of the Act is between that which is 'normal' and that which is 'abnormal' or 'unusual' as a regular activity, judged by an objective population standard'.[51] If the adviser thinks about normal day-to-day activities in this way, he is unlikely to go far wrong.

4. Work-related Activities

2.49 The orthodox view used to be that work-related activities were not normal day-to-day activities. The 2006 Guidance states that: 'Normal day-to-day activities do not include work of any particular form because no particular form of work is 'normal' for most people. In any individual case, the activities carried out might be highly specialized. For example, carrying out delicate work with specialized

---

47 [2001] IRLR 605, EAT.

48 The 1996 Guidance, Part 2, para C2 did say that account should be taken of how far an activity was normal for *most* people in deciding whether it was a normal day-to-day activity. That paragraph has now been replaced by the 2006 Guidance, Part 2, paras D5–6.

49 *Ekpe v Commissioner of Police of the Metropolis* [2001] IRLR 605, EAT, at para 39.

50 [1999] IRLR 680, EAT.

51 *Ekpe v Commissioner of Police of the Metropolis* [2001] IRLR 605, EAT, at para 32.

tools may be a normal working activity for a watch repairer, whereas it would not be normal for a person who is employed as a semi-skilled worker. The Act only covers effects which go beyond the normal differences in skill and ability.'[52]

2.50 That paragraph of the 2006 Guidance is wrong, for two reasons. First, in pointing out that no particular form of work is normal for *most* people, it repeats the mistake made in the 1996 Guidance about non work-related activities. As pointed out by the EAT in *Ekpe*, it is not a matter of what the majority do. The question is whether or not the activity is a normal day-to-day one. Many forms of work involve perfectly normal day-to-day activities. Subject to the point made in the next paragraph, it is only work which involves highly specialized skills which might not be described as a normal day-to-day activity.

2.51 Second, and more importantly, it is inconsistent with EC law. In considering the meaning of disability in the context of the Framework Directive, the ECJ has ruled that 'the concept of disability must be understood as referring to a limitation which results in particular from physical, mental or psychological impairments and which hinders the participation of the person concerned in professional life.'[53] In EC law, therefore, instead of denying the relevance of work-related activities to the question whether or not a person can be called disabled, the definition of disability is expressly linked to a person's ability to participate in professional life.

2.52 That principle has now been recognized by the EAT. In *Paterson v The Commissioner of Police of the Metropolis*,[54] the claimant was a police officer who had achieved the rank of chief inspector despite the fact that he was dyslexic. He complained that he had been discriminated against on the grounds that his employers failed to make sufficient adjustments for him when undertaking examinations for promotion to the rank of superintendent. The tribunal found that he was at a significant disadvantage compared with his peers when taking these examinations, but held that these were not normal day-to-day activities, and, therefore, held that he was not disabled.

2.53 The EAT allowed the claimant's appeal. Its view was that, even without reference to EC law and the decision reached by the ECJ in *Chacon*, carrying out an assessment or examination was properly to be described as a normal day-to-day activity, even if it did relate to work. Furthermore, it pointed out that DDA 1995, s 1 had to be read in a way which gives effect to EC law. The EAT thought that could be done simply by giving a meaning to day-to-day activities which encompassed

52 The 2006 Guidance, Part 2, para D7.

53 *Chacon Navas v Eurest Colectividades SA* [2006] IRLR 706, ECJ, at para 43.

54 [2007] IRLR 763, EAT.

the activities which are relevant to participation in professional life. Appropriate measures had to be taken to enable a worker to advance in his or her employment. Since the effect of the claimant's disability might adversely affect promotion prospects, then it must be said to hinder participation in professional life.[55]

This is an important decision. Although it had previously been recognized that many types of work might involve normal day-to-day activities, this was only thought to be relevant in the sense that a claimant's ability to carry out such activities at work (boiling the kettle, climbing the stairs etc), could clearly form part of the evidential basis for assessing whether the claimant was adversely affected in his ability to carry out normal day-to-day tasks in general.[56] The decision in *Paterson* goes further, however, in including within the meaning of a normal day-to-day activity, activities (such as the taking of an examination) which are relevant to the claimant's ability to participate in life at work on an equal footing. The decision also has significant implications for what is meant by a 'substantial' adverse effect. See the discussion at paragraphs 2.58–2.64 below. **2.54**

The potential ramifications of this decision are far-reaching. Take, for example, a professional footballer who loses an eye in an accident. As a result, he can no longer play well enough to justify selection in the team, and he is dismissed. Would such a person satisfy the statutory definition of disability? If the person were able to function well enough with one eye to cope with the normal demands of day-to-day life, the conventional answer would be no. Although playing football might well be described as a normal day-to-day activity (what is abnormal about it?), playing it so well that you can make a living out of it would take it beyond the range of normal day-to-day activities. That, at any rate, is the view expressed in the Guidance.[57] If the approach in *Paterson* is adopted, however, day-to-day activities should be given a meaning which encompasses the activities which are relevant to participation in professional life. For the professional footballer, that means being able to see well enough to be able to play to the requisite high standard. If he cannot, because he has lost an eye, according to the *Paterson* analysis, he would presumably satisfy the statutory definition of disability.[58] **2.55**

It should be noted, however, that there is nothing in the Framework Directive which requires an employer to recruit or maintain in employment a person who is not competent to perform the essential functions of the post concerned. In the above example, the football club would not be required to keep a job open for the **2.56**

---

55 Ibid at paras 66–67.

56 See, for example, *Law Hospital NHS Trust v Rush* [2001] IRLR 611, CS. See also the 2006 Guidance, Part 2, para D9.

57 The 2006 Guidance, Part 2, para D8.

58 The 2006 Guidance, Part 2, para D8.

person who had lost an eye and could no longer play well enough to perform the essential functions required of a professional footballer. However, the football club might still be obliged to make a reasonable adjustment for him. It might, for example, be reasonable to transfer him to a post on the coaching staff.[59]

2.57 The relevance of work-related activities has also been recognized in a case where a person's impairment only had a substantial adverse effect on his ability to carry out normal day-to-day activities whilst he was at work.[60] The claimant had occupational asthma, the adverse effects of which were exacerbated by the fumes in the foundry where he worked, but subsided when he was away from work. The EAT held that, in assessing whether a disability has a substantial and long-term effect on someone's ability to do every day tasks, it was not appropriate to confine the evaluation to the extent to which the claimant was disabled only in a normal day-to-day environment. The symptoms which the claimant suffered from at work were not to be ignored simply because the work was specialized and unusual. The fact that the claimant was only adversely affected whilst at work did not mean that he was denied the protection of the DDA 1995.

E. Substantial Adverse Effect

1. Meaning of 'Substantial'

2.58 A 'substantial' adverse effect in this context simply means one that is more than minor or trivial. It does not mean one that is very large. According to the 2006 Guidance, the requirement that an adverse effect on normal day-to-day activities should be a substantial one reflects the general understanding of disability as a limitation going beyond the normal differences in ability which may exist among people.[61] This message is reinforced by a series of examples in which guidance is given as to what might, and what might not, constitute a 'substantial' adverse effect on someone's ability to carry out normal day-to-day activities in relation to each of the list of capacities.[62]

2.59 Although that guidance sounds simple enough on the surface, it is not quite as straightforward as it sounds. The question concealed within it is whether, in assessing what is substantial, the tribunal should only consider the claimant's abilities, and how his impairment affects his own ability to cope with normal day-to-day activities; or whether it should be measuring the claimant's impairment

---

59 See discussion in chapter 4 at para 4.107.

60 *Cruickshank v VAW Motorcast Ltd* [2002] ICR 729, [2002] IRLR 24, EAT.

61 The 2006 Guidance, Part 2, para B1.

62 The 2006 Guidance, Part 2, paras D15-D27.

against an objective standard of how people in general cope with normal day-to-day activities. To put it in a slightly different way, what account should be taken of the fact that the claimant might have been well above the average in terms of his ability to cope with normal day-to-day activities before suffering an impairment which means that he can now only cope in an average way?

That difference in approach is revealed by the way in which the 2006 Guidance deals with two of the factors which it mentions as meriting consideration when assessing whether the impact of an impairment is substantial. First, it states that the time taken by a person with an impairment to carry out a normal day-to-day activity should be considered when assessing whether the effect of that impairment is substantial. That time should be compared with the time it might take *a person* who did not have the impairment to complete an activity.[63] Second, it states that another factor to be considered is the way in which a person with that impairment carries out a normal day-to-day activity. In this instance, it states that the comparison should be with the way that *the person* might be expected to carry out the activity if he or she did not have the impairment.[64] There are two different approaches here. One compares the claimant with others. The other compares him with himself. Which is to be preferred? **2.60**

The statutory definition set out in DDA 1995, s 1 makes it clear that the second approach is the correct one. The comparison to be made is between the claimant's ability to carry out normal day-to-day activities with the impairment, and his ability to carry out those activities without the impairment. How someone else copes with those same activities is simply not relevant. The claimant will satisfy the statutory definition if *his ability* to carry out normal day-to-day activities is affected in the required way.[65] **2.61**

That was the approach favoured by the EAT in *Paterson*, discussed at paragraphs 2.52–2.56 above. The tribunal in that case had been much influenced by the fact that the claimant police officer had managed to achieve a very senior position in the organization before failing the examination required to enable him to be promoted to superintendent. It accepted that he would be at a definite disadvantage in the high pressure situation of an exam at that level when compared with his colleagues who did not have dyslexia, but found that the correct comparison **2.62**

63 The 2006 Guidance, Part 2, para B2. Note that the 1996 Guidance made the comparison with the person himself in his unimpaired state, ie as per the comparison drawn in the 2006 Guidance, Part 2, para B3.

64 The 2006 Guidance, Part 2, para B3.

65 See, for example, *Leonard v Southern Derbyshire Chamber of Commerce* [2001]IRLR 19, EAT, in which the EAT stated that the tribunal should concentrate on what the claimant cannot do or can only do with difficulty, rather than on the things that he can do. This focus would avoid the danger of a tribunal concluding that as there are still many things that a claimant can do, the adverse effect cannot be substantial.

should be with the ordinary average norm of the population as a whole. On that basis, it held that he did not satisfy the statutory definition (as very few people would have even been qualified to take this exam in the first place).

2.63 As already noted, the EAT held that this was the wrong approach. The correct approach is to ask how the claimant himself would have performed, but for the impairment in question, not how the impairment affects his ability when compared with the population as a whole. The fact that a person might have been an 'over achiever' compared with the average person before being impaired is immaterial in assessing whether the impairment has a substantial effect. As stated in *Paterson:*

> Once it was accepted that the disability affected Mr Paterson's ability to progress in his profession, the only reasonable inference was that it had a substantial effect on his day-to-day activities. Any other conclusion would mean that because of the effects of his dyslexia, he would in practice face a glass ceiling; he would not be able to compete adequately in the promotion stakes beyond a certain level.[66]

2.64 In summary, therefore, although the DDA 1995 requires a certain level of objectivity in considering what is a substantial adverse effect on a person's ability to carry out normal day-to-day activities, this does not come from making a comparison between the claimant's ability to cope with day-to-day activities and how others cope. Rather, it comes from the somewhat elastic concept of what is a 'normal' day-to-day activity. Hitherto, the higher the level of skill required for a particular activity, the less likely it was that the activity would be seen as a normal one. The decision in *Paterson* seems to herald a new approach.

2. Coping Strategies

2.65 As was pointed out in *Goodwin*,[67] disabled people often adjust their lives and circumstances to enable them to cope for themselves. If a person's coping strategies are so successful that his impairment ceases to have a substantial adverse effect on his ability to carry out normal day-to-day activities, does that mean that he no longer satisfies the statutory definition?

2.66 The answer to that question lies in what it is *reasonable* to expect the disabled person to do. If a person can reasonably be expected to behave in such a way that the impairment ceases to have a substantial adverse effect on his ability to carry out normal day-to-day activities, he would no longer meet the definition of disability.[68] For example, a teacher suffering from lower back pain might be

---

66 *Paterson v The Commissioner of Police of the Metropolis* [2007] 763, EAT, at para 32.

67 *Goodwin v The Patent Office* [1999] IRLR 4, EAT.

68 See the 2006 Guidance, Part 2, para B7.

expected to give up his hobby of marathon running if that enabled him to cope with commuting into work on the train in the rush hour. He might not, however, be expected to give up his hobby of gardening. The more a person has to modify his behaviour to cope with a normal day-to-day activity, the less likely it is that his coping strategy will take him outside the ambit of the definition.

Account should also be taken of situations where a person avoids doing things which, for example, cause pain, fatigue or substantial social embarrassment. The 2006 Guidance gives an example of a woman with a persistent stammer who avoids using the telephone and giving verbal instructions at work. It would not be reasonable to conclude that a person who employed such an avoidance strategy was not a disabled person. Furthermore, coping strategies can break down, particularly in stressful situations.[69] **2.67**

These provisions seem to be at odds with the aim of the legislation. Compare, for example, the provisions relating to the effect of medical treatment—which, in broad terms, is to be disregarded in assessing whether a person satisfies the statutory definition (see below at paragraphs 2.71—2.77). Why, on the one hand, should a tribunal be told to ignore the fact that a person's impairment is not causing him any substantial adverse effect because it is being controlled by medication, when, on the other, it is told to take account of the fact that a person may be able to mitigate the effects of his impairment by altering his behaviour? **2.68**

There is no satisfactory answer to that question. However, any suggestion by a respondent that a claimant does not satisfy the statutory definition because he should have adapted his behaviour in order to cope better with normal day-to-day activities is unlikely to be greeted with much enthusiasm by the tribunal. Although no express reference was made to coping strategies in *Vicary*, the EAT had no difficulty in that case in disposing of the tribunal's suggestion that the claimant's inability to carry a washing basket, a bag of shopping, a suitcase, briefcase or hand-held handbag were all activities which were capable of being modified to prevent or reduce the effects of the impairment, on the basis that she could rely upon shoulder bags, rather than hand-held bags; and on the basis that she could carry washing in small quantities and shopping in trolleys, unloading it in small quantities. **2.69**

The EAT said that this was a misunderstanding of the task confronting a tribunal: **2.70**

> The fact that a person is able to mitigate the effects of their disability does not mean that they are not disabled within the meaning of the Act. It seems to us obvious that it would be a substantial impairment on a normal day-to-day activity if the applicant

[69] The 2006 Guidance, Part 2, paras B8-B9. For a case on coping strategies, see *Commissioner of Police of the Metropolis v Virdi* UKEAT/0338/06, EAT.

could not use a hand-held bag or carry washing, other than in small quantities, or unload her shopping trolley other than in small quantities.[70]

3. Deduced Effects

2.71 The DDA 1995 provides that an impairment which would be likely to have a substantial adverse effect on the ability of the person concerned to carry out normal day-to-day activities, but for the fact that measures are being taken to treat or correct it, is to be treated as having that effect. Measures include, in particular, medical treatment and the use of a prosthesis or other aid. An exception is made in the case of the impairment of a person's sight, to the extent that the impairment is correctable by spectacles or contact lenses. In that instance alone, a claimant cannot claim to be disabled within the meaning of the DDA 1995 if wearing glasses or contact lenses would correct the impairment.[71]

2.72 These provisions are easy enough to understand but are likely to raise difficult questions of proof. Take, for example, the person who suffers from depression and who has been on medication for a number of years. In such a case, the medical evidence would have to consider the ongoing effect of the medication in order to assist the tribunal to determine the difficult question of the likely extent of the person's impairment, but for the fact that treatment was continuing (the so-called 'deduced effects').

2.73 The burden of proof falls on the claimant. He must prove that, but for the ongoing treatment, he would be suffering from an impairment with the requisite adverse effects. In one case, the claimant stated that she had had an anxiety neurosis for a number of years. She was undergoing psychotherapy treatment for this and claimed that her condition would deteriorate and that full symptoms would return if this treatment were to cease. However, she had produced no medical evidence to support that contention. The Court of Appeal rejected her claim, noting that:

> In any deduced effects case of this sort, the claimant should be required to prove his or her alleged disability with some particularity. Those seeking to invoke this peculiarly benign doctrine under para 6 of the schedule should not readily expect to be indulged by the tribunal of fact. Ordinarily, at least in the present class of case, one would expect clear medical evidence to be necessary.[72]

2.74 Is this really a peculiarly benign doctrine? Whilst it is true to say that the claimant who takes advantage of the deduced effects doctrine will benefit from the protection of the DDA 1995 without suffering the adverse effects required by the

70 *Vicary v British Telecommunications plc* [1999] IRLR 680, EAT, at para 15.

71 DDA 1995, sch 1, para 6.

72 *Woodrup v London Borough of Southwark* [2003] IRLR 111, CA, at para 13.

statutory definition, it should not be forgotten that he will still have the underlying impairment, and this will still feature on his personnel record. Furthermore, he may suffer adverse effects from his medication. Take, for example, the claimant with ulcerative colitis who treats his condition with steroids. The medication may keep the symptoms of his condition under control, but it may in turn cause unpleasant side-effects. For both reasons, the person who is taking measures to control his impairment merits the protection of the DDA 1995.

It has been held by the EAT[73] that the deduced effects doctrine only applies to continuing treatment, not to treatment which has been completed. Furthermore, where the effect of the continuing medical treatment is to create a permanent improvement rather than a temporary improvement, such permanent improvement should be taken into account, as measures are no longer needed to treat or correct it once the permanent improvement has been established. Thus, for example, the medical evidence before the tribunal may demonstrate that a course of cognitive behavioural therapy has achieved a permanent improvement in a claimant's moderate depressive disorder, so that it can now be described as mild, albeit ongoing. The claimant continues to receive therapy. The question then is whether, if treatment were stopped at the relevant date, would the person, notwithstanding such benefit as had been obtained from prior treatment, still have an impairment which would have the relevant adverse effect?[74] **2.75**

That makes good sense. If the improvement is permanent, there is no need to rely on the continuing treatment provisions, because the continuing treatment has ceased to have an effect on the impairment in question (at least in terms of degree). Furthermore, the claimant will still qualify for protection as someone with a past disability if it lasted for the requisite period. On the other hand, if the final outcome of the treatment cannot be determined, or if it is known that removal of the medical treatment would result in either a relapse or a worsened condition, the medical treatment must be disregarded under DDA 1995, sch 1, para 6.[75] **2.76**

Although the word 'measures' is not defined, DDA 1995, sch 1, para 6 provides that it includes, in particular, medical treatment and the use of a prosthesis or other aid. The EAT has held that having counselling sessions with a consultant clinical psychologist constitutes 'medical treatment'.[76] In another case, the EAT held that plates and pins which had been surgically inserted into the claimant's ankle some 20 years before might well count as 'an aid', much as the use of a stick **2.77**

---

73 *Abadeh v British Telecommunications plc* [2001] IRLR 23,EAT.
74 *Woodrup v London Borough of Southwark* [2003] IRLR, 111, CA, at para 4.
75 Ibid at para 31.
76 *Kapadia v London Borough of Lambeth* [2000] IRLR 14, EAT.

by a person who has difficulty walking would amount to an aid. Much would depend on whether or not the plates and pins were still performing any function, such that they could count as a 'continuing measure', and the evidence had failed to address this question. The case was, therefore, remitted to the tribunal to determine whether the metalwork was giving any ongoing support to the functioning of the claimant's ankle. If not, it followed that a permanent improvement had been effected, with the result that there was no need to consider how the ankle would function without the metalwork.[77]

4. Progressive Conditions

2.78 Special provision is made for progressive conditions by DDA 1995, sch 1, para 8(1) which provides that where:

(a) a person has a progressive condition (such as cancer, multiple sclerosis or muscular dystrophy or HIV infection);
(b) as a result of that condition, he has an impairment which has (or had) an effect on his ability to carry out normal day-to-day activities; but
(c) that effect is not (or was not) a substantial adverse effect,

he shall be taken to have an impairment which has such a substantial adverse effect if the condition is likely to result in his having such an impairment.[78]

2.79 In fact, following amendments made by the DDA 2005, three of the four progressive conditions specifically mentioned in DDA 1995, sch 1, para 8(1) (cancer, multiple sclerosis and HIV infection—but not muscular dystrophy) are now deemed to amount to disabilities for the purposes of the DDA 1995. There is no need for a person suffering from one of these conditions to prove that he has an impairment with the statutory adverse effects. He is deemed to be a disabled person from the moment when he is diagnosed as having the condition.

2.80 In order to take advantage of the provisions relating to progressive conditions, the claimant has to prove, therefore, that he has some impairment which has (or had) some effect on his ability to carry out normal day-to-day activities. The words in brackets show that the claimant does not have to be suffering any adverse effects at all at the time when his status as a disabled person is being considered (that is, the date of the alleged discriminatory act). He may be completely symptom-free at that time. What matters is that he has at some stage suffered some effect, and that it is likely that he will suffer some substantial adverse effect at some time in the future. No time scale is prescribed within which the substantial adverse effect has to occur.

---

77 *Carden v Pickerings Europe Ltd* [2005] IRLR 720, EAT.
78 A non-exhaustive list of progressive conditions can be found in the 2006 Guidance, Part 2, para B18.

It is, as always, for the claimant to prove that he has a progressive condition with the requisite features if he is to be treated as a disabled person for the purposes of the DDA 1995. He will, therefore, have to demonstrate that it is more likely than not that he will suffer *substantial* adverse effects in the future. In the normal case, this will be a matter for expert medical opinion, although the EAT has suggested that it might be possible to discharge the onus of proof by statistical evidence.[79] Although DDA 1995 sch 1, para 8(1) is silent on the point, it is suggested in the 2006 Guidance that the long-term condition will still have to be met.[80] There is no reason why that should not be the case. The claimant will have to prove, therefore, not only that he will suffer some substantial adverse effect at some point in the future, but also that the substantial adverse effect will be likely to last for at least 12 months. **2.81**

A person with a progressive condition which currently has no effect on day-to-day activities may also be covered by the provisions of DDA 1995, sch 1, para 8(1) where the effects of treatment for that condition give rise to a further impairment which does have an effect on normal day-to-day activities. That was the effect of the Court of Appeal decision in *Kirton v Tetrosyl Limited*,[81] a case in which the claimant underwent surgery for asymptomatic prostate cancer, as a result of which he was left with some minor urinary incontinence. The tribunal had found that the incontinence did not have a substantial adverse effect on the claimant's ability to carry out normal day-to-day activities. Whilst it was prepared to infer that the prostate cancer was likely to result in the claimant having an impairment with the statutory effects at some stage in the future (despite the surgery), the incontinence was not going to get any worse. As a result, it decided that the claimant did not fall within the statutory definition of disability, because the impairment from which he was suffering (incontinence) did not result from his progressive condition (prostate cancer). It resulted from the surgery. **2.82**

The Court of Appeal allowed an appeal from this decision, ruling that the word 'result' in DDA 1995, sch 1, para 8(1)(b) should not be so narrowly construed as to exclude an impairment which results from a standard and common form of operative procedure for the cancer. Furthermore, it did not matter that the impairment presently and indirectly caused by the cancer (urinary incontinence) did not have a substantial adverse effect and was not going to have such an effect in the future. The fact remained that the cancer was likely to get worse, and the **2.83**

[79] *Mowat-Brown v University of Surrey* [2002] IRLR 235, EAT. This case was decided before the change in the law relating to deemed disabilities such as multiple sclerosis. The claimant was held not to satisfy the statutory definition because the consultant neurologist who reported on his condition said that it was not possible to give an accurate prognosis for any individual with multiple sclerosis because of the variable nature of the condition.

[80] See the second example given in the 2006 Guidance, Part 2, para B18.

[81] [2003]IRLR 353, CA.

Court of Appeal (adopting a purposive construction) thought that that was enough to bring the case within the provisions of DDA 1995, sch 1, para 8(1).

2.84 Although the Court of Appeal's decision stretches the statutory language to its limit (the paragraph is surely referring to the worsening of the impairment caused by the condition, not the condition itself?), the importance of this decision has been considerably diminished, now that cancer (of whatever form) is deemed to be a disability without any examination of its adverse effects.[82]

2.85 Finally, even if the treatment for a progressive condition is completely successful, it may cause some other impairment which has a substantial adverse effect on a person's normal day-to-day activities. An example is given in the 2006 Guidance of a person who has progressing and uncontrollable ulcerative colitis. As a result, he has a colostomy. Although he no longer suffers any adverse effects from the colitis, following his operation, his bowel actions can only be controlled by a sanitary appliance.[83] That clearly has a substantial (and long-term) adverse effect on the person's ability to carry out normal day-to-day activities, and he, therefore, satisfies the statutory definition of disability.

5. Severe Disfigurements

2.86 An impairment which consists of a severe disfigurement is to be treated as having a substantial adverse effect on the ability of the person concerned to carry out normal day-to-day activities.[84] As a result, there is no need for a claimant who is severely disfigured to prove that his normal day-to-day activities have been affected in any way at all (although he will still have to prove that the disfigurement is long-term). This exception to the general requirement imposed by the DDA 1995—that a person's functionality must be impaired before he can qualify as a disabled person—is made for obvious reasons. If an employee is likely to be discriminated against simply because of the way he looks (as opposed to the way he functions) then he needs protection.

2.87 Scars, birthmarks, limb or postural deformation (including restricted bodily development), or diseases of the skin are all examples of disfigurements given in

---

[82] DDA 1995, sch 1, para 6A.

[83] The 2006 Guidance, Part 2 Para B19. Note that the example given is not illustrative of the point made in para B19 about progressive conditions and their treatment. In the example, the person is currently suffering substantial adverse effects as a result of his treatment. He does not need to rely on DDA 1995, sch 1 para 8. Note also that, in describing a situation in which the effect of an impairment caused by treatment for a progressive condition is likely to become substantial in the future, para B19 differs from the factual position in *Kirton*, where the impairment caused by the treatment (incontinence) was not going to deteriorate.

[84] DDA 1995, sch 1 para 3(1). No regulations have as yet been made under DDA 1995, sch 1 para 3(2).

the 2006 Guidance, which also notes that assessing severity will be mainly a matter of the degree of the disfigurement. It goes on to make the obvious point that it may be necessary to take account of where the disfigurement in question is (for example, on the back as opposed to the face).[85] Whilst that observation strictly applies only to the question whether a person should be deemed to be disabled in the first place, it is also, of course, relevant in deciding whether discrimination has taken place. Take, for example, a woman with a badly scarred leg who turns up for a job interview wearing trousers and is denied a job as a receptionist. She will not succeed with a claim that this was on account of, or in any way related to, disability if the person interviewing her could not see her leg and had no idea that it was scarred in this way.

Causation was the issue for the Court of Appeal of Northern Ireland in the case of *Cosgrove v Northern Ireland Ambulance Service*.[86] Mr Cosgrove had applied for a job with the respondent as an emergency ambulance person, but a doctor who examined him in a pre-employment medical examination found that he suffered from psoriasis of such severity that he was unfit for the post. The doctor said that this was because of the risk of cross-infection of patients and the substantially increased risk of infection that would arise for Mr Cosgrove himself. **2.88**

A tribunal held that the element of Mr Cosgrove's skin condition that had led to the refusal of employment was not the disfigurement inherent in the psoriasis but the propensity of the condition to become infected or to cause cross-infection. The Northern Ireland Court of Appeal agreed: **2.89**

> It is clear that the differential treatment of the appellant did not arise as a result of his disfigurement. He was not employed because it was judged that he was at risk of infection and that his condition carried the danger that he would infect others. These considerations have nothing to do with his being disfigured.

In concentrating on the reason lying behind the treatment of Mr Cosgrove, the Northern Ireland Court of Appeal made the point that the impairment (psoriasis) did not consist of a severe disfigurement, although it clearly included it. It ruled that impairments within the meaning of DDA 1995, sch 1, para 3(1) related solely to a condition of disfigurement, and not to a condition one aspect of which was disfigurement. **2.90**

That surely goes too far. If one aspect of a condition is that it is seriously disfiguring, why should it matter that the condition has other aspects as well? If Mr Cosgrove had been turned down for the job because his psoriasis was unsightly, why should it not be *deemed* to be a disability under DDA 1995, sch 1, para 3(1) just because **2.91**

[85] The 2006 Guidance, Part 2, para B21.
[86] [2007] IRLR 397, NI CA.

it also happened to carry with it a risk of infecting others, and therefore could not be described as a 'condition of disfigurement'? There is no reason why the provisions relating to severe disfigurements should be limited in this way. Causation should be the key to determining the issue.

2.92 For the purposes of DDA 1995 sch 1, para 3(1), a severe disfigurement is not to be treated as having a substantial adverse effect on the ability of the person concerned to carry out normal day-to-day activities if it consists of:

(a) a tattoo (which has not been removed); or
(b) a piercing of the body for decorative or other non-medical purposes, including any object attached through the piercing for such purposes.[87]

F. Long-term Adverse Effect

1. Statutory Definition of 'Long-term'

2.93 DDA 1995, sch 1, para 2 provides as follows:

> (1) The effect of an impairment is a long-term effect if—
> (a) it has lasted at least 12 months;
> (b) the period for which it lasts is likely to be at least 12 months; or
> (c) it is likely to last for the rest of the life of the person affected.
>
> (2) Where an impairment ceases to have a substantial adverse effect on a person's ability to carry out normal day-to-day activities, it is to be treated as continuing to have that effect if that effect is likely to recur.

2. The 12-month Period

2.94 The key point to bear in mind when considering these provisions is that the relevant date for determining whether the effect of the impairment has lasted for 12 months, or that it is likely to do so, or that a substantial adverse effect is likely to recur, is the date of the act of discrimination which is the subject of the complaint. Unless his claim is founded on a past disability, the claimant must satisfy the statutory definition of disability at the date of the alleged act of discrimination ('the relevant date').

2.95 The first and most straightforward situation to consider is the case where the effect of an impairment has *in fact* lasted at least 12 months as at the relevant date and is substantial. A person who developed a serious hearing impediment over a year ago, for example, is likely to have suffered an adverse effect which remained very much the same throughout the period. (Even if he was fitted with a hearing

[87] The Disability Discrimination (Meaning of Disability) Regulations 1996, reg 5.

aid after, say, three months and could then hear perfectly well as a result, the adverse effect would still be treated as continuing because of the provisions relating to deduced effects, discussed at paragraphs 2.71–2.77 above.) If that effect can be described as substantial, there will be no difficulty in proving that the person satisfies the statutory definition.

Moreover, it is not necessary for the effect to be the same throughout the period. As noted in the 2006 Guidance, the effect may change, and activities which were initially very difficult may become easier. The effect might even disappear temporarily. Other effects may develop and the initial effect may disappear.[88] All that matters is that, taken as a whole, the overall effects of the impairment on the person's ability to carry out normal day-to-day activities last for the requisite period and are sufficiently significant to be described as 'substantial'. **2.96**

The second situation to consider is the impairment which had a substantial adverse effect on the claimant's ability to carry out day-to-day activities more than a year before the relevant date, but then ceased to have that effect before it had lasted at least 12 months. The symptoms may have eased off so that they can no longer be described as having a substantial effect. They may even have ceased completely because the condition has gone into remission. In this case, the claimant will not satisfy the statutory definition unless he can prove that the substantial adverse effect is likely to recur in the future (see paragraphs 2.100–2.113 below). If he can do so, the adverse effect in question is treated as continuing, even if he is completely symptom-free at that time.[89] **2.97**

Third, there is the claimant who has an impairment, the effect of which has not yet lasted for a period of 12 months at the relevant time. In that situation, how does one assess whether an effect of an impairment is likely to continue for at least 12 months? The 2006 Guidance says that, in assessing the likelihood of an effect lasting for 12 months, account should be taken of the total period for which the effect exists. This includes any time before the point at which the alleged incident of discriminatory behaviour which is being considered by the tribunal occurred. Account should also be taken of both the typical length of such an effect on an **2.98**

---

88 The 2006 Guidance, Part 2, para C6.

89 See, for example, *British Gas Trading Limited v Scott* UKEAT/0322/07, EAT, where the claimant suffered a dislocation of her left patella in July 2002, made a full recovery by the start of 2003, and then dislocated the same patella in July 2005. The EAT held that the tribunal was entitled to hold that the claimant had an impairment which continued even though there were no adverse effects between the two dislocations. The impairment was the claimant's increased risk of dislocating the patella. The tribunal was also entitled to conclude that, as at the date when she was subsequently dismissed in September 2005, it was more likely than not that she would suffer further dislocations, thus bringing her within the statutory definition of a disabled person.

individual, and any relevant factors specific to the individual (for example, general state of health or age).[90]

2.99 Fourth, there is the case of the person who has an impairment, the adverse effects of which are likely to last for the rest of his life. This is to be treated as long-term, even if the adverse effects have not lasted for 12 months at the relevant date and are unlikely to do so because the person is expected to die before then. This could theoretically apply in the case of a person who is very old, but in an employment context it is only likely to be of any relevance in the case of terminal illnesses.

3. Recurring Conditions

2.100 As noted in paragraph 2.93 above, where an impairment ceases to have a substantial adverse effect on a person, it is to be treated as continuing to have that effect if that effect is likely to occur. Guidance on the application of these provisions has been given by the EAT in the case of *Swift v Chief Constable of Wiltshire Constabulary*.[91]

2.101 Mrs Swift was a civilian communications officer who had been off work for two lengthy periods between February 2001 and July 2002 suffering from a recognized psychiatric condition—moderately severe adjustment reaction with predominant symptoms of low mood and anxiety. When she returned to work, she brought complaints of disability discrimination. At the tribunal hearing, Mrs Swift conceded that the impairment resulting from her illness (problems with memory and concentration) had ceased to have a substantial adverse effect on her ability to carry out normal day-to-day activities by the time she came back to work. However, she claimed that she was still a disabled person because she fell within the definition of someone with a 'recurring condition'. The tribunal dismissed her complaint on the grounds that she had not shown that her disability was likely to recur.

2.102 The EAT dismissed her appeal, holding that the tribunal had been entitled to find that she had not proved that the substantial adverse effect in question (problems with memory and concentration) was likely to recur. In considering the application of DDA 1995, sch 1, para 2(2), the EAT said that a tribunal should ask itself the following questions:

(a) First, was there at some stage an impairment which had a substantial adverse effect on the applicant's ability to carry out normal day-to-day activities?

---

90 The 2006 Guidance, Part 2, paras C2-C3.

91 [2004] ICR 909, [2004] IRLR 540, EAT.

(b) Second, did the impairment cease to have a substantial adverse effect on the applicant's ability to carry out normal day-to-day activities?
(c) Third, what was the substantial adverse effect?
(d) Fourth, is that substantial adverse effect likely to recur?[92]

Although Mrs Swift had had occasional panic attacks and sleepless nights after coming back to work, the EAT ruled that the tribunal was perfectly entitled to hold that this did not constitute a recurrence of the substantial adverse effect in question, namely problems with memory and concentration, and that Mrs Swift had not established that this substantial adverse effect was likely to recur. The EAT stressed the point that it was the substantial adverse effect which had to recur, not the illness: **2.103**

> In our judgment, the 1995 Act contemplates that an illness, physical or mental, may run its course to a conclusion but leave behind an impairment. This is why para 1(1) of Schedule 1 provides that 'mental impairment' includes an impairment resulting from a clinically well recognised mental illness.[93] Once an illness ceases, and an impairment from the illness ceases to have a substantial adverse effect, it will no doubt generally be the case that the substantial adverse effect will recur only if the illness recurs. So it will always be relevant for the tribunal to consider whether the illness is likely to recur. But it is possible to envisage circumstances where an impairment resulting from an illness may again have a substantial adverse effect without the illness itself recurring. There may, for example, be a change in surrounding circumstances which increases the effect of the impairment. The question for the tribunal is whether the substantial adverse effect is likely to recur, not whether the illness is likely to recur.[94]

What is noticeable about this analysis is the emphasis on the need for the adverse effect to be the *same one* as occurred before. See questions (c) and (d) posed by the EAT set out in paragraph 2.102 above. Whilst it is fair to say that the statutory language of DDA 1995, sch 1, para 2(2) does point in that direction (see the double use of 'that effect'), it is hard to see why it is necessary for the same adverse effect to recur if the claimant is to benefit from these provisions. Why should it not be a different adverse effect? If an impairment is capable of adversely affecting a person in more than one way, why should a claimant be prevented from claiming that he has a recurring condition just because it is not the same adverse effect which has recurred? Furthermore, this requirement is at odds with what is said in the 2006 Guidance, Part 2, para C6 quoted in paragraph 2.96 above. **2.104**

The likelihood of recurrence should be considered taking all the circumstances of the case into account. This should include what the person could reasonably be **2.105**

92 Ibid at paras 19–26.

93 Para 1(1) of the Schedule has since been repealed, but the point made here remains valid.

94 *Swift v Chief Constable of Wiltshire Constabulary* [2004] ICR 909, [2004] IRLR 540, EAT, at para 34.

expected to do to prevent the recurrence. For example, the person might reasonably be expected to take action which prevents the impairment from having such effects (for example, avoiding substances to which he is allergic). However, the possibility that a person's coping strategies might break down (for example, because a routine is not followed or because a person is in an unfamiliar environment) should be taken into account when assessing the likelihood of a recurrence.[95]

4. Likelihood of Recurrence: Post-Discrimination Evidence

2.106 It is now clear that the decision which the tribunal is required to make as to the likelihood of recurrence should be based on the evidence available at the time, and not on what in fact happened after the relevant date. Thus, the fact that a claimant actually suffered a recurrence of his condition after the relevant date (the discriminatory act) and before the tribunal hearing, is irrelevant and must not be taken into account.

2.107 That important principle was decided by the Court of Appeal in *Richmond Adult Community College v McDougall*.[96] In that case, the claimant had a history of mental illness. She suffered from persistent delusional disorder and a schizo-affective disorder, as a result of which she was admitted to hospital between November 2001 and February 2002. She was then discharged from hospital and, as at the date when the respondent college withdrew a job offer which it had made to her in April 2005, there had been no recurrence of these disorders. Although the claimant was in fact subsequently recommitted to hospital under the Mental Health Act 1983 following a recurrence of her condition in August 2005, there was no evidence before the tribunal that there was any likelihood of a recurrence *as at the date of the acts complained of*. On that basis, the tribunal held that the claimant was not a disabled person within the meaning of the DDA 1995.

2.108 The EAT allowed an appeal against this decision. Relying on a principle applicable to the assessment of damages[97] which proceeds on the basis that where facts are available, they are to be preferred to prophecies, it held as follows:

> In determining whether a condition is likely to recur…it is relevant to consider not only those matters extant at the date the tort was committed, but those occurring up to the date of the hearing…On the issue of whether the claimant's mental impairment would be likely to recur at the date of her rejection for a job in 2005, it was

[95] The 2006 Guidance, Part 2, para C8.

[96] [2008] EWCA Civ 4, [2008] ICR 431, [2008] IRLR 227, CA.

[97] The so-called Bwllfa principle, named after the case of *Bwllfa and Merthyr v Pontypridd Waterworks Company* [1903] AC 426. See also *Golden Strait Corporation v Nippon Yusen* [2007] UKHL 12, [2007] 2AC 353, [2007] 2WLR 691, [2007] 3 All ERI, HL.

> relevant to consider that it had in fact recurred when she was recommitted under the Mental Health Act...[98]

The Court of Appeal overturned this decision. It ruled that the principle referred to above had no application in relation to issues of liability: **2.109**

> Liability in this case turned on whether the claimant was a disabled person at the relevant time. That required a determination of the question whether, as at that date, her impairment was 'likely to recur'. That had to be answered exclusively by reference to evidence relating to the then likelihood of such recurrence. In short, the statute requires a prophecy to be made. It does not permit recourse to evidence as to subsequent events.[99]

Prior to this decision, there had been conflicting decisions at EAT level on this issue. In *Greenwood v British Airways plc*,[100] the EAT (HHJ Clark presiding) had expressed itself quite satisfied that the tribunal should consider the adverse effects of the claimant's condition up to the tribunal hearing. It relied in part on the fact that the original guidance had said that 'in assessing the likelihood of an effect lasting for any period, account should be taken of the total period for which the effect exists. This includes any time before the point when the discriminatory behaviour occurred as well as time afterwards'.[101] **2.110**

In *Latchman v Reed Business Information Limited*,[102] on the other hand, the EAT (Lindsay J (President) presiding) held that it was not what has actually later occurred but what could earlier have been expected to occur which is to be judged. That view was supported by the EAT in *Spence v Intype Libra Limited*[103] (Elias J presiding). It dismissed the relevance of the original guidance relied on in *Greenwood* by stating simply that it was wrong. **2.111**

The Court of Appeal in *McDougall* preferred the reasoning in *Latchman* and *Spence*. It follows that *Greenwood* and cases which are based on it are no longer good law and should not be relied on. Part of the reasoning of the Court of Appeal in *McDougall* was that it would be unfair to judge whether or not an employer had committed a wrong in taking a discriminatory decision by looking at what happened later. Pill LJ said this: **2.112**

> The central purpose of the Act is to prevent discriminatory decisions and to provide sanctions if such decisions are made. Whether an employer has committed such a

98 *McDougall v Richmond Adult Community College* UKEAT/0589/06, [2007] IRLR 771.

99 Ibid at para 35 per Rimer LJ. See also *Croal v Network Rail Infrastructure Ltd* [2008] UKEAT 0506/07.

100 [1999] ICR 969, [1999] IRLR 600, EAT.

101 The 1996 Guidance, Part 2 para B8. That passage has now been omitted from the 2006 Guidance.

102 [2002] ICR 1453, EAT.

103 [2007]All ER (D) 261, EAT, at para 28.

> wrong must, in my judgment, be judged on the basis of the evidence available at the time of the decision complained of...

2.113 There is considerable force in that reasoning. As stated by the Court of Appeal in another case[104] dealing with disability-related discrimination, discrimination requires the employer to have a certain state of mind. If all the evidence available at the time shows that an employee is not disabled because the adverse effect of his impairment is unlikely to recur (and provided that the employer has carried out proper enquiries into the matter), why should an employer be found to have committed an act of discrimination just because, as matters (unexpectedly) turn out, the adverse effect does in fact recur?

G. Excluded Impairments

1. The Disability Discrimination (Meaning of Disability) Regulations 1996

2.114 As noted at the beginning of this chapter at paragraph 2.15, these regulations provide that certain conditions are deemed not to amount to impairments for the purposes of the DDA 1995, regardless of the effect they have on a person's ability to carry out normal day-to-day activities. These are as follows:

(i) addiction to, or dependency on, alcohol, nicotine, or any other substance (unless the addiction was originally the result of administration of medically prescribed drugs or other medical treatment);
(ii) the condition known as seasonal allergic rhinitis (for example, hayfever), except where it aggravates the effect of another condition;
(iii) tendency to set fires;
(iv) tendency to steal;
(v) tendency to physical or sexual abuse of other persons;
(vi) exhibitionism;
(vii) voyeurism.[105]

2.115 However, the fact that a person has one of these excluded conditions does not necessarily mean that he cannot be a disabled person for the purposes of the DDA 1995. He may have an accompanying impairment which meets the requirements of the statutory definition. Even if this impairment is caused by an excluded condition, he may still qualify as a disabled person. For example, a person who is

104 *Taylor v OCS Group Ltd* [2006] IRLR 613, CA.

105 The Disability Discrimination (Meaning of Disability) Regulations 1996, regs 3–4, made pursuant to powers contained in DDA 1995, sch 1, para 1(2).

addicted to alcohol may also have depression or liver damage as a result. While such a person could not claim to be disabled on the grounds of his alcohol addiction, he could still satisfy the definition as a result of the effects of his depression or liver damage.[106]

Whilst a claimant might develop an impairment as a result of an excluded condition, as in the example given above, it is also the case that he might develop an excluded condition as a result of an impairment. In both cases, difficult questions can arise in determining whether a person satisfies the statutory definition of a disabled person under the DDA 1995. The latter situation arose for consideration in *Murray v Newham Citizens Advice Bureau Ltd.*[107] Mr Murray disclosed at a job interview the fact that he had been in prison for stabbing a neighbour in 1993, at which time he had been diagnosed as a paranoid schizophrenic. He was not offered the job and complained that he had been discriminated against contrary to the DDA 1995. The tribunal concluded that the reason why Mr Murray was not offered the job was the concern that he might be placed under stress in the job he was applying for and react in a violent way. The tribunal acknowledged that the stabbing incident was a direct result of Mr Murray's illness but ruled that his tendency to violence was a condition which was excluded by the 1996 Regulations. **2.116**

The EAT allowed Mr Murray's appeal. It reasoned that 'conditions' within the meaning of DDA 1995, sch 1, para 1(2)(b) (pursuant to which the 1996 Regulations were made) referred to free-standing conditions, and not to those conditions which were the direct consequence of a physical or mental impairment. Mr Murray's tendency to violence was not a free-standing condition, but a result of his paranoid schizophrenia. He was, therefore, protected by the DDA 1995. **2.117**

A similar issue arose in *Power v Panasonic UK Ltd.*[108] Ms Power was an area sales manager who went off work sick following an increase in her work load. She was both depressed and drinking heavily. The tribunal considered that the core issue for it to decide was whether Ms Power became clinically depressed and turned to drink, or whether her alcohol addiction had produced depression. The tribunal was not satisfied that the depression was not a symptom of alcohol addiction and rejected her claim. **2.118**

The EAT said that this was the wrong approach and allowed an appeal against this decision. It ruled that it was not material to a decision as to whether a person **2.119**

106 The 2006 Guidance, Part 2, para A14.

107 [2003] IRLR 340, EAT.

108 [2003] IRLR 151, EAT.

was suffering a disability within the meaning of the DDA 1995 to consider how the impairment in question was caused. 'What is material is to ascertain whether the disability which they have at the material time is a disability within the meaning of the Act or whether, where it is relevant, it is an impairment which is excluded by reason of the Regulations from being treated as such a disability'.[109] It, therefore, remitted the case for rehearing.

2.120 A different approach informed the EAT's decision in *Edmund Nuttall Ltd v Butterfield*.[110] In that case, Mr Butterfield had committed two offences of indecent exposure and one of dangerous driving on his way home from a business trip. The next day he broke down and was admitted to hospital. He was later sentenced to a three year community rehabilitation order with a condition of medical treatment, and was also disqualified from driving for two years. It transpired that he had been exposing himself to females over an 18 month period. When interviewed by his employers, Mr Butterfield told them about the driving ban but said nothing about the offences of indecent exposure. However, the employers subsequently found out about these and dismissed him on the grounds that they had lost trust and confidence in him as a result of the lies he had told.

2.121 The tribunal upheld Mr Butterfield's disability discrimination claim. It held that Mr Butterfield had only committed the offences of indecent exposure because he had a mental illness, depression. In line with the decision in *Murray*, it therefore ruled that he was protected by the DDA 1995, and that he had been discriminated against on grounds of disability.

2.122 The EAT allowed the employers' appeal. It was not persuaded that the concept of 'free-standing conditions' introduced in *Murray* was helpful. In its view, the critical question was one of causation. It asked itself what was the reason for the less favourable treatment, here dismissal of the claimant? If the reason (or at least an effective cause) was the legitimate impairment, then prima facie discrimination, subject to the defence of justification, would be made out; if the reason was the excluded condition and not the legitimate impairment, then the claim would fail.[111] It was clear to the EAT that the sole reason for the dismissal in Mr Butterfield's case was the excluded condition. The company took its decision that he must be dismissed, not because he suffered from a depressive illness, but because he had committed offences which could bring the company into disrepute and then lied about them. He was, therefore, not protected by the DDA 1995.

---

109 Ibid at para 12.

110 [2005] IRLR 751, EAT.

111 Ibid at para 29. See further the discussion in chapter 15 of *London Borough of Lewisham v Malcolm* [2008] UKHL 43, [2008] 4 All ER 525, [2008] IRLR 700 HL.

This case is clearly at odds with the case of *Murray*, where the EAT concentrated on what had caused the excluded condition in deciding whether or not it should allow the claimant's claim to be disabled. In *Butterfield*, the EAT concentrated more on what had caused the alleged discrimination. If it was an excluded condition, as it decided it was, then the claimant could not claim the protection of the DDA 1995, even if the excluded condition was the result of a legitimate impairment. **2.123**

The reasoning in *Butterfield* could lead to harsh decisions being made. Take, for example, the person who is suffering from a condition which causes anxiety. He tries to alleviate the symptoms of his condition through drinking, and he becomes addicted to alcohol (in other words, the converse of the tribunal's finding in *Power*). This leads to absenteeism from work, as a result of which he is dismissed. Following the reasoning in *Butterfield*, such a person would not benefit from the protection of the DDA 1995 because it was the addiction to alcohol which led to the dismissal, and that addiction does not qualify as an impairment by virtue of the 1996 Regulations. The person's protestations that it was only his anxiety which led to the addiction in the first place would count for nothing. **2.124**

However, there is nothing in the 1996 Regulations which says that they are not to apply if a valid impairment caused the excluded condition. Their effect could be rendered nugatory if tribunals were to be allowed to bypass them in that way. Although the reasoning in *Butterfield* does pay due regard to what the 1996 Regulations actually say, and therefore seems preferable to the reasoning in Murray, guidance from the Court of Appeal on this issue is much needed. **2.125**

H. Deemed Disabilities

1. Transitory Provisions of the DDA 1995

Any person whose name was on the register of disabled persons maintained under the Disabled Persons (Employment) Act 1944, s 6, both on 12 January 1995 and on 2 December 1996, was deemed to have a disability and hence to be a disabled person for the purposes of the DDA 1995 for an initial period of three years, that is, until 1 December 1999, without having to satisfy the requirements of the statutory definition of disability contained in the DDA 1995.[112] Thereafter, any such person had to satisfy the statutory requirements in the normal way. **2.126**

Although the transitory provisions referred to above are likely to be of historical interest only in relation to anyone whose claim is based on a present disability, **2.127**

112 2 December 1996 was the date when DDA 1995, sch 1, para 7 came into force.

they remain of value in relation to those who are not currently disabled but whose claim is based on the fact that they had a disability in the past. Those who satisfy the requirements of DDA 1995, sch 1, para 7 are deemed to have had a disability for the three year period from 2 December 1996 to 1 December 1999.

2. Blind and Partially Sighted Persons

2.128 A person who is certified as blind or partially sighted by a consultant ophthalmologist, or is registered as such in the register maintained by the local authority, is deemed to meet the statutory definition of disability.[113] There is, therefore, no need for such a person to prove that he is impaired in any way.

3. Cancer, HIV Infection and Multiple Sclerosis

2.129 As already noted at paragraph 2.79 above, as a result of amendments made by the DDA 2005, cancer, HIV infection[114] and multiple sclerosis are now deemed to amount to disabilities for the purposes of the DDA 1995.[115] There is no need for a person suffering from one of these conditions to prove that he has an impairment with the statutory adverse effects. He is deemed to be a disabled person from the moment when he is diagnosed as having the condition. Although provision is made for regulations to provide that these deeming provisions are not to apply to cancers of a prescribed description, no such regulations have as yet been passed.[116]

I. Proving Disability

1. Burden of Proof

2.130 It is for the claimant to prove, on the conventional balance of probabilities, that he was a disabled person within the meaning of the DDA 1995 at the relevant time.[117] The relevant time is the date of the act of discrimination which is the subject of the complaint. For obvious reasons, if the employer does not accept that a claimant employee was disabled at the relevant time and requires him to prove it, that issue will often be tried as a preliminary issue. There is no point hearing a complaint about discrimination if the claimant does not qualify for protection.

---

[113] Disability Discrimination (Blind and Partially Sighted Persons) Regulations 2003.

[114] Defined by DDA 1995, sch 1, para 9 as meaning infection by a virus capable of causing the Acquired Immune Deficiency Syndrome.

[115] DDA 1995, sch 1, para 6A.

[116] DDA 1995, sch 1, para 6A(2).

[117] *Morgan v Staffordshire University* [2002] IRLR 190, EAT at para 20.

The claimant will need to focus, therefore, on the evidence needed to prove or disprove the issue of disability at an early stage of the proceedings, such as at the case management discussion which is routinely now ordered in employment cases with a view to defining the issues once the parties have stated their respective cases. For example, is there an issue about the nature of the impairment? Is there an issue about the nature of the adverse effect upon normal day-to-day activities caused by the claimant's impairment? Is there disagreement over how long the adverse effect is likely to last, or about the likelihood of a condition recurring? Is it a reasonable adjustments case? If so, is there a need to prove how and when the impairment might have been expected to manifest itself to the employers? In short, what is the claimant trying to prove? If the claimant does not focus on the issues which he will have to prove to demonstrate that he meets the statutory definition of disability at an early stage, there is a real risk that the evidence adduced will fail to address key issues.[118] **2.131**

2. Expert Evidence

As noted by the EAT in *Morgan*,[119] there will be many cases where the illness is sufficiently marked for the claimant's GP, by letter, to prove it in terms which satisfy the DDA 1995. However, there will frequently be a need for expert medical evidence on the claimant's condition and prognosis. Such expert evidence is particularly likely to be needed in cases of mental impairment, despite the removal of the provision in the DDA 1995 that mental impairment only includes an impairment resulting from, or consisting of, a mental illness if the illness was a clinically well-recognized one.[120] **2.132**

Guidelines intended to provide a framework as to how expert evidence should be collected in cases before the employment tribunal were given by the EAT in *De Keyser Ltd v Wilson*.[121] Parties and their advisers should follow those guidelines if possible, because they are at risk as to costs if they do not. The key message to emerge from the guidelines is that, save where one side or the other has already committed itself to the use of its own expert (which is to be avoided in the absence of special circumstances), the joint instruction of an expert is the preferred course. If a party does want to rely on expert evidence and has already obtained its own **2.133**

[118] See, for example, *The Governors of the Lord Grey School v Pavlou* UKEAT/0363/07, [2007] All ER(D) 249 in which the EAT allowed an appeal because there was no proper medical evidence to support the tribunal's conclusion that the claimant's depression would have continued (and therefore qualify as long term) if untreated with medication.

[119] *Morgan v Staffordshire University* [2002] IRLR 190, EAT, at para 20.

[120] See para 2.32 above. As noted there, to the extent that they are aimed at proving that a mental illness is clinically well-recognized, the observations made in *Morgan* about the possible routes to establishing the existence of mental impairment within the DDA 1995 can be disregarded.

[121] [2001] IRLR 324, EAT. See para 10.60.

expert's report, advance notice should be given to the other side and a copy of the expert's report should be provided.[122]

2.134 Even where a joint expert has provided a report on the issue of disability, a party will not be prevented from instructing and calling its own expert witness, if dissatisfied with the report of the joint expert. However, that party will have to show that there is a good (rather than fanciful) reason for wanting to call its own expert after a joint expert has been instructed.[123] Thus, in one case, the EAT accepted that the employer should be entitled to instruct its own expert in an attempt to demonstrate that the symptoms allegedly suffered by the claimant were either not genuine or were the result of a mental impairment. The employer's argument that the claimant was not suffering from any physical impairment within the meaning of the DDA 1995 could not be described as fanciful in all the circumstances, especially in view of the substantial value placed on the claim by the claimant.[124]

3. Role of the Tribunal

2.135 The tribunal should adopt a purposive construction in deciding whether a claimant meets the statutory definition of a disabled person.[125] That decision is for the tribunal to make on the basis of all the evidence. It is not the role of the medical expert to give an opinion on that question. It is not the task of the medical expert to tell the tribunal, for example, what is a normal day-to-day activity. Nor is it for the expert to conclude that the adverse effects caused by a claimant's physical impairment are substantial. The expert can—and should—explain what the adverse effects are, but it is for the tribunal to judge whether or not they are substantial within the meaning of the DDA 1995.[126]

2.136 On the other hand, the existence and/or extent of an impairment, particularly a mental impairment, is very much a matter of expert medical opinion. In *Morgan*, the EAT cautioned tribunals against the dangers of forming a view on mental impairment from the way the claimant gives evidence:

> Aside from the risk of undetected, or suspected but non-existent, play-acting by the claimant and that the date of the hearing itself will seldom be a date as at which the presence of the impairment will need to be proved or disproved, tribunal members will need to remind themselves that few mental illnesses are such that their symptoms

---

[122] *Goodwin v The Patent Office* [1999] IRLR 4, EAT.

[123] The test established in the personal injury case of *Daniels v Walker* [2000] 1 WLR 1382, CA.

[124] *Hospice of St Mary of Furness v Howard* [2007] IRLR 944, EAT.

[125] *Goodwin v The Patent Office* [1999] IRLR 4, EAT.

[126] *Abadeh v British Telecommunications plc* [2001] IRLR 23, EAT.

are obvious all the time and that they have no training or, as is likely, expertise, in the detection of real or simulated psychiatric disorders.[127]

Should tribunals adopt a more proactive, interventionist or inquisitorial role than normal in disability cases? In *Goodwin v The Patent Office*,[128] Morison J appeared to indicate that this should be the case, when he pointed out that some disabled persons might be unable or unwilling to accept that they suffered from any disability; and that it might be symptomatic of their condition to deny it. On that basis, he suggested that such people might need direct assistance from the tribunal at the hearing. **2.137**

Whilst those observations may well be true, the Court of Appeal has subsequently stated that it would not be helpful to describe the role of the tribunal in that way. It pointed out that the role of the tribunal is to adjudicate on disputes between the parties on issues of fact and law, adding that it is not the duty of the tribunal to obtain evidence or to ensure that adequate medical evidence is obtained by the parties. That was a matter for the parties and their advisers. Sensible and sensitive use of the tribunal's case management powers would provide an opportunity for explanations to be given to unrepresented claimants prior to the hearing, thereby enabling justice to be done.[129] **2.138**

In the final analysis, the role of the tribunal is to decide on the issue of disability by asking itself the four questions set out in paragraph 2.03 at the beginning of this chapter, as formulated in *Goodwin*: **2.139**

(a) Does the claimant have an impairment which is either mental or physical?
(b) Does the impairment have an adverse effect on the claimant's ability to carry out normal day-to-day activities?
(c) Is the adverse effect upon the claimant's ability substantial?
(d) Is the adverse effect upon the claimant's ability long-term?[130]

Parties and their advisers should approach the issue of disability in the same way, using the statutory guidance as appropriate. **2.140**

127 *Morgan v Staffordshire University*[2002] IRLR 190, EAT, at para 20.
128 [1999] IRLR 4, EAT.
129 *McNicol v Balfour Beatty Rail Maintenance Ltd* [2002] IRLR 711, CA, at para 26.
130 *Goodwin v The Patent Office* [1999] IRLR 4, EAT.

3

DISCRIMINATION IN EMPLOYMENT: THE AMBIT OF PART II OF THE DDA 1995

A. Introduction

3.01 Part II of the DDA 1995 prohibits discrimination against disabled people in the employment field. The aim of this chapter is to explain how Part II works and to describe its ambit. It addresses three main questions:

(a) Who is protected against discrimination?
(b) What is the scope of the protection?
(c) Who is liable for any discrimination which takes place?

3.02 Notwithstanding its title, Part II covers a broad spectrum of workers in a range of occupations, not just employees. Although the main focus of this chapter will be on the protection afforded to employees, the other categories of workers covered by Part II will be briefly covered as well.

3.03 Part II begins with two sections which define what is meant by discrimination and harassment and which apply equally to all the categories of workers covered by Part II.[1] These sections were introduced following amendments made to the DDA 1995 by the 2003 Regulations.[2] As a result, there are now four different types of discrimination under the disability legislation, together with a statutory tort of harassment, as follows:

(a) discrimination for a disability related reason, defined in DDA 1995, s 3A(1);
(b) discrimination arising out of a failure to comply with a duty to make reasonable adjustments, defined in DDA 1995, s 3A(2);
(c) direct discrimination, defined in DDA 1995, s 3A(5);
(d) victimization, defined in DDA 1995, s 55;[3]
(e) harassment, defined in DDA 1995, s 3B.[4]

3.04 It is important to appreciate that these sections do no more than define what is meant by discrimination. They do not make it unlawful. A complaint can only be presented to an employment tribunal if the discrimination in question is rendered unlawful in a way specified in Part II of the DDA 1995. One of the central questions to be addressed in this chapter, therefore, is what acts of discrimination are made unlawful by Part II? As will be seen, that question depends on who is making the complaint. Although the protection afforded to the categories of

---

1 DDA 1995, ss 3A & 3B.

2 The Disability Discrimination Act 1995 (Amendment) Regulations 2003, which changed the section numbers of reason-related disability discrimination and the duty to make reasonable adjustments; and introduced direct discrimination for the first time. They came into force on 1 October 2004.

3 Victimization is a form of discrimination. See definition in DDA 1995, s 55(1).

4 The meaning of these different types of discrimination, and harassment, are analyzed in detail in chapters 4–8.

worker covered by Part II is broadly speaking the same, different sections of the DDA 1995 apply, depending on the category of worker concerned. The ambit of Part II is covered in Part B of this chapter.

For an employee, the relevant section is DDA 1995, s 4. It is this section which makes it unlawful for an employer to discriminate against a disabled person, and it does it by reference to each stage of the employment relationship, from application for the job through to termination of the employment relationship. A consideration of this section forms the main subject matter of Part C of this chapter. Other sections of the DDA 1995 make discrimination unlawful in a range of occupations. Those sections are considered in Part D. The question of who is liable for the discrimination is dealt with in Part E. **3.05**

Practitioners should read chapters 7–9 of the Code of Practice 2004. Chapter 7 contains detailed guidance on the avoidance of discrimination in the recruitment of employees, and chapter 8 does the same in relation to those who are employed. Chapter 9 looks at discrimination in occupation more generally, covering the specific occupations covered by the DDA 1995 and explaining, where applicable, any differences in the nature of the protection provided. **3.06**

B. Who Is Protected?

1. Employees

Statutory Definition

DDA 1995, s 4 makes it unlawful for an employer to discriminate against employees and applicants for employment. DDA 1996, s 16A makes it unlawful for an employer to discriminate against former employees.[5] 'Employment' is defined in DDA 1995, s 68 as 'employment under a contract of service or of apprenticeship or a contract personally to do any work, and related expressions are to be construed accordingly'. **3.07**

This is a broader definition of an employee than that contained in ERA 1996 which is restricted to 'an individual who has entered into or works under (or, where the employment has ceased, worked under) a contract of employment'.[6] The DDA 1995, in common with the other discrimination statutes, extends its protection not only to those employed under *a contract of service* (or of apprenticeship) but also to those who have entered into *contracts personally to do any work*. **3.08**

---

5 See para 3.115.
6 ERA 1996, s 230.

'Employed under a Contract of Service'

3.09 It will usually be obvious whether or not a worker is employed under a contract of service, but a worker's status is not always clear cut. Many people still work without the benefit of a written contract of employment. Many more obtain work through the medium of employment agencies. In such circumstances, the precise nature of the legal relationship between the person providing the work and the person doing it is sometimes far from clear. The status of agency workers, in particular, has been the subject of much litigation.

3.10 Although a detailed consideration of the law in this area is beyond the scope of this book, given that the protection afforded to disabled workers by the DDA 1995 varies according to the status of the worker making the complaint, it is important to summarize briefly what the law requires of an employment relationship.

3.11 **The Multiple Test.** Over the years, a number of tests have been devised by the courts to identify whether a worker is an employee. Although there is no single test which is determinative of the issue, the test most commonly used is the multiple test which states that there are three essential elements which must be present in a contract of employment:

(a) mutuality of obligation between the employer and the employee;
(b) an obligation on the employee to work personally;
(c) the employee must to be subject to the control of the employer.[7]

3.12 **Mutuality of Obligation.** This phrase is not particularly illuminating in itself. The parties to any contract must be obliged to do something for each other.[8] However, in the specific context of a contract of employment, the phrase is used to make the point that there must be some obligation on the employer to provide work, and some obligation on the employee to perform it. This mutuality of obligation was described as an 'irreducible minimum' requirement of a contract of employment in a case where power station guides were employed on a casual as required basis, and were held not to be employees because they were free to accept or refuse any work which they might be offered.[9] It is because they are not obliged to work that voluntary workers are generally held not to be employees.[10]

3.13 It is a question of fact and degree in each case whether the requirement of mutuality of obligation is made out. A worker can be an employee even if he is not required to work all the time, but only on individual engagements as and when required,

[7] *Ready Mixed Concrete (South East) Ltd v Minister of Pensions* [1968]2 QB 497; [1968]1 All ER 433.

[8] As pointed out in *Cotswold Developments Construction Ltd v Williams* [2006] IRLR 181, EAT.

[9] *Carmichael v National Power plc* [2000] IRLR 43,HL at para 18.

[10] See, for example, *South East Sheffield Citizens Advice Bureau v Grayson* [2004] IRLR 353, EAT.

provided that each engagement can be seen as a separate contract of service within each of which the necessary mutuality of obligation exists.[11]

3.14 **Personal Service.** The second condition requires the employee to provide his services *personally*. If a worker is under no obligation to carry out the work himself, but can delegate it to somebody else, this condition will not be met and the worker will not be an employee.[12] However, a limited power to delegate will not necessarily be held to be inconsistent with a contract of employment.[13]

3.15 **Control.** The third condition is that the employer must have ultimate control over the person engaged to carry out work if it is to be a contract of employment. In *Montgomery v Johnson Underwood Ltd*,[14] the claimant had been on the books of an employment agency through which she was sent to work as a receptionist for the same client company for more than two years. She argued that she was employed by the employment agency. The Court of Appeal held that she was not. The absence of sufficient control by the employment agency over her daily tasks was inconsistent with a contract of employment. Control was one of the necessary elements in a contract of employment.

3.16 As with mutuality of obligation, the control test comes into sharp focus when considering the status of agency workers. Who employs an agency worker? The agency or the end-user? Which of the two is ultimately in control of the agency worker? Both? Or neither? See the discussion at paragraphs 3.27–3.37 below.

3.17 **The Overall Picture.** Unless the three elements described above are all present, the contract under consideration cannot be a contract of employment. Even if all three elements are present, that is still not determinative of the question. It is necessary to step back and look at the overall picture in order to decide whether a person is an employee, or is carrying on a business on his own account.[15] Factors which might indicate that the worker was not an employee would include, for example, the fact that he provided his own equipment and support staff and took a degree of financial risk in the operation. Factors indicating employment would include the fact that the worker was paid for holidays and during sickness absence.[16]

3.18 An important point to bear in mind is that the terms of the contract may be oral, or written, or a mixture of the two. The assessment of an individual's employment status should be based on evidence about the entire relationship existing between

---

11 *Cornwall County Council v Prater* [2006] IRLR 362,CA.

12 *Express & Echo Publications Ltd v Tanton* [1999] IRLR 367, CA.

13 *Macfarlane v Glasgow City Council* [2001] IRLR 7, EAT.

14 [2001] IRLR 269, CA.

15 *Hall v Lorimer* [1994] IRLR 171, CA, at para 11.

16 See factors set out in *Market Investigations Ltd v Minister of Social Security* [1969] 2QB 173 at pp.184–5.

the parties, not just the written documents. Unless it is clear that the written documents were intended to constitute the entire agreement between the parties, in assessing the employment status of the individual, the court or tribunal should try to obtain an overall picture of the work relationship between the parties.[17]

3.19 Increasingly, the courts have been willing to look beyond the written terms of an agreement and to look at the reality of the situation in determining whether or not a contract of employment exists. In one case, for example, the claimant had been supplied by an employment agency to work for the Royal National Lifeboat Institute. The written agreement entered into between RNLI and the claimant provided that the claimant was a temporary worker and stated that the agreement should not be construed as constituting any relationship of employer and employee. It also stated that the agreement 'constituted the whole agreement between the parties'. Even so, the EAT held that, in the circumstances of this case, it was permissible for the tribunal to look beyond the written terms of the agreement and, looking at the working relationship as a whole, to find that the claimant was an employee of RNLI.[18]

'A Contract Personally to do Work'

3.20 The second limb of the statutory definition of employment in DDA 1995, s 68 is '*a contract personally to do any work*'. This wording is very similar to the extended definitions of employment contained in the SDA 1975 and the RRA 1976,[19] and it is clearly wide enough to include the self-employed, that is, those who provide their *services* pursuant to contracts entered into with their customers or clients, rather than providing *themselves* as workers subject to the control of an employer. The concept of a contract for the engagement of personal work or labour has been described by the EAT as a 'wide and flexible one, intended by Parliament to be interpreted as such'.[20]

3.21 However, mutuality of obligation is still required. In *Mingeley v Pennock & Ivory*,[21] the Court of Appeal held that an independent taxi driver could not bring a race discrimination claim against the respondent company for whom he worked because it was entirely up to him whether he chose to work or not. He was not

17 *Carmichael v National Power* [2000] IRLR 43, HL.

18 *Royal National Lifeboat Institution v Bushaway* [2005] IRLR 674, EAT. See also *Consistent Group Ltd v Kalwak* [2007] IRLR 560, EAT, where the EAT upheld a finding that there was a contract of employment between an employment agency and its workers even though the contract was clearly drafted with the intention of avoiding employment obligations.

19 SDA 1975, s 82, RRA 1976, s 78.

20 *Quinnen v Hovells* [1984] IRLR 227,EAT.

21 [2004] IRLR 373, CA.

obliged to work and, therefore, fell outside the extended definition of employment under the RRA 1976.

So is personal service. There must be a contract under which there is an obligation on the contracting party *personally* to carry out work or labour.[22] As to that, the test which has come to be applied by the courts in interpreting the discrimination statutes is that of dominant purpose. Is there any obligation imposed on a contracting party *personally* to carry out work or labour? If so, is that obligation the dominant purpose of the contract?[23] **3.22**

Two cases under the DDA 1995 illustrate the point. In *Sheehan v Post Office Counters Ltd*,[24] a sub-postmaster had a contract with Post Office Counters Ltd for the provision of post office services. Although it was accepted that the sub-postmaster was personally responsible for managing the business and liaising with the respondent, it was held that the dominant purpose of the contract was the regular and efficient carrying out of post office services. The sub-postmaster did not have to carry out these services himself. This was not, therefore, a contract personally to do work within the statutory definition. **3.23**

Similarly, in *J Hawkins v N Darken (t/a Sawbridgeworth Motorcycles)*[25] a driver entered into a contract to collect and deliver goods, but he did not have to do the work himself. He could send someone else to do it. The Court of Appeal held that he was not an employee within the extended statutory definition of employment in DDA 1995, s 68. **3.24**

2. Contract Workers

Statutory Definition

DDA 1995, s 4B makes discrimination against contract workers unlawful. 'Contract worker' is defined in DDA 1995, s 4B(9) as follows: **3.25**

> 'principal' means a person ('A') who makes work available for doing by individuals who are employed by another person who supplies them under a contract made with A;
>
> 'contract work' means work so made available; and
>
> 'contract worker' means any individual who is supplied to the principal under such a contract.

---

22 The fact that the work undertaken personally pursuant to the contract is provided to a third party will not take it outside the statutory definition. See *Burton v Higham (t/a Ace Appointments)* [2003] IRLR 257, EAT.

23 Answered in the affirmative in *Loughran and Kelly v Northern Ireland Housing Executive* [1998] ICR 828; [1998] IRLR 593, HL; and in the negative in *Patterson v Legal Service Commission* [2004] IRLR 153, CA.

24 [1999] ICR 734, EAT.

25 [2004] EWCA Civ 1755, CA.

3.26 Workers who enter into contracts to provide their personal services to people who do not employ them under a contract of employment are already protected from discrimination as a result of the extended definition of employment under DDA 1995, s 68 discussed above. The provisions of DDA 1995, s 4B protect, in addition, workers who do not personally enter into such contracts, but who are supplied to carry out work under contracts made by their employers. Such workers would include, for example, employees who are seconded out by their employers to work for another organization; or sub-contractors who carry out work for a main contractor pursuant to a contract made between their employer and the main contractor.

Agency Workers

3.27 The provisions of DDA 1995, s 4B are also apt to protect the sizeable proportion of the workforce whose services are made available to employers through employment agencies. As will be seen in part D of this chapter, what DDA 1995, s 4B does is to make the end-user (that is, the person providing the work) liable as principal for any unlawful discrimination against the agency worker. The fact that the end-user might not actually employ or contract directly with the agency worker in question is immaterial. The agency worker will still be protected.

3.28 Given that agency workers who are sent out to work for principals by their employers will be protected against discrimination by principals by virtue of DDA 1995, s 4B, it might be thought that the much litigated question of the employment status of agency workers is of little significance in the context of discrimination law. If the end-user is liable for any discrimination as a principal anyway, is there any point in asking whether the worker is, in fact, employed by the end-user?

3.29 The answer to that is that it may well make a difference. What if the employment agency is held not to be an employer of the agency worker who is sent out to work for the principal? In that event, the agency worker would not fall within the statutory definition of a contract worker set out above, and the end-user would not be liable as a principal. It would only be liable if it was held to be an employer of the agency worker.

3.30 **Implied Contracts.** In dealing with this problem, in recent years the courts have shown themselves willing to *imply* a contract of employment between the agency worker and the end-user. However, that trend has now been reversed, and a contract will not be implied unless it is strictly necessary.

3.31 The leading case in this area was the Court of Appeal decision in *Dacas v Brook Street Bureau (UK) Ltd.*[26] Mrs Dacas had worked as a cleaner for Wandsworth

[26] [2004] IRLR 358, CA.

London Borough Council for several years. She was registered with an employment agency, Brook Street Bureau, which had been responsible for finding her the job with the council in the first place. When she was dismissed, she claimed unfair dismissal against both, but the tribunal held that she was an employee of neither.

The Court of Appeal upheld the finding that she was not employed by the employment agency. Although she received her pay from Brook Street, the employment agency was not obliged to provide her with work and she was not obliged to take it. Furthermore, the employment agency did not exercise any day-to-day control over her work. (She therefore failed the mutuality of obligations and control tests described above).[27] **3.32**

Although Mrs Dacas did not appeal against the tribunal's decision that she was not an employee of the council, Mummery LJ went on to suggest that, in cases involving triangular arrangements of this kind, the outcome which would accord with practical reality and common sense, if it was factually and legally permissible to do so, was that the worker had an implied contract of service with the end-user. He said that employment tribunals should consider whether or not there was an implied contract of employment in every case where the issue arose. Sedley LJ went so far as to say that an inexorable inference would arise in favour of such a contract if the arrangements had been in place for a year or more. **3.33**

The guidance given by Mummery LJ in Dacas was subsequently approved by the Court of Appeal in *Cable & Wireless plc v Muscat*.[28] However, it emphasized the point that a contract of employment should only be implied where it was necessary to give business reality to a transaction.[29] **3.34**

The same point has now been emphatically made by the Court of Appeal in *James v London Borough of Greenwich*.[30] In this case, the claimant's services had been supplied to the council for a number of years by employment agencies. Written agreements between the claimant and the employment agencies expressly provided that her work would not give rise to a contract between her and the council. On returning to the council after a period of sickness absence, the claimant was told that she was no longer required because the agency had sent a replacement. When she claimed unfair dismissal, a tribunal rejected her claim that she had become an employee of the end-user and the EAT dismissed her appeal. **3.35**

27 See paras 3.12 and 3.15.

28 [2006] IRLR 354, CA.

29 See also *Craigie v London Borough of Haringey*, EAT UKEAT/0556/06, [2007] All ER (D) 82, EAT; *Cairns v Visteon UK Ltd*, EAT UKEAT/0494/06, [2007] ICR 616, [2007] IRLR 175; and *Wood Group Engineering (North Sea) Ltd v Robertson*, UKEAT/0081/06.

30 [2008] EWCA Civ 35, [2008] ICR 545, [2008] IRLR 302, CA.

In doing so, it offered the following guidance to tribunals in dealing with this issue:

(a) The issue in agency cases is whether the way in which the contract is in fact performed is consistent with the agency arrangements or whether it is only consistent with an implied contract between the worker and the end-user;
(b) The key feature is not just the fact that the end-user is not paying the wages, but that it cannot insist on the agency providing the worker at all;
(c) When agency arrangements are genuine and accurately represent the actual relationship between the parties (as is likely to be the case when there is no pre-existing contract between the worker and end-user), it will be rare that there will be evidence entitling the tribunal to imply a contract between the worker and the end-user;
(d) The mere fact that an agency worker may have worked for an end-user for a considerable period of time does not justify the implication of a contract between the worker and the end-user on the ground of necessity;
(e) It will be easier for a tribunal to infer a contract of employment with the end-user where the agency arrangements are superimposed on an existing contractual relationship between the worker and the end-user.

3.36 The Court of Appeal dismissed an appeal against this decision. It expressly approved the guidance given by the EAT, and Mummery LJ noted that future appeals would have little prospect of success where the decision had been reached by applying the correct test of necessity as described in the EAT's guidance. The question of whether an agency worker is an employee of an end-user is a question to be decided in accordance with the common law principles of implied contract. It was not for the courts or tribunals to extend employment protection rights to agency workers. That was a matter for Parliament.[31]

3.37 As a result of this decision, only rarely will an agency worker now be able to demonstrate that he is an employee of the end-user. As already noted, this will not matter if the worker in question satisfies the definition set out in DDA 1995, s 4B(9) referred to in paragraph 3.25 above, because he will then have a claim against the end-user as a principal. However, the practitioner should be alert to the different possibilities when framing a claim under the DDA 1995. The safe course to take where doubt exists about the employment status of a claimant is to bring claims in the alternative against the agency and the end-user.

---

[31] Note that a Private Member's Temporary and Agency Workers (Equal Treatment) Bill is currently being considered by Parliament, the purpose of which is to provide for the protection of temporary and agency workers and to require the principle of equal treatment to be applied to them.

Limited Companies. There does not need to be a direct contractual link between the worker supplied to work for the principal and the agency supplying him. A limited company can be interposed. That issue was determined by the Court of Appeal in *Abbey Life Assurance Company Ltd v Tansell.*[32] Mr Tansell was a computer consultant who provided his services through a limited company. He placed his name with an employment agency which specialized in placing computer personnel, and a contract was entered into between the employment agency and Mr Tansell's limited company to supply Mr Tansell's services to Abbey Life. Mr Tansell then developed diabetes and his services with Abbey Life were terminated. He complained of disability discrimination. The Court of Appeal held that he was a contract worker within the meaning of the DDA 1995 and, therefore, was eligible to bring a claim. It ruled that he had been supplied to work for the principal within the meaning of the statutory definition, despite the fact that his limited company was the entity supplied to the principal by the employment agency, not him personally. Provided there was an unbroken chain of contracts between the individual and the end-user of his services, the end-user was a principal for the purposes of the DDA 1995, and the individual was a contract worker. **3.38**

3. Other Categories of Worker

Specific provision is made in Part II of the DDA 1995 for the following categories of worker: **3.39**

(a) office-holders;
(b) partners;
(c) barristers;
(d) advocates;
(e) members of trade organizations;
(f) applicants for, or holders of, professional or trade qualifications;
(g) those seeking or undertaking practical work experience;
(h) members of local authorities;
(i) police officers.

The protection against discrimination and harassment afforded to the above categories of worker is substantially the same as that provided for employees. See Part D of this chapter. **3.40**

32 [2000] IRLR 387, CA.

4. Miscellaneous

Personal Representatives

3.41 A complaint brought under the discrimination statutes survives the death of the complainant. The Court of Appeal so held in the case of *Harris v Lewisham & Guy's Mental Health NHS Trust*[33] in which it allowed an appeal against the EAT's decision that a claim under the discrimination legislation must be regarded as a right of a largely personal nature which could not be continued after the death of the claimant.

3.42 The Court of Appeal ruled that a claim for compensation for discrimination is a cause of action within the meaning of the Law Reform (Miscellaneous Provisions) Act 1934, s 1(1), which provides that 'on the death of any person . . . all causes of action . . . vested in him shall survive . . . for the benefit of his estate'. There was nothing in the discrimination statutes which took away the right of a personal representative conferred by the 1934 Act. A claim of disability discrimination can, therefore, be brought on behalf of a disabled person by his personal representatives after his death.

Carers etc—Associative Discrimination

3.43 There is currently no provision in the DDA 1995 which specifically provides protection against discrimination based on a person's association with a disabled person, as opposed to his own disability. However, following the decision of the ECJ in *Coleman v Attridge Law*[34], tribunals will now have to strive to interpret DDA 1995 in a way which does provide protection against direct discrimination and harassment based on a person's association with a disabled person.[35]

3.44 The facts of the case were as follows. Ms Coleman was employed by Attridge Law as a legal secretary. She was not herself disabled, but was the carer of a disabled person, her son. She made various allegations against her employer, the thrust of which were that she had been abused and insulted, and treated less favourably than her colleagues, due to the fact that her child was disabled. When she complained of discrimination, the tribunal referred the case to the ECJ to determine whether the Framework Directive provided protection against associative disability discrimination. If it did, and if the DDA 1995 could be read consistently with such a construction, the claimant had a valid cause of action.

3.45 The employers' appeal against that referral was dismissed by the EAT which accepted that it was not clear whether or not the Framework Directive did prohibit associative discrimination. However, if it did, it ruled that the DDA

33 [2000] IRLR 320, CA.

34 [2008] All ER (D) 245, ECJ.

35 [2007] IRLR 88.

1995 was capable of being interpreted so as to include associative discrimination without distorting the words of the Statute and consistent with the domestic courts' responsibility to arrive at a construction which ensures that the Framework Directive is fully effective.

The ECJ has now ruled that the Framework Directive had to be interpreted as meaning that the prohibition of direct discrimination was not limited to people who were themselves disabled. Where an employer treated an employee who was not himself disabled less favourably than another employee was, had been or would be treated in a comparable situation, and the less favourable treatment of that employee was based on the disability of his child, whose care was provided primarily by that employee, such treatment was contrary to the prohibition of direct discrimination laid down by art 2(2)(a) of the Framework Directive. The same applied to the provisions of the Framework Directive prohibiting harassment.[36] **3.46**

This is a landmark decision which significantly extends the protection afforded by the DDA 1995. As noted above, the EAT has already concluded that, even as presently drafted, the relevant provisions of the DDA 1995 are capable of interpretation so as to include associative discrimination without distorting the words of the Statute and consistent with the domestic courts' responsibility to arrive at a construction which ensures that the Framework Directive is fully effective.[37] Given that the statutory definitions of direct discrimination and harassment contained in the DDA 1995 are both expressly defined by reference to the disabled person's disability (and no-one else's), it is somewhat surprising, to say the least, that the EAT, and now the tribunal, have felt able to reach this conclusion. It seems clear to the authors that additional wording will have to be interpolated into the Statute to make it fully compliant with the Framework Directive as interpreted by the ECJ in *Coleman*.[38] **3.47**

Volunteers

Generally speaking, volunteers will not be protected because, in view of the need for mutuality of obligation in a contract of employment, they will not satisfy the statutory definition of 'employment' found in DDA 1995, s 68. See, for example, *South East Sheffield Citizens Advice Bureau v Grayson*,[39] in which the EAT **3.48**

---

36 [2008] All ER (D) 245, ECJ.

37 [2004] IRLR 353, EAT. The tribunal now hearing Ms Coleman's case has reached the same conclusion at a pre-hearing review. It held that, on the basis of the ECJ decision, and in the absence of express and unambigous indications to the contrary, the DAA 1995 must be held to cover associative discrimination as well.

38 For the power of the courts to do this, compare, for example, *Litster v Forth Dry Dock Engineering Ltd* [1989] IRLR 161, HL, in which the House of Lords inserted words into the Transfer of Undertakings (Protection of Employment) Regulations 1981 in order to make them comply with EC Directive 77/187 relating to employee rights on transfers of a business.

39 [2004] IRLR 353, EAT.

overruled the tribunal's decision that volunteers at the CAB were engaged under a contract of employment within the meaning of DDA 1995, s 68(1). The EAT held that the critical question was whether the volunteers were contractually obliged to do work for the bureau. On the facts of the case, it decided that there was no such obligation. The volunteers did not have to work. They, therefore, did not satisfy the statutory definition.[40]

5. Territorial Ambit

3.49 The provisions of DDA 1995, ss 4 and 4B, relating to employees and contract workers apply only to employment or contract work done at an establishment in Great Britain.[41]

3.50 DDA 1995, s 68 (the interpretation section) provides that employment is to be regarded as being employment at an establishment in Great Britain if:

(a) the employee does his work wholly or partly in Great Britain; or
(b) the employee does his work wholly outside Great Britain, and
  (i) the employer has a place of business at an establishment in Great Britain;
  (ii) the work is for the purposes of the business carried on at the establishment; and
  (iii) the employee is ordinarily resident in Great Britain—
    (a) at the time when he applies for, or is offered, the employment; or
    (b) at any time during the course of the employment.

3.51 That definition applies to contract workers as well. The part of it which is likely to cause most difficulty in practice is in deciding whether the employee (or contract worker) who is working wholly outside Great Britain is nevertheless doing the work for the purposes of a business carried on by his employer within Great Britain.[42] This is a question of fact in each case.

3.52 No express provision is made for the other categories of worker protected by the DDA 1995. It is assumed that the same territorial ambit would apply.

6. Exemptions

Armed Forces

3.53 Although the protection against discrimination and harassment provided by the DDA 1995 applies to Crown employees in the same way that it applies to

---

[40] See also *Melhuish v Redbridge Citizens Advice Bureau* [2005]IRLR 419, EAT.
[41] DDA 1995, ss 4(6) and 4B(8).
[42] For a case on this issue, see *Williams v University of Nottingham*, EAT/0124/07, [2007] IRLR 660. See also *Lawson v Serco Ltd* [2006]ICR 250,HL.

employees generally, no such protection exists for members of the armed forces who have disabilities. They are specifically excluded from the ambit of the DDA 1995.[43]

C. Discrimination Against Employees

1. Statutory Framework

As pointed out in paragraph 3.04 at the start of this chapter, discrimination as defined by the DDA 1995 is not automatically unlawful. It is only unlawful if it occurs in circumstances covered by the DDA 1995. The first task facing the practitioner, therefore, is to identify the sort of discrimination which is the subject of the complaint. The next task is to consider whether such discrimination occurred in any of the circumstances made unlawful by the DDA 1995. **3.54**

For employees, the principle section which makes discrimination and harassment unlawful is DDA 1995, s 4. It is worth setting out its key provisions in full at the outset: **3.55**

> S 4 **Employers: discrimination and harassment**
> (1) It is unlawful for an employer to discriminate against a disabled person—
> (a) in the arrangements which he makes for the purpose of determining to whom he should offer employment;
> (b) in the terms on which he offers that person employment; or
> (c) by refusing to offer, or deliberately not offering, him employment.
> (2) It is unlawful for an employer to discriminate against a disabled person whom he employs—
> (a) in the terms of employment which he affords him;
> (b) in the opportunities which he affords him for promotion, a transfer, training or receiving any other benefit;
> (c) by refusing to afford him, or deliberately not affording him, any such opportunity; or
> (d) by dismissing him, or subjecting him to any other detriment.
> (3) It is also unlawful for an employer, in relation to employment by him, to subject to harassment—
> (a) a disabled person whom he employs; or
> (b) a disabled person who has applied to him for employment.

It should be noted that these provisions apply to all employers, however small.[44] Indeed, with regard to the provisions relating to applicants for employment, the prospective employer may not yet employ anyone at all. 'Employer' is expressly **3.56**

[43] DDA 1995, s 64.

[44] As originally enacted, the DDA 1995 had a specific exemption from its provisions for employers employing less than 15 employees. That exemption was removed by the 2003 Regulations.

defined to include a person who has no employees but is seeking to employ another person.[45]

2. Discrimination in Recruitment

'Arrangements'

3.57 DDA 1995, s 4(1)(a)makes it unlawful for an employer to discriminate against a disabled person in the *arrangements* which he makes for the purpose of determining to whom he should offer employment.

3.58 The meaning of 'arrangements' is very wide.[46] The arrangements in question are not confined to those which an employer makes in deciding who should be offered a specific job, but also include arrangements for deciding who should be offered employment more generally.[47] This clearly raises the possibility that an employer might discriminate against a disabled person whom he has never met and who has not even applied for a job yet. The matters considered under the headings below are all 'arrangements' for determining who should be offered employment.

Job Descriptions

3.59 Job descriptions can easily lead to unlawful discrimination against disabled people. The main point to bear in mind when considering this area is that, if the requirements stipulated for the job constitute 'arrangements' within the meaning of DDA 1995, s 4(1)(a), they will also constitute a 'provision, criterion or practice' for the purposes of DDA 1995, s 4A. If a disabled applicant for employment is substantially disadvantaged as a result, the duty to make adjustments will arise. Furthermore, if a disabled applicant cannot comply with the requirements of the job for a reason relating to his disability and is not offered it as a result, this will amount to less favourable treatment within the meaning of DDA 1995, s 3A unless the employer can justify the job requirements which he has laid down. It is in relation to these two kinds of discrimination that problems are most likely to arise for employers when stipulating job requirements.

3.60 Employers should, therefore, give careful thought to the following matters when drawing up job descriptions or person specifications:

the inclusion of unnecessary or marginal requirements;

blanket exclusions (that is, exclusions which do not take account of individual circumstances);

---

45 DDA 1995, s 18D(2).

46 See *Archibald v Fife Council* [2004] IRLR 651, HL per Lady Hale at para 62; *Smith v Churchill Stairlifts plc* [2006]IRLR 41, CA. Note also that "arrangements" are by definition included within the term 'provision, criterion or practice' for the purposes of Part II DDA 1995, see DDA 1995, s 18D.

47 The Code of Practice 2004, para 7.6.

stating that a certain personal, medical or health-related characteristic is essential or desirable for the performance of the job;

specifying that applicants must have certain qualifications for the job.[48]

Advertisements

The word 'arrangements' seems clearly apt to encompass within its broad remit a **3.61**
job advertisement. However, the Court of Appeal in *Difolco v NTL Group Ltd*[49] has cast doubt on this apparently straightforward proposition. In rejecting a claimant's claim that her employers had failed to comply with its duty to make reasonable adjustments by failing to offer her an alternative job which had been advertised on a part-time basis, the Court of Appeal pointed out that no duty to make reasonable adjustments could possibly arise in circumstances where the claimant had never applied for the job. (She had not). It went on:

> If the mere fact of advertising for a full-time job can constitute an 'arrangement' for the purposes of DDA 1995, then on the face of it, it would potentially discriminate against the whole innominate class of possible disabled applicants for the job.

That surely goes too far. It is hard to understand how a job advertisement placed **3.62**
by an employer could *not* constitute an arrangement for the purposes of DDA 1995, s 4(1)(a). The purpose of the advertisement is clearly to identify applicants for the job. What is that if not an arrangement made for the purpose of determining to whom an employer should offer employment?

A better analysis is that a job advertisement is indeed an arrangement which has the **3.63**
potential to be discriminatory, but the duty to make adjustments only arises if and when the disabled person is, or has notified the employer that he may be, an applicant for that employment.[50] Since nothing in DDA 1995, s 4A imposes any duty on an employer in relation to a disabled person if the employer did not know, and could not reasonably be expected to know, that the disabled person concerned was, or may be, an applicant for the employment,[51] the Court of Appeal could have relied on the employer's lack of knowledge to defeat the claimant's claim in *Difolco*, without casting doubt on whether a job advertisement was an arrangement.[52]

Specific provisions are contained in the DDA 1995 relating to discriminatory job **3.64**
advertisements.[53] In short, it is unlawful for a person offering a job, to publish an

[48] See the Code of Practice 2004, paras 7.7–7.10 and the examples given there. The observations made above relating to disability-related discrimination must now be read in the light of the House of Lords decision in *London Borough of Lewishan v Malcolm* [2008] UKHL 93, [2008] 4 All ER 525, [2008] IRLR 700, HL.

[49] [2006] EWCA Civ 1508, CA.

[50] DDA 1995, s 4A(2).

[51] DDA 1995, ss 4A(2) and (3).

[52] See also *Cardiff Women's Aid v Hartup* [1994] IRLR 390, EAT.

[53] DDA 1995, s 16B.

advertisement (or cause it to be published) which indicates, or might reasonably be expected to indicate, that the success of a person's application for the job may depend to any extent on his not having any disability, or any particular disability; or that the person determining the application is reluctant to make reasonable adjustments. Legal action in respect of discriminatory advertisements can only be taken by the EHRC.[54]

3.65 On the other hand, the DDA 1995 does not prevent job advertisements saying that the employer would welcome applications from disabled people. The Code of Practice 2004 notes that this would be a positive and public statement of the employer's policy. Indeed, there is nothing to prevent an employer from discriminating positively in favour of disabled people, and the DDA 1995 does not prevent jobs being advertised as open only to disabled people.[55] As noted by Baroness Hale in *Archibald v Fife Council*,[56] in that the DDA 1995 expects reasonable adjustments to be made to cater for the special needs of disabled people, it necessarily entails an element of more favourable treatment.

Selection, Assessment, and Interview Arrangements

3.66 The thrust of the message delivered to employers by the Code of Practice 2004 is that they should be pro-active in thinking about disability. That is particularly important in the arrangements made for assessing and interviewing applicants for employment whose personal circumstances will be unknown to the employer. Thus, for example, when inviting a job applicant to attend an interview, it would be good practice for an employer to ask whether any adjustments might be needed to enable him to participate fully in the process, and what those adjustments might be.[57]

3.67 That is simple common sense, and it accords with the overriding principle which employers must observe in this area: when selecting applicants for employment, they should ensure that, so far as possible, there is a level playing field. Where an employer knows, or ought to know, that an applicant has a disability and is likely to be at a substantial disadvantage because of the employer 's recruitment arrangements, to the extent that it is reasonable to do so, adjustments will have to be made to ensure that the disadvantage is removed and that the disabled applicant can compete on equal terms with non-disabled applicants. If the reasonable adjustments are not made, this will amount to unlawful discrimination.

---

[54] Equality Act 2006, s 25.

[55] Local authorities which are required to appoint on merit by Local Government and Housing Act 1989, s 7 are an exception to this.

[56] [2004] IRLR 651, HL.

[57] The Code of Practice 2004, para 7.24.

An example of a case relating to interview arrangements is *Ridout v T C Group*.[58] In this case, a claimant was shortlisted for interview. Despite the fact that she had told the employers about her epilepsy, and despite the fact that she arrived with sunglasses and made some comments about the fluorescent lighting in the room in which the interview took place, a tribunal rejected her claim that the employers had been in breach of a duty to make reasonable adjustments in respect of the physical arrangements for the interview. **3.68**

The tribunal thought that the claimant could have been much more forthcoming about what she regarded as being required. The EAT dismissed an appeal against this decision, holding that the tribunal was entitled to conclude that no reasonable employer could be expected to know, without being told in terms by the claimant, that the arrangements which were made for the interview might disadvantage her.[59] **3.69**

The decision in this case demonstrates how important it is for the claimant not to be reticent about mentioning any adjustments which he may think are required. Part of the reasoning of the EAT was that it was undesirable that an employer should be required to ask a disabled person numerous questions about his disability. The EAT thought that it would be wrong if, merely to protect themselves from liability, the prospective employers had to ask a number of questions which they would not have asked of somebody who was able-bodied. It said that people must be taken very much on the basis of how they present themselves. **3.70**

Although it is of course undesirable that disabled people should be subjected to questioning which they may well find intrusive, this is a case which could easily have been decided in favour of the claimant. Once she had made a comment about the lighting, and given that the employers knew that she had epilepsy, it was surely not asking too much to expect the employers to move the interview to a room where there was no fluorescent lighting, even if only as a precautionary measure. **3.71**

Useful guidance in this area can be found in the Code of Practice 2004. Employers and their advisers should study it and take note of its recommendations. It deals with, and answers, the following questions: **3.72**

(a) When should an employer short-list a disabled person for interview?
(b) What adjustments might an employer have to make when arranging or conducting interviews?
(c) What about aptitude or other tests in the recruitment process?

[58] [1998] IRLR 628, EAT.
[59] See also at para 4.151.

(d) When can an employer ask questions about a disability?
(e) Can a disabled person be required to have a medical examination?[60]

3.73 **Terms of Offers of Employment.** DDA 1995, s 4(1)(b) makes it unlawful for an employer to discriminate against a disabled person in the terms on which he offers that person employment. That is self-explanatory. An employer should not offer a job to a disabled person on terms which are less favourable than those which would be offered to other people. Take the example of a person with a history of depression who is offered employment with a six month probationary period, even though other employees are only required to serve a three month probationary period. This will amount to direct discrimination and will be unlawful.[61]

3.74 A requirement that a disabled person should undergo a medical test as a condition of an offer of employment, is a term upon which employment is offered and is potentially discriminatory. Even if this condition is applied to all to whom job offers are made, it is a provision, criterion or practice which may place the disabled person at a substantial disadvantage, therefore giving rise to the duty to make adjustments.

3.75 In *Paul v National Probation Service*,[62] the claimant, who suffered from a chronic depressive illness, was offered a job, subject to a satisfactory occupational health report. The occupational health adviser asked for a report from the claimant's GP, instead of from the consultant psychiatrist who was treating him. When she received the report, she took the view that the post would be too stressful for the claimant, and the job offer was withdrawn.

3.76 The EAT ruled that the tribunal had erred in dismissing his complaint, and that it had misidentified the arrangements (this was a case under the old law) which placed the claimant at a substantial disadvantage. It had, therefore, failed to consider potential adjustments which the employers could have made, including obtaining specialist advice from the claimant's consultant on his fitness for the post in question; speaking further to the claimant and, if appropriate, referring the matter back to the occupational health adviser; and taking steps in relation to adjusting the job they had offered.[63]

3.77 **Refusal to Offer Employment.** DDA 1995 s 4(1)(c) makes it unlawful for an employer to discriminate against a disabled person by refusing to offer, or deliberately not offering, him employment.

---

60 The Code of Practice 2004, paras 7.19–7.31. See also paras 6.14–6.16.
61 The Code of Practice 2004, para 7.32.
62 [2004] IRLR 191, EAT.
63 See also *Hammersmith & Fulham LBC v Farnsworth* [2000] IRLR 691, EAT.

That includes the withdrawal of an offer which has been made on a conditional basis. That is what happened in *Kenny v Hampshire Constabulary*.[64] The claimant, who had cerebral palsy and used a wheelchair, needed assistance with urinating. Although he was the best candidate for the job, his job offer was withdrawn because the employers were unable to find volunteers to help him with his personal care functions. The EAT found that an employer's duty to make reasonable adjustments under the old DDA 1995, s 6 was related to job-related matters only and did not go so far as to oblige the employer to provide a carer to assist an employee with his personal care functions. A line had to be drawn on the extent of the employer's responsibilities in providing adjustments to accommodate a disabled employee. It is doubtful whether this case would have been decided the same way under the duty to make adjustments imposed on employers by DDA 1995, s 4A which is not specifically restricted to job-related matters and is in much broader terms. In any event, the withdrawal of the offer was clearly covered by the provisions of DDA 1995, s 4(1)(c), even if discrimination was not made out.[65] **3.78**

The section does not include, however, the situation where an employee has been dismissed and seeks reinstatement on appeal. A refusal by an employer to reinstate an employee on the order of a tribunal does not fall within DDA 1995, s 4(1)(c).[66] **3.79**

3. Discrimination Against Employees

DDA 1995, s 4(2) makes it unlawful for an employer to discriminate against a disabled person whom he employs: **3.80**

(a) in the terms of employment which he affords him;
(b) in the opportunities which he affords him for promotion, a transfer, training or receiving any other benefit;
(c) by refusing to afford him, or deliberately not affording him, any such opportunity; or
(d) by dismissing him, or subjecting him to any other detriment.

Furthermore, DDA 1995, s 4(3)(a) makes it unlawful for an employer, in relation to employment by him, to subject to harassment a disabled person whom he employs. **3.81**

The component parts of DDA 1995, s 4(2) are dealt with in sequence below. **3.82**

64 [1999] IRLR 76, EAT.
65 See also para 4.24.
66 *Rhys-Harper v Relaxion Group plc* [2003] ICR 867, HL.

Terms of Employment

3.83 There is nothing in DDA 1995, s 4(2)(a) which requires the terms of employment in question to be contractual. Employers will frequently provide their employees with company handbooks and policies relating to a range of matters, such as sickness, redundancy, and health and safety. Such documents may, or may not, have contractual effect, but they will still form part of the terms of employment afforded to the employee for the purposes of DDA 1995, s 4(2)(a).

3.84 Terms of employment should not discriminate against disabled employees, and the employer should consider whether any reasonable adjustments need to be made to the terms and conditions which would otherwise apply. For example, an employer's standard terms and conditions of employment might state the hours when employees were expected to be at work. It is likely to be a reasonable adjustment to change these hours for someone whose disability means that he has difficulty using public transport during rush hours.[67]

Performance-related Pay

3.85 An obvious area in which disabled people might suffer a disadvantage is that of performance-related pay. This problem area is specifically covered by the Code of Practice 2004.[68] It notes that if, on the ground of disability, an employee is denied the opportunity to receive performance-related pay, this is likely to be direct discrimination. Even if less favourable treatment of an employee in relation to performance-related pay is not directly discriminatory, it may amount to disability-related discrimination unless the employer can show that it is justified.[69] If an employee has a disability which adversely affects his rate of output, the effect may be that he receives less under a performance-related pay scheme than other employees. The employer must then consider whether there are reasonable adjustments which would overcome this substantial disadvantage. Examples are given.

Sick Pay

3.86 Terms and conditions of employment frequently provide for sick pay to be paid to employees who are away sick, over and above their statutory entitlement. Typically, such sick pay schemes will entitle the sick employee to full pay for a specified period, followed by a period on half pay. The entitlement will then cease. Clearly, sickness absence may well be caused by an employee's disability,

67 The Code of Practice 2004, para 8.4.

68 The Code of Practice 2004, paras 8.5–8.6.

69 Although following *London Borough of Lewisham v Malcolm* [2008] UKHL 43, [2008] 4 All ER 525, [2008] IRLR 700, HL this may no longer be the case. See para 5.17 et seq.

and it is not surprising that disability discrimination claims have frequently been made in relation to the operation of such schemes. However, following the decisions of the EAT and then the Court of Appeal in *O'Hanlon v Commissioners for HM Revenue and Customs*,[70] such claims are now very unlikely to succeed.

In *O'Hanlon*, the claimant, who suffered from clinical depression, had exhausted her entitlement to full pay and then half pay, under a scheme operated by the respondent as a result of her frequent absences from work. She argued that she should have been paid in full during her entire sickness absence on the basis that this would have been a reasonable adjustment for her employer to make. Alternatively, she argued that periods of absence which were due to her disability (clinical depression) should not have been aggregated with periods of sickness absence which were not related to her disability. She also claimed disability-related discrimination, arguing that her employer had treated her less favourably for a reason related to her disability through halving her pay after 26 weeks and paying nothing after 52 weeks (in accordance with the terms of the scheme). **3.87**

The EAT rejected her arguments. It held that the duty to make reasonable adjustments would only very rarely require employers to give higher sick pay to a disabled person than would be payable to a non-disabled person who did not suffer the same disability-related absences. To do so would amount to a form of wage fixing for the disabled sick. Furthermore, it might act as a disincentive to return to work which would not accord with the purpose of the legislation. With regard to disability-related discrimination, the EAT accepted that a reduction in pay due to a sickness absence caused by disability was less favourable treatment for a disability-related reason, but said that it was justified by the extra cost and the potential difficulties which it would create for employment relations if disabled people were to be paid more than non-disabled people.[71] **3.88**

The Court of Appeal fully endorsed the EAT's decision, saying that it saw much force in the EAT's conclusion that it would be a rare case where giving a greater level of sick pay to a disabled employee would ever be a reasonable adjustment. Further, it said that the EAT's decision that any disability-related discrimination was justified could not be faulted. There were powerful economic reasons for the terms of the scheme to be adhered to, since it would cost a significant amount to **3.89**

[70] [2006] IRLR 840, EAT; and [2007] IRLR 404, CA.

[71] Note that the EAT's decision on disability-related discrimination should now be read in the light of the decision of the House of Lords in *London Borough of Lewisham v Malcolm* UKHL 43, HL, [2008] 4 All ER 525, [2008] IRLR 700, HL in which their Lordships held that *Clark v Novacold* ([1999] 2 All ER 977; [1999] ICR 951; [1999] IRLR 318, CA, the long-established Court of Appeal authority on identifying the comparator for the purposes of disability-related discrimination, had been wrongly decided. See chapter 5 for a full discussion of this case.

pay full pay to all disabled employees who were absent from work in circumstances where their pay would otherwise be reduced.

3.90 The one crumb of comfort which disabled employees can take from these judgments is the observation made by Hooper LJ in the Court of Appeal that it might be a reasonable adjustment to pay a greater level of sick pay to a disabled employee where the employer had caused the absence in the first place by failing to make a reasonable adjustment which would have enabled the employee to remain at work.[72]

Training

3.91 It is unlawful for an employer to discriminate against a disabled person in the opportunities which he affords him for training, or by refusing to afford him, or deliberately not affording him, any such opportunity.[73]

3.92 The Code of Practice 2004 deals with this statutory provision under the heading 'Induction, training and development'. Although 'induction' and 'development' are not specifically mentioned in DDA 1995, s 4(2)(b), the section is clearly wide enough to cover both. Examples are given of ways in which an employer might make reasonable adjustments in order to avoid disabled people being placed at a substantial disadvantage in relation to their training. Thus, an employer may need to alter the time or the location of the training for someone with a mobility problem, make training manuals, slides or other visual media accessible to a visually impaired employee (perhaps by providing Braille versions or having them read out) or ensure that an induction loop is available for someone with a hearing impairment.[74]

3.93 Once it is appreciated that the duty to make adjustments requires positive steps to be taken to eliminate disadvantages experienced by disabled people, much of this is plain common sense. A more subtle point lies behind the observation in the Code of Practice 2004 that employers must not discriminate in selection for training.[75] A disabled person might not apply for training because he thinks that he could not cope with it as a result of his disability. That is not an excuse for the employer not to consider him for the training in question in the first place. Failure to do so could well amount to discrimination.

---

[72] For an example of a case where the employer had caused the employee's disability, see *Nottinghamshire County Council v Meikle* [2004] IRLR 703, CA. See also paras 4.102–4.105.

[73] DDA 1995, ss 4(2)(b) and 4(2)(c).

[74] The Code of Practice 2004, para 8.8.

[75] Ibid.

Benefits

3.94 The embargo on discrimination applies to the receipt of any other benefit as well. The range of potential benefits or 'perks' offered to employees as part of their employment package is, of course, potentially endless. The benefit does not have to be contractual. DDA 1995, s 4(2)(b) would apply to the provision of non-contractual benefits as well. The Code of Practice 2004 notes the following examples: canteens, meal vouchers, social clubs and other recreational activities, dedicated car parking spaces, discounts on products, bonuses, share options, hairdressing, clothes allowances, financial services, healthcare, medical assistance/insurance, transport to work, company car, education assistance, workplace nurseries, and rights to special leave.[76]

3.95 As with all other aspects of the working relationship, the employer must ensure that benefits are made available to employees in a way which does not discriminate against disabled people. The duty to make reasonable adjustments may well arise. The Code of Practice 2004 gives the example of dedicated car parking spaces made available at work. It is likely to be a reasonable adjustment for the employer to allocate one of the dedicated spaces to a disabled employee who finds it very difficult to get from the public car parks further away. This is just one small example of the way in which the duty of reasonable adjustments might entail an element of positive discrimination in favour of a disabled person.[77]

3.96 Specific exemption is made for benefits of any description which the employer provides to the public, or to a section of the public which includes the disabled employee, if the employer is concerned with the provision of benefits of that description to the public.[78] What this is aimed at are benefits which the employer is providing to members of the public generally, not just for its employees. That is because the provision of those benefits relates to the employer's activities as a service provider rather than as an employer. The exemption will not apply, however, if the benefit to employees is materially different (for example, at a discount) or is governed by the contract of employment, or relates to training.

Promotion and Transfer

3.97 As with training and benefits, DDA 1995, s 4(2)(b) outlaws discrimination by an employer against a disabled employee in the opportunities afforded for promotion or transfer, as well as by refusing to afford him, or deliberately not affording him, any such opportunity. In all of these areas, the outlawing of discrimination extends beyond the decision not to promote, transfer, train or confer a benefit on

[76] The Code of Practice 2004 para 8.10.
[77] The Code of Practice 2004 para 8.10.
[78] DDA 1995, s 4(4).

the disabled person. Opportunities for promotion, transfer, training or the receipt of a benefit are covered as well.

3.98 A transfer to an alternative job is frequently an issue in disability discrimination claims when a disabled employee is no longer able to carry out the job for which he has been employed, and this will often be seen as a reasonable adjustment. In *Archibald v Fife Council*,[79] the claimant was employed by the respondent council as a road sweeper. Following an operation, she was confined to a wheelchair and was no longer able to carry out her job. The House of Lords held that the duty of reasonable adjustments could include transferring without competitive interview a disabled employee from a post she could no longer do to a post which she could do. Furthermore, the employer's duty might extend to moving the disabled person to a post at a slightly higher grade. A transfer could be upwards as well as sideways or downwards.

3.99 A refusal to promote an employee for a reason related to his disability will also be discriminatory, unless the employer can justify it. See, for example, *Greenwood v British Airways*,[80] in which the claimant claimed that he had been discriminated against when his employers refused to promote him because of his sickness record.

Dismissal or any Other Detriment

3.100 Finally, DDA 1995, s 4(2)(d) makes it unlawful for an employer to discriminate against a disabled person by dismissing him, or subjecting him to any other detriment.

3.101 **Dismissal.** A disabled person will be taken to have been dismissed for the purposes of the DDA 1995 if:

(a) he is expressly dismissed; or
(b) the period for which he is employed expires without his employment being immediately renewed on the same terms; or
(c) he gives notice, or does some other act to bring his employment to an end, in circumstances in which he is entitled to terminate it without notice by reason of the conduct of his employer (constructive dismissal).[81]

3.102 Constructive dismissals have only been expressly included within the ambit of the DDA 1995 following the amendments made by the 2003 Regulations. Prior to that, there were conflicting authorities on the question whether a constructive

[79] [2004] IRLR 651, HL.
[80] [1999] IRLR 600, EAT. This should now be read in the light of *London Borough of Lewisham v Malcolm* [2008] UKHL 43, [2008] 4 All ER 525, [2008] IRLR 700, HL.
[81] DDA 1995, s 4(5).

dismissal counted as a dismissal for the purposes of DDA 1995, s 4(2)(d). The question was finally resolved by the Court of Appeal in *Nottinghamshire County Council v Meikle*.[82] In that case, the claimant resigned as a result of her employer's persistent failure to agree to adjustments which she needed in order to enable her to return to work after sickness absence. The Court of Appeal held that this was a dismissal within the meaning of the section.

Inevitably, situations may arise where it is impossible for a disabled employee to continue at work because he can no longer carry out the job and he faces dismissal by reason of incapacity. However, there will also be other situations in which the dismissal of a disabled person fails to be considered. The disabled person may be dismissed for misconduct. He may face redundancy. He may be selected for compulsory ill health retirement. His fixed term contract may have expired. He may have walked out in response to a fundamental breach of contract by his employer entitling him to terminate his employment and claim constructive dismissal. All of these situations fall within the ambit of DDA 1995, s 4(2)(d), and the employer must take care to ensure that any dismissal is not discriminatory and therefore unlawful. **3.103**

Incapacity. It would be justifiable to terminate the employment of an employee whose disability makes it impossible for him to perform the main functions of his job any longer, if an adjustment such as a move to a vacant post elsewhere in the business is not practicable or otherwise not reasonable for the employer to have to make.[83] Provided correct procedures were followed, such a dismissal would be neither unfair nor discriminatory. **3.104**

Following *Archibald v Fife Council*,[84] the employer will have to consider whether a transfer upwards or promotion might be a reasonable adjustment to make if this would have the effect of keeping the disabled employee in employment. Ultimately, however, the DDA 1995 does not impose an absolute obligation on an employer to refrain from dismissing an employee who is absent from work as a result of his disability.[85] **3.105**

Useful guidance to employers on managing disability or ill health is given in the Code of Practice 2004 at paragraphs 8.15–8.23. Having made the general point that employers will often find that it is of benefit to their organization to retain a disabled employee where possible, rather than having to recruit and train a new member of staff, the Code of Practice 2004 deals with the issue of job retention in the context both of the disabled employee whose condition worsens, and the **3.106**

[82] [2004] IRLR 703, CA. For a decision going the other way, see *Commissioner of Police of the Metropolis v Harley* [2003] IRLR 263, EAT.

[83] The Code of Practice 2004, para 8.24.

[84] [2004] IRLR 651, HL.

[85] See, for example, *Royal Liverpool Children's Trust v Dunsby* [2006] IRLR 351, EAT.

disabled employee with a stable impairment who is faced with a change in the nature of his job.

3.107 The difficult question of confidential information and the extent to which an employer is entitled to let other staff know about an employee's disability is also addressed. Two points, in particular, are worth noting. First, sometimes a reasonable adjustment will not work without the co-operation of other employees, so that it may become necessary for the employer to tell one or more of the disabled person's colleagues about his disability (which may not be obvious). Second, the DDA 1995 does not prevent a disabled person from keeping a disability confidential from an employer. However, if he does so, unless the employer could reasonably be expected to know about it anyway, the employer will not be under a duty to make a reasonable adjustment.[86]

3.108 **Misconduct.** Where the dismissal of a disabled person is being considered by reason of misconduct, the employer may have to consider whether the misconduct was caused by the disability - and, therefore, whether he should modify the sanction he would normally apply. Take the example of a woman who shouts at her line manager in front of work colleagues and uses inappropriate language. The employer would usually consider dismissal as a sanction for such behaviour, but takes into account the fact that she was in great pain on the day in question because of her disability and instead issues a warning. This is likely to be a reasonable adjustment to make.[87]

3.109 Furthermore, the employer will have to consider whether any reasonable adjustments need to be made to the disciplinary or dismissal process where the dismissal of a disabled person by reason of misconduct is being considered. The Code of Practice 2004 gives an example of a young man with learning difficulties being allowed to bring a friend, rather than a work colleague, to a disciplinary hearing.[88]

3.110 **Redundancy.** When setting criteria for redundancy selection, employers should consider whether any proposed criterion would adversely impact upon a disabled employee. If so, it may be necessary for the employer to make reasonable adjustments. For example, it is likely to be a reasonable adjustment to discount disability-related sickness absence when assessing attendance as part of a redundancy selection scheme. Some employers use 'flexibility' as a selection criterion for redundancy (for example, willingness to re-locate or to work unpopular hours, or ability to carry out a wide variety of tasks). An employer should carefully

---

[86] The Code of Practice 2004, paras 8.21–8.23.

[87] The Code of Practice 2004, para 8.26.

[88] The Code of Practice 2004, para 8.26. See also *Taylor v OCS Group Ltd* [2006] IRLR 613, CA.

consider how to apply this criterion to a disabled employee as it might be discriminatory.[89]

Detriment. DDA 1995, s 4(2)(d) concludes by making it unlawful for an employer to discriminate against a disabled person whom he employs by subjecting him to any other detriment. The use of the word 'other' indicates that the detriment cannot consist of any of the unlawful acts already created by the section, and that this is a catch-all expression designed to cover any other discriminatory behaviour in the workplace not already catered for. **3.111**

The term has been given a wide meaning. It has been held that a detriment exists if a reasonable worker would, or might, take the view that the treatment was in all the circumstances to his detriment.[90] Although an unjustified sense of grievance will not suffice, it is not necessary for the claimant to demonstrate any physical or economic consequence of an action in order for it to amount to a detriment. The matter is looked at from the point of view of the person alleging detriment, and it suffices if he thinks that the treatment was to his detriment. However, his opinion must be a reasonable one to hold. The test is, therefore, not wholly subjective.[91] **3.112**

It is no longer necessary to argue that harassment amounts to a detriment in order to bring a claim. Harassment is now unlawful in its own right and has its own statutory definition under the DDA 1995. Furthermore, it is specifically provided that 'detriment' does not include conduct falling within the definition of 'harassment'.[92] Note, however, that the exclusion does not apply to pressurizing a person to discriminate by subjecting or threatening to subject him to any detriment. Conduct which amounts to harassment will still count for that purpose.[93] **3.113**

Harassment

Finally, DDA 1995, s 4(3) makes it unlawful for an employer, in relation to employment by him, to subject to harassment a disabled person whom he employs or a disabled person who has applied to him for employment. It should be noted that the harassment in question must relate in some way to the employment. The meaning of harassment for these purposes is covered in chapter 8. **3.114**

---

89 The Code of Practice 2004, para 8.25. See also *Kent County Council v Mingo* [2000] IRLR 90, EAT.

90 *Chief Constable of West Yorkshire v Khan* [2001]IRLR 830, HL.

91 *Shamoon v Chief Constable of the Royal Ulster Constabulary (Northern Ireland)* [2003] ICR 337, [2003] IRLR 285, HL.

92 DDA 1995, s 18D.

93 DDA 1995, s 16C.

4. Discrimination Against Former Employees

3.115 DDA 1995, s 16A applies to relationships which have come to an end, including employment relationships. It makes it unlawful for an employer to discriminate against a former employee by subjecting him to a detriment, or by subjecting him to harassment, where the discrimination or harassment arises out of, and is closely connected to, the employment relationship. For example, a disabled person working as a sales consultant has to go back to his former workplace for a meeting to finalize handover of his customer files to his replacement. On arrival, he is verbally abused by one of his former colleagues. The abuse relates to his disability. This is unlawful.[94]

3.116 It is also unlawful to victimize a person (whether or not he is disabled) after his employment has come to an end.[95] Take the example of an employer who gives a poor reference for an ex-employee who is disabled, referring to his disability as being a hindrance. This is an untrue reflection of the standard of work carried out by the disabled person. The poor reference was given because the ex-employee had brought a claim of disability discrimination against his former employer. Consequently, it is unlawful.[96]

3.117 Finally, an employer's duty to make reasonable adjustments also applies in respect of a former employee who is a disabled person.[97] The Code of Practice 2004 gives the example of a former employee with life-time membership of the works social club who is no longer able to access the club because of a mobility impairment. Once the employer becomes aware of the problem, he will need to consider making reasonable adjustments. The appropriate comparators in this last example would be former employees of the same employer who are not disabled. A hypothetical comparator can be used if necessary.[98]

5. Exemptions

National Security

3.118 As originally enacted, the DDA 1995 excluded from liability any act done for the purposes of safeguarding national security. Following amendments made by the 2003 Regulations, that blanket defence no longer operates in relation to the employment provisions of the DDA 1995. DDA 1995, s 59(2A) now provides that any act done for the purpose of safeguarding national security is not made

---

94 The Code of Practice 2004, para 8.28. See also paras 8.07–8.11.

95 DDA 1995, s 55.

96 The Code of Practice 2004, para 8.29. See also *Bond v Hackney Citizens Advice Bureau* [2003] IRLR 484, HL, where the House of Lords upheld the claimant's right to make a claim against the CAB for refusing to give her a reference after she had been dismissed.

97 DDA 1995, ss 16A(4)-(6).

98 The Code of Practice 2004, paras 8.30–31.

unlawful by Part II of the DDA 1995 if the doing of the act was justified by that purpose. Any employer who seeks to defend discriminatory behaviour on the grounds of national security will now have to show that it was justified for that purpose.

Statutory Authority

DDA 1995, s 59(1) excludes from liability any act done: **3.119**

(a) in pursuance of any enactment;
(b) in pursuance of any instrument made by a Minister of the Crown under any enactment; or
(c) to comply with any condition or requirement imposed by a Minister of the Crown (whether before or after the passing of this Act) by virtue of any enactment.

The House of Lords has held that the words 'in pursuance of any instrument' in the equivalent provision in RRA 1976 should be construed narrowly, so that only acts done *in necessary performance of an express obligation* contained in the instrument are covered. The exemption does not extend to include also acts done *in exercise of a power or discretion* conferred by the instrument.[99] **3.120**

This means that nothing is made unlawful by the DDA 1995 if it is required by an express statutory obligation. However, it is only in cases where a statutory obligation is specific in its requirements, leaving an employer with no choice other than to act in a particular way, that the provisions of the DDA 1995 may be overridden. **3.121**

DDA 1995, s 59 was successfully relied on by the employers in *Lane Group plc & North Somerset Council v Farmiloe*.[100] The claimant, who was employed as a warehouseman in the employers' warehouse, suffered from psoriasis as a result of which he was unable to wear the protective footwear which, following a risk assessment, the employers required all persons working in their warehouse to wear. The employers decided to make an exception for the claimant because of his medical condition, but the senior Health and Safety officer of the local authority told them that they could not do this because 'you cannot opt out of Health and Safety'. No alternative jobs could be found for the claimant and he was, therefore, dismissed. The EAT allowed an appeal against the tribunal's decision that the employers had discriminated against the claimant. It held that there was an absolute duty on the employers to comply with the Personal Protective Equipment at Work Regulations 1992 and that, by virtue of DDA 1995, s 59, this took precedence over the disability discrimination legislation. **3.122**

99 *Hampson v Department of Education and Science* [1981] IRLR 302, HL.
100 UKEAT/0352/03/DA & UKEAT/0357/03/DA, [2004] All ER (D) 8.

3.123 It is in the context of health and safety legislation that this exemption is most likely to be raised as a defence by employers. However, such defences will be carefully scrutinized. If employers are too easily allowed to sidestep the duties they owe to disabled employees by citing health and safety reasons, the whole purpose of the DDA 1995 would be defeated.

D. Discrimination Against Other Categories of Worker

1. Statutory Framework

3.124 Specific sections of the DDA 1995 outlaw discrimination and harassment against other categories of worker in much the same way as DDA 1995, s 4 outlaws discrimination and harassment in respect of employees. DDA 1995, s 16A dealing with relationships which have come to an end, applies to all these categories of worker as well. The definitions of discrimination and harassment contained in DDA 1995, ss 3A and 3B remain the same and apply to all categories of worker who are protected by the DDA 1995.

3.125 Guidance on discrimination in occupation is contained in chapter 9 of the Code of Practice 2004.

2. Contract Workers[101]

3.126 DDA 1995, s 4B(1) makes it unlawful for a principal, in relation to contract work, to discriminate against a disabled person who is a contract worker:

(a) in the terms on which he allows him to do that work;
(b) by not allowing him to do it or continue to do it;
(c) in the way he affords him access to any benefits or by refusing or deliberately omitting to afford him access to them; or
(d) by subjecting him to any other detriment.[102]

3.127 DDA 1995, s 4B(2) makes it unlawful for a principal, in relation to contract work, to subject a disabled contract worker to harassment.

3.128 Although the above provisions are similar to those which relate to employees, they are not identical because they are specially tailored to cover the relationship between a contract worker and a principal. For that reason, there is no express prohibition

---

[101] For the definition of a 'contract worker', see para 3.25 of this chapter.

[102] Under the DDA 1995 as originally enacted, these provisions were to be found in s 12. This was the section relied on by the claimant in *Abbey Life Assurance Co Ltd v Tansell* [2000] IRLR 387, CA. See para 3.38 above.

on discriminating against a contract worker in, for example, the opportunities which the principal affords him for promotion. That would be inapposite in the case of a contract worker. However, as noted in the Code of Practice 2004:

> The effect of the Act is that, where a person is a principal for the purposes of the Act, he is treated as if he were, or would be, the actual employer of the disabled contract worker. Therefore, the same principles relating to discrimination apply to a principal as to an employer.[103]

The duty to make reasonable adjustments applies to principals in the same way that it applies to employers. However, a principal is not required to make a reasonable adjustment which the disabled contract worker's employer is already under a duty to make.[104] What this means in practice is that the principal is responsible for any additional reasonable adjustments which might need to be made as a result of the principal's own arrangements or premises. For example, the principal may need to make an adjustment to his premises to cater for a contract worker who uses a wheelchair. **3.129**

The employer's duty to make reasonable adjustments is also extended in the case of contract workers. If the contract worker is likely to be substantially disadvantaged on each occasion when he is supplied to a principal to do contract work by a provision, criterion or practice applied by, or physical feature of premises occupied by, all or most of the principals to whom he is or might be supplied, the employer is under a duty to make a reasonable adjustment.[105] **3.130**

This additional duty on the employer only arises if the contract worker is likely to be affected in this way each time he is supplied for work. The employer would have to make reasonable adjustments to overcome the disadvantage wherever it might arise, rather than taking separate steps in relation to each principal. Take the example of a blind secretary employed by an employment business who is supplied to other organizations for secretarial work. Her ability to access standard computer equipment places her at a substantial disadvantage at the offices of all, or most of, the principals to whom she might be supplied. The employment business provides her with a specially adapted portable computer and Braille keyboard.[106] **3.131**

There is clearly potential for the disabled contract worker to fall between two stools here. The employer might think that a reasonable adjustment is the responsibility of the principal to make, and vice versa. Alert to this possibility, the Code of Practice 2004 notes that it is good practice for the principal and the employer **3.132**

---

103 The Code of Practice 2004, para 9.6.
104 DDA 1995, ss 4B(6) and (7).
105 DDA 1995, ss 4B(4) and (5).
106 The Code of Practice 2004, para 9.10.

to co-operate with each other, to discuss what adjustments should be made, and who should make them.[107]

3. Office-Holders

3.133 Office-holders are brought within the scope of the disability discrimination legislation by virtue of DDA 1995, ss 4C–4F. Examples of office-holders include company directors, judges, and chairmen or members of non-departmental public bodies. What the holders of such offices or posts have in common is that they are not regarded as 'employees' by the law, even though they may be similar to employees in providing services personally under the direction of another in return for remuneration.[108] Most political posts are excluded.[109]

3.134 In order to qualify for protection, the office or post in question must satisfy one or more of the following conditions:

(a) The office or post is one to which persons are appointed to discharge functions personally under the direction of another person, and in respect of which they are entitled to remuneration.
(b) The office or post is one to which appointments are made by a Minister of the Crown, a government department, the National Assembly of Wales or any part of the Scottish Administration.
(c) The office or post is one to which appointments are made on the recommendation of, or subject to approval of, a person referred to in paragraph (b) above.[110]

3.135 DDA 1995, s 4D makes it unlawful to discriminate against or harass office-holders, or applicants for such offices. DDA 1995, s 4E imposes a duty to make reasonable adjustments in relation to office-holders. The prohibitions against discrimination and harassment, and the duty to make reasonable adjustments, are all similar to the provisions relating to employees contained in DDA 1995, ss 4 and 4A. A useful summary of these provisions can be found in the Code of Practice 2004 at paragraphs 9.14–9.22.

3.136 In relation to office-holders, the person responsible for the duties imposed by the DDA 1995 is defined as the 'relevant person'.[111] As noted in the Code of Practice

---

107 The Code of Practice 2004, para 9.12.

108 The Code of Practice 2004, para 9.14. See also the discussion in *Percy v Church of Scotland Board of Natural Mission* [2006] IRLR 195, HL.

109 DDA 1995, s 4C(5).

110 DDA 1995, s 4C(3).

111 DDA 1995, s 4F.

2004, the person on whom the duties are imposed depends on the circumstances. It may be:

(i) the person with power to make the appointment;
(ii) the person or body with power to recommend or approve the appointment;
(iii) the person with power to determine the terms or working conditions of the appointment (including any benefit or physical feature); or
(iv) the person with power to terminate the appointment.[112]

4. Partners

Partners are covered by DDA 1995, ss 6A–6C. Partnership generally involves a contract between the partners to engage in a business with a view to profit.[113] The provisions only apply to partners in the true legal sense of the word. They do not apply to salaried partners, who, generally speaking, are not true partners but employees of the firm for whom they work.[114] **3.137**

DDA 1995, s 6A makes it unlawful for a firm to discriminate against or harass disabled partners or applicants for partnership in the firm. Again, the provisions are very similar to those contained in DDA 1995, s 4 relating to employees. Indeed, the Code of Practice 2004 notes that the effect of the Act is to give a partner, or applicant for partnership, similar rights against the firm to those of an employee or job applicant against an employer. The same applies where people are proposing to form themselves into a partnership and a disabled person is a prospective partner. Limited liability partnerships are also covered.[115] **3.138**

The duty to make reasonable adjustments applies to partnerships in the same way that it applies to employers. See DDA 1995, s 6B. There is, however, one major difference. Whereas an employee cannot be required to contribute towards the cost of making a reasonable adjustment which his employer makes on his behalf, a prospective or actual partner in a firm may have to make a contribution. That is the effect of DDA 1995, s 6B(4) which states that the cost of carrying out the reasonable adjustment shall be treated as an expense of the firm. Provided that the disabled person in whose favour the reasonable adjustment was made is, or becomes, a partner in the firm, he can be required to contribute a reasonable amount towards the cost, particular regard being paid to the proportion in which he is entitled to share in the firm's profits. **3.139**

---

112 The Code of Practice 2004, para 9.22.

113 See Partnership Act 1890, s 1.

114 If the salaried partner does not show profits, this is an important factor suggesting that he is not a true partner, although it is not necessarily conclusive. See, for example, *M Young Legal Associates v Zahid* [2006] EWCA Civ 613, CA.

115 The Code of Practice para 9.27 and DDA 1995, s 6C.

5. Barristers and Advocates

3.140 DDA 1995, s 7A(1) makes it unlawful for a barrister or a barrister's clerk to discriminate against a disabled person in relation to any offer of a pupillage or tenancy. DDA 1995, s 7A(2) makes it unlawful for a barrister or barrister's clerk to discriminate against existing pupils or tenants. Harassment of a prospective or actual pupil or tenant is made unlawful by DDA 1995, s 7A(3). Again, the wording of these sections closely follows that contained in DDA 1995, s 4 relating to employees.

3.141 Disabled pupils, tenants and applicants for pupillage or tenancy are, therefore, protected from internal discrimination against them by fellow barristers or barristers' clerks. In addition, DDA 1995, s 7A(4) makes it unlawful for any person to discriminate against a disabled person or to subject him to harassment in relation to the giving, withholding or acceptance of instructions to a barrister. It would, therefore, be unlawful for a solicitor to refuse to instruct a barrister merely because he has a disability.[116] That would amount to direct discrimination. Furthermore, it would potentially be unlawful for a solicitor to refuse to instruct a disabled barrister because, due to his disability, it would take longer for him to comply with the instructions. Unless the solicitor could justify the need for the instructions to be turned around quickly, that might amount to discrimination for a reason related to the barrister's disability.[117]

3.142 Barristers and their clerks are under the same duty to make reasonable adjustments in respect of pupils, tenants and applicants for pupillage or tenancy as is imposed on employers in respect of their employees by DDA 1995, s 4A.[118] The duty applies to each member of chambers. The duty does not, however, extend to solicitors. They are under no duty to make a reasonable adjustment in relation to disabled barristers instructed by them.

3.143 Very similar provisions to those set out above in relation to barristers in England and Wales apply to advocates in Scotland. Due to the fact that advocates in Scotland do not practise from sets of chambers, the scope of the sections covering advocates is limited to their duties towards prospective and actual pupils. See DDA 1995, ss 7C–7D. As noted in the Code of Practice 2004, advocates in Scotland tend to practise from home. Where a disabled pupil is taken on by an advocate who practises from home, this may affect the extent of the adjustments which it is reasonable for the advocate to make.[119]

---

116 The Code of Practice 2004, para 9.37.

117 However, see now chapter 5 and the decision in *London Borough of Lewisham v Malcolm* [2008] UKHL 43, [2008] 4 All ER 525, [2008] IRLR 700, HL.

118 DDA 1995, s 7B.

119 The Code of Practice 2004, para 9.41.

6. Trade Organizations

Members of trade organizations are covered by DDA 1995, ss 13–14. A 'trade organization' is defined as: 3.144

(a) an organization of workers;
(b) an organization of employers; or
(c) any other organization whose members carry on a particular profession or trade for the purposes of which the organization exists.

DDA 1995, s 13 makes it unlawful for a trade organization to discriminate against, or harass, its members, or applicants for its membership, in terms very similar to those contained in DDA 1995, s 4 relating to employers. DDA 1995, s 14 imposes on the trade organization a duty to make adjustments in relation to disabled members of the organization or disabled applicants for membership. Again, this duty is very similar to that imposed on employers by DDA 1995, s 4A. It should be noted that a separate Code of Practice has been issued by the EHRC relating to trade organizations and qualifications bodies, to which reference should be made for further guidance in this area.[120] 3.145

7. Qualifications Bodies

A qualifications body is defined to mean any authority or body which can confer, renew or extend a professional or trade qualification, but it does not include bodies responsible for schools, local education authorities in England or Wales or education authorities in Scotland.[121] As mentioned in the preceding paragraph, a separate Code of Practice has been issued by the DRC in relation to qualifications bodies.[122] 3.146

DDA 1995, s 14A(1) makes it unlawful for a qualifications body to discriminate against a disabled person: 3.147

(a) in the arrangements which it makes for the purpose of determining upon whom to confer a professional or trade qualification;
(b) in the terms on which it is prepared to confer a professional or trade qualification on him;
(c) by refusing or deliberately omitting to grant any application by him for such a qualification; or

---

120 The Disability Discrimination Act 1995 Code of Practice for Trade Organisations, Qualification Bodies and General Qualifications Bodies 2008.

121 DDA 1995, s 14A(5).

122 The Disability Discrimination Act 1995 Code of Practice for Trade Organisations, Qualification Bodies and General Qualifications Bodies 2008.

(d) by withdrawing such a qualification from him or varying the terms on which he holds it.

3.148 The justification defence for discrimination set out in DDA 1995, s 3A is modified for qualifications bodies so that it takes the form of the justification defence for indirect discrimination in the other discrimination statutes. DDA 1995, s 14A(3) provides that justification is to be measured by reference to a 'competence standard', which is defined as 'an academic, medical or other standard applied by or on behalf of a qualifications body for the purpose of determining whether or not a person has a particular level of competence or ability'.[123]

3.149 In determining whether the application by a qualifications body of a competence standard to a disabled person constitutes discrimination, the application of the standard is justified for the purposes of DDA 1995, s 3A(1)(b) if, but only if, the qualifications body can show that:

(a) the standard is, or would be, applied equally to persons who do not have his particular disability; and
(b) its application is a proportionate means of achieving a legitimate aim.

3.150 DDA 1995, s 14A(2)makes it unlawful for a qualifications body, in relation to a professional or trade qualification conferred by it, to subject to harassment a disabled person who holds, or applies for, such a qualification.

3.151 DDA 1995, s 14B sets out the duty to make adjustments which applies to qualifications bodies. It is in the same terms as the duty to make adjustments which applies to employers, adapted as necessary.[124] However, it specifically does not relate to a competence standard. No duty is imposed on a qualifications body to make any adjustments to a competence standard in order to accommodate disabled people.

8. Practical Work Experience

3.152 Those seeking practical work experience are covered by DDA 1995, ss 14C–14D, inserted by the 2003 Regulations. 'A placement provider' is defined as meaning any person who provides a work placement to a person whom he does not employ. 'Work placement' is defined as meaning practical work experience undertaken for a limited period for the purposes of a person's vocational training.[125]

3.153 DDA 1995, s 14C(1) makes it unlawful for placement providers to discriminate against a disabled person seeking or undertaking a work placement. DDA 1995,

---

123 DDA 1995, s 14A(5).

124 For a case under this section, see *Project Management Institute v Latif* [2007] IRLR 579, EAT.

125 DDA 1995, s 14C(4).

s 14C(2) outlaws harassment. DDA 1995, s 14D imposes a duty on placement providers to make reasonable adjustments. These provisions are all very similar to those contained in DDA 1995, ss 4 and 4A relating to employers.

It should be noted that there may be a dual responsibility to make reasonable adjustments when disabled people are sent on a work placement, both on the sending organization and on the placement provider. As with the situation where an employer and a principal are expected to co-operate to ensure that appropriate adjustments are made in relation to contract workers, so in this area, it would be reasonable to expect the sending organization and the placement provider to co-operate in the case of those sent on work placements.[126] **3.154**

9. Local Authorities

The relationships between locally-electable authorities and their members are governed by DDA 1995, ss 15A–15C. These sections apply, inter alia, to the Greater London Authority; county councils; county borough councils; district councils; and London borough councils.[127] In much the same way as the other relationships covered above, these sections make it unlawful for local authorities to discriminate against their members. **3.155**

DDA 1995, s 15B(1) makes it unlawful for an authority to discriminate against a disabled person who is a member of the authority: **3.156**

(a) in the opportunities which it affords the disabled person to receive training, or any other facility, for his carrying-out of official business;
(b) by refusing to afford, or deliberately not affording, the disabled person any such opportunities; or
(c) by subjecting the disabled person to any other detriment in connection with his carrying out of official business.

DDA 1995, s 15B(2) makes it unlawful for an authority to subject a disabled person who is a member of the authority to harassment in connection with his carrying-out of official business. **3.157**

DDA 1995, s 15C imposes a duty on authorities to make adjustments where a provision, criterion or practice applied by, or on behalf of, an authority or any physical feature of premises occupied by, or under the control of, such an authority, places a disabled person who is a member of the authority at a substantial disadvantage, in comparison with members of the authority who are not disabled persons, in connection with his carrying-out of official business. **3.158**

126 The Code of Practice 2004, paras 9.42–9.50.
127 For a full list, see DDA 1995, s 15A.

Disability Equality Duty

3.159 It is relevant to note here that new obligations for public authorities are imposed by the disability equality duty which was introduced by the DDA 1995, s 49A, and which came into force on 4 December 2006. The disability equality duty requires a public authority, when carrying out its functions, to have due regard to the need:

(i) to eliminate unlawful disability discrimination;
(ii) to eliminate harassment of disabled persons that is related to their disabilities;
(iii) to promote equality of opportunity between disabled persons and other persons;
(iv) to take steps to take account of disabled persons' disabilities, even where that involves treating disabled persons more favourably than other persons;
(v) to promote positive attitudes towards disabled persons;
(vi) to encourage participation by disabled persons in public life.

3.160 Full guidance as to the operation of the disability equality duty can be found in a Code of Practice published by the DRC.[128] It has also published a guide specifically dealing with the operation of the disability equality duty in the employment field. No private legal rights are created for employees of such public authorities by the disability equality duty, and further discussion of it is, therefore, beyond the scope of this book.

10. Police

3.161 Specific provision is made for police officers by DDA 1995, s 64A which was inserted by the 2003 Regulations and which provides that the holding of the office of constable shall be treated as employment:

(a) by the chief officer of police as respects any act done by him in relation to a constable or that office;
(b) by the police authority as respects any act done by them in relation to a constable or that office.

3.162 Police officers, therefore, now have the same rights as other employees under Part II of the DDA 1995. They are treated as being in the employment of the chief officer of police for the purposes of the provisions of the DDA 1995 which impose vicarious liability for the acts of others.[129] The chief officer of police is, therefore, liable for acts of discrimination carried out by his officers. Proceedings should be brought against the chief officer of police and/or the police authority.

---

128 The Duty to Promote Disability Equality: Statutory Code of Practice.
129 DDA 1995, s 64A(2) and s 58.

E. Who Is Liable?

1. Primary Liability

As seen in the preceding section of this chapter, the DDA 1995 pins primary liability for unlawful acts of discrimination on those responsible for the unlawful act concerned. For example: **3.163**

(a) The employer is liable for unlawful acts of discrimination against his employees.
(b) The principal is liable for unlawful acts of discrimination against contract workers, although the employer can also be liable (for example, for a failure to make a reasonable adjustment).
(c) The 'relevant person' is liable for unlawful acts of discrimination against office holders.
(d) The firm is liable for unlawful acts of discrimination against partners.
(e) Barristers or their clerks (and anyone giving instructions to a barrister) are liable for unlawful acts of discrimination against pupils and tenants, and advocates are similarly liable in Scotland;
(f) Placement providers are liable for unlawful acts of discrimination against those undertaking work placements; and
(g) The chief officer of police and / or the police authority are liable for unlawful acts of discrimination against police constables.

2. Secondary Liability

Employers

Additional protection for employees is provided by DDA 1995, s 58(1) which states that: **3.164**

> anything done by a person in the course of his employment shall be treated for the purposes of this Act as also done by his employer, whether or not it was done with the employer's knowledge or approval.

An employer is, therefore, made liable for the discriminatory acts of his employees in the course of their employment, whether or not they were done with the employer's knowledge or approval. The employer will only be able to defend the claim if he can show that he took reasonable steps to prevent the acts in question from occurring.[130] **3.165**

In the Course of Employment. The central issue in determining whether or not an employer is vicariously liable for the acts of his employee at common law **3.166**

130 DDA 1995, s 58(5).

is whether or not the employee could be said to be acting in the course of his employment when he carried out the tortious act. The traditional approach to the question was to ask whether the act complained of was an act which the employee was authorized to do, albeit carried out in an improper way. Or was the employee on a frolic of his own?

3.167 That approach was rejected in a harassment case brought under RRA 1976.[131] The EAT had found that the appalling acts which had been committed against a 16 year old boy could not, by any stretch of the imagination, be described as having been done in the course of employment, in the sense of being an improper mode of performing tasks which the perpetrators were employed to do. The Court of Appeal decided that the 'course of employment' test in RRA 1976 (and, therefore, the other discrimination statutes as well) was not the same as the test for vicarious liability at common law. The purpose of the vicarious liability provisions in the discrimination statutes was to deter harassment in the workplace by making the employer liable for the unlawful acts of employees, while providing a defence for the conscientious employer who has used his best endeavours to prevent such harassment.[132]

3.168 The common law test has also now been changed. The question to be asked is whether the employee's wrongful acts were so closely connected with the nature of the employment that it would be just and fair to hold the employer liable.[133] The test for determining whether an employee is acting in the course of his employment is, therefore, now likely to be looked at in very much the same way, whether it is a case of vicarious liability at common law or secondary liability under the discrimination legislation. Although each case will depend on its own facts, the requirement to give a purposive construction to the discrimination statutes, together with the existence of a defence for the employer who has done what he can to prevent acts of discrimination, will make it a relatively rare case in which an employer will manage to escape liability by arguing that his employee was not acting in the course of his employment.[134]

3.169 Liability can even attach to an employer whose employee commits a tort when working for someone else. See the Court of Appeal decision in *Viasystems (Tyneside) Ltd v Thermal Transfer (Northern) Ltd*,[135] where it was held that two employers could both be vicariously liable for the negligence of an employee at the same time. According to Lord Justice Rix, 'the possibility of dual responsibility provides a coherent solution to the problem of the borrowed employee . . . what one

131 *Jones v Tower Boot Co Ltd* [1997] ICR 254, CA; [1997] IRLR 168.

132 See *Jones v Tower Boot Co Ltd* [1997] IRLR 168.

133 See *Lister v Helsey Hall* [2001]IRLR 472, HL.

134 For such a case, see *Sidhu v Aerospace Composite Technology* [2000] IRLR 602, CA; and compare *Chief Constable of Lancashire Police v Stubbs* [1999] IRLR 81, EAT.

135 [2005] IRLR 995, CA.

is looking for is a situation where the employee in question, at any rate for relevant purposes, is so much a part of the work, business or organization of both employers that it is just to make both employers answer for his negligence'.

The Statutory Defence. DDA 1995, s 58(5) provides as follows: **3.170**

> In proceedings under this Act against any person in respect of an act alleged to have been done by an employee of his, it shall be a defence for that person to prove that he took such steps as were reasonably practicable to prevent the employee from—
>
> (a) doing that act; or
> (b) doing, in the course of his employment, acts of that description.

In considering what steps they might take to prevent employees from carrying out acts of discrimination against disabled people, employers should pay careful attention to the advice given in chapter 2 of the Code of Practice 2004. As noted there, employers are more likely to comply with their duties under the DDA 1995, and to avoid the risk of legal action being taken against them, if they implement anti-discriminatory policies and practices, that is equality policies or diversity policies.[136] Courts and tribunals must take into account any part of the Code of Practice 2004 that appears to them relevant to any question arising in any proceedings.[137] Employers seeking to rely on the statutory defence would, therefore, be well advised to pay careful attention to what the Code of Practice 2004 has to say in this area. **3.171**

Although recognizing that large and small employers are likely to have different kinds of anti-discriminatory policies, the Code of Practice 2004 suggests that it is advisable for all employers to take the following steps: **3.172**

(i) establish an anti-discriminatory policy and communicate it to all employees and agents of the employer;
(ii) provide disability awareness and equality training to all employees, especially those who have responsibility for managing, recruiting or training employees themselves;
(iii) inform employees and agents that conduct which breaches the policy will not be tolerated, and respond quickly and effectively to any breaches;
(iv) monitor the effectiveness of the policy;
(v) address acts of discrimination as part of disciplinary rules and procedures;
(vi) have complaints and grievance procedures;
(vii) have clear procedures to deal with harassment;

136 The Code of Practice 2004, para 2.12.
137 DDA 1995, s 51(5).

(viii) establish a policy in relation to disability-related leave and monitor its effectiveness;
(ix) consult with disabled employees;
(x) regularly review the effectiveness of reasonable adjustments made and act on the finding of those reviews;
(xi) keep clear records of decisions taken in respect of each of these matters.

3.173 It is important for employers to note the emphasis placed on monitoring the effectiveness of the policy. Paying lip service to the disability legislation by drawing up a policy and then doing nothing to implement it is not going to be good enough. The tribunal will want to know what steps the employer has taken to ensure that the policy is effective.

3.174 It is also imperative that the employee (typically the equality officer) who is called to give evidence to the tribunal about the anti-discriminatory steps taken by the employer is master of his brief. Nothing is more likely to sabotage an employer's DDA 1995, s 58 defence than an equality officer who is not familiar with the detail of his employer's equality policy.

3.175 Guidance on the steps that an employer should take in order to be able to rely upon the DDA 1995, s 58 defence has been given by the EAT.[138] The first step was to identify whether the employer took any steps at all to prevent the employee doing the act or acts which were the subject of the complaint. Secondly, having identified what steps, if any, the employer took, the tribunal should consider whether there were any further steps which the employer could have taken which were reasonably practicable. Whether or not such further steps would have been successful in preventing the acts of discrimination in question is not determinative of the issue. An employer should not be able to get out of taking reasonably practicable steps on the back of an assertion that, whatever reasonably practicable steps it took, it would have made no difference (the 'why bother?' approach).

3.176 The Court of Appeal has since cast doubt on that last proposition in a case in which it held that the tribunal was entitled to reject a claim on the basis that the suggested alternative measures proposed by the claimant in a sex discrimination case would have had little or no effect.[139] In summary, an employer's statutory defence will be assessed by reference to whatever the tribunal considers it would have been reasonably practicable for it to have done in the circumstances of any particular case.

---

138 *Canniffe v East Riding of Yorkshire Council* [2000] IRLR 555, EAT.
139 *Croft v Royal Mail Group plc* [2003],ICR 1425, CA.

Principals

Principals are made liable for the acts of others by DDA 1995, s 58(2) which provides that 'anything done by a person as agent for another person with the authority of that other person shall be treated for the purposes of this Act as also done by that other person'. That applies whether the authority was express or implied; or whether it was given before or after the act in question was done.[140] **3.177**

This provision was considered by the EAT in *Lana v Positive Action Training in Housing (London) Ltd.*[141] In this case, the claimant was placed by the respondent organization (with which the claimant had a training contract) as a trainee with another company. That company informed the respondent that it wanted to dispense with the claimant's services, shortly after she had announced that she was pregnant. The respondent then terminated her training contract because it did not have any work to give her. The EAT ruled that the company with which the claimant had been placed was acting as the agent of the respondent, which was liable for any discriminatory acts performed by it pursuant to this section. **3.178**

The reasoning of the EAT was that liability under this section will arise not only when an agent has been authorized by the principal to do a discriminatory act (this would be unduly restrictive), but also where authority has been given to do an act which *could* be carried out by the agent in a discriminatory manner. Here, the company with whom the claimant had been placed could legitimately terminate the claimant's placement. It did not have to do it in a discriminatory way, however, and accordingly, the respondent was liable for its actions. **3.179**

3. Aiding Unlawful Acts

Own Acts

An employee or agent for whose discriminatory acts an employer or principal is liable under the provisions described above will himself be liable for the same acts under DDA 1995, s 57, which provides as follows: **3.180**

> (1) A person who knowingly aids another person to do an unlawful act is to be treated for the purposes of this Act as himself doing the same kind of unlawful act.
> (2) For the purposes of subsection (1), an employee or agent for whose act the employer or principal is liable under section 58 (or would be so liable but for section 58(5)) shall be taken to have aided the employer or principal to do the act.

Under DDA 1995, s 57(2), an employee or agent can therefore be made liable for his own acts. It will be noted, however, that the claim against the employee or **3.181**

140 DDA 1995, s 58(3).
141 [2001] IRLR 501, EAT.

agent under this section will only succeed if the employer or principal is, in fact, liable under the secondary liability provisions discussed above (or would be but for the statutory defence).

3.182 The possibilities are, therefore, as follows:

(a) *Both employer and employee (or principal and agent) are liable:* The employer because he is liable for the discriminatory acts of his employee committed in the course of his employment, and he fails to make out the statutory defence; the employee because he is deemed to have aided the unlawful act of the employer;
(b) *Only the employee is liable:* The employee has committed a discriminatory act in the course of his employment but the employer makes out the statutory defence. Even so, the employee remains liable under DDA 1995, s 57. For a case where this happened under the equivalent provisions of RRA 1976, see *Yeboah v Crofton*.[142]
(c) *Neither the employer nor the employee is liable:* The employer is not liable because the employee was not acting in the course of his employment when he committed the discriminatory act: The employee is not liable because he is not aiding an unlawful act.

3.183 In a rather circular way, therefore, under DDA 1995, s 57(2) an employee can be held liable for aiding his employer to commit an unlawful act when it was he himself who committed the act of discrimination for which the employer is held liable.

Aiding Another

3.184 An employee or agent (or indeed anyone else) can also be liable for knowingly aiding another person to do an unlawful act under DDA 1995, s 57(1). In those circumstances, he is treated as having done the same kind of unlawful act himself.

3.185 The nature and extent of the knowledge required to be caught by this subsection was considered by the EAT in *Allaway v Reilly*.[143] In this case, a firemaster was accused of aiding his employer to discriminate on grounds of sex against a former employee. The employee had been dismissed and the complaint against the firemaster related to the way in which he had handled the disciplinary proceedings which led to the dismissal. He sought unsuccessfully to be excluded as a respondent to the claim, and the EAT dismissed his appeal against this decision. The criterion of knowledge was to be given a broad interpretation.

142 [2002] IRLR 634, CA.
143 [2007] IRLR 864, EAT.

> Discrimination does not have to be what he intended nor does it have to have been his motive. It is enough that, on the evidence, the conclusion can be drawn that discrimination as the probable outcome was within the scope of his knowledge at the time. It would not need to be in the forefront of his mind nor would he need to have specifically addressed his mind to it.[144]

Allaway was a case where the employee was held to have aided his employer to carry out an unlawful act of discrimination. A person can also be held personally liable for aiding acts of discrimination carried out by other employees. That was the decision of the Court of Appeal in *Gilbank v Miles*[145] in which the manager of a hairdressing salon was held liable for the acts of her fellow employees because she had consciously encouraged them to discriminate. **3.186**

There is a defence against liability under this section for knowingly aiding another to do an unlawful act if a person acts in reliance on a statement made to him by that other person that the act would not be unlawful and it is reasonable for him to believe that statement.[146] **3.187**

4. Instructions and Pressure to Discriminate

It is unlawful for a person who has authority over another person, or in accordance with whose wishes that other person is accustomed to act, to instruct him to do any act which is unlawful under Part II of the DDA 1995, or to procure, or attempt to procure, the doing by him of any such act.[147] It is also unlawful to induce, or attempt to induce, a person to do any act which contravenes Part II of the DDA 1995 by providing, or offering to provide, him with any benefit, or subjecting him or threatening to subject him to any detriment.[148] These provisions are self-explanatory. Only the EHRC may bring proceedings in respect of a contravention of DDA 1995, s 16C.[149] **3.188**

144 Per Lady Smith at Para. 15
145 [2006] IRLR 538, CA.
146 DDA 1995, s 57(3).
147 DDA 1995, s 16C(1).
148 DDA 1995, s 16C(2).
149 DDA 1995, s 17B(1).

4

THE DUTY TO MAKE REASONABLE ADJUSTMENTS

A. Introduction

4.01 The duty to make reasonable adjustments aims to remove impediments that prevent disabled persons from integrating fully into the workplace. It reflects a social model of disability in which functional limitations arising from a disability do not necessarily restrict a disabled person's ability to participate fully in society; rather, environmental factors such as the format of a building or an employer's working practice lead to the disabled being unnecessarily disadvantaged.

4.02 The DDA 1995 does not prohibit indirect discrimination. Instead, the reasonable adjustments duty requires employers and others to make reasonable adjustments where any of their 'provisions, criteria or practices'[1] place a disabled person at a substantial disadvantage when compared with non-disabled persons. Although the duty only requires adjustments to be made if they are reasonable, it will require employers to take positive action for disabled people that they would not be required to take for others.[2]

4.03 The duty to make reasonable adjustments for employees was previously contained in DDA 1995 s 6 and was commonly called the 'Section 6 Duty'. Respondents were able to defend a failure to comply with a Section 6 Duty by arguing that the failure was justified. In October 2004 s 6 was moved to s 4A and the defence of justification was removed.[3] An employer may now only defend a failure to make an adjustment by arguing that the duty did not arise or that the adjustment in question was not reasonable.

B. The Statutory Framework

4.04 The most significant provisions in Part II of the DDA 1995 directly affecting the general duty to make reasonable adjustments for employees are set out below.

[1] See para 4.25 for a detailed discussion of what constitutes a PCP.

[2] *Archibald v Fife Council* [2004] UKHL 32, [2004] 4 All ER 303, [2004] ICR 954, [2004] IRLR 651, HL, per Lady Hale at para 57.

[3] See the 2003 Regulations that were implemented to give effect to Article 5 of the Framework Directive which requires reasonable accommodations to be made for disabled persons.

DDA 1995, s 4A is set out in full, the other sections are summarized for simplicity.

Section 4A—Employers: duty to make adjustments

(1) Where—

(a) a provision, criterion or practice applied by or on behalf of an employer; or

(b) any physical feature of premises occupied by the employer;

places the disabled person concerned at a substantial disadvantage in comparison with persons who are not disabled, it is the duty of the employer to take such steps as it is reasonable, in all the circumstances of the case, for him to have to take in order to prevent the provision, criterion or practice, or feature having that effect.

(2) In subsection (1) the disabled person concerned means—

(a) in the case of a provision, criterion or practice for determining to whom employment should be offered, any disabled person who is, or has notified the employer that he may be an applicant for that employment;

(b) in any other case a disabled person who is—

(i) an applicant for the employment concerned;

(ii) an employee of the employer concerned.

(3) Nothing in this section imposes any duty on an employer in relation to a disabled person if the employer does not know and could not reasonably be expected to know—

(a) in the case of an applicant, or potential applicant, that the disabled person concerned is, or may be, an applicant for the employment, or

(b) in any case, that that person has a disability and is likely to be affected in the way mentioned in subsection (1).

- **Section 3A(2)** provides that a person *discriminates* against a disabled person if he fails to comply with a duty to make reasonable adjustments imposed on him in relation to the disabled person.
- **Section 4** sets out the circumstances in which a breach of the duty to make adjustments constitutes *unlawful* discrimination.
- **Section 16A(4)** requires reasonable adjustments to be made even after the employment relationship has ended.
- **Section 17A** gives the tribunal jurisdiction to hear a complaint of unlawful discrimination and describes the remedies which a tribunal may award. Section 17A(1C) sets out who bears the burden of proof.
- **Section 18A and Schedule 4, Part 1** (together with the Disability Discrimination (Employment Field) (Leasehold Premises) Regulations 2004 (SI 2004/153)) set out the nature of the adjustments required to premises if the employer does not own the building it occupies.
- **Section 18B(1)** provides a list of factors which the tribunal must take into account when considering whether an adjustment is reasonable.
- **Section 18B(2)** lists examples of steps which a person may need to take in order to comply with a duty to make reasonable adjustments.

- **Section 18D(2)** defines PCP to include 'arrangements'.
- **Schedule 3, section 3(3)(b)** provides that any act extending over a period shall be treated as done at the end of that period, and **section 3(3)(c)** provides that a deliberate omission shall be treated as done when the person in question decided upon it.

1. The Basic Framework

4.05 Not all discrimination is prohibited by the DDA 1995. A remedy under DDA 1995, s 17A can only be claimed for *unlawful* discrimination. Although a failure to comply with the reasonable adjustments duty amounts to discrimination (DDA 1995, s 3A(2)), it will only be *unlawful* discrimination if the circumstances fall within DDA 1995, s 4. If the circumstances do not fall within s 4 then the disabled person concerned has no sustainable complaint. DDA 1995, s 4 is dealt with elsewhere in this work but must be considered in every inquiry into whether a reasonable adjustment should have been made.[4]

4.06 Section 4A sets out the substance of the duty to make adjustments for employees.[5] DDA 1995, s 4A(1) requires an employer to make reasonable adjustments to prevent its PCP (or a physical feature of its premises) from placing the *disabled person concerned*[6] at a substantial disadvantage in comparison with someone who is not disabled.

4.07 DDA 1995, ss 4A(2) and 4A(3) describe the circumstances in which s 4A(1) applies. Sub-section 4A(2) provides that both disabled employees and disabled applicants for employment qualify as a *disabled person concerned.* Sub-section 4A(3) provides that an employer is only under a duty to make adjustments for the disabled person if he has a specified degree of knowledge. (See paragraph 4.135).

2. Applying the Statutory Provisions

4.08 In *Morse v Wiltshire County Council* [1998] IRLR 352, the EAT determined that *three* steps were essential to a proper consideration of an allegation that a respondent has failed to make a reasonable adjustment. A fourth step, not dealt with in *Morse* but which must also be considered, is how the employer's knowledge affects its duty.[7]

---

[4] Section 4 DDA 1995, s 4 is discussed in detail in chapter 3.

[5] Other sections of the DDA 1995 require adjustments to be made in favour of other workers categories. See para 4.15.

[6] See para 4.16.

[7] DDA 1995, s 4A(3). See also *Secretary of State for Work and Pensions v Macklin* UKEAT/0370/07, [2008] All ER (D) 413, EAT; *Chief Constable of Lincolnshire Police v Weaver* UKEAT/0622/07, [2008] All ER (D) 291, EAT.

While this four-step process provides valuable guidance to the practitioner it should be noted that a tribunal is not obliged to expressly refer to each step. As long as it is clear from the judgment that the tribunal has applied the correct statutory test it will not be found to have made an error.[8] **4.09**

The First Step asks whether the person is entitled to make a claim. For the duty to be actionable, the discrimination must fall within the circumstances prescribed by DDA 1995, s 4. The claimant must also fall within a category of persons entitled to make a claim; that is, be a disabled employee, a disabled applicant for employment or a disabled contractor etc. Only those provisions particular to the duty to make adjustments are dealt with in this chapter. Other relevant considerations such as whether a person is disabled, an employee or a contractor, and the effect of DDA 1995, s 4 are dealt with elsewhere.[9] **4.10**

The Second Step: once it is established that the person is entitled to make a claim (and consequently under what section of the DDA 1995 the claim should be made), the next question is whether the duty to make adjustments has arisen. In the employment context this involves looking at whether any of the PCPs applied by, or on behalf of, the employer (or any features of premises occupied by the employer) place the disabled person concerned at a substantial disadvantage when compared to non-disabled persons. If the answer to this question is in the affirmative, the duty to make reasonable adjustments will have arisen. **4.11**

The Third Step is a consideration of what steps it was reasonable, in all the circumstances, for the employer to have to take to alleviate the disadvantage caused by the PCP/feature identified in Step 2. The nature and extent of the identified disadvantage will influence the kind of adjustments that are likely to be considered reasonable. Tribunals are required to have regard to the factors set out in DDA 1995, s 18B(1) when considering the duty to make adjustments and so an examination of this section forms an integral part of Step 3.[10] In practice it is helpful to use DDA 1995, s18B(1) as a framework for the consideration of whether an alleged adjustment is reasonable. **4.12**

A Fourth Step is identifying the extent to which the employer knew of the disability and the effects of the disadvantage caused by the PCP.[11] Both the existence and the nature of the duty are affected by the employer's actual or constructive knowledge of these matters and so a consideration of that knowledge is a necessary step in the assessment of what the duty was and whether it was breached.[12] Although the **4.13**

[8] *Beart v HM Prison Service* [2003] EWCA Civ 119, [2003] ICR 1068, CA.

[9] Chapter 2 contains a comprehensive discussion of the meaning of disability and chapter 3 contains a discussion of s 4 and the definition of employees, contractors and others etc.

[10] For a discussion of DDA 1995, s 18B(1) See para 4.74.

[11] DDA 1995, s 4A(3).

[12] See para 4.135.

authors refer to this as a fourth step, the reality is that if the employer disputes that it has the requisite degree of knowledge, it will be necessary to deal with this issue when scrutinizing whether the duty to make adjustments arises.

C. Step One—Is the Person Entitled to Make a Claim?

4.14 A person must be disabled before an employer is required to make reasonable adjustments for them. The issue of whether a person can claim disability discrimination by association was considered by the ECJ in the case of *Coleman v Attridge Law*.[13] The scope of the reasonable adjustments duty is not affected by this decision. The Framework Directive expressly limits the reasonable adjustments duty to 'persons with disabilities'.[14] *Coleman v Attridge Law* is discussed further at paragraph 3.43.

1. Employees, Contractors and Others

4.15 The aim of the reasonable adjustment provisions in Part II of the DDA 1995 is to integrate disabled people into the workforce *whatever* the position or office they hold. Although Part II is frequently referred to as the Part dealing with employment, many other work relationships are covered in it. The DDA 1995 requires reasonable adjustments to be made in respect of the following:

employees (DDA 1995, s 4A);
contract workers (DDA 1995, s 4B(4));
office-holders (DDA 1995, s 4E);
partnerships (DDA 1995, s 6B);
barristers (DDA 1995, s 7B);
advocates (DDA 1995, s 7D);
members of trade organizations (DDA 1995, s 14);
holders of a professional or a trade qualification (DDA 1995, s 14B);
persons undertaking practical work experience (DDA 1995, s 14D);
members of local authorities (DDA 1995, s 15C);
police officers (DDA 1995, s 64).[15]

---

13 [2008] EUECJ C-303/06, [2008] ICR 1128, [2008] IRLR 722.

14 Article 5 of the Framework Directive which requires the provision of measures to accommodate the needs of 'a person with a disability'. See also Recital 17.

15 The duty to make adjustments in respect of each of these persons is summarised in chapter 3. The substance of the duty to make adjustments in each of these situations is based around the social model of disability. They are therefore similar but adapted to the particular circumstances in which they are intended to apply.

An employer's duty under DDA 1995, s 4A is to make reasonable adjustments for the *disabled person concerned*;[16] it is not to make adjustments to accommodate disabled persons generally. Policies or adjustments adopted by the employer with the aim of dealing with disabled persons *as a group* do not relieve the employer from its duty to deal with each individual disabled person.[17] **4.16**

Employers have a duty to make adjustments for four categories of disabled persons: **4.17**

(a) persons who have informed the employer that they are, or may be, applying for a job (DDA 1995, s 4A(2)(a));
(b) applicants for a position (DDA 1995, s 4A(2)(b)(i));
(c) employees (DDA 1995, s 4A(2)(b)(ii)); and
(d) ex-employees (DDA 1995, s 16A).[18]

Employers are only required to make adjustments to PCP for determining to whom employment should be offered if the person requiring the adjustment has either applied for the job or has notified the employer that he may be applying for the job.[19] **4.18**

D. Step Two—How Does the Duty to Make Adjustments Arise?

The duty to make adjustments arises where a PCP or a physical feature of an employer's premises places the disabled person concerned at a substantial disadvantage in comparison with persons who are not disabled. Only once this occurs will an employer be required to take reasonable steps to prevent the PCP or physical feature from having the disadvantageous effect.[20] A good checklist for identifying whether the duty has arisen is provided in *Smiths Detection Watford Ltd v Berriman*:[21] **4.19**

> **Identifying Whether the Duty to Make Adjustments has Arisen**
> Identify:
> (a) the relevant PCP of the employer;
> (b) the relevant physical features of the premises occupied by the employer;

16 See chapter 2 for the meaning of disability and disabled person concerned.

17 Para 5.4 of the Code of Practice 2004.

18 For DDA 1995, s 16A see para 3.115. Before s 16A came into force it was unclear whether the duty to make adjustments applied in respect of a dismissal or to a person who had left employment. This was because of controversy over whether the old DDA 1995, s 6(2) narrowed the scope of the duty to make adjustments. See *Burke J in Baynton v South West Trains* [2005] ICR 1730 (paras 21 and 31), EAT. See also *Morse v Wiltshire County Council* [1998] IRLR 352, EAT; *Clark v TDG Ltd (t/a Novacold)* [1999] 2 All ER 977, [1999] ICR 951, [1999] IRLR 318, CA; *Fu v London Borough of Camden* [2001] IRLR 352, EAT; *Relaxion v Rhys Harper*[2003] ICR 867, HL.

19 DDA 1995, s 4A(2)(a).

20 See *Secretary of State for Work and Pensions v Macklin* UKEAT/0370/07, [2008] All ER (D) 413, EAT per Clarke J at paras 29 to 32.

21 UKEAT/0144/05, [2005] All ER (D) 56, EAT.

(c) the non-disabled comparators (where appropriate); and
(d) the nature and extent of the substantial disadvantage suffered by the claimant. This step may involve a consideration of the cumulative effect of both the PCP and physical feature and looking at the overall picture.[22]

1. Provisions, Criteria, and Practices

4.20 The phrase 'provision, criterion and practice' replaced the old term 'arrangements' in October 2004.[23] The definition of PCP includes the term 'arrangements'[24] so case law identifying 'arrangements' under the old s 6(1) is still useful in identifying a PCP. A discussion of the meaning of arrangements is, therefore, a logical place to begin an examination of what qualifies as a PCP.

The Meaning of Arrangements

4.21 In *Archibald v Fife*[25] Lady Hale gave a very broad interpretation to the term 'arrangements'. The claimant was a road sweeper who became disabled after an operation. As a result of her disability she was no longer able to perform any manual work including road sweeping. All of the jobs available at her level within the council were manual jobs. She was interviewed for over one hundred clerical jobs at a higher grade but was unsuccessful. She was dismissed for incapacity. Lady Hale, examining whether any of the council's 'arrangements' put the claimant at a substantial disadvantage, stated that:[26]

> Subject to [the old s 6(2)[27]] the term 'arrangements' is undefined. It could clearly relate to the council's redeployment policy, but in this case that did not put Mrs Archibald at a substantial disadvantage compared with anyone else. It could equally apply to the terms on which Mrs Archibald held her road sweeping job. An employer's arrangements for dividing up the work he needs to have done into different jobs are just as capable of being 'arrangements' as are an employer's arrangements for deciding who gets what job or how much each is paid. Some employers might combine cooking and bottle-washing in one job while others might treat them quite differently. The job descriptions for all their posts are 'arrangements' which they make in relation to the terms, conditions and arrangements on which they offer employment. Also included in those arrangements is the liability of anyone who becomes incapable of fulfilling the job description to be dismissed.

---

22 See *Smiths Detection Watford Ltd v Berriman* UKEAT/0144/05, (2005) All ER (D) 56, EAT at para 85. Serota J reiterated this test in *The Environment Agency v Rowan* UKEAT/0060/07/DM, [2008] IRLR 20, EAT. See also *London Borough of Barnet v Ferguson* UKEAT/0220/06 [2006] All ER (D) 192, EAT.

23 As a result of the 2003 Regulations introduced in response to the Framework Directive.

24 See DDA 1995, s 18D(2).

25 [2004] IRLR 651, HL.

26 [2004] IRLR 651, HL, at para 62. Note Lady Hale's comment that the definition of arrangements was restricted by the now repealed s 6(2).

27 See further para 4.24.

The Court of Appeal gave a similarly broad interpretation to arrangements in *Smith v Churchill Stairlifts*.[28] Mr Smith had lumbar spondylosis and applied for a job with the respondent selling radiator cabinets. He was successful at interview and was invited to the next stage of selection, a training course. Before the course took place the respondent decided that it wanted its sales staff to carry the actual cabinets when visiting clients. The respondent assumed that, since the cabinets were very heavy, the claimant would be unable to lift them and withdrew its offer of a place on the training course. None of the nine other able-bodied persons invited on the course had their offers withdrawn even though it later transpired that three of them were also unable to lift the cabinets. The Court of Appeal considered that the following qualified as arrangements: **4.22**

(i) that in order to do the job of selling, employees had to carry a full-sized radiator cabinet;
(ii) that the offer of participation in the course would be withdrawn if the claimant was, or was believed to be, unable to carry a cabinet.[29]

The offer of participation in a training course (or its withdrawal) had nothing to do with the operation of either a contractual term or a formal policy. Such a broad interpretation of arrangements covers practically any action taken by the respondent so long as the circumstances fall within DDA 1995, s 4[30] and the action affects a disabled person to whom the duty to make adjustments is owed.[31] **4.23**

When using case law on the meaning of 'arrangements', practitioners should bear in mind that the old s 6(2), which acted as an additional restriction on the circumstances in which the duty to make adjustments applied, has been repealed and was not re-enacted with the remainder of the old s 6.[32] *Kenny v Hampshire Constabulary*[33] is perhaps the most frequently cited case in which a substantial disadvantage was found **not** to be caused by an 'arrangement' but is also a good illustration of a case which is unlikely to be followed because of the repeal of s 6(2). Mr Kenny had cerebral palsy and required assistance going to the toilet. The respondent withdrew its offer of employment for a number of reasons but principally because it was unable to find a volunteer who would assist him going **4.24**

28 [2005] EWCA Civ 1220, [2006] ICR 524, [2006] IRLR 41, CA.

29 Per Maurice Kay LJ at para 40 (see also the useful discussion at paras 30 to 34).

30 Section 4 is discussed in detail in chapter 3.

31 See ss 4A(2) and s 16A(4)-(6) DDA discussed at paras 3.80 and 3.115 above.

32 The old s 6(2) restricted the application of the Section 6 duty to 'any term, condition or arrangements on which employment, promotion, transfer, training or any other benefit is offered or afforded'.

33 [1999] ICR 76, [1999] IRLR 76, EAT.

to the toilet. The EAT held that the old s 6(2) narrowed the scope of the duty so that it did not require an employer to provide a carer to meet the disabled employee's personal needs. Since the old s 6(2) no longer applies, it is doubtful whether *Kenny* or other similar cases would be decided in the same way today.

The Meaning of Provision, Criterion or Practice

4.25 The phrase 'provision, criterion or practice' appears in the SDA 1975 and RRA 1976 as well as the DDA 1995 and was considered in the context of the SDA 1975 by the EAT in *British Airways v Starmer*.[34] BA imposed a rule that if a pilot had less than 2,000 hours flying experience, the pilot could not reduce his or her flying hours to below 75 per cent of the full-time requirement. The claimant wanted to work 50 per cent of her full-time hours. Neither party sought to challenge the 2,000 hours requirement but the employee claimed that the PCP that placed women at a particular disadvantage were that:

> in order to continue working for BA she would have to work either full-time or for the equivalent of 75 per cent of full-time; or
>
> that in order to continue working for BA she would have to work for the equivalent of more than 50 per cent of full-time.

4.26 Burton J's analysis of the PCP in *Starmer* shows that the meaning of PCP under the amended DDA 1995 will be broader than the old term *arrangements*. PCP will be given a broader meaning than *arrangements* for three reasons. Firstly because the DDA 1995, like the SDA 1975, incorporates the pre-amendment term *arrangements* into the definition of PCP[35], secondly because EC law prohibits states from reducing protection against discrimination[36], and finally because, wherever possible, a consistent interpretation should be given to the main anti-discrimination enactments.[37]

4.27 Given that the meaning of *arrangements* was so broad and that *arrangements* are incorporated into the meaning of PCP, it should be rare for there to be a dispute over whether something qualifies as a PCP.[38]

---

[34] [2005] IRLR 862, EAT. In this case Burton J considered the meaning of PCP under the amended SDA 1975. The pre-amendment SDA 1975 referred to 'requirement or condition' rather than PCP.

[35] DDA 1995, s 18D(2) is the equivalent of SDA 1975, s 82 because it expressly incorporates *arrangements* into the definition of PCP.

[36] Article 8(2) of The Framework Directive contains a prohibition on regressive legislation.

[37] See *Rhys-Harper v Relaxion Group* [2003] UKHL 33, [2003] IRLR 484, HL.

[38] Although it should be noted that the old DDA, 1995 term *arrangement* was interpreted very broadly whereas the phrase *requirement or condition* under the old SDA 1975 had a narrower meaning.

4.28 Since it is tempting to treat the phrase 'Provision, criterion or practice' as a term with its own meaning, the ordinary and natural meaning of each of the words, as given in the Shorter Oxford English Dictionary, is set out here as a reminder of their individual significance:

Dictionary Definition of Provision, Criterion and Practice

Provision:

2 The action or an act of providing something; the fact or condition of being provided. Freq. in **make provision,** make prior arrangement or preparation (for), supply necessary resources (for) . . .

3 A supply of necessaries or materials provided, esp. of food and drink . . .

4 (A clause or division of) a legal or formal statement providing for some particular matter or making a stipulation or condition; a proviso.

5 Something provided or arranged in advance; a measure or measures taken beforehand; a precaution.

Criterion [Plural—Criteria]:

1 A principle, standard or test by which a thing is judged, assessed or identified.

2 A (supposed) organ or faculty of judging.

Practice:

1**a** The habitual doing or carrying out of something; usual or customary action or performance; action as opp. to profession, theory knowledge etc.

3**a** The action of scheming or planning;

5**a** The action of doing something; performance, operation; method of action or working.

5**b** An action, a deed; in pl., doings, proceedings;

6 An exercise; a practical treatise.[39]

The Meaning of Physical Features

4.29 DDA 1995, s 4A(1)(b) requires reasonable adjustments to be made in relation to any permanent or temporary physical features of premises occupied by employers that places a disabled person at a substantial disadvantage.

4.30 The employer need not own the premises but must occupy them. 'Occupier' is not defined in the DDA 1995. The common law definition is broad. Any person who exercises some degree of control over the premises will be considered an occupier at common law and premises may have more than one occupier.[40]

---

39 See the *Shorter Oxford English Dictionary* (5th edn).

40 See *Wheat v E Lacon & Co Ltd* [1966] 1 All ER 582 at pages 591 to 592. Although this case deals with the meaning of occupier under the Occupier's Liability Act 1957, it is consistent with the common law definition (see Lord Denning at page 593).

4.31 DDA 1995, s 18D(2) defines a physical feature to include:

> any feature arising from the design or construction of a building on the premises;
>
> any feature on the premises or any approach to, exit from, or access to, such a building;
>
> any fixture, fitting, furnishing, furniture, equipment, or material in, or on, the premises;
>
> any other physical element or quality of any land comprised in the premises.

4.32 More specifically, a physical feature includes steps, stairways, kerbs, exterior surfaces and paving, parking areas, building entrances and exits (including escape routes), internal and external doors, gates, toilet and washing facilities, lighting and ventilation, lifts and escalators, floor coverings, signs, furniture, and temporary movable items.[41]

4.33 The Code of Practice 2004 gives two examples of physical features in a workplace placing a disabled person at a substantial disadvantage.[42] The first example is of a person with a hearing impairment who finds it difficult to work in an open-plan office with hard floors. The open-plan layout and the hard floors are the physical features. They place the disabled person at a substantial disadvantage because, compared to non-disabled persons, he finds it very difficult to hear. The second example is of a workplace with glass doors that present a hazard to a visually impaired employee. The hazard is a substantial disadvantage caused by the physical feature, the glass doors.

4.34 The duties of employers who occupy their premises under a lease are discussed from paragraph 4.161 below.

2. The Comparator, the Disadvantage, and the Disability

4.35 When considering whether the PCP cause a substantial disadvantage, the DDA 1995 requires a comparison to be made between the 'disabled person concerned' and persons who are not disabled. This is a different comparison from that made under the SDA 1975 or the RRA 1976.

4.36 For example, in indirect sex discrimination cases the question is whether women *as a group* are placed at a particular disadvantage.[43] By contrast, the test under the DDA 1995 is concerned with a disadvantage caused to the *individual* disabled

41 Code of Practice 2004 para 5.10.
42 Code of Practice 2004 para 5.9.
43 The provisions in RRA 1976, s 1 are materially the same.

person rather than disabled persons generally. The *like for like* comparisons under the direct discrimination provisions of the SDA 1975 and RRA 1976 are also inappropriate for reasonable adjustments claims because of the positive nature of the reasonable adjustments duty.[44] Since positive action in this context means that the employer is required to take action to remove a disadvantage that may not be required for a non-disabled person, it is likely to be an admission of liability to say that the disabled person has been treated in the same way as non-disabled persons.

The comparators for determining whether someone is at a substantial disadvantage in a reasonable adjustments claim are identified by reference to both the alleged disadvantage and the PCP. The current approach was set out in the leading case of *Smith v Churchill Starlifts*.[45] Firstly, the PCP and the alleged disadvantage are identified. Then the comparative exercise asks whether the disadvantage is substantial in comparison with persons firstly who are not disabled[46] and secondly, who are not disadvantaged by the PCP. **4.37**

To illustrate, take an employer who has a rule that applicants who are unable to type at 55 words per minute or faster will not be offered an interview. The claimant is disabled by arthritis which means she cannot type at more than 40 words per minute. She is refused an interview but the non-disabled people who were able to fulfil the criterion were all offered interviews. The PCP is the criterion that the person must be able to type at 55 words per minute before an interview is offered and the alleged disadvantage is that the claimant has not been offered an interview. The comparison is made with applicants who were not disabled, who were able to type at more than 55 words per minute and who were therefore offered an interview. The claimant is substantially disadvantaged compared to these comparators because they were offered an interview, whereas she was not. **4.38**

Smith v Churchill Stairlifts[47] provides a good illustration of how the comparison exercise works in practice. The facts of this case are recited at paragraph 4.22 above. Two of the PCP identified by the Court of Appeal were: **4.39**

(i) that in order to do the job of selling, employees had to carry a full-sized radiator cabinet;
(ii) that the offer of participation in the course would be withdrawn if the claimant was, or was believed to be, unable to carry a cabinet.

---

[44] Per Baroness Hale in *Archibald v Fife* [2004] UKHL 32, [2004] 4 All ER 303, [2004] ICR 954, [2004] IRLR 651, HL, at para 57.

[45] *Smith v Churchill Stairlifts* [2005] EWCA Civ 1220, [2006] ICR 524, [2006] IRLR 41, CA, per Maurice Kay LJ at para 40.

[46] *Smith v Churchill Stairlifts* [2005] EWCA Civ 1220, [2006] ICR 524, [2006] IRLR 41, CA, per Maurice Kay LJ at para 34.

[47] [2005] EWCA Civ 1220, [2006] ICR 524, [2006] IRLR 41, CA.

4.40 Using the first PCP the comparators were the 6 out of 9 able-bodied candidates who were subject to the requirement to lift the cabinets but were not disadvantaged by it because they could carry the cabinets and so were not rejected. Using these comparators the claimant was subject to a disadvantage. Using the second PCP the comparators were the 9 other non-disabled people who had been successful and accepted onto the course. Using this PCP the only person suffering a disadvantage as a result of his perceived inability to lift a cabinet was the claimant. The claimant had, when compared with non-disabled persons, been placed at a substantial disadvantage by having the offer of a place on the training course withdrawn.

4.41 When, the PCPs were considered as a whole, the Court of Appeal considered that it was obvious that the claimant had been placed at a substantial disadvantage compared with non-disabled persons.

4.42 The comparison exercise suggested in *Smith v Churchill* may well be incorrect. When the pool for comparison compares the disabled person's treatment only with those that are disadvantaged, this assumes the question for which the comparator question is asked. Was there a disadvantage? A better comparison would surely be with all persons who were subjected to the PCP. Applying this analysis to the first PCP in *Smith v Churchill*, all 9 able-bodied candidates who applied for the job would be comparators: three of whom were also unable to lift the cabinets. Using the second PCP in *Smith v Churchill* the comparators were the 9 other candidates, all of whom were accepted onto the course. Using this new comparison exercise, the claimant would still be disadvantaged by the second PCP but it would be a question of fact as to whether the claimant was disadvantaged by the first PCP.

4.43 *Smith v Churchill* illustrates the importance of choosing the correct PCP[48] and shows how the comparator changes depending on the PCP that are identified. If the incorrect PCP and/or comparator are identified, a claim can quite easily be lost, particularly since the burden of proof requires the claimant to prove facts from which a tribunal could deduce that a duty has arisen.[49]

---

[48] See also *NTL Group Ltd v Difolco* [2006] EWCA Civ 1508.

[49] For another example of the importance of selecting the right PCP see *Paul v National Probation Service* [2004] IRLR 190, EAT. In *Paul* the claimant had a chronic depressive illness and in 2001 applied for a part-time post as a community service supervisor. He was offered the job subject to a satisfactory occupational health report. The occupational health report recommended that the claimant was not suitable for the post and he was offered the job of handyman instead. The tribunal considered that the relevant arrangement was the requirement to undertake an occupational health assessment. The EAT considered that the relevant arrangement was the result of the actual assessment and the employer's reaction to it rather than the simple requirement to undertake the assessment (see paragraphs 23 to 25). For further discussion of the burden of proof see para 10.80.

3. The Extent of the Disadvantage

The claimant must actually suffer a disadvantage as a result of the application of the PCP. In *Cave v Goodwin*,[50] for instance, the employer sent a disciplinary letter containing allegations of misconduct to an employee whom it knew had a learning disability. However, the employer failed to make any adjustments, such as reading the letter to him, to ensure that he was able to understand it. Ordinarily this would cause a claimant a substantial disadvantage but in this case the claimant knew all about the allegations of misconduct because he had discussed them with members of staff. He was not, therefore, disadvantaged by being unable properly to understand the letter.[51] **4.44**

A duty to make adjustments arises only if the disadvantage caused to the claimant by the PCP is substantial. A substantial disadvantage is one that is more than minor or trivial.[52] This is consistent with the interpretation given to 'substantial' where it appears elsewhere in the DDA 1995.[53] It is not a high threshold and in practice a disadvantage has to be clearly trivial to be treated as insubstantial.[54] **4.45**

The nature of the claimant's disability determines both whether the disadvantage is linked to the disability and also the extent of the disadvantage. For instance, a person with a hearing impediment in one ear may not be at a *substantial* disadvantage by being required to use a standard auditory telephone because he is able to use his other ear to answer the telephone. On the other hand, a person who is profoundly deaf in both ears will be substantially disadvantaged compared to a non-disabled person if he is required to use a standard telephone because he will not be able to use it. The latter employee may require a visual telephone that turns speech into text in order to prevent the disadvantage of not being able to use the telephone. In each case the nature of the individual's disability and the working environment determines whether there is a disadvantage, how serious the disadvantage is, and what adjustments will be required. An employer who simply labels a person as deaf and then implements a standard set of adjustments without examining the nature of the person's disability, may well fail to identify the adjustments required for the disabled person concerned.[55] **4.46**

---

50 [2001] EWCA Civ 391.

51 See *Cave v Goodwin* [2001] EWCA Civ 391 para 50.

52 Code of Practice 2004 para 5.11. See also *Cave v Goodwin* [2001] EWCA Civ 391.

53 See *Heinz v Kenrick* [2000] ICR 491, EAT for a discussion of the meaning of substantial in the context of the test of justification. See *Vicary v British Telecom plc* [1999] IRLR 680, EAT for a discussion of the meaning of substantial in the context of the meaning of disability. See also para 2.58 above.

54 In *London Underground v Bragg* UKEAT/847/98 Lindsay J doubted whether a claimant who had a hearing impairment which required him to turn up the television and which made it difficult only occasionally to hear speech, had a substantial adverse affect.

55 See *Cave v Goodwin* [2001] EWCA Civ 391.

4.47 Another example is provided by two persons who are suffering from cerebral palsy with varying degrees of severity. Cerebral palsy is a non-progressive condition and a person with mild cerebral palsy may still manage to mobilize well and be able to use stairs effectively. Another person may be suffering from more severe symptoms, be a wheelchair user and so need a ramp or a lift. The requirement to use the stairs would, therefore, place the latter person at a disadvantage but not the former. The nature of the individual's cerebral palsy determines what disadvantages, if any, are suffered as a result of the employer's PCP and what adjustments are required to prevent those disadvantages.

4.48 Although for the purposes of determining whether a claimant satisfies the definition of disability DDA 1995, sch 1, s 8, requires a tribunal to find that an adverse effect on day-to-day activities is substantial if it is likely to have a substantial adverse effect in the future, no such requirement is included in relation to substantial disadvantages caused by PCP. The DDA 1995 does not require adjustments to be made at present even if the adjustment will be required in the future.[56]

Medical Advice

4.49 Tribunals and employers are unlikely to be medically qualified and unless they examine the medical or other evidence, they may not be equipped to determine whether the disadvantage in question was caused by the disability or what the gravity of any disadvantage was. An employer who does not seek medical advice and assumes that a disabled person is affected by a PCP in a particular way may find that his assumptions are incorrect. Where a reasonable employer would have sought medical assistance and would consequently have known that the employee was suffering a substantial disadvantage, the employer's ignorance of the disadvantage will not relieve him of a failure to make reasonable adjustments to prevent it.[57]

4.50 In practice, medical advice or evidence frequently plays an important role in identifying the nature and the extent of the disadvantage and the type of adjustment that is reasonable,[58] and should be sought where possible.

The Future—Assessing whether the Disadvantage is Substantial

4.51 It is possible that the comparative exercise used in *Smith v Churchill*[59] requires further refinement in addition to that suggested at 4.42 above. The present test

[56] See para 2.78.
[57] See para 4.160.
[58] See para 4.149 for a discussion of when and what medical advice an employer is expected to seek.
[59] See para 4.35.

quantifies the disadvantage by comparing how the PCP affects what the claimant *can* achieve, with persons who are not disadvantaged. However, the examination of whether a person is substantially disadvantaged by an employer's PCP arguably requires a comparison between what the disabled person can achieve, and what the disabled person could have achieved, without his disability.

This interpretation of 'substantial' is consistent with the interpretation of 'substantial adverse effect' in DDA 1995, s 1[60] and also with the fact that the duty is owed to the individual disabled person. In *Paterson v The Commissioner of Police for the Metropolis*[61] the employer argued that an adverse effect (in the context of DDA 1995, s 1) could only be described as 'substantial'[62] by comparing how the employee performed with the population at large, rather than by examining the effect of the disability on the individual employee. Using this test, an employee who was highly intelligent but who was disabled by mild dyslexia, did not suffer a substantial adverse affect on his day-to-day activities because his performance was still significantly better than the average able-bodied person. **4.52**

This argument was rejected by the EAT which held that one should consider what the individual would have been able to do without the impairment, and compare it to what he can actually do.[63] This comparison revealed that the claimant was substantially disadvantaged because without his disability he would have been able to compete more effectively at a higher level. **4.53**

The EAT accepted the submission that interpreting 'substantial adverse effect' without having regard to what the claimant could have achieved, but for the disability, would have a devastating affect on the operation of the legislation and undermine the purpose of the DDA 1995. Any other conclusion, Elias J held, 'would mean that because of the effect of his dyslexia, he would in practice face a glass ceiling; he would not be able to compete adequately in the promotion stakes beyond a certain level.' Furthermore, Elias J considered this interpretation consistent with *Chacon Navas v Eurest Colectividades SA*[64] in which the ECJ stated that 'disability' referred to a limitation resulting from a physical or mental impairment and which hinders the participation of the person concerned in **4.54**

---

60 This provides that a person has a disability if he has a physical or mental impairment, which has a *substantial and long-term adverse affect* on his ability to carry out normal day-to-day activities. See paras 2.58 to 2.64.

61 *Paterson v Commissioner for the Metropolis* UKEAT/0635/06/LA, [2007] ICR 1522, [2007] IRLR 763, EAT. See also *Edwards v Mid Suffolk District Council* [2001] IRLR 190 at para 42, EAT.

62 The case concerned the meaning of substantial in the phrase 'substantial and long-term adverse effect on day-to-day activities' contained in DDA 1995, s 1.

63 See *Paterson v The Commissioner of Police for the Metropolis* UKEAT/0635/06/LA, [2007] ICR [2007] IRLR 763, EAT at para 68.

64 [2006] IRLR 706, ECJ.

professional life.[65] The hindrance of participation in professional life was exactly the sort of disadvantage from which Mr Paterson suffered.

4.55 Although Elias J did not address directly whether the substantial disadvantage in DDA 1995, s 4A should be approached in the same way as the substantial adverse effect in DDA 1995, s 1, the reasoning that Elias J applied in *Paterson* is equally relevant to both sections.

4.56 The following example illustrates how the observations of Elias J in *Paterson* might be incorporated into the substantial disadvantage comparison. An employer stipulates that all persons able to type more than 80 words per minute will be offered an interview. A disabled applicant, who suffers from arthritis, cannot comply with this PCP as he can only type at 50 words per minute. In these circumstances, the comparator according to *Smith v Churchill*,[66] is a non-disabled person, who is able to type at at more than 80 words per minute and who is therefore offered an interview. The claimant will be substantially disadvantaged even if he was unable to type at 80 words per minute before he developed arthritis, and is, therefore, not at an actual disadvantage. Using the *Paterson* test, a more accurate assessment of the disadvantage is made: the person who was unable to type at 80 words per minute before they began to suffer from a disability would not suffer a substantial disadvantage and vice versa.

4.57 The principle drawback with this approach is that the capabilities of the disabled person without his disability may be difficult, or often impossible, to identify. It also has the rather unfortunate effect of appearing to measure the disadvantage according to the claimant's disability rather than the PCP. It may, perhaps, be sensible to use evidence of the claimant's capabilities, but for the disability, where it is available and reliable, but to use the *Smith v Churchill*[67] comparison exercise where the evidence is unavailable or speculative.

E. Step Three—What Adjustments Must an Employer Make?

1. The Objective Test

4.58 The question whether an adjustment is reasonable is judged objectively but takes into account what is reasonable for the disabled person concerned.[68] Where a

65 ECJ at para 42.
66 [2005] EWCA Civ 1220, [2006] ICR 524, [2006] IRLR 41, CA. See paras 4.35 to 4.43.
67 [2005] EWCA Civ 1220, [2006] ICR 524, [2006] IRLR 41, CA.
68 See para 4.76 for a discussion of how the interaction of the PCP and the substantial disadvantage determines what adjustments are required. *Smith v Churchill Stairlifts Plc* [2005] EWCA Civ

PCP causes a claimant a substantial disadvantage, the employer will be required to make any, and all, adjustments which *the tribunal considers* would have been reasonable[69] to prevent the substantial disadvantage. It is not a test that asks whether the respondent's actions fell within a band of reasonable responses.

An employer may hold a view that is genuine, relevant to the circumstances and which provides a more than insignificant reason for not making an adjustment but the tribunal may still find that it would have been reasonable to make it.[70] An employer may also argue that an adjustment was unreasonable even if it did not consider it at the time[71] and it is perfectly possible for there to be an 'entirely fortuitous and unconsidered compliance'.[72] **4.59**

There is no duty to make an adjustment that does *nothing* to alleviate the disadvantage or which might only *possibly* do something to alleviate the disadvantage.[73] The adjustment must itself mitigate or prevent or shield the employee from something.[74] The relevant question is whether the employer did, or did not, make an adjustment that had some practical consequence of preventing or mitigating the difficulties faced by the disabled person at work. **4.60**

Before 2007, a line of authority developed, following the case of *Mid-Staffordshire General Hospital NHS Trust v Cambridge*,[75] to the effect that an employer who gave no consideration to making adjustments would breach the duty.[76] Subsequently, a number of EAT cases in 2006 and 2007 overruled **4.61**

1220, [2006] ICR 254, [2006] IRLR 41; *NCH Scotland v McHugh* UKEATS/0010/06; *Williams v J Walter Thompson Group* [2005] EWCA Civ 133, [2005] IRLR 376; *British Gas Services v McCaull* [2001] IRLR 60, EAT; *Jones v Post Office* [2001] EWCA Civ 588, [2001] IRLR 384; *Morse v Wiltshire County Council* [1998] IRLR 352, EAT.

69 Code of Practice 2004 para 5.18.

70 Per Lord Justice Maurice Kay in *Smith v Churchill Stairlifts* [2005] EWCA Civ 1220, [2006] ICR 524, [2006] IRLR 41 at para 50.

71 *British Gas Services Limited v McCaul* [2001] IRLR 60, EAT, at para 43.

72 Per Elias J in *Tarbuck v Sainsbury Supermarkets* [2006] IRLR 664, EAT, at para 71. See also *Fu v London Borough of Camden* [2001] IRLR 186; *Home Office v Collins* [2005] EWCA Civ 598; *British Gas Services v McCaull* [2001] IRLR 60, EAT; *Sylvia Hay v Surrey County Council* [2007] EWCA Civ 93; *Cave v Goodwin* [2001] EWCA Civ 391. It is also irrelevant that the employer deliberately adopted a policy which operated to the disadvantage of disabled people *Chief Constable of Lincolnshire Police v Weaver* UKEAT/0622/07, EAT.

73 This is also consistent with the pre-*Tarbuck* position in cases such as *Beart v HM Prison Service* [2003] IRLR 238, CA, in which it was held that an adjustment could still be considered reasonable even if it could not be guaranteed to work in the sense of totally removing the disadvantage. The authors suggest reading Lindsay J's judgment in the EAT (EAT/650/01). See paras 4.61–4.65.

74 *The Environment Agency v Rowan* UKEAT/0060/07/DM per Serota J, obiter, at para 61.

75 [2003] IRLR 566, EAT.

76 See also *Southampton City College v Randall* [2006] IRLR 18, EAT; *Rothwell v Pelikan Hard Copy Scotland Ltd* [2006] IRLR 24, EAT; *Humphries v Chevler Packaging Ltd* UKEAT/0224/06.

Mid-Staffordshire;[77] the most influential amongst these was the case of *Tarbuck v Sainsbury Supermarkets*.[78]

4.62 *Tarbuck* held that consulting with a disabled person about the adjustments which might be required was not a reasonable adjustment (even though it was in many cases a necessary pre-requisite to actually making one). This was because the consultation itself does *nothing* to remove a disadvantage.[79] All it does is inform the respondent what adjustments might be necessary.

4.63 In *The Environment Agency v Rowan*[80] the suggested adjustment concerned a trial period. The claimant had a bad back and her symptoms included an inability to sit for long periods and a need for bed rest. She argued that the respondent should have allowed her to work from home for a trial period. Serota J considered that, like a consultation, a trial period was a useful tool for determining whether an adjustment would be effective, but it did not itself do anything to alleviate a disadvantage. This is, of course, a question of fact. There may be circumstances, as there may be with a consultation, in which the trial period constitutes a benefit by itself.[81]

4.64 If the adjustment which the employer neglected would have been an *effective* adjustment, the tribunal may then address the question of whether it would also have been a *reasonable* adjustment. The tribunal must then consider the relative effectiveness of the adjustment (or lack of it) as one factor, amongst all the other circumstances, and determine whether the adjustment was reasonable.[82]

4.65 The *Tarbuck* line of authorities have mirrored developments in the burden of proof. It has been made clear that the claimant bears the burden of proving that a particular adjustment was prima facie reasonable[83] and so must be able to identify an adjustment that would have been effective and which was not implemented. Where the tribunal finds that the respondent has failed to make an

---

77 *London Borough of Barnet v Ferguson* UKEAT/0220/06/DA; *NCH Scotland v McHugh* UKEATS/0010/06/MT; *Fowler v London Borough of Waltham Forest* UKEAT/0116/06/DM; *Heathrow Express v Jenkins* UKEAT/0497/06MAA; *HM Prison Service v Johnson* [2007] IRLR 951, EAT; *Scottish and Southern Energy & Mackay* UKEATS/0075/06. A particularly thorough review of the authorities is contained in *London Borough of Camden v Price-Job* UKEAT/0507/06, UKEAT0054/07.

78 [2006] IRLR 664, EAT.

79 Although the EAT did leave open the possibility that on occasions consultation might constitute a benefit by itself.

80 UKEAT/0060/07/DM.

81 A similar decision was reached in respect of the requirement to undertake a sufficient medical assessment before dismissal, in *London Borough of Camden v Price-Job* UKEAT/0507/06, UKEAT/0054/07.

82 DDA 1995, s 18B(1)(a)

83 See para 10.75 and *Project Management Institute v Latif* [2007] IRLR 579, EAT.

adjustment, it must identify, giving sufficient detail, the nature of the adjustment.[84]

A Continuing Duty?

In *Humphries v Chevler Packaging Ltd*[85] the EAT considered the question of when time starts to run in reasonable adjustments cases. Mrs Humphries was employed as a full-time machine operator/packer. She became unable to do her job because of a disability that gave her pain in her right arm and shoulder. She was offered alternative work on lower pay as a cleaner, which she rejected. She eventually went on sick leave for 18 months, at the end of which she resigned. She claimed that the respondent had failed to make adjustments to facilitate her return to work. **4.66**

The tribunal found that time, for the purposes of limitation, ran from when the employer made it clear that no further adjustment would be made because a failure to make an adjustment was an omission to which DDA 1995, sch 3, s 3(3)(c) and s 3(4) applied. These sections provide that an omission occurs when: **4.67**

(a) the person in question decided upon it (DDA 1995, sch 3, s 3(3)(c)); or
(b) when the person in question did an act that was inconsistent with the omitted act (DDA 1995, sch 3, s 3(4)(a)); or
(c) if he has done no such inconsistent act, when the period expires within which he might reasonably have been expected to do the omitted act if it was to be done (DDA 1995, sch 3 s 3(4)(b)).

Since a breach of the duty to make reasonable adjustments was an omission, time began to run when the employer decided not to make the adjustment. In *Humphries* this was more than 7 months before the claim was presented and so the limitation period had expired and the tribunal did not have jurisdiction to hear the claim. In the EAT, Reid J upheld the tribunal's decision that the failure to make an adjustment was an omission and stated that the failure to make an adjustment was not a continuing act.[86] **4.68**

Humphries effectively decides that the duty to make adjustments is extinguished once an employer decides not to make a particular adjustment. However, the EAT did not consider, by reference to the terms of the duty itself rather than DDA 1995, sch 3, whether the duty to make an adjustment is, by its nature, a continuing duty. There was also no real discussion about whether a failure to **4.69**

[84] *HM Prison Service v Johnson* [2007] IRLR 951, EAT.
[85] EAT/0224/06.
[86] Per Reid J at para 24.

make an adjustment is a continuing omission.[87] Instead, the focus was on DDA 1995, sch 3, s 3(3) and (4). The purpose of these sections is to govern when time begins to run for the purposes of a claim. Time limits do not determine whether or not a duty to make adjustments arises or whether a breach of such a duty is a continuing act or omission.

4.70 There is an argument, contrary to the decision in *Humphries*, that the duty to make adjustments does impose an ongoing duty. The duty requires employers to take positive steps to prevent an existing disadvantage. While the disadvantage continues to exist, so does the duty to take steps to prevent it, and there is nothing in the statutory language that limits this interpretation. The EAT in *Humphries* perhaps misunderstood this aspect of the duty because it followed the now overruled line of authorities,[88] holding that the duty could be breached if the employer failed to consider an adjustment.[89] It is now well established that the reasonable adjustments test is an objective one that is concerned with what the employer did and did not do, and that what the employer did or did not consider, is irrelevant.[90] If the employer's consideration of the adjustment is irrelevant to whether the duty arises or is breached, how can the very existence of the duty depend on when an act or omission was decided upon?

4.71 There is also an argument in the alternative, that a failure to remedy a disadvantage is a continuing omission. In *Littlewoods Organisation Plc v Traynor*[91] the claimant successfully argued that a failure to implement measures dealing with an act of discrimination constituted a continuing act of discrimination. This is particularly relevant to the reasonable adjustments duty.[92]

4.72 If the decision in *Humphries* is correct, an employer could decide on the day he employed a disabled person[93] never to make any adjustments to assist him. The consequence of this would be that the duty would not arise on any subsequent day the employee was employed. If the employee did not present a claim within

---

87 A series of omissions may also constitute a continuing act: *Commissioner of Police of the Metropolis v Hendricks* [2002] EWCA Civ 1686. See also *Littlewoods Organisation Plc v Traynor* [1993] IRLR 154, EAT.

88 *Southampton City College v Randall* [2006] IRLR 18, EAT. This case was one of those in a line of authorities following *Mid-Staffordshire General Hospital NHS Trust v Cambridge* [2003] IRLR 566, EAT. This line of authorities was overruled by *Tarbuck v Sainsburys Supermarkets* [2006] IRLR 664, EAT. See para 4.61.

89 See Reid J at para 24 and paras 4.61 to 4.62.

90 See para 4.58–4.65.

91 [1993] IRLR 154, EAT. See also *Smith v Network Rail Infrastructure* UKEAT/0047/07/DA, EAT, and para 10.17.

92 For a discussion of time limits, see para 10.13.

93 The employee does not even need to be aware that a decision has been made for time to run: see *Swithland Motors Plc v Clarke* [1994] ICR 231, EAT. See further para 10.24.

three months of the day he started work, he would have no remedy and the employer would not be under a duty to make any further adjustments. This is surely contrary to the aims of the Framework Directive[94] and the DDA 1995 to ensure the integration of disabled persons into the workplace and society. Only a continuing duty to make adjustments, which enables the disabled person to fully participate throughout the period of employment, is truly compatible with the aims of the Framework Directive.

2. Determining Whether an Adjustment is Reasonable

An employer will only breach the duty to make adjustments if he has not taken such steps as were reasonable, in all the circumstances of the case, for him to take in order to prevent the PCP or physical feature, having a substantial adverse affect. **4.73**

DDA 1995, s 18B(1) sets out certain factors which *must* be taken into account when considering whether or not it is reasonable to make an adjustment. Although it is compulsory to have regard to DDA 1995, s 18B, a tribunal's failure to mention it in its reasons is likely to be treated in the same way as a failure to mention the Code of Practice 2004: as long as it is clear that the tribunal has properly considered the issue of reasonableness, the EAT is unlikely to interfere with the decision.[95] It is good practice, however, to refer the tribunal to relevant parts of DDA 1995, s 18B(1). The list of factors, although not intended to be exhaustive,[96] is certainly a useful place to begin a consideration of what adjustments are reasonable, particularly when dealing with more substantial adjustments. **4.74**

> **DDA 1995, s 18B(1)—Reasonableness**
> 18B(1) In determining whether it is reasonable for a person to have to take a particular step in order to comply with a duty to make reasonable adjustments, **regard shall be had**, in particular, to—
>
> (a) the extent to which taking the step would prevent the effect in relation to which the duty is imposed;
> (b) the extent to which it is practicable for him to take the step;
> (c) the financial and other costs which would be incurred by him in taking the step and the extent to which taking it would disrupt any of his activities;
> (d) the extent of his financial and other resources;
> (e) the availability to him of financial or other assistance with respect to taking the step;

94 Directive 2000/78/EC.

95 See, for instance, *Travis v Electronic Data Systems* [2004] EWCA Civ 880 and *Project Management Institute v Latif* [2007] IRLR 579, EAT paras 41–43. But note the case of *Nichols v The Governors of Kingsley School* EAT/0206/03 in which the EAT remitted a case to the tribunal to consider the effect of a particular paragraph of the Code of Practice 2004.

96 See the Code of Practice 2004. At para 5.27.

(f) the nature of his activities and the size of his undertaking;
(g) where the step would be taken in relation to a private household, the extent to which taking it would—
  (i) disrupt that household; or
  (ii) disturb any person residing there. [emphasis added]

The Step must be Effective

4.75 The Code of Practice 2004 suggests that the effectiveness and practicability of a particular adjustment should be considered first. If a step will be completely ineffective an employer is not required to take it.[97] As many effective adjustments should be made as are needed and as are reasonable.[98]

4.76 The nature of the PCP and the substantial disadvantage it causes the disabled person are highly relevant to what adjustments will be effective.[99] The disadvantage is inevitably linked to the claimant's disability and the effectiveness of an adjustment may well depend on evidence of the limitations causing the disadvantage.[100] Expert assistance from an occupational therapist or other medical specialist is obviously the kind of assistance most likely to help an employer understand what adjustments will be effective.

4.77 It is insufficient to find, as the tribunal at first instance did in *Smiths Detection Watford Ltd v Berriman*,[101] that an adjustment would be effective simply because it was what the claimant had requested. The claimant must prove a prima facie case that a particular adjustment would have prevented the disadvantage and could be considered reasonable.[102] If a claimant is unable to return to work in any capacity, no duty to make adjustments arises until he is fit to return to some form of work.[103]

Practicability

4.78 The question of whether something is practicable does not merely ask whether something is physically possible. It requires an assessment of the time, trouble, effort and difficulty in performing a particular task. If an adjustment can be made without practical difficulty then it will be practicable to make the adjustment.

97 See para 4.60
98 Code of Practice 2004, paragraph 5.18.
99 See paras 4.37 et seq.
100 *Jones v Post Office*[2001] IRLR 384, CA; *Fu v London Borough of Camden* [2001] IRLR 186, EAT; *Edwards v Mid Suffolk District Council* [2001] IRLR 190, EAT; *Morgan v Staffordshire University* [2002] IRLR 190, EAT at 195; *Sylvia Hay v Surrey County Council* [2007] EWCA Civ 93, CA, at para 37.
101 UKEAT/0144/05.
102 *Project Management Institute v Latif*[2007] IRLR 579, EAT. See paras 10.75 to 10.88
103 *Secretary of State for Work and Pensions v Heggie* UKEAT/0482/07/JOJ.

In health and safety law, if something is not possible in the light of current knowledge and technology then it will not be practicable.[104] There is no reason why this meaning should not also apply in the context of the DDA 1995.

There is no reference to 'reasonable' practicability in s 18B probably because the question of the *extent* to which an adjustment is practicable is simply one of the circumstances to be taken into account when assessing whether it is reasonable in all the circumstances to make the adjustment. Thus, the more impracticable it is to make the adjustment, the weightier the argument that the adjustment is unreasonable. **4.79**

The Financial Cost and the Disruption

If an adjustment is practicable and will be effective, the financial cost of the adjustment and the disruption that making it might cause are the next most significant issues. Adjustments that cost little or nothing and which are not disruptive are likely to be considered reasonable. **4.80**

The significance of the cost of an adjustment may depend upon the value of the employee's experience to the employer.[105] An employer may have to spend at least as much on an adjustment to enable the retention of a disabled person (including any retraining) as he would have to spend on recruiting and training a replacement for the disabled person.[106] The more valuable an employee, the more likely it is than an employer will be required to spend substantial sums on an adjustment.[107] The value of an employee will depend on the following factors: **4.81**

(i) the amount of resources (such as training) invested in the employee;
(ii) the employee's length of service;
(iii) the employee's level of skill and knowledge;
(iv) the level of the employee's pay.

It is legitimate in some circumstances to take into account the cost of the adjustment should the employer be required to make it for more than one person. In *O'Hanlon v Commissioners for HM Revenue & Customs*[108] the Court of Appeal upheld the EAT's distinction between a single claim, turning on its own facts, where the cost is limited to an adjustment for that individual and a claim which, **4.82**

104 See Parker J in *Adsett v K and L Steelfounders and Engineers Ltd* [1953] 1 All ER 97 (a case under the Factories Act 1937). This case was affirmed in the Court of Appeal [1953] 2 All ER 320.

105 See Code of Practice 2004 paras 5.31 and 5.32.

106 See Code of Practice 2004 at para 5.31.

107 See Code of Practice 2004, para 5.33.

108 [2007] IRLR 404, [2007] ICR 1359, CA. See also *The Chief Constable of Lincolnshire Police v Weaver* UKEAT/0622/07 and the Code of Practice 2004 para 5.42.

if successful, would inevitably affect many others and have very significant financial as well as policy implications for the employer.[109]

4.83 Clearly, the more disruption that an adjustment causes, the less reasonable it will be. So, for instance, an adjustment that required other employees to assist a disabled person to go to the toilet might be considered less reasonable than simply installing a toilet that had a hand rail and was accessible from a wheelchair.

The Extent of the Employer's Financial Resources

4.84 The cost of the adjustment should not be considered in isolation. The extent of the financial resources of the organization being asked to make the adjustment will be an important factor in determining whether the adjustment is unreasonably expensive. A wealthy investment bank will be required to do more than a small charity shop.

4.85 Larger organizations may well be expected to have a specific budget for making reasonable adjustments. However, each case should still be considered individually and there may be circumstances in which an employer may have to spend more than any figure it has allocated.[110]

4.86 The resources available to the employer *as a whole* should be taken into account.[111] The respondent's corporate structure may be relevant to the funds available to it. A shop, forming part of a large corporation which has a chain of stores, is unlikely to persuade the tribunal that its resources are the resources of the shop alone rather than the company that owns it.

4.87 The extent of the respondent's financial resources played a significant role in the decision in *Murphy v Slough Borough Council*.[112] In that case the claimant was a teacher whose disability prevented her from having a child. She arranged a surrogate birth and requested paid maternity leave to enable her to bond with the child. The Governing Body of the school turned down her request and said that the school's financial resources would only allow them to offer her unpaid leave. The school was unable to recover the costs of her paid leave as it would have been able to do had the claimant received statutory maternity pay. The cost of the leave was the equivalent of funding two pupils for a year. The school's budget was also in deficit. The school's financial resources were such that it was unreasonable to

109 The EAT at para 68.
110 Code of Practice 2004 para 5.36.
111 Code of Practice 2004 para 5.36.
112 [2005] ICR 721, CA.

make the adjustment.[113] Pill J indicated that if the school had had the resources of the Local Education Authority, the result may well have been more favourable to the claimant.

The availability of financial assistance with respect to making the adjustment is obviously relevant to any argument that the adjustment is too expensive. As has been seen above in *Murphy,* the unavailability of financial assistance can mean that the strain on the respondent's finances is greater than might otherwise be the case. In *Williams v J Walter Thompson Group Ltd*[114] the tribunal was unimpressed with the suggestion that a training course costing £4,500 was too expensive when £3,500 could have been financed through the Access to Work scheme. **4.88**

Nature of the Employer's Activities and the Size of the Undertaking

All employers, irrespective of their size, now have a duty to make reasonable adjustments.[115] However, the size of the employer and the extent of its resources may still be relevant to the extent to which an employer is required to make adjustments. An employer with a large number of staff is likely to have to make more significant efforts to reallocate duties or to identify a suitable alternative post than a small employer, irrespective of its financial resources. A plea of poverty is not an answer to a failure to make an organizational change that costs little or nothing. **4.89**

Private Households

Since the repeal of the small-employer exemption, even private households are required to comply with the DDA 1995. When considering whether an adjustment required of a private household is reasonable, should be had to the extent to which making it would disrupt the household or disturb any person residing there.[116] **4.90**

Planning Permission and Building Regulations

The DDA 1995 does not override the statutory requirements to obtain planning permission or building regulations approval where necessary.[117] Alterations to the employer's premises may require planning permission, particularly if the **4.91**

---

[113] Per Keene LJ at para 41. Although this case concerned disability-related discrimination, the Court of Appeal indicated that it was inconceivable that the circumstances that justified disability-related discrimination would not also render the adjustment unreasonable.

[114] [2005] IRLR 376, CA.

[115] The exemption for small employers contained in DDA 1995, s 7 was removed by the 2003 Regulations with effect from 1 October 2004.

[116] DDA 1995, s 18B(1)(g).

[117] Code paras 12.3 to 12.5.

building is listed. Building regulations approval can also be required in a wide variety of situations.

4.92 The simple fact that planning permission or building regulations approval may be required in order to make an adjustment, does not relieve the employer of the duty to make it. It is only if the permission or approval is refused that the employer or landlord will have a defence under DDA 1995, s 59.[118] The Code of Practice 2004 even suggests,[119] perhaps unrealistically, that an employer might be required to appeal any refusal to grant planning permission or to give building regulations approval before it can rely on the refusal. The cost of any required application is relevant to whether or not it is reasonable to have to make it.

4.93 Although the alteration of an existing building must comply with the building regulations,[120] the fact that a building satisfies the requirements of the building regulations is irrelevant to the duty to make adjustments.[121]

4.94 If the building is a new one, it may already comply with the British Standard BS8300. BS8300 is the code of practice for the design and construction of new buildings and prescribes an approach that is designed to meet the needs of disabled people. The Code of Practice 2004 suggests that it is unlikely to be reasonable to have to make an adjustment to a building that meets the standards set out in BS8300.

Other Factors to Consider

4.95 The factors listed in the Code of Practice 2004 and DDA 1995, s 18B are not exhaustive. The Code of Practice 2004 itself provides some examples of factors, not listed in DDA 1995, s 18B(1), which might affect a tribunal's consideration of whether the adjustment was reasonable. Those factors are:

(i) the effect on other employees;
(ii) adjustments that have been made for other disabled persons;
(iii) the extent to which the disabled person is willing to co-operate.[122]

4.96 A tribunal should have regard to all cogent reasons why a particular adjustment is, or is not, reasonable irrespective of whether the reason is listed in the Code of Practice 2004 or DDA 1995, s 18B(1).

4.97 For instance, it may be relevant that an employer knew what adjustments were required before it recruited the claimant. In *Williams v J Walter Thompson*

118 See para 4.126.
119 See Code of Practice 2004 para 12.5.
120 SI 2000/2531.
121 See Code of Practice 2004 paras 12.7 to 12.8.
122 See Code of Practice 2004 para 5.42.

Group Ltd[123] the respondent recruited the claimant to do a specific job doing Lotus Notes development work. The claimant was totally blind and required training and new or adapted software/equipment to use Lotus Notes. The respondent knew this before it offered the job to the claimant. After 18 months the respondent had provided only one day of training and had failed to make any adjustments to allow the claimant to do her work. The respondent claimed that its failure to make reasonable adjustments was justified[124] because the technological changes required to make the changes were substantial and expensive. The Court of Appeal considered that since the respondent had recruited the claimant knowing the type of adjustments that it would have to make, it was not the response of a reasonable employer then to refuse to make those adjustments even if they turned out to be expensive or difficult.

An employer's blameworthy conduct may make it more reasonable to make an adjustment than it would have been had the employer not done anything wrong. In *Meikle v Nottinghamshire County Council*[125] an employer's previous failure to make reasonable adjustments to PCPs which were disadvantaging the claimant, made her so ill that she became unable to work. Because the employers caused her illness, it was unjustifiable for the employer not to adjust its policy of not paying employees who were absent from work and to pay the claimant during her absence. But for such a default, an employer is not normally required to pay a disabled employee more sick leave than a non-disabled employee.[126] **4.98**

3. Common Adjustments

A list of common adjustments is provided by DDA 1995, s 18B(2): **4.99**

Section 18B(2)—Common Adjustments

(a) making adjustments to premises;
(b) allocating some of the disabled person's duties to another person;
(c) transferring him to fill an existing vacancy;
(d) altering his hours of working or training;
(e) assigning him to a different place of work or training;
(f) allowing him to be absent during working or training hours for rehabilitation, assessment or treatment;
(g) giving, or arranging for, training or mentoring (whether for the disabled person *or any other person*);
(h) acquiring or modifying equipment;

123 [2005] IRLR 376, CA.

124 The defence of justification was abolished by the 2003 Regulations with effect from 1 October 2004 but the reasoning in this case is equally applicable to the test of reasonableness.

125 [2005] ICR 1.

126 See *O'Hanlon v Commissioner for HM Revenue and Customs* [2007] IRLR 404, [2007] ICR 1359, [2007] EWCA Civ 283, CA at paras 70 to 73. See also paras 4.102 and 4.131.

(i) modifying instructions or reference manuals;
(j) modifying procedures for testing or assessment;
(k) providing a reader or interpreter;
(l) providing supervision *or other support.*[127]

4.100 In February 2002 a study carried out on behalf of the Department for Work and Pensions researched the type of adjustments which had been considered by tribunals and which were recorded on the database of Part II cases held at Bury St Edmunds.[128]

4.101 Practitioners should note that 7.6 per cent of the known adjustments involved an adjustment that was not listed in s 18(B)(2): ample warning that s 18(B)(2) should not be treated as exhaustive.

Nature of adjustments where known	Number of cases	Per cent of total cases
Transfer to an existing vacancy	139	20.8
Reallocation of duties	101	15.1
Acquiring or modifying equipment	75	11.2
Alteration to working hours	75	11.2
Assignment to different place of work	75	11.2
Adjustments to premises	33	4.9
Giving or arranging training	30	4.5
Modifying procedures for testing or assessment	25	3.7
Leave of absence for rehabilitation assessment or treatment	21	3.1
Providing a carer or support worker	18	2.7
Providing supervision	15	2.2
Modifying instructions or reference manuals	5	0.7
Providing a reader or interpreter	4	0.6
Other	51	7.6
Total number of cases	667	

127 The words in italics were added by the 2003 Regulations and were not included in the old s 6(3). The Code of Practice 2004, at para 5.18, provides helpful practical examples for each of these adjustments.

128 Monitoring the Disability Discrimination Act 1995 (Phase 2) by Sarah Leverton. The above table is compiled using the data in Table 44 of her report.

Sick Pay

Where a disabled employee does not receive pay during his absence from work he may be substantially disadvantaged by the PCP that he must be fit for work to be paid.[129] The crucial question in these circumstances is not whether there is a substantial disadvantage, but whether it will be reasonable to make the adjustment of paying the employee while he is absent. **4.102**

In the vast majority of cases it will not be considered a reasonable adjustment to pay a disabled employee more sick pay than other employees. The position was succinctly summarized in a paragraph by Elias J in the EAT whose judgment was upheld by the Court of Appeal:[130] **4.103**

> In our view it will be a very rare case indeed where the adjustment said to be applicable here, that is merely giving higher sick pay than would be payable to a non-disabled person who in general does not suffer the same disability related absences, would be considered necessary as a reasonable adjustment . . . although we do not rule out the possibility that it could be in exceptional circumstances.

Claims that additional sick pay should be paid as a reasonable adjustment are likely to fail. However, the judgments of the Court of Appeal and EAT confirm that it is not a legal impossibility and that an employer can be required to pay additional sick pay in exceptional circumstances. **4.104**

Nottinghamshire County Council v Meikle[131] provides a good example of what might qualify as an exceptional circumstance. The employers had previously failed to make other reasonable adjustments. Consequently, Mrs Meikle was absent from work for longer than she would have been, had those adjustments been made. The employer was required to make an adjustment to its normal sick pay because the employer's previous default had the knock-on effect of making the failure to adjust the claimant's sick pay unjustified. Although the justification defence has been abolished, this reasoning applies equally well to the assessment of reasonableness. **4.105**

Modifying Standards of Performance

Employers who require particular standards of performance from their employees which a disabled person cannot meet, will place a disabled person at a disadvantage. Assuming that disadvantage is substantial, is it reasonable to have to **4.106**

---

129 See Elias J in *O'Hanlon v Commission for HM Customs* [2006] IRLR 840, EAT at paras 54 to 57. Elias J's judgment was approved on appeal at [2007] IRLR 404. See also *London Clubs Management v Hood* [2001] IRLR 719, EAT.

130 See Elias J in *O'Hanlon v Commission for HM Customs* [2006] IRLR 840, EAT at para 67 and the Court of Appeal's approval at [2007] IRLR 404, CA.

131 [2005] ICRI, CA, at paras 70 to 74.

adjust that standard to accommodate them? What standard of performance can an employer reasonably expect from a disabled employee? The short answer is that an employer is entitled to demand that a disabled person meets the standards required in order properly to perform the essential functions of the job.

4.107 Recital 17 of the Framework Directive makes it clear that the Directive 'does not require recruitment, promotion, maintenance in employment or training of an individual who is not competent, capable and available to perform the essential functions of the post concerned or to undergo the relevant training, without prejudice to the obligation to provide reasonable accommodation for people with disabilities.' This has also been the approach of the tribunals in the UK. In *Mulligan v Commissioner for Inland Revenue*[132] the EAT stated that 'the assessment of performance is a wholly separate issue from the duty to make reasonable adjustments which does not extend necessarily to lowering the quality of work or volume of work being demanded of the appellant.'[133]

4.108 The Framework Directive makes it clear that the DDA 1995 should not require the employer to engage someone who is unable to fulfil the **essential** functions of the post. This does not mean that the disabled person may not demand adjustments to any aspect of performance. Adjustments can, and should be, made to anything other than the essential functions of the post.[134]

4.109 Where an employee could only continue to perform the role if an adjustment was made to the essential function of the post, the only reasonable adjustment is likely to be a transfer to an alternative available vacancy.[135]

Modifying Procedures for Testing or Assessment (Including Disciplinary and Grievance Procedures)

4.110 While it may not be a reasonable adjustment for an employer to alter its standards of performance or competence, it may well be reasonable for it to alter its

---

132 EAT/691/99.

133 The situation is also similar with regard to competence standards. In *Hart v Chief Constable of Derbyshire* EAT/0403/07 the disabled person was seeking to qualify as a police officer even though she was unable to meet the required standards of performance that were necessary for the post. The EAT considered the situation analogous to adjustments required of qualifications bodies: qualifications bodies are required to make reasonable adjustments to any PCP *except* a competence standard (s 14B DDA 1995) and are not required to lower their standards in order to alleviate a substantial disadvantage. The claimant in *Hart* required an adjustment relieving her from having to achieve competence with respect to a core part of a police officer's duties and the EAT upheld the tribunal's decision that this was not a reasonable adjustment.

134 It should also be noted that performance standards are not excluded from the PCP for which adjustments are required to be made, in the same way that competence standards are excluded from the definition of PCP in respect of qualifications bodies.

135 *Archibald v Fife Council* [2004] IRLR 651, HL.

methods of assessing that performance or competence. The disabled person must be given the opportunity to participate in the testing or assessment process in as full a way as reasonably possible. Similar considerations apply to the conduct of disciplinary and grievance procedures. Where necessary, the procedures must be adjusted to ensure that the disabled person concerned can use them effectively.

Reasonable adjustments should also be made for candidates attending job interviews. The most difficult aspect of dealing with applicants for employment is establishing what the employer knew, or did not know, about the applicant's disability. The employer's knowledge of the disability should be thoroughly investigated as should any declarations made by the claimant regarding his disability.[136] **4.111**

A failure to make an adjustment to a disciplinary procedure can result in a very substantial award of damages, particularly if the procedure ends with the dismissal of the employee. Making adjustments such as changing the employee's representative; changing the time and venue for the meeting; providing additional written explanations of the procedure or of the allegations; and holding the meetings closer or further apart in time than they would be normally, cost little more than making an extra effort and yet, if they are not made when required, the resulting financial consequences can be disastrous. **4.112**

Whether an adjustment to a disciplinary procedure is reasonable is a question of fact. For instance, the Code of Practice 2004 suggests that allowing a young man with learning disabilities to bring a friend rather than a colleague to a disciplinary hearing would be a reasonable adjustment. However, in *Cave v Goodwin*,[137] the tribunal found, in exactly those circumstances, that the claimant was not substantially disadvantaged by the absence of his friend because (a) his disability affected his writing and reading rather than his speech, (b) he had been accompanied at his disciplinary hearing (albeit not by his choice of representative) and (c) he had shown himself, during the hearing before the tribunal, to be capable of representing for himself. The contrast between the findings in this case and the recommendation in the code of Practice 2004 is a good reminder that even when, on the face of it, a reasonable adjustment has not been made, the claimant must still show that he has suffered a disadvantage. **4.113**

Tribunals are unlikely to accept an argument that it was unreasonable to make an adjustment because the employee was facing disciplinary proceedings that were **4.114**

136 See further paras 4.135 to 4.160.
137 EWCA Civ 391.

likely to result in his dismissal.[138] However, this will be a question of fact in each case. Exceptionally, if the proposed adjustment causes very substantial disruption or is very expensive and the disciplinary proceedings are very near completion, there may be an argument that it was only reasonable to make the adjustment at the conclusion of the disciplinary process.

4.115 Proper medical advice can play an important role in ensuring that the outcome of the assessment or procedure is as fair as possible. It should be remembered, however, that cases such as *Paul v National Probation Service*[139] can no longer be relied upon as authority for the proposition that a medical assessment is, itself, a reasonable adjustment.[140]

4.116 Following *The Environment Agency v Rowan,*[141] it is also doubtful whether a trial period either for modifying a procedure, or as an assessment as to whether an adjustment will work, will qualify as a reasonable adjustment itself, although an employer who failed to conduct such a trial period may well struggle to show that the adjustment would not have been effective.

Transfers to an Existing Vacancy

4.117 Where a disabled person is dismissed because he is incapable of performing his job, a tribunal will inevitably ask whether it would have been reasonable to transfer the person to an existing vacancy. A disabled person may also wish to be transferred to a different role because he finds the work too difficult or stressful. Transfers are the most frequently cited reasonable adjustment in DDA 1995 claims.[142]

4.118 In most cases the question will not be as simple as whether or not the transfer itself is reasonable. The terms of the transfer such as how the employee is required to apply for the new role, the pay in the new job, the hours of work etc., will all play a part in the assessment of reasonableness. For instance, in *Archibald v Fife*,[143] once the claimant became incapable of doing her road sweeping job, the respondent required her to undertake competitive interviews for the jobs which she applied for because they were at a higher grade. The House of Lords considered that, even though the roles were at a higher grade, it would have been reasonable

138 In *Beart v HM Prison Service* (2003) IRLR 238, CA, the Court of Appeal upheld a tribunal's finding that a respondent failed to make a reasonable adjustment by not transferring an employee to a different workplace because she was facing a serious disciplinary charge.

139 [2004] IRLR 190, EAT.

140 See the discussion of *Tarbuck v Sainsbury's Supermarket* [2006] IRLR 664, EAT at para 4.61. For a discussion of the role of medical advice in the duty to make adjustments see paras 4.149 to 4.160.

141 UKEAT/0060/07/DM. See para 4.63.

142 See the table at para 4.101.

143 *Archibald v Fife Council* [2004] IRLR 651, HL.

simply to transfer the claimant to one of the existing vacancies rather than requiring her to undertake competitive interviews.[144]

The following questions will typically arise where a transfer is being considered. Will it be unduly disruptive to the employer's undertaking or to other employees? Will the training be unreasonably expensive? Will the transfer be effective to prevent the disadvantage? Does the size of the employer's undertaking make the transfer unreasonable? **4.119**

In most cases it is likely to be unreasonable to have to create a new role for a disabled employee but the DDA 1995 does not, as a matter of law, preclude the creation of a new post in substitution for an existing post.[145] **4.120**

The claimant will have to show that there was an existing vacancy to which it would have been reasonable to have transferred him, before the burden of proof shifts to the employer.[146] Where the claimant is suggesting that he should have been transferred, he should seek early disclosure of all the employer's vacancies for the relevant period of time in order to identify a suitable post. **4.121**

4. Health And Safety

Maintaining a balance between the obligations imposed by the health and safety legislation and the obligations imposed by the DDA 1995, can be difficult.[147] For example, health and safety law obliges employers to do everything reasonably practicable to reduce the risks to their employees' safety to the lowest possible level.[148] Some of the required adjustments under the DDA 1995 might hinder the employer's efforts to reduce the risk to other employees or the disabled person, and some adjustments may even increase the risk. Deciding which course of action to take in these circumstances can be problematic. **4.122**

In January 2007 the Health and Safety Commission and the DRC issued a joint statement stating that health and safety 'should never be used as a false excuse to justify discriminatory treatment' and indicated that 'it will be the exception rather than the rule to exclude disabled people from particular jobs and tasks.' **4.123**

---

144 Employers are not required to employ a disabled person who is incapable of performing the job after reasonable adjustments have been made for them. See paras 4.106 to 4.109.

145 *Southampton City College v Randall* [2006] IRLR 18, EAT. In this case the respondent's workforce was undergoing a restructure and the manager had a free hand in creating new job roles. The tribunal therefore found that, since the manager had a blank sheet of paper, it would have been reasonable to have created a new role for the claimant.

146 *Project Management Institute v Latif* [2007] IRLR 579, EAT.

147 Health and Safety reasons were cited in 14.3% of cases where the (now repealed) justification defence was relied upon (Sarah Leverton, Monitoring the Disability Discrimination Act 1995 (Phase 2), DRC in-house report Table 45).

148 Health and Safety At Work Act 1974, s 2(1).

4.124 The Code of Practice 2004 also cautions employers against assuming that disabled people necessarily represent a risk to health and safety and warns that making stereotypical assumptions about the health and safety implications of disability can constitute direct discrimination.[149]

4.125 An employer who has legitimate health and safety concerns about making an adjustment may argue that the adjustment is not appropriate in two ways. Firstly, he may argue that health and safety concerns render the adjustment unreasonable. Alternatively, if his action or omission was necessary to comply with health and safety legislation then he may argue that he was acting lawfully in pursuance of statutory authority under DDA 1995, s 59. The precise overlap and/or distinction between these two defences is unclear.

DDA 1995, s 59

4.126 Where an employer refuses to make an adjustment because of health and safety concerns, DDA 1995, s 59 may provide a defence. That section provides that no act is rendered unlawful that is done in pursuance of:

(a) any enactment;
(b) any instrument made under any enactment;
(c) to comply with any condition or requirement imposed by a Minister of the Crown.[150]

4.127 This section provides a blanket protection for those acts which are performed 'in pursuance' of a statutory obligation such as a health and safety obligation.[151] It is possible to construe 'in pursuance of' either broadly, to mean any acts done by the employer in *purported* compliance with the health and safety legislation, or narrowly, to mean only those acts *necessary* to compliance with the health and safety legislation.

4.128 In *Hampson v Department of Education and Science*[152] the House of Lords considered the meaning of 'in pursuance of' in the context of RRA 1976, s41(1)(b). Their Lordships held that the narrow interpretation of 'in pursuance of' was the correct interpretation and that the defence was restricted to those acts *necessary* for the performance of an express statutory obligation. There is no reason to interpret DDA 1995, s 59 differently.

149 Code of Practice 2004 paras 6.7 to 6.13.

150 DDA 1995, s 59 is dealt with further in paras 3.119–3.123.

151 The EAT described the health and safety legislation as trumping the DDA 1995 in *Lane Group Plc & North Somerset Council v Farmiloe* UKEAT/0532/03/DA and UKEAT/0357/03/DA.

152 [1990] 3 WLR 42, HL.

The point can be illustrated by way of an example. Take s 2(1) of the Health and Safety at Work etc. Act 1974 ('HSA'). This section confers no right of action in civil proceedings for a breach of the HSA but does impose a general duty on all employers to do everything reasonably practicable to ensure the health and safety of their employees. An employer will have to show that its failure to make an adjustment was necessary in order for it do everything reasonably practicable to ensure the health and safety of its employees under HSA s 2(1). If the employer could have satisfied its health and safety obligations in a way which would have allowed it to make the adjustment, the omission to make the adjustment would not then be necessary to comply with HSA s 2(1),[153] and so the employer's DDA 1995, s 59 defence will fail. **4.129**

In order to identify whether the act was done in pursuance of the relevant piece of legislation, the practitioner must understand thoroughly the duties imposed by the legislation in question.[154] **4.130**

Health and safety arguments might also be used to support an *employee's* argument that a particular adjustment was reasonable. In *Smith v Churchill Stairlifts*[155] the employer imposed a requirement to carry very heavy MDF radiator cabinets to clients' houses for demonstration purposes. The employer successfully argued at first instance that the decision to use the heavy cabinets rather than a lighter mock-up was a legitimate commercial requirement. Although the employer lost on other grounds, it may have been possible to use the *Manual Handling Operations Regulations 1992* to prevent the employer from arguing that commercial expediency required heavy cabinets to be used, as those regulations require employers to avoid the need for employees to undertake any lifting which involves a risk of them being injured.[156] **4.131**

The Importance of a Suitable and Sufficient Risk Assessment

An important part of an employer's duty to ensure, so far as is reasonably practicable, the health and safety of his employees at work, is the requirement to carry out an assessment of the risks in the workplace. Since an employer's act or omission in pursuance of health and safety legislation must be *necessary* in order for the DDA 1995, s 59 defence to apply, an employer which has not conducted a suitable and sufficient risk assessment may well have difficulties persuading a **4.132**

---

153 For further reading on the conflict between the health and safety legislation and duties under the DDA see *Lane Group Plc & North Somerset Council v Farmiloe* UKEAT/0532/03/DA and UKEAT/0357/03/DA and *R (A,B,X & Y) v East Sussex County Council* (No.2) [2003] EWHC 167.

154 A discussion of the health and safety legislation is beyond the scope of this text.

155 [2005] EWCA Civ 1220, [2006] ICR 524, [2006] IRLR 41.

156 See reg 4 of the Manual Handling Operations Regulations 1992.

tribunal that its actions were necessary to comply with its health and safety obligations. However, a risk assessment is unlikely itself to qualify as a reasonable adjustment.[157]

4.133 It is not clear how tribunals will approach the question of whether a suitable and sufficient risk assessment has been carried out. In the context of justification of less favourable treatment, cases such as *KF Bartlett v Toms*[158] suggest that unless the employer's risk assessment is clearly unreasonable, he is likely to be able to rely on its conclusions.[159] In *Jones v Post Office*[160] the Court of Appeal held that a tribunal cannot go to the extent of disagreeing with a risk assessment which is properly conducted, based on the properly formed opinion of suitably qualified doctors, and which produces an answer which is not irrational.[161] However, these cases are not relevant where an employer is seeking to rely on DDA 1995, s 59 or on an argument that the adjustment was reasonable because both of these latter tests judge the employer's actions objectively without regard either to the range of reasonable responses test or the material and substantial test. DDA 1995, s 59 requires the act or omission under health and safety legislation to be *necessary* to comply with the statutory obligation and the reasonable adjustments test entitles the tribunal to come to a different conclusion to the employer even if the reason for the employer's actions is material to the circumstances of the case and substantial.[162]

4.134 Risk assessments under the Management of Health and Safety at Work Regulations 1999 and most other pieces of health and safety legislation such as the Manual Handling Regulations 1992 are required to be 'suitable and sufficient'.[163] The Code of Practice 2004 also provides that a health and safety risk assessment should be tailored to the disabled person concerned and should consider what the risk would be after reasonable adjustments have been made.[164] A general policy for employees that does not take into account the individual's attributes, is not only likely to constitute unjustifiable less favourable treatment; it may not be suitable and sufficient to assess the risk to the disabled person con-

---

157 See para 4.62.

158 UKEAT/0131/04/ILB.

159 The EAT allowed an appeal because the tribunal substituted its own view of the employer's assessment of risk. See also *London Underground Ltd v Bragg* EAT/847/98.

160 [2001] IRLR 384, CA.

161 See *Jones v Post Office* [2001] IRLR 384, CA per Pill LJ at para 27. This case concerned the (now abolished) defence of justification in the context of a reasonable adjustments claim.

162 See para 4.59.

163 For instance, reg 3(1) of the Management of Health and Safety at Work Regulations 1999 provides that every employer shall make a suitable and sufficient assessment of the risks to the health and safety of his employees to which they are exposed whilst they are at work.

164 Code of Practice 2004 para 6.13.

cerned. A list of dos and don'ts when undertaking a risk assessment for a disabled person is published on the Health and Safety Executive's website.[165]

F. Step Four—Knowledge

Since the test for whether an adjustment is required is objective,[166] a tribunal may consider an adjustment to be reasonable even if the employer was not aware of its existence. The DDA 1995 remedies this potentially unjust state of affairs by providing the respondent with a knowledge defence. This knowledge defence is a defence only in the sense that the state of an employer's knowledge of the disability or its effects can determine both whether the duty has actually arisen and if so, what the nature of that duty is. **4.135**

The provisions governing how an employer's knowledge affects the duty to make adjustments are contained in DDA 1995, s 4A(3). **4.136**

> **Section 4A(3)—The Knowledge Defence**
> 4A(3) Nothing in this section imposes a duty on an employer in relation to a disabled person if the employer does not know, and could not reasonably be expected to know:
> (a) in the case of an applicant or potential applicant, that the disabled person concerned is, or may be, an applicant for the employment;
> (b) in any case, that the person has a disability and is likely to be affected in the way mentioned in subsection (1).

In any claim by an employee that there has been a failure to make reasonable adjustments, the employer may assert that the duty to make adjustments did not arise because it did not know that the person had a disability and was therefore likely to be placed at a substantial disadvantage by the relevant PCP. **4.137**

If the claimant is an applicant for employment or potential applicant, the employer has an additional knowledge defence if he did not know, and could not reasonably be expected to know, that the person was an applicant. **4.138**

1. Knowledge and the Duty to Make Adjustments

An employer will not be under a duty simply because he knows that a person is disabled. He must also know that the person is likely to be substantially disadvantaged by a PCP. This requirement for knowledge of the disadvantage caused by a PCP is often neglected by practitioners. **4.139**

---

165 <http://www.hse.gov.uk/disability/risk.htm>.

166 See para 4.58 et seq.

4.140 An employer may know that a person is disabled even if he is unaware that the person qualifies as a 'disabled person' under the DDA 1995. Take the example of an employer who provides an uncomfortable plastic chair to an employee suffering from long-term back pain. It is enough that the employer is aware that the employee is suffering from a physical impairment that makes it difficult for the employee to sit for extended periods of time. The employer cannot escape liability if he is ignorant of the fact that the person concerned qualifies as disabled under the DDA 1995. The employer has sufficient knowledge if he knows that an employee has a physical or mental impairment which has a substantial and long-term adverse effect on that employee's ability to carry out normal day-to-day activities.[167]

4.141 In addition to knowing that the employee is disabled, the employer must also know that the disabled person is likely to be placed at a substantial disadvantage by the employer's PCP. The employer's knowledge of the likelihood of the claimant suffering a substantial disadvantage can define the extent of the adjustments that the employer is required to make. This was recognized in *Ridout*[168] in which Morrison J stated, at paragraph 23:

> Subsection (6) [of the Section 6 Duty] requires the tribunal to measure the extent of the duty, if any, against the actual or assumed knowledge of the employer both as to the disability and its likelihood of causing the individual a substantial disadvantage in comparison with persons who are not disabled.

4.142 The employer is only required to take action to prevent PCP causing substantial disadvantages which it knows, or ought to know, about. If the employer does not, and ought not, know about the substantial disadvantage caused by a particular PCP, it is not required to make an adjustment to prevent that disadvantage. In *Ridout* the EAT held that no employer could be expected to know that the PCP that they had put in place for interviewing the claimant might disadvantage the claimant unless she told them about it. Even though the claimant required adjustments (and it would have been simple to make them), the duty to make the adjustments did not arise.

4.143 This is an important and often overlooked aspect of the duty to make reasonable adjustments and can have a profound effect on the way that a case is presented and resolved. The lack of reported cases on this issue suggests that it is a defence which is currently neglected by employers.

2. Constructive Knowledge

4.144 An employer need not have actual knowledge in order for the duty to make reasonable adjustments to arise because constructive knowledge is sufficient.

---

167 See para 5.32.

168 *Ridout v TC Group* [1998] IRLR 628, EAT.

DDA 1995 s, 4A(3) only relieves an employer from the duty to make reasonable adjustments if he did not actually know and 'could not reasonably be expected to know' of the disability or the substantial disadvantage caused by the PCP. If a reasonable employer could be expected to know of the disability or its effects, then he will have constructive knowledge and cannot rely on his own ignorance in his defence.

The test of reasonableness in DDA 1995, s 4A(3) is the range of reasonable responses test.[169] Where, for instance, an employer relies on a properly formed opinion from a medical practitioner he will not be in breach of the duty, provided his use of the opinion fell within the range of reasonable responses open to him.[170] This approach is derived from the approach taken to an employer's reliance on medical advice in *Jones v Post Office*.[171] It sets a much less rigorous hurdle for employers to cross than the objective test used to determine whether an adjustment is reasonable.[172] **4.145**

Whether a reasonable employer in the circumstances would have known, of the disability and its effects, involves a broad enquiry into what the employer would have known at the time, given (a) the facts known to the employer and (b) what it would have discovered had it conducted a reasonable enquiry. In *Chief Constable of Avon Constabulary v Dolan*[173] the EAT upheld the tribunal's decision to impose constructive knowledge on the Chief Constable. The tribunal had relied on the following reasons: **4.146**

(a) the fact that the symptoms of the claimant's psychiatric disorder were evident;
(b) the deterioration in the claimant's performance;
(c) the claimant's own self-assessment which stated that he had a physical or mental impairment which had a substantial long-term adverse affect on his day-to-day activities;

169 The range of reasonable responses test is discussed in the context of unfair dismissal in *Post Office v Foley* [2000] IRLR 827, CA and *Iceland Frozen Foods v Jones* [1982] IRLR 439, EAT.

170 *Chief Constable of Avon Constabulary v Dolan* [2008] UKEAT/0522/07.

171 [2001] IRLR 384. Although *Jones v Post Office* is concerned with whether an employer's lack of knowledge justified disability-related discrimination, Clark J in *Chief Constable of Avon Constabulary v Dolan* [2008] UKEAT/0522/07, at para 16, recommended the use of the *Jones v Post Office* approach for DDA 1995, s 4A(3).

172 The question whether the respondent can justify its actions is not a strict test. It only requires that the reason for its actions is material to the circumstances of the case and substantial. This is much less onerous than the test of reasonableness that is applied to the adjustment duty (see paras 4.73 et seq.). A tribunal can find that an adjustment would have been reasonable even if the employer had reasons for not making it that were material to the circumstances of the case and substantial.

173 [2008] UKEAT/0522/07 at para 11.

(d) the guidance to the police service which required supervising officers to enquire whether or not the officer's condition fell within the DDA 1995;
(e) the Code of Practice 2004, which states at paragraph 5.12 that an employer must do all it can reasonably be expected to do to find out whether the employee has a disability.

4.147 In *Department of Work and Pensions v Hall,* [174] the EAT upheld a decision that the employer had constructive knowledge of the claimant's disability based on the following facts:

(a) the claimant had completed a disabled person's tax credit form and given it to the respondent's Human Resources Department;
(b) a member of the interview panel had known the employee for some time in a private capacity and knew of her disability;
(b) the claimant had become volatile and disruptive at work;
(c) the claimant refused access to her medical records;
(d) the claimant refused to provide information about her health in her application form.

4.148 In the circumstances of both these cases the respondent had constructive knowledge that the employee was a disabled person. In neither of these cases was there an examination of whether the employer had constructive knowledge of the way in which the claimant was likely to be affected by the PCP. This part of the knowledge defence should not be neglected.

3. Medical Advice

4.149 This section considers the nature of an employer's obligation to seek medical advice when contemplating an adjustment. Issues relevant to the presentation of medical evidence to a tribunal are dealt with in chapter 10.

4.150 Medical advice can obviously be expensive and employers with limited budgets may be reluctant or unable to pay for advice that may prove to be unnecessary. Does for instance, the fact that an employee behaves in an eccentric manner mean that a reasonable employer must ask him to see a doctor for an assessment of his mental health? There are unfortunately no fixed guidelines for when it might be reasonable to ask an employee to submit to a medical examination. What is reasonable will depend very much on all the circumstances of the individual case. However, given that the employer's conduct only has to fall within the range of reasonable responses, employers have a broad discretion.

---

174 [2005] All ER D 128, EAT.

4.151 The assessment of what type of enquiry is reasonable, involves striking a balance which neither requires the claimant to 'harp on' about his disability nor obliges the respondent to interrogate him about it.[175] In *Ridout v TC Group*[176] a person with epilepsy who applied for a job, declared on her application form that her epilepsy was controlled by medication. She was interviewed in a room with fluorescent lighting. Although she commented that the lighting might disadvantage her, she did not complain about it further. The EAT found that it was reasonable for the employer could not resonably be expected to anticipate any problems and was entitled to rely on the claimant's account of her own disability, without embarking upon an investigation of its own.

4.152 If an employer would ordinarily have been expected to make enquiries about its employee's health then it must have a good reason for not making them. In *London Borough of Hammersmith & Fulham v Farnsworth*[177] the employer engaged an independent occupational health physician to screen the health of an employee to whom it had offered a job. The physician expressed his concern that the claimant's work might be affected by his medical condition. The council argued that it did not make further enquiries because it was concerned to safeguard the applicant's privacy and that it, therefore, did not know that the claimant was disabled. This self-denying argument was rejected. The claimant had clearly been willing to disclose his medical problems to the employer's agent and so the argument that it was respecting the claimant's privacy was unsustainable. Once the employer had discovered the medical condition it was under a duty to find out more about it.

4.153 Since the duty is owed to the disabled person concerned, a blanket approach or policy determining when medical examinations should be procured, without regard to the individual, is unlikely to be reasonable in every case.

The Quality of the Medical Advice and Reliance upon It

4.154 The question of what medical evidence an employer is required to procure when determining what adjustments to make was considered in the context of disability-related discrimination in *Jones v Post Office*.[178] Kay LJ stated at paragraph 32:

> Where evidence (medical or otherwise) which was not available to the employer is put before the tribunal, provided the employer has taken into account all the evidence reasonably available to it, including, if medical issues are raised, sufficiently well qualified expert medical evidence, then the fact that other evidence is available by the time of the hearing cannot render the treatment unjustified.

175 *Ridout v TC Group* [1998] IRLR 628, EAT at para 25. See also *Jama v Alcohol Recovery Project* UKEAT/0602/06/RN.

176 [1998] IRLR 628, EAT.

177 [2000] IRLR 691, EAT.

178 [2001] IRLR 384 CA.

4.155 Arden LJ addressed the issue at paragraph 39:

> Employers are not obliged to search for the Holy Grail. It is sufficient if their conclusion is one which on a critical examination is found to have substance.

4.156 Although employers are not required to search for the Holy Grail, it is important that the respondent chooses an appropriate medical expert with a relevant qualification.[179]

4.157 The employer must also endeavour to ask the expert relevant questions. In *Chief Constable of Avon & Somerset Constabulary v Dolan* the EAT expressed the view that it was 'extraordinary' that the respondent had never asked its doctor to comment on whether the claimant was disabled within the meaning of DDA 1995 s 1. The fact that the doctor did not mention that he considered the claimant to be disabled did not prevent the employer from being fixed with constructive knowledge.

4.158 While an employee is not required to harp on about his disability, he is expected to co-operate with the employer's requests for information. In *Jama v Alcohol Recovery Project*[180] the claimant was suffering from post-traumatic stress disorder. He ignored frequent requests to attend the respondent's occupational health service and to provide information from his general practitioner. The EAT upheld a decision that since the claimant had failed to co-operate with the medical experts or to produce any other evidence, the respondent could not be fixed with constructive knowledge of his disability even though the claimant had told them in terms that he was suffering from post-traumatic stress disorder.

4.159 If two contradictory medical opinions are received, it may be reasonable for the employer to seek a third medical opinion.[181] However, so long as the medical opinion that the respondent chooses to rely on is suitably qualified, it is unlikely that a tribunal could properly interfere with the decision to rely on that opinion as opposed to any other.[182] An employer will be entitled to rely on such an opinion even if it contradicts what he has been told by the claimant about the disability.[183]

4. Knowledge of the Adjustment and Reasonableness

4.160 Ignorance of the availability of an adjustment is not a defence to a reasonable adjustments claim under DDA 1995, s 4A. Take the example of a blind school teacher who is unable to read the school timetable. The school knows that the

179 See also *Surrey Police v Marshall* EAT/774/01.
180 UKEAT/0602/06/RN.
181 *British Gas v Breeze* (unreported, EAT, 13 September 1998).
182 *KF Bartlett v Toms* UKEAT/0131/04.
183 *Farley v The Prison Service* EAT/359/01 per Holland J at para 7(c).

teacher is blind and that the use of a printed school timetable puts him at a substantial disadvantage when compared to his non-disabled colleagues. The school made no adjustments. If the tribunal finds that it would have been a reasonable adjustment to provide a Braille printout of the timetable the employer will have breached the duty even if it was unaware that there was such a thing as Braille.

G. Obligations in Respect of Leases

Employers who own their own building are very likely to have the power to make the adjustments to that building that their statutory duty under the DDA 1995 requires them to make. The situation may be different for employers who occupy premises under a lease or a sub-lease. An employer may be prevented, by the terms of the lease, from making the alterations that the DDA 1995 requires of him. **4.161**

DDA 1995, s 18A and Part 1 of Schedule 4 deal with this scenario by implying a mechanism into leases by which the employer can require his immediate landlord to give his reasonable consent to alterations to the premises.[184] If the employer does not take advantage of this mechanism by seeking the immediate landlord's consent in the prescribed way, he is prevented from relying on any constraint attributable to the fact that he occupies the premises under a lease, when defending a reasonable adjustments claim.[185] **4.162**

If either the immediate or superior landlord unreasonably withhold their consent to the alterations, the DDA 1995 allows them to be joined as a party to the discrimination claim by either the claimant or the employer. If this occurs the landlord can be ordered to make the required alteration or to pay compensation.[186] **4.163**

1. Terms Implied into Leases

DDA 1995, s 18A(1) applies where a person, who owes a duty to make reasonable adjustments, occupies premises under a lease. A 'lease' includes a tenancy, sub-lease, sub-tenancy and an agreement for a lease, tenancy, sub-lease or sub-tenancy.[187] 'Sub-lease' means any sub-term created out of, or deriving from, a **4.164**

184 A similar term is implied into a lease between the immediate landlord and any superior landlord. See para 4.164 below.

185 DDA 1995 sch 4, pt 1, s 1.

186 DDA 1995 sch 4, pt 1, s 2(6).

187 DDA 1995 s 18A(3).

leasehold interest and 'sub-tenancy' means any tenancy created out of, or deriving from, a superior tenancy.[188]

Terms Implied Into Lease By DDA 1995—Section 18A(2)

18A(2) Except to the extent to which it expressly so provides, the lease shall have effect by virtue of this subsection as if it provided—

(a) for the occupier to be entitled to make the alteration with the written consent of the lessor;
(b) for the occupier to have to make a written application to the lessor for consent if he wishes to make the alteration;
(c) if such an application is made, for the lessor not to withhold his consent unreasonably; and
(d) for the lessor to be entitled to make his consent subject to reasonable conditions.

4.165 Regulation 9[189] has the effect of implying the same terms (as are implied into the lease between the employer and the immediate landlord) into any superior lease under which the premises are held. This ensures that, where the occupation of premises is subject to a series of sub-tenancies, each lease along the chain is altered to require the landlord to grant his reasonable consent to proposed alterations to the premises.

4.166 Leases which already impose conditions on the alteration of the employer's premises or allow the lessor to impose conditions if that employer seeks its consent to an alteration, are overridden. DDA 1995, s 18A(4) provides that such leases must be treated, for the purposes of DDA 1995, s 18A(1), as leases in which the occupier is not entitled to make alterations and so any requests for the landlord's consent may be made in accordance with the statutory mechanism rather than the provisions in the lease.

2. The Mechanism for Seeking the Landlord's Consent

4.167 Where an employer occupies premises under a lease or sub-lease and the duty to make adjustments requires him to alter the premises, he must apply in writing to his immediate landlord for the landlord's consent to the alterations.

4.168 There is no express requirement for the employer's application to contain any detail of the alterations that he is proposing to make, although common sense suggests that it is sensible for the employer to give as much detail as possible. Even if the

[188] Disability Discrimination (Employment Field) (Leasehold Premises) Regulations 2004 SI2004/153, reg 8.

[189] Disability Discrimination (Employment Field) (Leasehold Premises) Regulations 2004 SI2004/153.

employer does not provide much detail at the application stage, reg 7[190] allows the landlord to grant his consent, subject to a condition requiring the employer to submit plans of the proposed alterations for the landlord's approval (which approval cannot be withheld unreasonably).[191]

4.169 If the employer occupies the tenancy under a sub-lease, his immediate landlord may be unable to grant his consent without himself seeking the superior landlord's consent. In these circumstances the immediate landlord must, within 21 days of receiving the application from the employer, either:

(a) reply consenting to or refusing the application; or
(b) reply indicating that he consents to the application subject to the consent of another person. If the landlord is required to seek another person's consent to the alterations he must do so within 21 days of the employer's request.[192]

4.170 The immediate landlord can be deemed to have withheld his consent in two ways. Firstly, if the immediate landlord does not reply to the employer's request in accordance with paragraph (a) above and secondly, if his own request for the other person's consent in accordance with paragraph (b) above is not in writing, does not state that the request is being made to comply with a duty to make adjustments and does not state that he, the immediate landlord, has given his conditional consent to the alterations.[193]

3. Reasonableness of Withholding Consent/Imposing Conditions

4.171 Although the Disability Discrimination (Employment Field) (Leasehold Premises) Regulations 2004 contain provisions that, in certain circumstances, deem the withholding of consent by the landlord to be reasonable or unreasonable,[194] no guidance is provided on the *general* approach to the question of whether the withholding of consent, or the imposition of conditions, is reasonable.

4.172 Although the authors are not aware of any cases discussing the issue of reasonableness under DDA 1995, sch 4, Part 1, s 2, the Code of Practice 2004 provides some guidance at paragraph 12.22. Whether withholding consent is reasonable

190 Ibid.
191 See para 4.171.
192 Disability Discrimination (Employment Field) (Leasehold Premises) Regulations 2004 SI2004/153, reg 4(2).
193 Disability Discrimination (Employment Field) (Leasehold Premises) Regulations 2004 SI2004/153, reg 4(4). Where a landlord initially fails to meet the requirements of reg 4(2) but does so at a later date see reg 4(3).
194 Regs 5 and 6.

will depend on all the circumstances. A trivial or arbitrary reason for withholding consent is almost certain to be unreasonable. If the alteration will result in a permanent reduction in the value of the landlord's premises, withholding consent is likely to be reasonable. If the proposed adjustment will cause significant disruption and inconvenience to other tenants, it may also be unreasonable. The need for planning permission or buildings regulation approval may also be a significant factor.[195] These considerations demonstrate that the question of reasonableness is likely to require a broad common sense approach that considers all the circumstances relevant to the individual case.

4. When Consent is Deemed to be Withheld Unreasonably

4.173 The immediate landlord will be deemed to have withheld his consent unreasonably in two situations: firstly, if the lease expressly provides that consent shall be given for alterations of the kind that the employer is seeking and secondly, where the immediate landlord has failed to request the consent of the superior landlord in the appropriate way.[196]

4.174 The immediate landlord's failure to seek his superior landlord's permission in the prescribed way leads to him being deemed not only to have withheld his consent[197] but also to him having done so unreasonably.[198]

5. When Consent is Deemed to be Withheld Reasonably

4.175 The immediate landlord will be deemed to have reasonably withheld his consent where there is a legally binding obligation (not contained in a lease) towards any person preventing alterations being made without his consent and where he has unsuccessfully sought that other person's consent.[199]

4.176 DDA 1995, 18B(3) also provides that, for the purposes of the reasonable adjustments duty, where any person, under any binding obligation,[200] is required to obtain the consent of another person to any alteration of the premises occupied by him, it is *always* reasonable for him to seek the consent of that person and

[195] See para 4.91.

[196] See para 4.167.

[197] See para 4.170.

[198] Reg 5(4).

[199] 'Binding obligation' is defined in reg 2 of the Disability Discrimination (Employment Field) (Leasehold Premises) Regulations 2004 SI2004/153 to mean a legally binding obligation (not contained in a lease) in relation to premises whether arising from an agreement or otherwise.

[200] Defined in 18B(5) to mean any legally binding obligation not contained in a lease in relation to the premises.

it is *never* reasonable for him to have to make the alteration without that person's consent.

6. Consent Subject to Reasonable Conditions

The landlord may give his consent subject to reasonable conditions. Regulation 7(1) provides that the following conditions, or conditions to similar effect, will be deemed to be reasonable: **4.177**

(a) that the occupier must obtain any necessary planning permission and any other consent or permission required under any enactment;
(b) that the occupier must submit any plans or specifications for the alteration to the landlord for approval (which must not be withheld unreasonably) and that the work must be carried out in accordance with the plans or specifications;
(c) that the landlord must be permitted a reasonable opportunity to inspect the works when they are completed;
(d) that the occupier must repay to the lessor the costs reasonably incurred in connection with the giving of his consent.

If the landlord could have reasonably withheld his consent, reg 7(2) provides that a condition requiring the employer to reinstate the premises to its original pre-alteration state will be reasonable. This gives the landlord the flexibility to agree to the alteration on the condition that his interest in the property is properly safeguarded. **4.178**

7. Remedies Against the Landlord

DDA 1995, sch 4 provides that the claimant or the employer can apply to join the immediate landlord and/or superior landlord[201] as a party on a complaint of discrimination under DDA 1995, s 17A. **4.179**

If the request is made before the hearing, the tribunal must grant it. If it is made at the hearing the tribunal may refuse it and if it is made after the hearing the tribunal must refuse it.[202] **4.180**

The tribunal may award a remedy against the landlord if it has unreasonably refused to consent to the alteration or has consented to the alteration subject to unreasonable conditions. The tribunal may grant one or more of: a declaration, **4.181**

201 Reg 9 Disability Discrimination (Employment Field) (Leasehold Premises) Regulations 2004 SI2004/153 alters para 2 sch 4 so that lessor includes any superior landlord.

202 Sch 4, pt 1, ss 2(2) to 2(4).

an order authorizing or directing the employer to make a specified alteration or compensation.[203]

4.182 The tribunal may not award compensation against the employer if it has made an order for compensation against the landlord. Aside from this, the tribunal may grant any of these remedies in addition to, or in substitution for those that it makes for the substantive complaint under DDA 1995, s 17A(2).[204]

H. Cases Listed by Adjustment

4.183 The following is a list of cases in which types of adjustment have been required. The list is not intended to be comprehensive and the adjustments are not always discussed in detail in them. Only cases in the EAT, Court of Appeal and House of Lords are listed. Cases are repeated where necessary.

Making adjustments to premises
Kenny v Hampshire Constabulary [1999] IRLR 76
Ball v London Borough of Waltham Forest UKEAT/0999/03 (adjustment to lighting)

Allocating duties to another person
Romec v Rudham UKEAT/0069/07

Transferring the person to fill an existing vacancy
Kent County Council v Mingo [2000] IRLR 90
Archibald v Fife Council [2004] IRLR 651
Tarbuck v Sainsbury Supermarkets [2006] IRLR 664

Transfer to non-existent vacancy
Southampton City College v Randall [2006] IRLR 18
Electronic Data Systems v Travis [2004] EWCA Civ 880

Altering the person's hours of working
Jones v Post Office [2001] IRLR 384
Callagan v Glasgow City Council [2001] IRLR 724

Altering a job description
Archibald v Fife [2004] IRLR 651

Assigning the person to a different place of work
Lanarkshire Primary Care NHS Trust v Naicker UKEAT/0003/05
Prison Service v Beart [2003] ICR 1068
Archibald v Fife [2004] IRLR 651

203 Sch 4, pt 1, ss 2(6) and 2(7).
204 Sch 4, pt 1, ss 2(8) and 2(9).

Allowing the person to be absent during working or training hours for rehabilitation, assessment or treatment
Ross Baxter v Power Lines Pipes & Cables Ltd UKEAT0068/04
Electronic Data Systems v Travis [2004] EWCA Civ 880

Giving, or arranging for, training or mentoring (whether for the disabled person or any other person)
Williams v J Walter Thompson Group Ltd [2005] IRLR 376
Stott v Governing Body of St Aelred's Catholic Technology College NHS Foundation Trust UKEAT0322/05
Simpson v West Lothian Council UKEAT/0049/04
Electronic Data Systems v Travis [2004] EWCA Civ 880

Acquiring or modifying equipment
Hay v Surrey County Council [2007] All ER (D) 199
Williams v J Walter Thompson Group Ltd [2005] IRLR 376
Fu v London Borough of Camden [2001] IRLR 186

Modifying instructions or reference manuals
Meikle v Nottinghamshire County Council [2004] EWCA Civ 859, [2004] IRLR 703

Modifying procedures for testing or assessment (including disciplinary and grievance procedures)
Taylor v OCS Group Ltd [2005] All ER (D) 344
Paul v National Probation Service [2004] IRLR 190
Electronic Data Systems v Travis [2004] EWCA Civ 880
Johnson & Johnson Medical v Filmer [2002] ICR 292
Cave v Goodwin [2001] EWCA Civ 391
Morse v Wiltshire County Council [1998] IRLR 352
Ridout v TC Group [1998] IRLR 628

Providing a reader or interpreter
Project Management Institute v Latif [2007] IRLR 579

Providing supervision or other support
Romec v Rudham UKEAT/0069/07
Paul v National Probation Service [2004] IRLR 190
Kenny v Hampshire Constabulary [1999] IRLR 76

Dismissing or moving a fellow employee
Barratt v Accrington and Rossingdale College UKEAT/099/06
Beart v HM Prison Service [2003] IRLR 238

Adjustment to payments for absence/sick leave
Fowler v London Borough of Waltham Forest UKEAT0116/06

O'Hanlon v Commissioners for HMRC [2007] ICR 1359
Murphy v Slough Borough Council [2005] IRLR 382
Meikle v Nottinghamshire County Council [2004] IRLR 703
Gowman v Ceredigion County Council UKEAT/0155/04
Bancroft v Mitie Property Ltd UKEAT0494/04
London Clubs Management v Hood [2001] IRLR 719

5

DISABILITY-RELATED DISCRIMINATION

A. Introduction

'Disability-related discrimination' is the shorthand expression used in the 2004 Code of Practice (and widely adopted elsewhere) when referring to the form of discrimination set out in DDA 1995, s 3A(1). Unlike the other equality statutes, there is at present no tort of indirect discrimination under the DDA 1995. Nor, when it was first enacted, was any provision made for direct discrimination. The intention was that 'disability-related discrimination' would be broad enough to encompass both.[1] This purpose was to be achieved by making it unlawful to discriminate against disabled people not only *on the ground of* their disability, but also *for a reason related to* their disability. Disability-related discrimination was, therefore, said to distinguish less favourable treatment which amounts to direct discrimination from a wider class of less favourable treatment which, although not amounting to direct discrimination, was nevertheless unlawful.[2] **5.01**

[1] *Clark v Novacold Ltd* [1999] 2 All ER 977; [1999] ICR 951; [1999] IRLR 318, CA, at para 65.
[2] Code of Practice 2004, para 4.29.

5.02 Over the years since the DDA 1995 was first enacted, this purpose has been achieved in the context of employment law by applying an objective, impersonal approach to the meaning of disability-related discrimination. Attention was focused on the difficulties which disabled people experienced at work as a result of their disabilities, rather than on the disability itself. Like was not compared with like. The comparison to be drawn was between those who suffered such difficulties as a result of disability, and those who did not. Discriminatory motive was completely irrelevant to the issue. If a disabled employee was treated less favourably at work because he had under-performed, disability-related discrimination would still have taken place, even if the employer had no idea that the reason for the employee's poor performance was due to a disability which he had not been told about. This lack of knowledge was only relevant to a defence of justification.[3]

5.03 That long-established understanding of the law of disability-related discrimination has now been turned on its head as a result of the decision of the House of Lords in *London Borough of Lewisham v Malcolm*,[4] in which it was held that the leading Court of Appeal case of *Clark v Novacold*,[5] which had stood unchallenged for nine years, had been wrongly decided. Although this was a housing case brought under a different part of the DDA 1995, the section which was in issue is in identical terms to DDA 1995, s 3A(1).[6]

5.04 In summary, their Lordships decided that *Clark v Novacold* applied the wrong test to the identification of the comparator for the purposes of disability-related discrimination. They decided that like should be compared with like, and that the correct comparator for a person absent from work, for example, as a result of a disability was a person also absent from work, but not because of disability. Knowledge, actual or imputed, was essential. An alleged discriminator could not be said to have discriminated against a disabled person for a reason related to his disability if he did not have the requisite degree of knowledge that the person was disabled in the first place. The physical or mental condition constituting the disability had to play a motivating part in the decision taken by the alleged discriminator to inflict on the disabled person the treatment complained of.

5.05 The ramifications of this decision are far-reaching. Unless *Malcolm* can be distinguished on the basis that it was a housing case under a different part of the DDA 1995, and not an employment case, the large body of case law which has developed following the decision in *Clark v Novacold* can no longer be relied on; the

3 *Heinz (HJ) & Co Ltd v Kenrick* [2000] ICR 491; [2000] IRLR 144, EAT, at para 27.

4 [2008] UKHL 43, [2008] 4 All ER 525, HL.

5 [1999] 2 All ER 977; [1999] ICR 951; [1999] IRLR 318, CA.

6 *London Borough of Lewisham v Malcolm* [2008] UKHL 43, at para 158.

Code of Practice 2004 will have to be rewritten; and the protection afforded to disabled people by the concept of disability-related discrimination will be greatly reduced. The government has already indicated that it is giving careful consideration to the implications of the judgment in *Malcolm*.

Can it be distinguished? That would appear to be very doubtful. By a majority, the House of Lords in *Malcolm* overruled *Clark v Novacold*, Lord Scott saying in terms that, in his opinion, *Clark v Novacold* had been wrongly decided. Furthermore, DDA 1995, s 24(1)(a) (the section under consideration in *Malcolm*) is in identical terms to DDA 1995, s 3A(1)(a). One possible argument open to claimants would be to argue that DDA 1995, s3A(1)(a) should be interpreted in a different way to *Malcolm* in order to comply with the Framework Directive, which requires member states to protect disabled employees from both direct and indirect discrimination. Since UK courts are required to give a purposive interpretation to the DDA 1995 so that it complies with the Framework Directive, a claimant might argue that the *Clark v Novacold* interpretation of the DDA 1995 is the only interpretation consistent with providing protection against indirect discrimination in accordance with the Framework Directive; and that it would be contrary to the Framework Directive and the general principle of equality in EC law to interpret s 3A(1)(a) in the way envisaged in *Malcolm*. However, it seems highly likely that Parliament will have to introduce legislation to amend the DDA 1995.[7] This chapter will, therefore, explain the law relating to disability-related discrimination as it stood before the intervention of the House of Lords. It will also consider how the law currently stands as a result. **5.06**

B. The Statutory Definition

The relevant subsections of DDA 1995, s 3A are as follows: **5.07**

> (1) For the purposes of this Part, a person discriminates against a disabled person if—
> (a) for a reason which relates to the disabled person's disability, he treats him less favourably than he treats or would treat others to whom that reason does not or would not apply, and
> (b) he cannot show that the treatment in question is justified.
>
> (3) Treatment is justified for the purposes of subsection (1)(b) if, but only if, the reason for it is both material to the circumstances of the particular case and substantial.
>
> (4) But treatment of a disabled person cannot be justified under subsection (3) if it amounts to direct discrimination falling within subsection (5).

7 Indeed, the goverment's consultation paper on improving protection for disability discrimination issued in November 2008 indicates that the goverment intends to replace disability-related discrimination with a new form of protection based on the concepts of indirect discrimination.

(6) If, in a case falling within subsection (1), a person is under a duty to make reasonable adjustments in relation to a disabled person but fails to comply with that duty, his treatment of that person cannot be justified under subsection (3) unless it would have been justified even if he had complied with that duty.

5.08 In considering a claim of disability-related discrimination, therefore, the following questions arise:

(a) What was the reason for the less favourable treatment?
(b) Did that reason relate to the claimant's disability?
(c) Was the treatment less favourable than the treatment of a person to whom that reason did not, or would not, apply?
(d) If so, was the treatment justified?

C. Less Favourable Treatment

1. Identification of the Correct Comparator

5.09 Unlike the other equality statutes, there is no express requirement under DDA 1995, s 3A(1) to make a like for like comparison between the disabled person and an able-bodied person whose relevant circumstances are the same, or not materially different, in order to establish whether there has been less favourable treatment. The reason for that is straightforward. In sex or race discrimination, the fact of being female, or of a different race, makes no difference to a person's ability to do the job, so that it is important to establish whether all other relevant circumstances, including abilities, are the same, in order to determine whether there has been any less favourable treatment. The whole point about disability, however, is that it can affect a disabled person's ability to carry out his job. Disability-related discrimination was intended to protect disabled people from less favourable treatment to which they were vulnerable because their ability to carry out their jobs was affected. A like for like comparison is, therefore, inappropriate.

5.10 However, DDA 1995, s 3A(1)(a) does still require some comparison to be made, because it requires the discriminator to treat the disabled person less favourably than he treats, or would treat, others to whom *that reason* does not, or would not, apply. The double use of the word 'would' in the subsection indicates that the comparator can be a hypothetical one if an actual one does not exist, but the question remains: what does *that reason* mean?

2. The Wide Construction: *Clark v Novacold*

5.11 This question was first considered by the Court of Appeal in *Clark v Novacold*.[8] Mr Clark was employed as a process operator by Novacold. It was a physically

[8] [1999] IRLR 318, CA.

demanding job. In August 1996, he suffered a back injury at work and was signed off sick. Medical reports were obtained which were unable to give any indication as to when he might be able to return to work. On that basis, Mr Clark was dismissed in January 1997. In considering Mr Clark's claim of disability-related discrimination, the Court of Appeal had to consider the identity of the comparator.

5.12 The employers argued that the words '*that reason*' in DDA 1995, s 3A(1)(a) referred back to the whole of the first clause of the paragraph, that is, 'for a reason which relates to the disabled person's disability'. That interpretation required not only the existence of a reason for the treatment, but also a causal link to the disability. On that approach, the correct comparator would be a person who was also incapable of working, but for a reason which did not relate to that disability. Since the employers would also have dismissed such a person, there was no less favourable treatment of Mr Clark and, therefore, no discrimination.

5.13 On Mr Clark's behalf, on the other hand, it was argued that the words '*that reason*' referred only to the first three words of the section '*for a reason*', and that the causal link between the reason for the treatment (absence from work) and the disability, was not the reason for the treatment. On that basis, the correct comparator would be someone who was still capable of working. The employers would have no reason to dismiss such a person, and therefore Mr Clark had been treated less favourably.

5.14 The Court of Appeal ruled in Mr Clark's favour. Mummery LJ pointed out that the section was ambiguous, and was capable of bearing either of the suggested meanings. However, he thought it more probable that Parliament meant '*that reason*' to refer only to the facts constituting the reason for the treatment, and not to include within that reason the added requirement of a causal link with disability. That was more properly to be regarded as the cause of the reason for the treatment than, as in itself, a reason for the treatment.[9]

5.15 Mummery LJ found support for his view in the example which had been given in Parliament when the Bill was being debated of a situation where dogs are not admitted to a café, with the effect that blind people would be unable to enter it. He said this:

> On the Novacold interpretation of the comparison to be made, the blind person with his guide dog would not be treated less favourably than the relevant comparator, ie 'others', to whom that reason would not apply, would be sighted persons who had their dogs with them. There could not therefore be any, let alone prima facie, discrimination. But the Minister specifically stated that this would be a prima facie case of disability discrimination, ie less favourable treatment, unless justified.

[9] Ibid at para 63.

> It could only be a case of less favourable treatment and therefore a prima facie case of discrimination, if the comparators are 'others' *without* dogs: 'that reason' for refusing access to refreshment in the café would not apply to 'others' without dogs.[10]

5.16 In a statute designed to protect disabled people from discrimination, that interpretation is surely correct. Why should the blind man who *needs* his dog in order to navigate across the restaurant without bumping into fellow diners be compared with a sighted person who *chooses* to bring his dog with him because he likes its company? Can it seriously be said that this is not a case of discrimination because both men have been refused entry and, therefore, treated in exactly the same way? If nothing else, it would surely qualify as indirect discrimination, as noted in Parliament, because a blind person is statistically more likely to have a dog with him. Disability-related discrimination was designed to cover such cases as well. However, this is no longer the law following the House of Lords decision discussed below.

3. The Narrow Construction: *London Borough of Lewisham v Malcolm*[11]

5.17 In February 2002, the London Borough of Lewisham ('the Council') let a flat to Mr Malcolm who was a homeless person. He suffered from schizophrenia. The tenancy was a secure tenancy and Mr Malcolm was entitled to exercise a right to buy the flat because he had previously been a tenant of the Council. He applied to do so, but before the transaction had been completed, he sublet the flat on an assured shorthold tenancy for a period of six months and moved out. This was a breach of the express terms of his tenancy agreement, and had the automatic effect that Mr Malcolm's tenancy was no longer a secure one. The Council found out and commenced possession proceedings. Mr Malcolm defended the proceedings on the basis that he was a disabled person. He argued that his schizophrenia had played a part in his decision to sublet the flat and that the Council was, therefore, seeking possession from him because of his disability.

5.18 The judge dismissed his defence, principally on the ground that the DDA 1995 was not brought into play at all where security of tenure was lost by operation of law. She also made findings of fact that Mr Malcolm was not a disabled person within the meaning of the DDA 1995, and that his decision to sublet his flat was a planned decision, closely linked to his proposed purchase of the flat on mortgage, and not an irrational act caused by his illness.

---

10 Ibid at para 69.

11 *London Borough of Lewisham v Malcolm* [2008] 4 All ER 525.

The Court of Appeal overruled this decision, finding that Mr Malcolm was disabled within the meaning of the DDA 1995; that there was an 'appropriate relationship' between the reason for the Council's actions and the illness; that his treatment had been less favourable than that of others to whom that reason did not apply; and (by a majority) that the fact that the landlord did not know of the disability did not preclude a finding of discrimination.[12] **5.19**

The House of Lords allowed the Council's appeal. One of the central points which arose for consideration was the identification of the comparators with whom Mr Malcolm should be compared when considering whether he had been treated less favourably than others. Were they (a) persons without a mental disability who had sublet a Lewisham flat and gone to live elsewhere, or (b) tenants of Lewisham flats who had not sublet or gone to live elsewhere, or (c) some other comparator group, and if so what?[13] **5.20**

By a majority of 4 to 1 on this point (Baroness Hale dissenting) it was held that *Clark v Novacold* had been wrongly decided and that a narrow construction should be given to the section. In deciding that the more natural comparison was with group (a), Lord Bingham rejected the *Clark v Novacold* approach for the reason given by Toulson LJ in the Court of Appeal: **5.21**

> The complainant is logically bound to be able to satisfy the requirement of showing that his treatment is less favourable than would be accorded to others to whom the reason for his treatment did not apply. For without the reason there would not be the treatment.[14]

Lords Scott, Brown and Neuberger reached the same conclusion, for much the same reason, Lord Scott going so far as to describe the comparison required by the *Clark v Novacold* as pointless and an emasculation of the statutory comparison.[15]

The same criticism can be levelled at the construction favoured by the House of Lords, which emasculates the whole concept of disability-related discrimination. In requiring like to be compared with like, it fails to recognize that the disabled worker does not choose to be off work sick; the blind man does not choose to take a dog with him to the restaurant; the man suffering from schizophrenia does not choose to take irrational decisions. Lord Scott says that *Clark v Novacold* was wrongly decided because the employers would have dismissed any employee who proposed to be absent from work for up to a year, whatever the cause of **5.22**

[12] *London Borough of Lewisham v Malcolm* [2007] EWCA Civ 763; [2008] 2 WLR 369; [2008] Ch 129, CA.

[13] *London Borough of Lewisham v Malcolm* [2008] 4 All ER 525, per Lord Bingham at para 13.

[14] *London Borough of Lewisham v Malcolm* [2008] 2 WLR 369, CA, at para 157.

[15] *London Borough of Lewishan v Malcolm* [2008] 4 All ER 525, per Lord Scott at paras 32–33.

the absence. The use of the word 'proposed' gives the game away. For the person suffering from a disability, this is not a matter of choice. In a passage in his judgment which is sure to raise hackles amongst disability organizations up and down the country, Lord Scott blames the dog for the treatment meted out to the blind man refused access to the restaurant![16]

5.23 Given the construction favoured by the House of Lords, it is hard to conceive of a situation in which a claim of disability-related discrimination might survive this comparative test. One possibility would be the employer who has a different attitude to mental and physical disabilities. There is nothing in DDA 1995, s 3A(1) which requires the comparison to be made with a non-disabled person; the comparison could also be made with a disabled person with a different sort of disability. If, for example, an employer treats an employee who is off work suffering from a mental illness less favourably than he treats (or would treat) an employee off work for the same amount of time with a physical impairment, then the statutory comparison required by the House of Lords might still be met. Beyond that situation, however, it is difficult to envisage circumstances in which a claim for disability-related discrimination could succeed, unless they also amounted to direct discrimination. As stated by Lord Brown, the approach to construction favoured by the House of Lords confines the section largely, if not entirely, to the proscription of direct discrimination only.[17]

D. The Disability-related Reason

1. The New Approach

5.24 The decision of the House of Lords in *Malcolm* also demands a new approach to the identification of the disability-related reason which is said to be responsible for the less favourable treatment. It will no longer be enough to identify a reason for the treatment and then demonstrate that the reason related to the claimant's disability on an objective basis. It will also be necessary to prove that the employer knew, or should have known, that the employee was disabled; and, crucially, that the disability played some part in his decision to treat the employee less favourably.

16 Ibid, per Lord Scott at para 35.
17 Ibid, per Lord Brown at para 114.

2. Identifying the Reason

The first task for the practitioner remains that of identifying the reason for the less favourable treatment which is the subject of the complaint.[18] Although there will usually be little difficulty with this, problems can be caused where the employer may have had more than one reason for acting as he did. For example, conduct and capability may both be an issue where an employee has been dismissed. The employer may claim that he dismissed the employee for misconduct, when the real reason was, in fact, capability. In such cases, 'the task of the court is to ascertain the *real reason* for the treatment, the reason which operates on the mind of the alleged discriminator. This may not be the reason given, and may not be the only reason, but the test is an objective one.'[19] **5.25**

3. Does the Reason Relate to Disability?

The second task is to demonstrate that the reason for the less favourable treatment relates to disability. Even before the change in approach required by *Malcolm*, it was possible for an employer to escape liability by arguing that the requisite causal connection between the reason and disability had not been made out, even if he knew full well that the claimant suffered from a disability. In *London Clubs Management Ltd v Hood*,[20] for example, the employer successfully argued that the reason why the claimant was not paid sick pay when he was absent from work for two weeks suffering from cluster headaches was not related to his disability, but was due to his manager's decision not to pay sick pay generally as there had been a high level of sickness amongst all employees. This was a managerial decision which applied across the board. It was not directed at the disabled claimant. **5.26**

The question whether the reason relates to the disability is one of fact.[21] The issue for the tribunal is likely to be whether a sufficiently close connection has been made out. In *Malcolm*, Lord Bingham recognized that it would be hard to decide whether or not there was an adequate connection in borderline cases. The only guidance he felt able to offer was that the expression 'relates to' was broader and less precise than the conventional language of causation. He took the expression to denote 'some connection, not necessarily close, between the reason and **5.27**

[18] Described as 'the material reason' in *Cosgrove v Caesar & Howie* [2001] IRLR, EAT, at para 5.
[19] *London Borough of Lewisham v Malcolm* [2008] 4 All ER 525, per Lord Bingham, at para 9.
[20] [2001] IRLR 719, EAT.
[21] *Clark v Novacold* [1999] IRLR 318, CA, per Mummery LJ at para 52.

the disability'.[22] Lord Neuberger thought that a 'broad and flexible effect' should be given to the words.[23]

5.28 The practitioner must therefore ensure that evidence is led to enable the tribunal to make a finding of fact that the reason for the treatment was causally linked to the requisite degree to disability. That point was emphasized by the EAT in *British Gas Services Ltd v McCaull*,[24] when allowing an appeal against a tribunal's decision that the claimant had been discriminated against because he had not been provided with information about an alternative job when he became unfit for his normal job as a result of epilepsy. The EAT pointed out that no evidence had been given as to why the information about the alternative job had not been provided. This could have been the result of managerial oversight or incompetence or some other reason which had nothing to do with the claimant's disability. The causal connection had not been made out.[25]

4. Knowledge

5.29 Prior to *Malcolm*, conflicting views had been expressed in the EAT on the need for the employer to know that his employee was disabled before he could be held liable for disability-related discrimination. In *O'Neill v Symm & Co Ltd*,[26] the EAT had held that knowledge of the disability, or at least the material features of it as set out in DDA 1995, Schedule 1 was relevant, and that an employer could not be held liable for disability-related discrimination if he did not have that knowledge.

5.30 In the subsequent case of *H J Heinz Co Ltd v Kenrick*,[27] the EAT took a different view. Lindsay J pointed out that there was nothing in the statutory language which required that the relationship between the disability and the treatment should be judged subjectively, through the eyes of the employer, so that the applicable test should be the objective one of whether the relationship existed, not whether the employer knew of it:

> Unless the test is objective, there will be difficulties with credible and honest yet ignorant or obtuse employers who fail to recognise or acknowledge the obvious.[28]

5.31 In *London Borough of Hammersmith & Fulham v Farnsworth*[29] the EAT went further, holding that the employers' knowledge of the claimant's disability was

[22] *London Borough of Lewisham v Malcolm* [2008] 4 All ER 525, per Lord Bingham at para 10.
[23] Ibid per Lord Neuberger at para 169.
[24] [2001] IRLR 60, EAT at para 34.
[25] See also *Edwards v Mid Suffolk District Council* [2001] ICR 616; [2001] IRLR 190, EAT.
[26] [1998] ICR 481; [1998] IRLR 233, EAT.
[27] *Heinz (HJ) & Co Ltd v Kenrick* [2000] ICR 491; [2000] IRLR 144, EAT.
[28] Ibid at para 25.
[29] [2000] IRLR 691, EAT.

simply irrelevant in deciding whether they treated her less favourably for a reason that related to her disability. The EAT noted that the decision in *O'Neill v Symm & Co* that actual knowledge was required was no longer good law in the light of the Court of Appeal decision in *Clark v Novacold.*

When this issue came before the House of Lords in *Malcolm*, their Lordships were unanimous in finding that some degree of knowledge was essential if there was to be a finding of disability-related discrimination. Lord Bingham agreed with what Toulson LJ had said on the subject in the Court of Appeal: **5.32**

> I do not believe that Parliament would have intended to make a person liable in tort for disability discrimination if that person had no awareness or grounds for awareness at the relevant time that the complainant was suffering from a disability or that his disability might have any connection with the matters giving rise to the treatment said to constitute unlawful discrimination.

He therefore concluded that knowledge, or at least imputed knowledge, was necessary.[30] Their other Lordships were in broad agreement, Baroness Hale and Lord Brown making the point that it was not necessary for the alleged discriminator to know that the disability was one which satisfied the statutory definition of disablement.

The judgments delivered in the House of Lords accord most closely with the approach taken by Lindsay J in *Heinz v Kenrick*. Their Lordships appeared willing to accept that the claimant should not have to go so far as to prove that the alleged discriminator actually knew that he was disabled (and certainly not so far as to prove that he knew that he was disabled by reference to the statutory definition of disability). Imputed (or constructive) knowledge would suffice. **5.33**

In practice, this is likely to mean that the claimant will have to prove that there were at least sufficient indications to put the employer on notice that disability might be in issue. Frequent absences from work due to sickness, for example, might suffice to put the employer on enquiry. So might an employee's conduct at work. The employer cannot bury his head in the sand and ignore signs which suggest that the claimant might be suffering from a disability. Any knowledge about the claimant's condition which the employer could have obtained from an occupational health physician, or indeed any other agent, will be taken into account.[31] Information will not be imputed to the employer, however, if it is gained by a person providing services to employees independently of the employer. **5.34**

---

30 *London Borough of Lewisham v Malcolm* [2008] 4 All ER 525, per Lord Bingham at para 18.
31 *London Borough of Hammersmith & Fulham v Farnsworth* [2000] IRLR 691.

That would include, for example, information obtained by an external counsellor, even if the employer had paid for the counselling service to be provided.[32]

5. Causation

5.35 Until recently, it was widely accepted that an alleged discriminator's motive or purpose for treating a disabled person less favourably for a reason connected with his disability was wholly irrelevant. All that mattered was that the discriminator had, in fact, treated the disabled person less favourably for a reason which, objectively assessed, related to his disability. Take the example given in *Heinz v Kenrick* of a postman who successfully conceals the fact that he has an artificial leg and can only walk for short distances at a time when he applies for a job. He is subsequently dismissed for being slow at his rounds, the employer presuming that this was caused by idleness or absenteeism. The EAT considered that this would have qualified as a case of disability-related discrimination, even though the employer had no idea that his employee's slowness was due to the fact that he had an artificial leg. (The employer's ignorance might, however, be highly-relevant to the question of justification.)[33]

5.36 Doubt was first cast on that understanding by the Court of Appeal in *Taylor v OCS Group Ltd*.[34] Mr Taylor was a profoundly deaf employee who was suspended for misconduct after it had been discovered that he had forwarded confidential emails from a colleague's computer to his own. At his disciplinary hearing, there was no interpreter present and Mr Taylor did not fully understand what was happening. Following the hearing, he was dismissed for gross misconduct. This decision was upheld following an appeal at which an interpreter had been present. The EAT overturned the tribunal's finding that Mr Taylor had been dismissed for misconduct, not for a reason related to his disability, on the basis that his inability to explain himself at the disciplinary hearing had contributed to his dismissal. That was a disability-related reason.

5.37 The Court of Appeal overruled this decision, and said this:

> In our view, the argument accepted by the Employment Appeal Tribunal and advanced before us by Ms Gill is fallacious. These provisions of the DDA are concerned with discrimination by an employer. Discrimination requires that the employer should have a certain state of mind. In the context of the DDA, an employer cannot discriminate against the employee unless he treats the disabled employee differently for a reason (present in his, the employer's mind) which is related to the employee's disability. It may be that in some cases an employer might have more than one reason for dismissing an employee; one reason might be misconduct and there might also be present in the employer's mind another reason which does relate to his

[32] Code of Practice 2004, para 5.16.

[33] *Heinz (HJ) & Co Ltd v Kenrick* [2000] IRLR 144, EAT, at para 25.

[34] [2006] IRLR 613, CA.

> disability such as the fact that the employee took a lot of time off work or had a lower productivity than other employees. The employer might decide to dismiss the employee for these combined reasons. In such a case, we would say that, if the disability-related reason had a significant influence on the employer's decision, that would be enough to found the conclusion that the dismissal was for a reason related to the employee's disability. We would add that it would be open to an ET to find that the employer's decision had been affected by the disability-related reason even though the employer had not consciously allowed that reason to affect his thinking. We would certainly accept that an employer could have an innate prejudice against disabled people just as some are prejudiced on the grounds of race or gender. What is important is that the disability-related reason must affect the employer's mind, whether consciously or subconsciously. Unless that reason has affected his mind, he cannot discriminate.[35]

The view of the Court of Appeal, therefore, was that an employer could only be liable for discrimination if the disability-related reason was present in his mind (consciously or sub-consciously) and had *a significant influence* on his decision. It is implicit in the decision that the employer has to be aware of the disability, or at least should have been aware of it. Reverting to the example of the postman, the employer would only be liable, according to the Court of Appeal, if he was aware that the postman was slow at doing his rounds because he had an artificial leg and this reason had a significant influence on his decision to dismiss him. A subjective element has therefore been in introduced into the test where none existed before. **5.38**

In *London Borough of Lewisham v Malcolm*, the House of Lords went even further. In particular, Lord Scott expressed the view that if the physical or mental condition that constitutes the disability has played no motivating part in the decision of the alleged discriminator to inflict on the disabled person the treatment complained of, the reason cannot relate to disability.[36] For the first time, motive has been introduced into the debate. That is the language of direct discrimination. **5.39**

6. Result of the New Approach

The result of the approach to disability-related discrimination laid down by the House of Lords is that disabled employees will have to rely more than ever on the employer's duty to make reasonable adjustments to achieve a level playing field in the workplace. There is no specific provision made for indirect discrimination. Disability-related discrimination (which was intended to cover indirect discrimination) has effectively been discarded. **5.40**

---

35 *Taylor v OCS Group Ltd* [2006] IRLR 613, CA, at para 72.

36 *London Borough of Lewisham v Malcolm* [2008] 4 All ER 525, HL, per Lord Scott at para 29.

5.41 Using again the example of the postman with the artificial leg, the approach required by the House of Lords leads to the following results:

(a) The correct comparator is not someone who carries out his rounds in an acceptable time, but someone who is unacceptably slow for a reason other than disability (such as idleness).
(b) If the employer would treat such a person in the same way as the postman (that is, by dismissing him) then there is no less favourable treatment and no discrimination.
(c) The employer would only discriminate against the postman if he treated him less favourably than the idle employee, that is, if he dismissed the postman with the artificial leg but kept on the idle one. (But why would he do that?)
(d) Even then, this would only amount to disability-related discrimination if the employer knew (or should have known) that the postman's slowness was caused by some disability, and if his less favourable treatment of him was motivated by that fact.

E. Justification

1. Overview

5.42 If Lord Brown was correct when he stated in *Malcolm*[37] that the approach adopted to DDA 1995, s 3A(1) by the House of Lords confined it largely, if not entirely, to the proscription of direct discrimination only, then justification is not an issue which need trouble the practitioner. Treatment cannot be justified if it amounts to direct discrimination. As stated by Baroness Hale, if the provisions on disability-related discrimination were to be given the narrow scope favoured by the majority in the House of Lords, then Parliament could simply have repealed the justification provision now found in DDA 1995, s 3A, instead of introducing the statutory tort of direct discrimination.[38]

5.43 To cater for the unlikely event that circumstances can still be found to exist in which a finding of disability-related discrimination, not amounting to direct discrimination, can be made, the law on justification as it stood before *Malcolm* is as set out below.

[37] [2008] 4 All ER 525, HL, at para 114.
[38] Ibid at para 81.

2. The Statutory Test

In summary, save for cases amounting to direct discrimination which can never be justified, less favourable treatment of a disabled person for a reason which relates to his disability will not amount to discrimination if it can be justified. For these purposes, treatment can be justified if, but only if, the reason for it is both material to the circumstances of the particular case and substantial. However, a person cannot justify such treatment if he has failed to comply with a duty to make reasonable adjustments in relation to the disabled person, unless the treatment would have been justified even if he had complied with that duty.[39] **5.44**

The statutory sequence is, therefore, as follows: **5.45**

(a) The disabled claimant shows less favourable treatment.
(b) The respondent shows that that treatment is justified if:
    (1) the reason for the less favourable treatment is both material to the circumstances of the particular case and substantial, unless
    (2) the employer is under a duty to make reasonable adjustments in relation to the claimant but fails [without justification] to comply with that duty, subject to the treatment being justified even if he had complied with that duty.[40]

3. The Role of the Tribunal

The leading case on justification is the Court of Appeal decision in *Jones v Post Office*.[41] The claimant in this case was a mail delivery driver who developed insulin-dependent diabetes. As a result, his employers first removed him from his driving duties altogether and then, following a review of the position, offered to allow him to return to limited driving duties only. When the claimant complained of discrimination, the employers sought to defend their decision on the basis that it had been justified in the circumstances. The tribunal reviewed the expert evidence and concluded that a correct appraisal of the claimant's medical condition would have led to the conclusion that it was, in fact, safe for the claimant to drive throughout his shift. The tribunal took the view that it was for it to determine the question of justification, and, therefore, found that the employers' defence of justification was not made out. **5.46**

---

39 See the statutory definition set out at para 5.7 above.

40 As set out in *Baynton v Saurus General Engineers Ltd* [2000] ICR 375; [1999] IRLR 604, EAT, at para 26. Note that the justification defence for a failure to comply with a duty to make reasonable adjustments was removed as from 1 October 2004—hence the square brackets above.

41 [2001] EWCA Civ 558; [2001] ICR 805; [2001] IRLR 384, CA.

5.47 The Court of Appeal ruled that the tribunal had approached the matter in the wrong way. The role of the tribunal was confined to considering whether the reason given for the less favourable treatment could properly be described as both material to the circumstances of the particular case and substantial:

> The respondent asserts in this case that the risk arising from the presence of diabetes is material to the circumstance of the particular case and substantial. Where a properly conducted risk assessment provides a reason which is on its face both material and substantial, and is not irrational, the tribunal cannot substitute its own appraisal. The employment tribunal must consider whether the reason meets the statutory criteria; it does not have the more general power to make its own appraisal of the medical evidence and conclude that the evidence from admittedly competent medical witnesses was incorrect or make its own assessment.[42]

5.48 The role of the tribunal, therefore, is to apply an objective test to the reason relied on by the employer and to the known facts. The approach is similar to the range of reasonable responses test applied in unfair dismissal cases. It is not for the tribunal to decide the matter itself. The same applies to an appellate court reviewing a decision taken by the tribunal.[43]

4. Meaning of 'Material'

5.49 In *Jones v Post Office*, Arden LJ pointed out that the word 'material' denoted the quality of the connection which must exist between, on the one hand, the employer's reason for discriminating against the employee and, on the other hand, the circumstances of the particular case. It meant that there must be a reasonably strong connection between the employer's reason for the treatment and the circumstances of the individual case. That interpretation was indicated by the use of the word 'material' rather than 'relevant' or 'applicable'.[44]

5.50 Furthermore, it was held in *Baynton v Saurus General Engineers Ltd*[45] that the tribunal should not consider the matter from the employer's point of view alone. What is material to the circumstances of the case include the circumstances of both the employer and the employee. The tribunal has to carry out a balancing exercise between those interests. In this case, the claimant was dismissed for long-term sickness at a time when he was due to see his consultant. There was no indication that the tribunal had balanced the desirability of awaiting the outcome of that consultation with the employers' need to dismiss. The EAT therefore allowed the claimant's appeal against the decision that his dismissal was justified.

---

42 *Jones v Post Office* [2001] IRLR 384, CA, at para 25.
43 *Williams v J Walter Thompson Group Ltd* [2005] EWCA Civ 133; [2005] IRLR 376, CA.
44 Ibid at paras 36–37.
45 [1999] IRLR 604, EAT, at para 38.

5. Meaning of 'Substantial'

When used elsewhere in the DDA 1995, the word 'substantial' is said to mean something which is more than minor or trivial.[46] In this context, it means more than that. To be substantial, the reason which the employer adopted as his ground for discrimination must carry real weight and, thus, be of substance.[47] **5.51**

6. The Link with Reasonable Adjustments

Whenever a tribunal is considering justification within the context of disability-related discrimination, it must ask itself whether the employer was under a duty to make reasonable adjustments in relation to the disabled person. That is because, if an employer has failed to comply with a duty to make reasonable adjustments, he cannot justify less favourable treatment of an employee unless such treatment would have been justified even if he had complied with the duty.[48] In effect, the tribunal has to ask itself the question 'would a reasonable adjustment have made any difference?' **5.52**

7. Knowledge

Before *Malcolm*, the question arose whether an employer had to know about a claimant's disability before it could rely on a defence of justification. In one case, it was held that an employer cannot discharge the onus of justifying disability discrimination when it did not apply its mind to what should be done during the employment because it was ignorant of the disability.[49] Subsequently, the EAT said that went too far. The fact that the employer did not know the disability existed might affect the justification issue but does not preclude it. What matters is to analyse the treatment meted out by the employer.[50] **5.53**

Following *Malcolm*, this, of course, is no longer a live issue. If an employer cannot be liable for disability-related discrimination because he does not have the requisite level of knowledge about the claimant's disability in the first place, the issue of justification simply does not arise. **5.54**

46 See Code of Practice 2004, para 5.11 and the 2006 Guidance, para B1.

47 *Jones v Post Office* [2001] IRLR 384, CA, per Arden LJ at para 39. That definition has now been imported into the Code of Practice 2004 at para 6.3.

48 DDA 1995, s 3A(6).

49 *Quinn v Schwarzkopf Ltd* [2001] IRLR 67, EAT.

50 *Callagan v Glasgow City Council* [2001] IRLR 724.

8. Health and Safety

5.55 Under health and safety law, it is the duty of every employer to ensure, so far as it is reasonably practicable, the health, safety and welfare at work of its employees. Part of the duty is a requirement for all employers to assess the risks to the health and safety of all employees in the work place and then to put in place measures that reduce the risks to as low a level as can reasonably be achieved. There is obviously scope for tension between the competing requirements of this principle and the DDA 1995. Can health and safety concerns justify less favourable treatment?

5.56 The answer to that question depends on the nature of the duty being considered. If it is an absolute one, health and safety comes first. See, for example, the EAT decision in *Lane Group & North Somerset Council v Farmiloe*[51] where health and safety laws justified the dismissal of the claimant, a warehouseman who was unable to wear protective footwear because of a skin condition, psoriasis. The employer had carried out a risk assessment that had identified a need for warehouse staff to wear safety footwear, but had been making an exception for Mr Farmiloe. A local health and safety inspector told the employer that he could not do this, on the basis that 'you can't opt out of health and safety'. No suitable alternative job being available for Mr Farmiloe, he was dismissed. The EAT held that the employer's justification defence was made out, because it had to comply with the relevant health and safety regulations. This was an absolute duty, and DDA 1995 s 59(1) provided that:

> 'nothing in this Act makes unlawful any act done—
> (a) In pursuance of any enactment; or
> (b) In pursuance of any instrument made by a Minister of the Crown under any enactment'.

5.57 It should be noted that, under the comparative test established in *Malcolm*, the employer would not have had to justify the dismissal anyway. The comparator would be a person who did not wear safety footwear, but for a reason not related to disability. This would include a person who simply preferred to wear his own, more comfortable footwear. The employer would have treated him in the same way. Therefore, there would have been no less favourable treatment, and no discrimination. Justification would never have become an issue. This only serves to reinforce the point that, as things stand post-*Malcolm*, disability-related discrimination has been rendered practically valueless.

---

51 UKEAT 0352/03 and 0357/03.

9. Sickness Absence and Sick Pay Schemes

The arrangements made for employees who are forced out of work as a result of disability have frequently come under scrutiny in disability-related discrimination claims. One issue is the amount of time for which the employer should allow the employee to remain on long-term sickness absence before dismissing him. Another is the extent to which an employer may be required to make adjustments to a standard company policy on payment of sick pay. There is, clearly, the potential for a person suffering from a disability which affects his attendance at work to exhaust his entitlement to company sick pay more quickly than an employee who is not disabled. That raises the question of whether it would be a reasonable adjustment for the employer to extend the disabled employee's entitlement under the scheme. If he chose not to, would he be able to justify that decision in a disability-related discrimination claim? **5.58**

In *O'Hanlon v Commissioners for HM Revenue & Customs*,[52] the EAT upheld the tribunal's conclusion that the duty to make reasonable adjustments did not require the claimant's employers to pay full pay to employees off work ill as a result of a disability-related illness when they had exhausted their entitlement under the company sick pay rules. In an emphatic judgment, the EAT held that it would be a very rare case indeed where such an adjustment would be considered necessary as a reasonable adjustment. Two reasons in particular were given. First, it would involve tribunals in usurping the management function of the employer. The tribunal would have to decide whether employers were financially able to meet the costs of modifying their policies by making these enhanced payments. In taking such a decision, the tribunals 'would be entering into a form of wage fixing for the disabled sick'. Second, the DDA 1995 was designed to recognize the dignity of the disabled and to require modifications which would enable them to play a full part in the world of work. It was not to treat them as objects of charity, which would for some people tend to act as a positive disincentive to return to work.[53] **5.59**

With regard to the claim for disability-related discrimination, although the EAT held that there was a prima facie case (on the *Clark v Novacold* interpretation of the law) that the claimant had been less favourably treated, the tribunal had found that there were powerful economic reasons for the rule adopted. It would cost a very significant sum to pay full pay to all disabled employees absent sick in circumstances where their pay would otherwise be reduced. On that basis, the EAT upheld the tribunal's conclusion on justification, adding the observation **5.60**

52 [2006] IRLR 840, EAT.
53 Ibid at paras 67–69.

that justification could simply be the fact that 'the employer considered it appropriate to pay those who attend work and contribute to the operation more than those whose absence prevents that'.[54]

5.61 The EAT's decision was upheld by the Court of Appeal, Hooper LJ describing the EAT's conclusion on justification as unassailable.[55] It has since been followed by the EAT in *Fowler v London Borough of Waltham Forest*.[56] Even before the change in the law heralded by *Malcolm*, therefore, the scope for disabled employees to claim discrimination as a result of an employer's refusal to change the normal operation of sick pay schemes was extremely limited. One case where it remained possible to argue that a change should be made to normal sick pay arrangements was where it was the employer's fault that the employee was off work sick in the first place.[57] Under the new law, this would not even constitute less favourable treatment, let alone discrimination which the employer could be called upon to justify.

54 Ibid at paras 90–91.

55 *O'Hanlon v Commissioners for HM Revenue & Customs* [2007] IRLR 404, CA, at para 68.

56 UKEAT/0116/06.

57 *Nottinghamshire County Council v Meikle* [2004] EWCA Civ 859; [2004] 4 All ER 97; [2004] IRLR 703, CA.

6

DIRECT DISCRIMINATION

A. Introduction

There were no provisions relating to direct discrimination in the DDA 1995 as originally enacted. Specific provisions relating to direct discrimination were only introduced into the DDA 1995 with effect from 1 October 2004 in order to comply with the Framework Directive. Partly for this reason, and partly because the test for direct discrimination is a restrictive one, there have been very few cases in this area. **6.01**

B. Statutory Definition

DDA 1995, s 3A(5) provides as follows: **6.02**

> A person directly discriminates against a disabled person if, on the ground of the disabled person's disability, he treats the disabled person less favourably than he treats or would treat a person not having that particular disability whose relevant circumstances, including his abilities, are the same as, or not materially different from, those of the disabled person.

This definition is broadly similar to the definitions found in the other equality statutes. Sex discrimination occurs when a woman is treated less favourably on **6.03** the grounds of her sex.[1] Race discrimination occurs when a person is treated less favourably on racial grounds.[2] However, three points should be made.

6.04 First, the definition specifically refers to *the disabled person's disability*. The comparison is to be made with a person not having *that particular disability*. This suggests that the comparator could be someone who has a different disability from the claimant, as well as someone who is not disabled at all. This would enable a claim to be brought against an employer who, for example, treated an employee with a mental disability less favourably than he treated an employee with a physical disability.

6.05 Second, the definition only expressly affords protection to the disabled person himself. That contravenes the Framework Directive, which, as held by the ECJ in *Coleman v Attridge Law*[3], covers associative discrimination as well. In this case, the claimant was a legal secretary who complained that she had been treated less favourably than her colleagues at work on the grounds that she had a disabled son. The ECJ ruled that the Framework Directive had to be interpreted as meaning that the prohibition of direct discrimination was not limited to people who were themselves disabled. Where an employer treated an employee who was not herself disabled less favourably than another employee was, had been or would be treated in a comparable situation, and it was established that the less favourable treatment of that employee was based on the disability of her child, whose care was provided primarily by that employee, such treatment was contrary to the prohibition of direct discrimination laid down by art 2(2)(a) of the Framework Directive.[4]

6.06 Third, the definition requires the relevant circumstances of the comparator, *including his abilities*, to be the same as, or not materially different from, those of the disabled person. That wording emphasizes the point that the comparison to be made is on a like for like basis. However, the definition also stipulates that the comparator must not have the *particular disability* suffered by the claimant. Clearly, the claimant's abilities might be compromised by the particular disability from which he suffers. Is that fact to be taken into account? This difficult issue is addressed in section D of this chapter.

---

1 SDA 1975, s 1.

2 RRA 1976, s 1.

3 [2008] All ER (D) 245, ECJ.

4 Despite the contrary view expressed by the EAT and the tribunal hearing this case, it would appear to the authors that additional words will have to be interpolated into the definition of direct discrimination in DDA 1995 in order to make it compliant with the Framework Directive. See the discussion in chapter 3 at 3.43–3.47.

C. The Reason For The Treatment

1. 'On the Ground of'

Treatment of a disabled person is 'on the ground of' his disability if it is caused by the fact that he is disabled or has the disability in question. In general, this means that treatment is on the grounds of disability if a disabled person would not have received it but for his disability. However, disability does not have to be the only (or even the main) cause of the treatment complained of—provided that it is an effective cause, determined objectively from all the circumstances.[5] Although there is no statutory basis for these assertions, they are uncontroversial, reflecting the position in discrimination law generally.[6] **6.07**

2. Stereotypical Assumptions

Direct discrimination is likely to occur if an employer makes generalized or stereotypical assumptions about a disability or its effects, rather than considering the individual abilities of the disabled person. An employer would not normally make such assumptions about a non-disabled person.[7] **6.08**

This passage in the Code of Practice 2004 was relied on by a tribunal in *Tudor v Spen Corner Veterinary Centre*.[8] The claimant worked as an animal nursing assistant and receptionist. She suffered a stroke in May 2005. While she was still in hospital in June 2005, she was told that she had gone blind. She was also told that it was impossible to say if, or when, she might recover her sight. The claimant's mother told the employers about what had happened and shortly afterwards, the claimant was informed that she was being dismissed and that her employment would terminate in July 2005. When the claimant brought a claim of disability discrimination, the tribunal was satisfied that the employers had made generalized and stereotypical assumptions about the claimant. The vet running the practice had given evidence that 'with blindness you do not recover', but at the time of dismissal she had no way of knowing whether this was the case or not. The vet simply assumed that the claimant would not recover her sight. No meeting had been arranged with the claimant before she had been dismissed, to discuss the matter, and no medical expert had been consulted. In the circumstances, direct discrimination had been made out. **6.09**

---

5 Code of Practice 2004, para 4.7.

6 See *James v Eastleigh Borough Council* [1990] 2 AC 751; [1990] 3 WLR 55; [1990] 2 All ER 607; [1990] ICR 554; [1990] IRLR 288, HL. See also *O'Neill v Governors of St. Thomas More School* [1997] ICR 33; [1996] IRLR 372, EAT.

7 Code of Practice 2004, para 4.8.

8 Case no. 2404211/05, IDS Brief 809.

3. Knowledge

6.10 Direct discrimination need not be conscious. People may hold prejudices that they do not admit, even to themselves. Furthermore, as the following example demonstrates, direct discrimination can occur even though the employer is unaware of a person's disability:

> An employer advertises a promotion internally to its workforce. The job description states that people with a history of mental illness would not be suitable for the post. An employee who would otherwise be eligible for the promotion has a history of schizophrenia, but the employer is unaware of this. The employee would, nevertheless, have a good claim for unlawful direct discrimination in relation to the promotion opportunities afforded to him by his employer. The act of direct discrimination in this case is the blanket ban on anyone who has had a mental illness, effectively rejecting whole categories of people with no consideration of their individual abilities.[9]

D. The Comparator

1. Relevant Circumstances

6.11 The statutory definition of direct disability discrimination requires a comparison to be made between the disabled person and an actual or hypothetical comparator in order to establish whether the disabled person has been treated less favourably on the grounds of his disability. The section stipulates that this comparator should satisfy two conditions:

(a) he must not have the particular disability which the disabled person has; and
(b) his relevant circumstances, including his abilities, must be the same as, or not materially different from, those of the disabled person.

6.12 If the actual or hypothetical comparator must not have the claimant's particular disability, but at the same time he must have abilities which are broadly speaking the same as the claimant's abilities, the following question arises. How does one deal with the fact that one of the relevant abilities of the disabled person might well be compromised as a result of his disability? When making the comparison, is one looking at the abilities of the disabled person as they would have been, but for his disability, or as they in fact are as a result of his disability?

6.13 The Code of Practice 2004 skates round this difficult question by stating that the effects of the disability *may be relevant* in some cases:

> Direct discrimination only occurs where the **relevant** circumstances of the comparator, including his abilities, are the same as, or not materially different from, those of the

9 Code of Practice 2004, para 4.11.

> disabled person himself. It is therefore important to focus on those circumstances which are, in fact, relevant to the matter to which the less favourable treatment relates. Although, in some cases, the effects of the disability may be relevant, the fact of the disability itself is not a relevant circumstance for these purposes. This is because the comparison must be with a person **not** having that particular disability.[10]

What this passage appears to be saying is that the effects of the disability are to be taken into account if they are relevant to the matter to which the less favourable treatment relates. Take the example given: **6.14**

> A disabled person with arthritis who can type at 30 words per minute (wpm) applies for an administrative job which includes typing, but is rejected on the grounds that her typing speed is too slow. The correct comparator in a claim for direct discrimination would be a person not having arthritis who also has a typing speed of 30 wpm (with the same accuracy rate).[11]

In this example, were it not for her arthritis, the woman rejected for the job would have had a faster typing speed. Her abilities have been compromised by her disability, and as a result she has to be compared with someone not having that particular disability who also types at the same slow rate. This demonstrates the restricted scope of this form of discrimination. If a requirement for the job is a typing speed of 50 words per minute, the employer would not give either person the job because both are too slow at typing. There would therefore be no less favourable treatment of the disabled person and no discrimination. There would only be direct discrimination if it could be shown that the employer would give the (hypothetical or actual) non-disabled applicant the job, despite her slow typing speed, when he would not give it to the disabled person. But why would an employer do that? Clearly, he would not; or if he did, the decision would not be based on ability. Only in that unlikely event might one be driven to the conclusion that any such decision was based on prejudice against the disabled person. **6.15**

In reality, of course, the employer is much more likely to take on an applicant who could type at the requisite speed of 50 words per minute. If he did so, this would not amount to direct discrimination because that applicant's relevant abilities are not the same as the disabled woman's abilities. She can type faster. It could only ever have amounted to disability-related discrimination, and it would not even be that following *London Borough of Lewisham v Malcolm*.[12] **6.16**

Where, on the other hand, the effects of the disability are not relevant to the matter to which the less favourable treatment relates, it is much easier to appreciate **6.17**

---

[10] Code of Practice 2004, para 4.20.
[11] Ibid, first example.
[12] See previous chapter.

that they should not be included as 'relevant circumstances'. Take the example of a disabled man with arthritis who applies for an administrative job which includes typing, but is rejected in favour of a non-disabled candidate. Because of his arthritis, the man has a slow typing speed and has difficulty walking. The job is entirely desk-based, and does not require the person doing it to be able to walk further than a few metres within the office. The comparator here would be a non-disabled candidate with the same slow typing speed, but it would not be necessary for the comparator to have mobility problems. The ability to walk further than a few metres is not relevant to the candidate's ability to do the job.[13]

2. The Clone Approach

6.18 The difficulty with identifying a suitable comparator is demonstrated by the case of *High Quality Lifestyles Ltd v Watts*,[14] the only appellate authority to date on this issue. The respondent employer was an organization providing residential care for people with learning difficulties, autistic spectrum disorders, and others with severely challenging behavioural problems. The claimant was a support worker. He lived in the residential home with the service users. Although he was HIV positive, he did not disclose this to his employers when he started his employment with them. He only told them about his condition at about the time when he was promoted after five months' employment. By that time, he had been scratched, lacerated and bitten by service users on a number of occasions. After he told his employers that he was HIV positive, he was suspended while they carried out a risk assessment, and then dismissed on the grounds that his position was untenable in the light of the risk assessment which had been made.

6.19 A tribunal upheld the claimant's claim of direct disability discrimination. It held that the hypothetical comparator should be a person in exactly the same position but without his disability. Such a person would have a communicable disease but it would not be HIV. The tribunal went on to find that the claimant had been dismissed because of the effect of his condition. He had, therefore, been dismissed on the grounds of his disability.

6.20 The EAT allowed an appeal against this decision. Quite correctly, it pointed out that the tribunal had failed to ask itself whether the hypothetical comparator which it had constructed would be treated any differently. Furthermore, the tribunal's approach to relevant circumstances was flawed:

> The error which the tribunal made . . . was in failing to impute relevant circumstances to the hypothetical comparator. The circumstances were not, as the tribunal found,

[13] Code of Practice 2004, para 4.21.

[14] [2006] IRLR 850, EAT.

> that the comparator should have a communicable disease. Assuming, as the tribunal correctly did, that the comparator has the same 'abilities, skills and experience', the comparator must also have some attribute, whether caused by a medical condition or otherwise, which is not HIV positive. This attribute must carry the same risk of causing to others illness or injury of the same gravity, here serious and possibly fatal. If the tribunal found that the comparator would have been dismissed, then the claimant has not been less favourably treated. The facts which it is necessary for the claimant to have proved, in order to shift the burden of proof to the respondent, is not only a workable model for the hypothetical comparator but also some evidential basis upon which it could be said by the tribunal that the comparator would not have been dismissed.[15]

The approach taken by the EAT in this case is extremely restrictive. In requiring the comparator to have some attribute which was not HIV but which carried the same risk of causing to others illness or injury of the same gravity, serious and possibly fatal, it required the comparator to have a condition which was HIV in all but name. This is dancing on the head of a pin. This comparison is similar to the clone comparator rejected by the Court of Appeal in a race discrimination case in which it was pointed out that, if the comparator's circumstances were to be identical in all respects but for race, then logically the only reason for less favourable treatment left remaining would be race.[16] **6.21**

3. The Broader Approach

A broader approach was taken to the identification of the comparator in *Tudor v Spen Corner Veterinary Centre*,[17] the case discussed in paragraph 6.09 above. Up to the decision to dismiss in that case, the employer had received sick notes lasting one week each and had no evidence as to whether the claimant would regain her sight. In those circumstances, the tribunal considered that an appropriate comparator would be an employee who had suffered a broken leg which meant she was unable to work and it was unclear when she might be able to resume work again. In respect of such an individual, the tribunal considered that the employer would not have made stereotypical assumptions on her likelihood of recovery or her ability to do the job again. **6.22**

Although an ability to see is presumably a relevant ability for a vet, as for most other jobs, it was omitted from the comparison made by the tribunal in *Tudor v Spen Corner Veterinary Centre* because the section demands that the comparator does not have the *particular* disability suffered by the claimant. In order to meet the conflicting requirements that the relevant abilities of the comparator should be the same, yet different because he must not have the particular disability in **6.23**

15 *High Quality Lifestyles Ltd v Watts* [2006] IRLR 850, EAT at para 48.
16 *Madden v Preferred Technical Group CHA Ltd* [2004] EWCA Civ 1178; [2005] IRLR 46.
17 Case no. 2404211/05.

question, the EAT in *High Quality Lifestyles Ltd v Watts* attempted to construct a disability for its comparator which was the same as HIV in all but name.[18] If the tribunal in *Tudor v Spen Corner Veterinary Centre* had tried to do the same, it would have had to construct a comparator who could not see, yet was not blind!

6.24 The difficulty is further demonstrated by the example given in the Code of Practice 2004 of a disabled person with a severe visual impairment who is refused a job as a bus driver because he fails to meet the minimum level of visual acuity which is essential for the safe performance of the job. It is suggested that a suitable comparator would be a person not having that particular disability (for example, a person who merely has poorer than average eyesight) who also fails to meet that minimum standard.[19] That is a fudge. In attempting to meet the conflicting demands of the section, the example attributes the same abilities to the comparator (he cannot see well enough to pass the test) but insists that he does not have the same disability (severe visual impairment). However, this is just a question of degree. The person with the severe visual impairment might have worse eyesight than the person with poorer than average eyesight, but neither can see well enough to meet the minimum standard. The disability which they share is that neither can see well enough to get a job as a bus driver.

6.25 The wording of the section presents real problems of construction. However, if any meaning is to be given to the concept of direct disability discrimination, the approach taken by the tribunal in *Tudor v Spen Corner Veterinary Centre* is to be preferred. The merit of this approach is that it does enable a meaningful comparison to be made. Following the House of Lords decision in *Malcom*[20] severely limiting the scope of disability-related discrimination, more claims of direct discrimination can be expected. Further guidance from the appellate courts is urgently needed in this area.

4. Relevance of Reasonable Adjustments

6.26 In making the comparison for the purposes of direct discrimination, the disabled person's abilities must be seen as they are. That remains the case, even if the employer has failed to make reasonable adjustments which would have had the effect of enhancing the disabled person's ability to do the job. On the other hand, if adjustments have been made which have had the effect of enhancing the disabled person's abilities, then it is those enhanced abilities which should be considered.[21]

---

18 This is particularly the case, given that disability is defined by reference to a person's abilities. See para 6.12.

19 Code of Practice 2004, para 4.20.

20 [2008] UKHL 43. See previous chapter for a discussion of this case.

21 Code of Practice 2004, para 4.22.

This point can be illustrated by the following examples. First, a disabled person who applies for an administrative job which includes typing is not allowed to use her own adapted keyboard (even though it would have been reasonable for the employer to allow this) and types a test document at 30 words per minute. Her speed with the adapted keyboard would have been 50 words per minute. A non-disabled candidate is given the job because her typing speed on the test was 45 words per minute with the same accuracy rate. This is not direct discrimination, as the comparator is a non-disabled person typing at 30 words per minute. (The disabled person would, however, have a good claim for a failure to make reasonable adjustments.) **6.27**

Second, a disabled person with arthritis who applies for a similar job is allowed to use an adapted keyboard and types a test document at 50 words per minute. A non-disabled candidate types at 30 words per minute with the same accuracy rate. However, the disabled candidate is rejected because of prejudice and the other candidate is offered the job instead. This is direct discrimination, as the comparator would be a person not having arthritis who could type at 50 words per minute.[22] **6.28**

5. Justification

Unlike disability-related discrimination, there is no defence of justification for treatment of a disabled person which amounts to direct discrimination. An employer can never be justified in treating a disabled person less favourably *on the grounds of* his disability. **6.29**

E. Proving Discrimination

Although the burden of proof lies on the claimant to prove that he was a disabled person within the meaning of the statutory definition at the time of the alleged act of discrimination, the reverse burden of proof applied to discrimination cases generally is applied to cases of disability discrimination by DDA 1995, s 17A(1C) which provides as follows: **6.30**

> Where, on the hearing of a complaint under subsection (1), the complainant proves facts from which the tribunal could, apart from this subsection, conclude in the absence of an adequate explanation that the respondent has acted in a way which is unlawful under this Part, the tribunal shall uphold the complaint unless the respondent proves that he did not so act.

This section reverses the burden of proof in cases of disability discrimination where the claimant proves facts from which an inference of unlawful **6.31**

[22] Code of Practice 2004, at para 4.22.

discrimination could be drawn. The employer must then show that it is more likely than not that its conduct was not unlawful. With specific reference to an allegation of direct discrimination, it means that an employee must prove facts from which it could be inferred in the absence of an adequate explanation that he has been treated less favourably on the ground of his disability than an appropriate comparator has been, or would be, treated. If the employee does this, the claim will succeed unless the employer can show that disability was not any part of the reason for the treatment in question.[23]

6.32 An illustration of the reverse burden of proof in action is provided by the case of *Bowerman v B&Q and Ors.*[24] The claimant in this case had Asperger's Syndrome which meant that he had difficulty communicating and socialising with others, and picking up subtle non-verbal communications. A female colleague at work made a complaint to the employer that the claimant had touched her inappropriately. Two other female members of staff made similar allegations when the complaint was investigated. Following a disciplinary hearing, the claimant was summarily dismissed for sexual harassment. However, an employee at one of B&Q's other stores, who did not have Asperger's Syndrome and who faced similar allegations, was not dismissed. Instead, he was moved to another store following a suspension. The tribunal found that the claimant had been directly discriminated against on the ground of disability by being dismissed, because he had been treated less favourably than the employee at the other store, whose relevant circumstances were not materially different. The claimant had, therefore, proved facts from which the tribunal could conclude, in the absence of an adequate explanation, that the employer had acted unlawfully.

23 Code of Practice 2004, at para 4.43. See also para 10.75 et seq.

24 ET Case No. 1400375/05, reported in IDS Brief 825, March 2007.

7

VICTIMIZATION

A. Introduction

The effectiveness of the DDA 1995 would be greatly reduced if employees were deterred from taking part in tribunal proceedings, either as witnesses or claimants, out of fear of reprisals from their employer.[1] Therefore, in order to ensure the proper functioning of the judicial process and the enforcement of its anti-discrimination provisions, the DDA 1995 seeks to prevent reprisals by offering protection to employees who perform certain acts. The DDA 1995 protects four acts. They are: **7.01**

(a) bringing proceedings under the DDA 1995;
(b) giving evidence or information in connection with proceedings under the DDA 1995;
(c) otherwise doing anything under, or by reference to, the DDA 1995: and
(d) alleging that any person has contravened the DDA 1995.

---

1 See Lord Bingham in *Derbyshire v St Helens Metropolitan Borough Council* [2007] ICR 841 [2007] IRLR 540, HL, at para 4: 'The right not to be discriminated against on the grounds of disability would be of limited value if the alleged discriminator were free, otherwise than by defeating the claim on its merits, to frustrate or interfere with the conduct of the proceedings in a way that undermined the integrity of the judicial process.'

For simplicity, the term 'protected act' will be used throughout this chapter to refer to these four acts.

7.02 The DDA 1995 prohibits employers from subjecting persons to less favourable treatment by reason that they have performed a protected act.[2] Since the *reason for* the treatment determines whether or not victimization occurs, it is the employer's subjective intention that governs liability. 'A' victimizes 'B' not only if A mistreats him because B *has* performed a protected act, but also if A mistreats him because he *believes or suspects* that B has performed, or is going to perform, a protected act.[3] 'A' is judged according to A's subjective motivation which may be conscious or subconscious.[4]

7.03 Since the purpose of the victimization provisions is to protect persons taking part in proceedings under the DDA 1995 or seeking to enforce the observance of it, one does not have to be disabled to make a victimization claim.[5] For instance, a person will be protected if he is giving evidence in connection with proceedings brought by a disabled person even if he himself is not disabled.

B. Statutory Framework

7.04 Victimizing a person contrary to DDA 1995, s 55 constitutes discrimination. DDA 1995, s 55 is not a free-standing cause of action. Like other acts of discrimination, victimization is only unlawful in the circumstances listed in DDA 1995, s 4. DDA 1995, s 4 is the gateway to a claim for victimization in the same way that it is for other discrimination claims under the DDA 1995. DDA 1995, s 4 is dealt with in more detail elsewhere in this work.[6]

Victimization DDA 1995 s 55(1)

55(1) For the purposes of Part 2 a person ('A') discriminates against another person ('B') if—

(a) he treats B less favourably than he treats or would treat other persons whose circumstances are the same as B's; and

(b) he does so for a reason mentioned in subsection (2).

---

[2] The word 'victimization' under the DDA 1995 is, therefore, different to 'victimization' in its everyday sense. A person can be victimized, in the everyday sense of the word, irrespective of the reasons for his treatment, whereas under the DDA 1995 a person only victimizes another if he does so by reason of his having performed a protected act.

[3] DDA 1995, s 55(2)(b).

[4] *Nagarajan v London Regional Transport* [2000] 1 AC 501, [1999] ICR 877, [1999] IRLR 572, HL.

[5] DDA 1995, s 55(5).

[6] See chapter 3.

The four protected acts—DDA 1995, s 55(2)(a)

55(2) The reasons are that —

(a) B has—
  (i) brought proceedings against A or any other person under this Act; or
  (ii) given evidence or information in connection with such proceedings brought by any person; or
  (iii) otherwise done anything under or by reference to this Act in relation to A or any other person; or
  (iv) alleged that A or any other person has (whether or not the allegation so states) contravened this Act; or

(b) believes or suspects that B has done or intends to do any of those things.

The statutory test can be usefully separated into a three stage enquiry: **7.05**

(a) Has the person performed a protected act in good faith?
(b) Has the claimant suffered less favourable treatment than a comparator?
(c) Was the claimant afforded that less favourable treatment because he had performed, or was about to perform, a protected act?

It is important to keep the three stages separate. It is particularly easy to confuse the second and third stages. The purpose of the second stage is to identify *whether* the victim was treated less favourably than others who had not performed a protected act. The third stage seeks to identify *why* the claimant was afforded the less favourable treatment. **7.06**

C. The Protected Acts

Discrimination occurs where a person is treated less favourably because he has performed a protected act. The claimant must identify which of the protected acts he seeks to rely on. Very often, because of the similar nature of each of the protected acts, he can, and should, rely on more than one.[7] **7.07**

1. Brought Proceedings—(DAA 1995, s 55(2)(a)(i))

The first protected act is bringing proceedings under the DDA 1995 against the discriminator or any other person. Whether someone has 'brought proceedings under the DDA 1995' is, for the most part, self-explanatory. For proceedings to be brought *under the DDA 1995* they must actually rely on one or more of the provisions contained in the DDA 1995.[8] **7.08**

[7] *Nagarajan v London Regional Transport* [2000] 1 AC 501, [1999] ICR 877, [1999] IRLR 572, HL.

[8] See para 7.14.

7.09 The situation is more complex when the victimization relates to the employer's conduct of its defence of proceedings under the DDA 1995. In *Chief Constable of West Yorkshire v Khan*,[9] a case under the identical provisions of the RRA 1976,[10] the House of Lords drew a material distinction between an employer who acted against an employee because proceedings existed and an employer who acted against an employee because the employee had brought proceedings. It was held that an employer was entitled to take steps to preserve its position in litigation, because this would be taking action because proceedings were in existence rather than because proceedings had been brought.[11]

7.10 In *Derbyshire & Ors v St Helens Metropolitan Borough Council (Equal Opportunities Commission & Ors intervening)*[12] the House of Lords cast doubt on the reasoning in *Khan* but arrived at a similar decision by a different route. Their Lordships held that action taken during the course of an employer's honest and reasonable conduct of its defence of a DDA 1995 claim was unlikely to constitute *unlawful* discrimination because it would not subject the claimant to a 'detriment' under s 4.[13]

7.11 Following *Derbyshire*, there is no need to use the distinction in *Khan* between 'bringing proceedings' and 'brought proceedings' to allow employers properly to conduct their own defence of discrimination claims. It is likely that *Khan* will be viewed as a case that turned very much on its own facts rather than as one that distinguished between victimization as a result of bringing proceedings and victimization as a result of conducting proceedings.

2. Giving Evidence or Information in Connection with Proceedings (DDA 1995, s 55(2)(a)(ii))

7.12 A person giving evidence or information is protected from less favourable treatment in so far as that giving of evidence or information is in connection with proceedings under the DDA 1995. Evidence or information will be given in connection with proceedings if it led to proceedings being brought.

7.13 Although it does not matter whether the evidence or information was given prior to, or after the, commencement of proceedings, the victimization itself must

---

9 [2001] UKHL 48, [2001] 1 WLR 1947, HL.

10 RRA 1976, s 2(1) prohibits less favourable treatment of a person who has 'brought proceedings against the discriminator or any other person under this Act'.

11 See Lord Nicholls at paras 29–31. See also *Cornelius v University College of Swansea* [1987] IRLR 141, CA, referred to by Lord Nicholls.

12 [2007] UKHL 16, [2007] ICR 841, HL.

13 See *Derbyshire v St Helens Metropolitan Borough Council* [2007] ICR 841, HL and para 3.111.

occur at a time when proceedings have actually been brought.[14] It should be noted that an internal complaint or grievance process is unlikely to constitute 'bringing proceedings'.[15]

3. Doing Anything under or by Reference to the DDA 1995—(DDA 1995, s 55(2)(a)(iii))

The next protected act is doing anything under, or by reference to, the DDA 1995 in relation to 'A' or any other person.[16] The interpretation of *under* is much narrower that the interpretation of *by reference to*. Where something is alleged to be done *under* the DDA 1995, the claimant must identify the specific provision of the DDA 1995 under which the protected act was carried out.[17] **7.14**

The phrase 'by reference to' was added in December 2005[18] and makes the DDA 1995 consistent with the SDA 1975 and RRA 1976.[19] It is intended to be a catch-all provision[20] protecting those actions which might have been missed by DDA 1995, ss 55(2)(a)(i), (ii), or (iv). In *Kirby v Manpower Services Commission*[21] the EAT considered that an allegation of a possible breach of the RRA 1976 was sufficient to qualify as having been made 'by reference' to the RRA 1976. This broad interpretation was adopted in another RRA 1976 case, *Aziz v Trinity Street Taxis Ltd.*[22] In *Aziz* the claimant recorded conversations with his employer because (i) he considered that he was being unfairly treated; (ii) the possibility was beginning to form in his mind that this might amount to racial discrimination; (iii) he considered that the tape recordings might help him establish this at a later date. The Court of Appeal considered that this was sufficient to mean that the tapes were made 'by reference to' the RRA 1976, because an act can be done by reference to the relevant legislation in a broad sense even if the doer does not focus his mind specifically on any particular provision of the Act or is not able to identify the Act itself.[23] There is no reason why the DDA 1995 should not be interpreted in the same way. **7.15**

---

14 See *Kirby v Manpower Services Commission* [1980] IRLR, 229, [1980] 1 WLR 725, EAT, per Slynn J at page 730D.

15 *British Telecommunications Plc v Grant,* EAT 816/92.

16 See para 7.04.

17 *Kirby v Manpower Services Commission* [1980] IRLR, 229, [1980] 1 WLR 725, EAT, per Slynn J at page 730F.

18 Disability Discrimination Act 2005, s 19(1).

19 See RRA 1976, s 2(1)(c) and SDA 1975, s 4(1)(c).

20 In the context of the RRA 1976 see *National Probation Service for England and Wales v Kirby* [2006] IRLR 580, EAT, per Clark J at paras 33 and 36.

21 [1980] 1 WLR 725, [1980] IRLR, 229, EAT.

22 [1988] IRLR 204, CA.

23 [1988] 1 IRLR 204, CA, per Slade LJ at para 29.

4. Alleging that a Person has Contravened the DDA 1995—(DDA 1995, s 55(2)(a)(iv))

7.16 The final protected act is the act of alleging that a person has contravened the DDA 1995. In order to qualify as a protected act the allegation need not state explicitly that a breach of the DDA 1995 has occurred but it must allege facts that are capable in law of breaching the DDA 1995.[24] In the sex discrimination case of *Waters v Commissioner of Police of the Metropolis*,[25] the acts complained of were very serious but they took place outside work and were, therefore, incapable of amounting in law to unlawful acts of discrimination. As a result the claimant was not protected by the victimization provisions.

7.17 It is arguable that the approach in *Waters* does not apply to the DDA 1995 because of differences in the legislative language. SDA 1975, s 4(1)(d) provides that the protected act is that the person victimized has:

> alleged that the discriminator or any other person has committed an act which (whether or not the allegation so states) would amount to contravention of this Act . . .

7.18 By contrast, DDA 1995, s 55 contains no equivalent to the words 'would amount to a contravention' but simply reads 'alleged that A or any other person has contravened this Act'. This would suggest that there is no requirement in the DDA 1995 for the allegations actually to amount to a contravention of the DDA 1995 before qualifying as a protected act.

7.19 However, since in most circumstances less favourable treatment afforded to a person by reason of their making an allegation contrary to DDA 1995, s 55(2)(a)(iv) will also be prohibited by DDA 1995, s 55(2)(a)(iii),[26] this argument is rendered academic where the case is pleaded sufficiently broadly to encompass a claim under both subsections.

5. Bad Faith

7.20 DDA 1995, s 55(4) provides that the victimization provisions do not apply to treatment accorded to a person if the allegations made by that person were both false *and* in bad faith.[27] Both falsity and bad faith are required and so a false

---

[24] *Waters v Commissioner of Police of the Metropolis* [1997] ICR 1073, HL.

[25] [1997] ICR 1073, HL.

[26] This overlap was acknowledged in *Kirby v Manpower Services Commission* [1980] IRLR 229, [1980] 1 WLR 726, EAT, at p.731.

[27] In whistleblowing cases under ERA 1996, s 43G, an allegation is made in bad faith if it was made for an ulterior purpose. However, it should be noted that Auld L J in *Street v Derbyshire Unemployed Worker's Centre* [2004] EWCA Civ 964 doubted, at para 41, that the meaning of good faith under the equal opportunities legislation was the same as the whistleblowing provisions of the ERA 1996.

allegation made in good faith will attract protection, as will a true allegation made in bad faith.[28]

Identifying whether an allegation is false is a simple question of fact that has nothing to do with the motive of the person making it. A false allegation is one that is wrong, erroneous or incorrect.[29] **7.21**

Bad faith may manifest itself in a wide variety of ways but in most cases whether an allegation is made in bad faith will depend upon whether the person making the allegation knew that the allegation was false when he made it or persisted with the allegation after discovering that it was false or misconceived. **7.22**

The purpose for which the claim is brought is not important but the claimant must believe in the claim.[30] Even if a person brings the claim for a collateral purpose, the claim is not made in bad faith so long as the claimant believes that the claim he is making has substance. In *HM Prison Service v Ibimidun*[31] the claimant brought a series of race discrimination claims against his employer. Although some claims succeeded, he was eventually dismissed for bringing a false race discrimination claim which he had brought to achieve a settlement by harassing his employer. The claimant claimed that his dismissal was victimization. The EAT held that since the allegations made by the claimant in his race discrimination claim were false, brought for a collateral purpose, and made in bad faith, the victimization claim must fail and he was found to have been fairly dismissed. **7.23**

D. Less Favourable Treatment

The requirement for treatment to be less favourable is best understood as a requirement for the claimant to have suffered some form of detriment before the discrimination is actionable[32]. For treatment to have been less favourable, the claimant must be treated worse than other employees. It is not enough to identify unfavourable treatment, as this does not demonstrate that the claimant has been treated less favourably than anyone else: the employer may simply treat everyone badly. Although the facts establishing less favourable treatment may, in many **7.24**

---

[28] Code para 4.35 provides that: 'the fact that a person has given evidence on behalf of an applicant in a claim which was unsuccessful does not, of itself, prove that his evidence was false or was not given in good faith'.

[29] See *GMB Union v Fenton* UKEAT/0484/04/RN and UKEAT/0798/02/RN and UKEAT/0046/03/RN per Burton J at para 41.

[30] *GMB Union v Fenton* UKEAT/0484/04/RN & UKEAT/0798/02/RN & UKEAT/0046/03/RN.

[31] UKEAT/0408/07/DA UKEAT/0517/07.

[32] See para 7.10.

cases, shed light on the reasons for the treatment, it is important to keep a clear conceptual distinction between whether there was less favourable treatment and whether treatment was afforded to a person by reason of a protected act.

7.25 The concept of less favourable treatment requires a comparison between the treatment accorded to the complainant and the treatment accorded to other people. The comparison under the DDA 1995 requires a comparison with:

(a) a person who has not performed a protected act;
(b) whose circumstances are otherwise the same;

but the claimant's disability must be disregarded.[33]

7.26 The comparison must be with a person who has not performed a protected act. Does this mean for instance, that where a person has brought proceedings under the DDA 1995, his treatment should be compared with a person who has brought proceedings under some other enactment? In the case of *Chief Constable of West Yorkshire v Khan*[34] the House of Lords held that the comparison, in these circumstances, should be with a person who had not done the protected act at all and that no further qualification, such as requiring the comparator to have acted under other some other enactment, was appropriate.[35]

7.27 Apart from not having performed the protected act, the comparator in a victimization case must be a person whose circumstances are the same as the claimant's. 'Circumstances' in this context means the circumstances in which the discrimination is made unlawful by DDA 1995, s 4.[36] In the same way that the comparator in a reasonable adjustments case is identified by reference to the substantial disadvantage and the PCP,[37] the comparator in a victimization case is identified by the nature of the detriment or other DDA 1995, s 4 circumstance that is applicable. In *Chief Constable of the West Yorkshire Police v Khan*[38] the claimant brought race discrimination proceedings against the respondent. During the course of those proceedings he asked to be provided with a reference so that he could apply to another police force. The respondent took the view that it was inappropriate to provide a reference about matters that were the subject of race discrimination

33 DDA 1995, s 55(3).

34 [2001] UKHL 48, [2001] 1 WLR 1947.

35 See *Chief Constable of West Yorkshire v Khan* [2001] UKHL 48, [2001] 1 WLR 1947 per Lord Nicholls at para 27 and Lord Hoffman at para 48; see also *Brown v TNT Express Worldwide (UK) Ltd* [2001] ICR 182.

36 See *Chief Constable of the West Yorkshire Police v Khan* [2001] UKHL 48, [2001] ICR 1065 per Lord Nicholls at paras 24 to 27 and Lord Mackay at paras 39 and 40. *Khan* was heavily criticized on other grounds in *St Helens Borough Council v Derbyshire and Ors* [2007] UKHL 16, [2007] IRLR 540.

37 *Smith v Churchill Stairlifts Plc* [2006] ICR 524, [2006] IRLR 41, CA, see para 4.35.

38 [2001] UKHL 48, [2001] ICR 1065.

proceedings and refused to provide one. The House of Lords considered that the comparator, in these circumstances, was a person employed in Great Britain and who had applied for a reference. On this basis it determined the claimant had been subjected to less favourable treatment.[39]

Since the purpose of the DDA 1995 is to protect anyone taking action under, or in relation to, the DDA 1995, a person's disability is irrelevant to the comparison.[40] Any person who has performed a protected act may make a victimization claim, provided that his circumstances fall within DDA 1995 s 4.[41] **7.28**

E. By Reason of the Protected Act

In order to succeed in a victimization claim, it is not sufficient merely to show that an employee who has performed a protected act has been treated less favourably than another person, as this might simply be a matter of chance. The victim must also show that the less favourable treatment occurred *by reason* of the protected act. There must be a causal connection between the employer's unlawful motive and the less favourable treatment. **7.29**

In *Chief Constable of West Yorkshire v Khan*[42] Lord Nicholls confirmed that the question of whether conduct was by reason of a protected act was judged subjectively:[43] **7.30**

> Contrary to views sometimes stated the . . . ingredient 'by reason that' does not raise a question of causation as that expression is usually understood. Causation is a slippery word, but normally it is used to describe a legal exercise... Sometimes the court may look for the 'operative cause', or the 'effective' cause. Sometimes it may apply a 'but for' approach.... The phrases 'on racial grounds' and 'by reason that' denote a different exercise: why did the alleged discriminator act as he did? What consciously or unconsciously, was his reason? Unlike causation, this is a subjective test . . . The reason why a person acted as he did is a question of fact.

Although the judgment in *Khan* came under serious attack in *Derbyshire v St Helens Metropolitan Borough Council*,[44] this passage from *Khan* was adopted[45] **7.31**

---

39 Per Lord Mackay at para 40. The case was decided against the claimant on other grounds.

40 DDA 1995, s 55(3) and s 55(5). See also *Wandsworth NHS Primary Care Trust v Obonyo* EAT 0237/05 for a case concerning the RRA 1976 in which the EAT considered that the claimant's race was irrelevant to the comparator even thought this was not made explicit under the RRA 1976.

41 *Bruce v Addleshaw Booth & Co* UKEAT/0404/03/MAA.

42 [2001] UKHL 48, [2001] 1 WLR 1947.

43 Lord Nicholls was considering the meaning of 'by reason that' in the context of the RRA 1976 at para 29.

44 [2001] UKHL 48, [2001] 1 WLR 1947.

45 See Lady Hale and Lord Bingham at paras 9 and 41 respectively.

and remains a helpful explanation of the correct approach. It should be noted though, that Lord Neuberger in *Derbyshire* preferred a more simple explanation than that given in *Khan* and gave the phrase 'by reason that' the simple meaning of 'because'.[46]

7.32 A subjective test is obviously appropriate since the guilty intention of the employer is the mischief against which the victimization provisions are aimed. Knowledge of the protected act must, therefore, be actual rather than constructive[47] but the intention can be subconscious.[48]

7.33 In *Nagarajan v London Regional Transport*[49] the House of Lords held that the unlawful motive need not be the only cause of the less favourable treatment but it must have had a significant influence on the treatment before it could be said to have caused the victimization.[50] A significant influence is an influence that is more than minor or trivial. Under the relevant principles of EC law (including the Burden of Proof Directive), member states are required to eradicate 'all discrimination whatsoever' and so the concept of 'significant influence' adopted by Lord Nicholls in *Nagarajan* must mean significant in the sense of 'more than trivial'. The principle of equal treatment cannot be breached by the trivial.[51]

---

46 See Lord Neuberger at paras 63 to 65 and 76.

47 *Allianz Cornhill v Fidler* UKEAT/0723/04.

48 *Nagarajan v London Regional Transport* [2000] 1 AC 501, [1999] ICR 877, [1999] IRLR 830.

49 [2000] 1 AC 501, [1999] ICR 877, [1999] IRLR 830.

50 *Nagarajan v London Regional Transport* [2000] 1 AC 501, [1999] ICR 877 Per Lord Nicholls at page 886E-F.

51 *Igen Ltd & Ors v Wong* [2001] ICR 931 per Gibson LJ at paras 36 & 37. See also *Villalba v Merril Lynch and Co. Inc* [2007] ICR 469 where the tribunal found that unconscious discrimination had no more than a trivial influence on the respondent's decision to treat the claimant less favourably and that there had, therefore, been no victimization. Even though the tribunal did not adopt the 'no influence whatsoever' approach, its decision was upheld in the EAT: see Elias J at paras 79 to 82.

8

HARASSMENT

A. Introduction

The 2003 Regulations, which came into force in October 2004, made harassment for a reason related to disability unlawful.[1] Before October 2004, claimants who were subjected to harassment had to make a claim under one of the other sections of the DDA 1995. Harassment under the DDA 1995 is not a form of discrimination[2] but is unlawful in its own right. It is comprised of the following elements: **8.01**

Unwanted conduct towards a person:
(a) that is afforded for a reason that is related to the victim's disability and
(b) that has the purpose or effect of the violation of a person's dignity *or* the creation of an intimidating, hostile, degrading, humiliating or offensive environment

[1] SI No 1673 reg 4.
[2] Harassment is not included within the meaning of discrimination under DDA 1995, s 3A.

8.02 A remedy for harassment may also be claimed in the civil courts under the Protection from Harassment Act 1997. Although this chapter is chiefly concerned with the prohibition of the harassment of employees under the DDA 1995, it will briefly discuss claims under the PHA 1997 and compare the advantages and disadvantages with proceeding in the tribunal or the civil courts.

8.03 The definition of harassment in the DDA 1995 mirrors the definitions in both the SDA 1975 and the RRA 1976.[3] There are no reported cases dealing with harassment under the DDA 1995 and most of the case law on harassment concerns sexual harassment. Although the relevant provisions of the SDA 1975 were amended with effect from 6 April 2008 by the Sex Discrimination Act 1975 (Amendment) Regulations 2008,[4] the pre-amendment SDA 1975 case law provides useful guidance on the interpretation of the harassment provisions of the DDA 1995.[5] References in this chapter to the SDA 1975 are, therefore, references to the SDA 1975 before its amendment by the Sex Discrimination Act 1975 (Amendment) Regulations 2008.

B. Statutory Framework

8.04 DDA 1995, s 3B contains the definition of harassment.

> **3B Meaning of 'harassment'**
>
> (1) For the purposes of this Part, a person subjects a disabled person to harassment where, for a reason which relates to the disabled person's disability, he engages in unwanted conduct which has the purpose or effect of—
>
> (a) violating the disabled person's dignity, or
>
> (b) creating an intimidating, hostile, degrading, humiliating or offensive environment for him.
>
> (2) Conduct shall be regarded as having the effect referred to in paragraph (a) or (b) of subsection (1) only if, having regard to all the circumstances, including in particular the perception of the disabled person, it should reasonably be considered as having that effect.

8.05 Harassment is made unlawful under the DDA 1995 in respect of the following:

(a) employees and applicants for employment (DDA 1995, s 4(3));
(b) contract workers (DDA 1995, s 4B(2));

---

3 SDA 1975, s 4A(1)(a) and RRA 1976, s 3A. In cases under the SDA 1975 (prior to 6 April 2008 when the Sex Discrimination Act 1975 (Amendment) Regulations 2008 came into force) and the RRA 1976 the provisions prohibited treatment afforded 'on the grounds' of sex or race.

4 SI 2008/656.

5 See paras 8.09 to 8.10. It should be noted that the SDA 1975 contains two additional instances of harassment that are not mirrored in the DDA 1995: firstly, the prohibition on unwanted verbal, non-verbal or physical conduct of a sexual nature (under SDA 1975, ss 4A(1)(b)) and secondly, less favourable treatment on the ground of the rejection of unwanted conduct (under1975, ss 4A(1)(c)). Care should be taken when using principles derived from cases based on those additional sections.

(c) office-holders (DDA 1995, s 4D(4));
(d) partners (DDA 1995, s 6A(2));
(e) barristers (DDA 1995, s 7A(4));
(f) advocates (DDA 1995, s 7C(3));
(g) membership of a trade organization (DDA 1995, s 13(3));
(h) an application for a professional or trade qualification (DDA 1995, s 14A2));
(i) practical work experience (DDA 1995, s 14C(2));
(j) members of locally-electable authorities (DDA 1995, s 15B(2)).[6]

Unlawful harassment can be committed after a person's contract of employment has come to an end provided that the harassment arises out of, and is closely connected to, the relevant relationship.[7] **8.06**

C. Conduct for a Reason Related to Disability

Harassment occurs when unwanted conduct is afforded to a person for a reason related to their disability. The question of whether conduct is for a reason related to disability appears at first sight to be a similar question to whether a person was treated less favourably for a reason related to disability under DDA 1995, s 3 A(i).[8] However, unlike disability-related discrimination, no comparator is required in harassment claims because there is no requirement for the purpose or the effect of the unwanted conduct to be less favourable than that which was accorded to others. The tribunal simply has to identify (1) whether there was unwanted conduct and (2) whether the unwanted conduct was afforded for a reason related to disability. **8.07**

1. Causation and Compliance with EC Law

The main distinction between harassment under the DDA 1995 and harassment under other equal opportunities legislation is the requirement for the harassment to be for a 'reason related to' the victim's disability rather than 'on the grounds' of his disability. Despite this difference, the requirement for the 'reason' or the 'grounds' for the treatment to be linked to a protected characteristic (such as sex or race) was common to all the harassment provisions until the SDA 1975 was amended by the Sex Discrimination Act 1975 (Amendment) Regulations 2008.[9] **8.08**

6 The relevant authorities are listed in DDA 1995, s 15A.

7 DDA 1995 s 16A(3). See para 3.115 et seq., for a discussion of DDA 1995, s 16A.

8 See *Mayor v Burgesses of the London Borough of Lewishan v Malcolm* [2008] UKHL 43 which overruled *Clark v TDG Ltd, (t/a Novacold)* [1999] IRLR 318, CA.

9 2008/656. The amendments take effect from 6 April 2008.

8.09 In *R (Equal Opportunities Commission) v Secretary of State for Trade and Industry*[10] Burton J considered whether the harassment provisions in the SDA 1975 were incompatible with the Equal Treatment Directive.[11] The EOC, as it then was, argued that the requirement, in the SDA 1975, for unwanted conduct to be afforded 'on the grounds of' sex narrowed the protection envisaged by the Equal Treatment Directive, which describes harassment as unwanted conduct 'related to' sex. Burton J accepted the EOC's argument that unwanted conduct that both 'related to' sex and that had the degrading purpose or effect would qualify as harassment under the Equal Treatment Directive irrespective of the *reason* for the treatment. The requirement for the conduct to be afforded 'on the grounds of' sex, therefore, imported an element of causation into the test that was not envisaged by the Equal Treatment Directive. Consequently, Burton J held that the harassment provisions of the SDA 1975 should be recast so as to eliminate this issue of causation and to make it compatible with the Equal Treatment Directive.

8.10 Burton J also indicated that the requirement, under the DDA 1995, for conduct to be for a 'reason related to' disability was likely to be incompatible with the Framework Directive for the same reasons.[12] The Framework Directive,[13] like the Equal Treatment Directive, describes harassment as taking the form of unwanted conduct 'related to' disability.[14] The DDA 1995 imported an element of causation into the test that was not anticipated by the Framework Directive.[15] For example, a man who makes office life difficult for a disabled employee might argue that the reason for his behaviour was not related to the claimant's disability but to the fact that he did not want to share his office with anyone: he would have been equally unwelcoming to a non-disabled employee. Even if the man mistreated the claimant by teasing him about his disability he would not be guilty of harassment under the DDA 1995 in the absence of a motive linked to disability.[16]

---

10 [2007] EWHC 483, [2007] ICR 1234, [2007] IRLR 327.

11 Equal Treatment Directive 76/207/EEC.

12 See *Equal Opportunities Commission v Secretary of State for Trade and Industry* [2007] EWHC 483, [2007] ICR 1234, [2007] IRLR 327, per Burton J at para 13.

13 2000/78/EC.

14 Article 2(3) Framework Directive. Note that the Framework Directive requires a person's dignity to be violated *and* the creation of an intimidating, hostile, degrading humiliating or offensive environment. The DDA 1995 is drafted more broadly, since it uses 'or' in place of the italicized 'and' above.

15 Since Burton J's decision in *Equal Opportunities Commission v Secretary of State for Trade and Industry* [2007] IRLR 327 the House of Lords has interpreted the meaning 'of reason related to' in an even narrower way than Burton J anticipated in *Mayor v Burgesses of the London Borough of Lewishan v Malcolm* [2008] UKHL 43. This case overruled the longstanding case of *Clark v TDG Ltd (t/a Novacold)* [1999] IRLR 318, CA. Cf. para 5.03.

16 For similar cases under the SDA 1975 see *Macdonald v Advocate General for Scotland and Pearce v Governing Body of Mayfield Secondary School* [2003] UKHL 24, [2003] IRLR 512 per Lord Nicholls at para 15. See also *Porcelli v Strathclyde Regional Council* [1986] ICR 564, Ct of Session,

The Sex Discrimination Act 1975 (Amendment) Act 2008, s 3 amended the definition of harassment in the SDA 1975[17] by removing 'on the ground of her sex, he engages in unwanted conduct that' and substituting it with 'he engages in unwanted conduct that is related to her sex or that of another person.' If the DDA 1995 was amended in a similar fashion then the fact that disability-related conduct was not afforded for a reason related to disability would not be a defence. Despite the clear indication given in the EOC case that the DDA 1995 does not comply with the Framework Directive in this respect, the government has given no indication that it intends to take any steps to amend the DDA 1995. **8.11**

D. Unwanted Conduct

If conduct is not unwanted the recipient will not be harassed even if the conduct would, ordinarily, be considered harassment. This defence is often relied upon in claims under the SDA 1975 where employers assert that the victim of the harassment did not mind the behaviour in question or, indeed, participated in it. **8.12**

The question of whether conduct is unwanted is clearly an extremely sensitive factual issue. The test is an objective one that takes into account the claimant's state of mind but is not determined by it.[18] *Driskel v Peninsula Business Services*[19] provides helpful guidance on how to approach the difficult question of whether the conduct was unwanted: **8.13**

> ***Driskel v Peninsula Business Services***
> The ultimate judgment...reflects an objective assessment by the tribunal of all the facts. That said, amongst the factors to be considered are the applicant's subjective perception of that which is the subject of complaint and the understanding, motive and intention of the alleged discriminator. Thus, the act complained of may be so obviously detrimental, that is, disadvantageous (see *Insitu*)[20] to the applicant as a woman by intimidating her or undermining her dignity at work, that the lack of any contemporaneous complaint by her is of little or no significance. By contrast she may complain of one or more matters which if taken individually may not objectively signify much, if anything, in terms of detriment. Then a contemporaneous indication of sensitivity on her part becomes obviously material as does the evidence of the alleged discriminator as to his perception. That which in isolation may not

Stewart v Cleveland Guest (Engineering) Ltd [1994] ICR 535, [1994] IRLR 440, EAT and *Brumfitt v Ministry of Defence* [2005] IRLR 4, EAT.

17 SDA 1975, s 4A(1)(a).

18 *Reed and Bull Information Systems Ltd v Stedman* [1999] IRLR 299, EAT and *Snowball v Gardner Merchant* [1987] ICR 719 at 724, [1987] IRLR 397, EAT.

19 [2000] IRLR 151, EAT.

20 *Insitu Cleaning Co Ltd v Heads* [1995] IRLR 4, EAT.

> amount to discriminatory detriment may become such if persisted in notwithstanding objection, vocal or apparent..... By contrast the facts may simply disclose hypersensitivity on the part of the applicant to conduct which was reasonably not perceived by the alleged discriminator as being to her detriment—no finding of discrimination can then follow.[21]

8.14 These principles translate, albeit roughly, into the context of the DDA 1995. Some are, obviously, more relevant than others. The important principle to note is that while the victim's own conduct and perception is relevant to whether the impugned conduct was unwanted, a broad array of other factors will also be relevant.

8.15 Factors such as whether a complaint was made at the time, the duration of the conduct and any contemporaneous indications of sensitivity from the victim are relevant. In the SDA 1975 the fact that a woman participated in talk about sexual matters,[22] or in sexual banter, may be relevant. There does not, however, need to be an explicit rejection of the conduct for it to be unwanted.[23] Conduct may be welcome from one person but not another, and the character of the claimant or of the respondent's employees will influence the tribunal's assessment of how the conduct was received.[24] In many cases the nature of the conduct itself is relevant: generally speaking, the more serious the conduct, the more likely it is that it will be found to be unwanted.

8.16 Horseplay in the workplace, particularly where the claimant joins in or encourages it, can heavily influence a decision as to whether conduct was wanted. In *Jones v ICS Cleaning Services Ltd*[25] the tribunal at first instance found that:

> Hardly a day went by in this workplace without what has been described before us as horseplay. This included men grabbing each others' genitals as a form of greeting; staff being held down, tickled and trousers removed; arm wrestling; mock fighting; writing an 'M' on peoples' foreheads as an indication that they had been 'managed'; spankings with the two foot ruler as a form of punishment 'meant in fun' as well as various kinds of banter. It is difficult to comprehend such behaviour and even more difficult to understand some of its being described only as 'horseplay'.

8.17 The tribunal also found however:

> that the applicant certainly instigated many of the acts complained of and that he himself made unwanted comments to Mr Cutmore as well as attempting to pull down Mr Cutmore's trousers and tickling him.

---

21 [2000] IRLR 151, EAT, per Holland J at para 12.

22 *Snowball v Gardner Merchant* [1987] ICR 318, [1987] IRLR 397, EAT.

23 *Reed & Anor v Stedman* [199] IRLR 299, EAT.

24 *Wileman v Minilec Engineering* [1988] ICR 318, [1988] IRLR 144, EAT.

25 EAT/811/99.

The EAT upheld the tribunal's decision that since the claimant himself had instigated much of the conduct himself, it was not unwanted and he had not suffered a detriment. His claim failed. **8.18**

The question of whether the claimant was a willing participant in the potentially unlawful conduct is one which tribunals should approach with care. Although older SDA 1975 cases such as *Wileman v Minilec Engineering Ltd*[26] (in which the tribunal considered that the claimant's provocative clothing was relevant to whether she had suffered a detriment) have questionable relevance to modern industrial relations, they do serve as reminders that the factual matrix within which harassment occurs is rarely straightforward and can lead to surprising results. Practitioners must not shy away from exploring difficult issues and putting their client's case. Although the authors have yet to come across a DDA 1995 claim in which it has been argued that the impugned conduct was not unwanted, this does not mean that it cannot, or should not, be pleaded if the circumstances require it. **8.19**

E. The Purpose or Effect of the Conduct

Once the unwanted conduct is shown to have been engaged in for a reason related to a person's disability, the claimant must show that it had either the purpose, or the effect, of violating his dignity or creating an intimidating, hostile, degrading, humiliating or offensive environment for him. **8.20**

If the purpose of the conduct was to violate the claimant's dignity or create an intimidating, hostile, degrading, humiliating or offensive environment for him, then the conduct constitutes harassment even if, in fact, the victim was not affected by it. The Code of Practice 2004 gives the example of a man with a learning disability who is called 'stupid' and 'slow' behind his back. The Code of Practice 2004 states that this would probably be harassment because the names were used with the *purpose* of humiliating him.[27] **8.21**

Similarly, a person whose conduct has the effect of violating a person's dignity or creating an intimidating, hostile, degrading, humiliating or offensive environment for him will be guilty of harassment even if he did not intend his actions to have that result. DDA 1995, s 3B(2) states that unwanted conduct shall be regarded as having the *effect* of violating a person's dignity or creating an intimidating, hostile, degrading, humiliating or offensive environment only if, having regard to all the circumstances, including in particular the perception of the **8.22**

---

26 *Wileman v Minilec Engineering* [1988] ICR 318, [1988] IRLR 144, EAT.

27 Code of Practice 2003 para 4.39.

disabled person, it should reasonably be considered as having that effect. This objective test is similar to the test of whether conduct is unwanted: the perception of the victim is taken into account but is not necessarily determinative and the tribunal should undertake a broad factual investigation. Since the test is objective, the tribunal will consider whether a reasonable person, in the position of the claimant, would find that the conduct violates his dignity etc. In *Smith v Vodafone UK Ltd*[28] the claimant was sitting at her desk with a punnet of melons. A manager walked over and stated 'you've got some lovely melons there.' He had made the remark innocently but then realized the connotations of what he had said, became embarrassed and apologized stating 'Oh sorry that did not sound right did it?' Importantly, the manager had never before made innuendoes or engaged in inappropriate behaviour. The tribunal found that, in the circumstances, even if there was a *double entendre*, a reasonable person would not have taken the words as a reference to her bosoms but as a joke in the manner of a seaside postcard or Carry On film pun!

1. Violating a Person's Dignity or Creating an Intimidating, Hostile, Degrading, Humiliating or Offensive Environment

8.23 The DDA 1995 does not require harassment to take any particular form. As shown by cases under the SDA 1975, harrassment may be verbal,[29] written[30] or physical.[31] Any conduct that has the purpose or effect of violating a person's dignity or creating an intimidating, hostile, degrading, humiliating or offensive environment for him will be capable of constituting harassment.

8.24 A person may be subjected to harassment by a number of incidents even if none of the incidents by themselves amounted to harassment.[32] This is because a series of acts which, individually, are innocuous, may constitute harassment when considered in totality.[33] The tribunal should endeavour to make findings of fact about each of the individual incidents before it proceeds to determine whether, taken as a whole, there has been harassment.

8.25 A good example of a course of conduct amounting to harassment is provided by *Green v Deutsche Bank Group Services*.[34] This case was brought under the

[28] *Smith v Vodafone* [2001] UKEAT0564/01.

[29] See *Insitu Cleaning Co Ltd v Heads* [1995] IRLR 4, EATand *(1) Reed and (2) Bull Information Systems Ltd v Stedman* [1999] IRLR 299, EAT.

[30] *HM Prison Service v Salmon* [2001] IRLR 425, EAT.

[31] *Porcelli v Strathclyde Regional Council* [1986] IRLR 134, Ct of Session.

[32] *Reed and Bull Information Systems Ltd v Stedman* [1999] IRLR 299, EAT.

[33] *Driskel v Peninsular Business Services Ltd* [2000] IRLR 151, EAT.

[34] [2006] IRLR 764.

Protection from Harassment Act 1997 but provides a useful example of how individual incidents can accumulate into serious harassment. Ms Green's colleagues ignored her, excluded her from conversations and group activities, burst out laughing when she walked past them, made crude and lewd remarks, removed papers from her desk, hid her post, removed or omitted her name from internal circulation lists and administrative records, and conducted loud conversations close to her chair, making it difficult for her to make or receive telephone calls. One individual in the office conducted a sustained campaign against her in an attempt to raise his own profile as against hers. He attempted to take over her work and undermine her in order to give outsiders the false impression that he was her boss. Although many of the incidents were trivial it was unsurprising, when the totality of the conduct was considered, that the court found that the claimant had been harassed.

Although harassment frequently involves a sustained campaign, a one-off act can **8.26** constitute harassment if it is sufficiently serious.[35] In the context of the SDA 1975, a manager who greeted an employee with the salutation '*Hiya big tits*' found himself in breach of the harassment provisions.[36] A similarly offensive comment about a person's disability would be likely to constitute harassment.

Both the Code of Practice 2004[37] and ACAS' leaflet '*Bullying and Harassment at* **8.27** *Work: a guide for managers and employers*' provide some helpful examples of harassment:

Examples of Conduct Amounting to Harassment provided by ACAS

(a) spreading malicious rumours, or insulting someone by word or behaviour (particularly on the grounds of age, race, sex, disability, sexual orientation and religion or belief);[38]
(b) copying memos that are critical about someone to others who do not need to know;
(c) ridiculing or demeaning someone—picking on them or setting them up to fail;[39]
(d) exclusion or victimization;[40]
(e) unfair treatment;

[35] Contrast this with the position under the Protection from Harassment Act 1997. See para 8.31 below.

[36] *Insitu Cleaning Co Ltd v Heads* [1995] IRLR 4, EAT.

[37] Code of Practice 2004 para 4.39.

[38] *Thomas & Ors v Robinson* [2003] IRLR 7, EAT; *Liversidge v Chief Constable of Bedfordshire* [2002] ICR 1135, [2002] IRLR 651, CA; *Driskel v Peninsula Business Systems* [2000] IRLR 151, EAT; *Chief Constable of the Lincolnshire Police v Stubbs* [1999] ICR 547, [1999] IRLR 81, EAT; *Reed and Bull Information Systems Ltd v Stedman* [1999] IRLR 299, EAT; *Insitu Cleaning Co Ltd v Heads* [1995] IRLR 4, EAT.

[39] *Reed and Bull Information Systems v Stedman* [1999] IRLR 299, EAT.

[40] *Chessington World of Adventures v Reed* [1997] IRLR 556, EAT.

(f) overbearing supervision or other misuse of power or position;
(g) unwelcome sexual advances—touching, standing too close, the display of offensive materials;[41]
(h) making threats or comments about job security without foundation;[42]
(i) deliberately undermining a competent worker by overloading and constant criticism;
(j) preventing individuals progressing by intentionally blocking promotion or training opportunities;
(k) physically assaulting someone.[43]

Examples of Harassment from the Code of Practice 2004 para 4.39

(1) A man with a stammer feels he is being harassed because his manager makes constant jokes about people with speech impairments. He asks his manager to stop doing this, but the manager says he is being 'oversensitive' as he habitually makes jokes in the office about many different sorts of people….
(2) A woman with depression considers that she is being harassed by her manager who constantly asks her if she is feeling alright despite the fact that she has asked him not to do so in front of the rest of the team. This could amount to harassment.

2. Conduct does not have to be Specifically Directed at the Claimant

8.28 The conduct may constitute harassment without being directed at the claimant. This may be either because the purpose of the conduct was to harass the claimant (perhaps by directing it a friend of the claimant) or because the actual effect of the conduct is such that it can be reasonably considered to have that effect regardless of whether it was aimed at him or not.[44]

F. Harassment and Direct Discrimination

8.29 Before harassment became a cause of action in its own right in October 2004, harassment claims were almost inevitably brought as direct discrimination claims based upon the premise that the victim has been subject to a 'detriment' under DDA 1995, s 4(2)(d). This type of harassment claim can no longer be brought as a direct discrimination claim and must be brought under DDA 1995, s 3B because DDA 1995, s 18D has, since October 2004, redefined 'detriment' to

[41] *Moonsar v Fiveways Express Transport* [2005] IRLR 9, EAT, *Porcelli v Strathclyde Regional Council* [1986] IRLR 134, Ct of Session.

[42] *Porcelli v Strathclyde Regional Council* [1986] IRLR 134, Ct of Session.

[43] *Jones v Tower Boot Company* [1997] ICR 254, [1997] IRLR 168, CA; *Bracebridge Engineering Ltd v Darby* [1990] IRLR 3, EAT.

[44] For a similar direct discrimination case see *Garry v London Borough of Ealing* [2001] IRLR 681, CA.

exclude harassment under DDA 1995, s 3B. The most sensible course, in most cases, will be for a claimant to plead harassment as the principal cause of action and direct discrimination in the alternative, and for the tribunal to consider them in that order. Harassment should be considered first to prevent the tribunal exceeding its jurisdiction by finding that the respondent directly discriminated against the claimant by harassing him.

The restriction on the definition of detriment does not apply to DDA 1995, s 16C(2) (the section dealing with giving instructions and placing pressure on people to discriminate)[45] and can, therefore, be brought as either a direct discrimination claim or an harassment claim. **8.30**

G. Protection from Harassment Act 1997

The Protection from Harassment Act 1997 came into force on 16 June 1997. PHA 1997, s 3 provides a civil remedy for anyone who is the subject of actual or apprehended harassment under PHA 1997, s 1. Damages may be claimed for any anxiety caused by, or any financial loss resulting from, the harassment. **8.31**

Section 1 PHA 1997—Protection From Harassment

(1) A person must not pursue a course of conduct—
   (a) which amounts to harassment of another, and
   (b) which he knows or ought to know amounts to harassment of the other.

(2) For the purposes of this section, the person whose course of conduct is in question ought to know that it amounts to harassment of another if a reasonable person in possession of the same information would think the course of conduct amounted to harassment of the other.

(3) Subsection (1) does not apply to a course of conduct if the person who pursued it shows—
   (a) that it was pursued for the purpose of preventing or detecting crime,
   (b) that it was pursued under any enactment or rule of law or to comply with any condition or requirement imposed by any person under any enactment, or
   (c) that in the particular circumstances the pursuit of the course of conduct was reasonable.

Section 7—Interpretation

7(1) This section applies for the interpretation of sections 1 to 5.
(2) References to harassing a person include alarming the person or causing the person distress.
(3) A 'course of conduct' must involve conduct on at least two occasions.
(4) 'Conduct' includes speech.

---

45 It should be noted that only the Disability Rights Commission can bring proceedings under DDA 1995, s 16C.

8.32 There are no restrictions on the persons who may take advantage of the PHA 1997 protection: for instance, the claimant does not have to be an employee and the harassment does not have to have anything to do with the workplace. Harassment under the PHA 1997 comprises three simple elements. Firstly, there must be a course of conduct, secondly, the course of conduct must amount to harassment and finally, the perpetrator must have known (or ought to know have known) that the course of conduct amounts to harassment.

8.33 The case of *Majrowski v Guy's and St Thomas' NHS Trust*[46] confirmed that an employer could be vicariously liable for the actions of employees who breached the PHA 1997 provided that those employees were acting in the course of their employment when the breach occurred.[47] Employees considering a harassment claim under the DDA 1995 should also consider the merits of bringing a claim in the civil courts under the PHA 1997.

1. Course of Conduct

8.34 PHA 1997, s 7 provides that conduct must occur on at least two occasions in order to constitute a 'course of conduct'. This contrasts with the position under the DDA 1995 where a single serious incident can constitute discriminatory harassment.[48]

2. The Meaning of Harassment under the PHA 1997

8.35 The course of conduct must amount to harassment. Harassment is not defined in the PHA 1997, but PHA 1997, s 7 indicates that actions causing a person alarm or distress are included within its scope. Furthermore, PHA 1997, s 7 defines 'conduct' under the PHA 1997 to include speech so that a course of conduct involving alarming or distressing verbal abuse will constitute harassment.

8.36 Action causing alarm or distress is sufficient to found a claim. There is no requirement for the harassment to cause any actual physical or psychiatric injury, but the quality of the harassment must go beyond the irritations, annoyances, even a measure of upset, that arise at times in everybody's day-to-day dealings with other

46 [2005] EWCA Civ 251, [2005] 2 QB 848, [2005] ICR 977, [2005] IRLR 340, CA.

47 The vicarious liability of employers under the DDA 1995 is dealt with in paras 3.166–3.169. There is increasingly little difference between the approach to vicarious liability at common law and under the DDA 1995. An employer will be vicariously liable for the actions of his employees where the torts of the employee 'are so closely connected with his employment that it would be fair and just to hold the employers vicariously liable' *Lister v Hesley Hall Ltd* [2001] ICR 665, HL. See also *Dubai Aluminium Co Limited v Salaam* [2002] UKHL 48 and *Hawley v Luminar Leisure* [2006] EWCA Civ 18.

48 See para 8.26.

people. There is a boundary between conduct which is unattractive, even unreasonable, and conduct which is oppressive and unacceptable.[49] To cross the boundary from the regrettable to the unacceptable, the gravity of the misconduct must be of an order to justify the sanctions of the criminal law under PHA 1997, s 2. Whether the conduct is sufficiently serious depends on the circumstances of the case; what might be harassment in the hospital ward may not be harassment on the factory floor or in the barrack room and vice versa.[50]

There is no requirement, under the PHA 1997, that the course of conduct be undertaken for any particular reason or related to any particular grounds such as disability but it must be directed at the victim.[51] **8.37**

3. Perpetrator Knows or Should Know that Conduct is Harassment

The final element of the test of harassment under the PHA 1997 is that the person must have known (or ought to have known) that his conduct amounted to harassment. PHA 1997, s 1(2) makes it quite clear that the test for whether a person ought to have known that his conduct would amount to harassment is an objective one. If a reasonable person in possession of the same information would have thought that the conduct amounted to harassment then the perpetrator will be guilty even if he did not anticipate the effect of what he was doing. **8.38**

Advantages and Disadvantages of a Claim under the PHA 1997

The advantages of bringing a claim under the PHA 1997 are:

(a) Public funding may be available to bring a claim.
(b) There is no statutory defence to a PHA 1997 claim.[52]
(c) Some of the legal costs of the claim may be recovered if the claimant wins.
(d) It may be possible to apply for injunctive relief, a remedy that is unavailable in the tribunal.
(e) There is no requirement to show that the conduct was afforded for a reason related to the claimant's disability.
(f) The test for whether the claimant experienced alarm or distress is subjective.
(g) The court may award an injunction to prevent harassment.
(h) The limitation period is six years.

49 *Majrowski v Guy's and St Thomas' NHS Trust* [2005] EWCA Civ 251, [2005] 2 QB 848, [2005] ICR 977. [2005] IRLR 340 per Lord Nicholls.

50 *Sunderland City Council v Conn* [2007] EWCA Civ 1492 per Gage LJ at para 12.

51 See *Banks v Ablex Ltd* [2005] EWCA Civ 172.

52 DDA 1995, s 58(5) states that: in proceedings under this Act against any person in respect of an act alleged to have been done by an employee of his, it shall be a defence for that person to prove that he took such steps as were reasonably practicable to prevent the employee from: (a) doing that act; or (b) doing in the course of his employment, acts of that description.

The disadvantages of bringing a claim under the PHA 1997 are:

(a) Costs may be awarded against the losing party under the PHA 1997.
(b) The burden of proof does not shift in a PHA 1997 claim.
(c) It is not possible to combine a PHA 1997 claim with a claim for unfair dismissal in the same action.
(d) No award can be made for injury to feelings short of being a recognised psychiatric illness.
(e) The claimant needs to prove that the offending conduct occurred on at least two occasions.
(f) The conduct needs to be directed at the victim.

9

REMEDIES

A. Statutory Framework

DDA 1995, s 17A(2) provides as follows: **9.01**

> Where an employment tribunal finds that a complaint presented to it under this section is well-founded, it shall take such of the following steps as it considers just and equitable—
> (a) making a declaration as to the rights of the complainant and the respondent in relation to the matters to which the complaint relates;
> (b) ordering the respondent to pay compensation to the complainant;
> (c) recommending that the respondent take, within a specified period, action appearing to the tribunal to be reasonable, in all the circumstances of the case, for the purpose of obviating or reducing the adverse effect on the complainant of any matter to which the complaint relates.

(3) Where a tribunal orders compensation under subsection (2)(b), the amount of the compensation shall be calculated by applying the principles applicable to the calculation of damages claims in tort or (in Scotland) in reparation for breach of statutory duty.
(4) For the avoidance of doubt it is hereby declared that damages in respect of discrimination in a way which is unlawful under this Part may include compensation for injury to feelings whether or not they include compensation under any other head.

9.02 The consideration of what is 'just and equitable' is concerned solely with which, if any, of the three orders to make and a tribunal may determine that it is just and equitable to make no award at all.[1] The tribunal has no power to award an injunction and cannot order reinstatement or re-engagement[2] as a remedy for disability discrimination.

9.03 Once a tribunal determines that it is just and equitable to award compensation, the quantum is determined by applying the principles applicable to the calculation of damages in tort claims in accordance with DDA 1995, 17A(3) and the concept of 'just and equitable' plays no further part in the assessment.[3] This is in contrast to the calculation of unfair dismissal awards under ERA 1996, s 123[4] where the quantum is determined according to justice and equity.

9.04 The statutory cap on the amount of compensation that can be awarded for unfair dismissal[5] does not apply to an action under the DDA 1995 and there is, therefore, no limit to the amount of compensation a tribunal can award.

B. Compensation Awarded in Like Manner to a Claim in Tort

9.05 The loss or damage for which compensation may be awarded in disability discrimination claims includes:

(a) past loss of earnings;
(b) future loss of earnings;
(c) other past and future financial losses including pension losses;
(d) injury to feelings;
(e) personal injury.

---

1 *O'Neill v Governors of St Thomas More Roman Catholic Voluntarily Aided Upper School* [1997] ICR 33 EAT & *Chief Constable of Manchester v Hope* [1999] ICR 338 EAT.

2 ERA 1996, ss 114 and 115 do not apply to claims under the DDA 1995 and there are no equivalent provisions contained in the DDA 1995.

3 *Hurley v Mustoe* [1983] ICR 422, EAT per Browne-Wilkinson J at page 425 paragraph G (this case concerns the very similar provision of the Sex Discrimination Act 1975).

4 ERA 1996, s 123 provides that 'the amount of the compensatory award shall be such amount as the tribunal considers just and equitable in the circumstances having regard to the loss sustained by the complainant in consequence of the dismissal in so far as that loss is attributable to action taken by the employer.'

5 See ERA1996, s 124.

DDA 1995, s 17A(3) requires compensation for disability discrimination to be awarded using the principles applicable to the calculation of damages in tort. Generally, in the law of tort, a person is entitled to be compensated for the loss or damage that he has suffered as a result of the tortious behaviour of another.[6] In so far as is possible, the law attempts to put the victim in the position that he would have been in had the tort not been committed.[7] **9.06**

It is unclear whether the statutory tort of discrimination require losses to be foreseeable before the claimant is compensated for them.[8] In *Essa v Laing Ltd,* [9] a case under the RRA1976, the Court of Appeal held that it was sufficient for the damage to flow directly and naturally from the discrimination. However, practitioners should note that Pill LJ[10] refused to be drawn on whether damages under the DDA 1995 were awarded on the same basis, stating at paragraph 39 that 'it is possible that, where discrimination takes other forms, different considerations will apply.' It is, therefore, unclear whether the principles set out in *Essa v Laing Ltd*[11] apply to cases other than the RRA 1976. Since this point has yet to be the subject of judicial determination, and arguments could legitimately be made either way, respondents may wish to argue that they should only be responsible for foreseeable damage. **9.07**

If all directly attributable losses can be recovered, the eggshell skull rule would not appear to be strictly relevant to the calculation of damages in discrimination cases. Damages will be payable even if no damage was foreseeable, so long as the damage is directly attributable to the unlawful conduct. **9.08**

It is worth emphasizing that, according to the *Essa v Laing Ltd*[12] formula, the link between the losses claimed and the tortious conduct of the employer must be direct. If the direct chain of causation is broken, for instance, where the claimant would in any event have resigned or been lawfully dismissed, then the respondent will not be responsible for the losses.[13] An unlawful termination is unlikely to **9.09**

---

6 See *Livingstone v Raynards Coal Co* (1880) 5 App Cas 25 per Lord Blackburn at p. 39.

7 See, for instance, the obiter dicta of Mr Justice Morison in *Ministry of Defence v Cannock* [1994] IRLR 509, EAT at para 124 and *Ministry of Defence v Wheeler* [1998] IRLR 23, CA.

8 *Essa v Laing Ltd* [2004] ICR 746, [2004] IRLR 313, CA. Lord Justice Rix's dissenting judgment provides a clear and helpful review of the issues. See also *Sheriff v Klyne Tuggs Lowestoft Ltd* [1999] ICR 170, CA.

9 [2004] ICR 746, [2004] IRLR 313, CA.

10 *Essa v Laing Ltd* [2004] ICR 746, [2004] IRLR 313, CA, per Pill LJ at para 32.

11 [2004] ICR 746, [2004] IRLR 313, CA.

12 [2004] ICR 746, [2004] IRLR 313, CA.

13 *Royal Mail Group Plc v Sharma UKEAT/0839/04/ILB; O'Donoghue v Redcar & Cleveland Borough Council* [2001] IRLR 615, CA; *Abbey National Plc v Formoso* [1999] IRLR 222, EAT. For a situation where a claimant was intending to resign in any event see *Ros (t/x Cherry Tree Day Nursery) v Fanstone* UKEAT/0273/07. See also *Gover & Ors v Property Care Ltd* [2006] EWCA Civ 286, CA.

break the chain of causation, since a tortfeasor cannot rely on his own wrong to escape liability.[14]

1. Joint and Several Liability

9.10 Although there is no specific provision in the DDA 1995 giving tribunals power to make a joint and several award,[15] more than one person may be responsible for an act of discrimination under the DDA 1995.[16] In *Ross v (1) Ryanair Limited (2) Stansted Airport Limited*[17], a case under Part III of the DDA 1995, Brooke LJ made a joint award of damages:

> Because a claim founded on unlawful discrimination contrary to the 1995 Act is treated pursuant to section 25(1) [Part III's equivalent of s 17A(3)[18]] in the same way as any other claim in tort, I can see no reason why we should not be able to order contribution as between Ryanair and STAL in the event that we are satisfied that they are both guilty of unlawful discrimination against Mr Ross.[19]

9.11 A joint and several award can be made because the tribunal is required to award compensation in like manner to claims in tort, and tortious principles require the court to attribute the share of blame between the parties according to the extent of their contribution.[20] In *Way v Crouch*[21] the EAT set out guidelines for tribunals considering making a joint and several award.

Guidelines for Making a Joint and Several Award from Way v Crouch

(i) In most cases it will be unnecessary to make a joint and several award of compensation. The present practice in tribunals of apportioning liability (where appropriate) between individual employees and employers works well in practice and does justice to the individual case;

(ii) if a tribunal does wish to make a joint and several award it should set out its reasons for doing so;

(iii) if a tribunal does consider it necessary to make a joint and several award it must have regard to s 2(1) of the Civil Liability (Contribution) Act 1978 which provides:

(1) Subject to Sub-section (3) below in any proceedings for contribution under Section (1) above the amount of the contribution recoverable from any person

---

14 *HM Prison Service v Beart* [2005] IRLR 56, CA.

15 Parties who are jointly liable share a single liability which each party can be held liable for. A party who is severally liable with others may be liable for the whole claim even where judgment has been obtained against the others. See the Glossary of the CPR at section G.

16 See para 3.164 et seq.

17 [2004] EWCA Civ 1751, CA.

18 Compensation under both part II and part III of the DDA 1995 is awarded in like manner to tort.

19 *Ross v (1) Ryanair Limited (2) Stansted Airport Limited* [2004] EWCA Civ 1751 at para 28.

20 See also *Way v Crouch* [2005] ICR 1362, [2005] IRLR 603, EAT; *Knightley v Johns* [1982] 1 ALL ER 851, CA and *Holtby v Brigham and Cowan* [2003] 3 ALL ER 421, CA.

21 [2005] ICR 1362, [2005] IRLR 603, EAT.

shall be such as may be found by the Court to be just and equitable having regard to the extent of that person's responsibility for the damage in question.

(iv) A person's responsibility for an act refers to both the extent to which each tort-feasor caused the damage and to their relative culpability;

(v) it is not permissible to make a joint and several award because of the financial resources of the respondent.

In the rare case when a practitioner needs to consider whether a joint and several award should be made, these guidelines provide a good framework for approaching the subject. The most important consideration is that the responsibility should be apportioned to reflect the relative culpability of the wrongdoers. Since the apportionment of liability is dependent upon fault, the fact that a particular respondent is insolvent or unable to pay compensation is *not* a sufficient reason for making a joint and several award.[22] **9.12**

2. Contributory Conduct

The Law Reform (Contributory Negligence) Act 1945 applies to the DDA 1995 and other discrimination legislation.[23] This means that compensation can be reduced if the claimant's own conduct amounts to negligence (or breach of a legal duty) and this has contributed to his own loss. **9.13**

Ordinary common law principles would also require contributory conduct to be taken into account when considering an award of compensation under the DDA 1995. In *Fife Council v McPhee*[24] the claimant had seriously impaired vision. He kept some money belonging to a client in contravention of his employer's policy. He did not give the client a receipt for the money and filled out a form incorrectly recording that the client did not have any money. He dissembled when his employer asked him about it. The tribunal found, amongst other things, that the claimant was unable to read the respondent's policy on dealing with client money, and that he was not provided with any assistance or with an opportunity to improve. The tribunal therefore found that the respondent had failed to make a reasonable adjustment and that the claimant had been unfairly dismissed. When awarding compensation for unfair dismissed, the tribunal found that the claimant had contributed to his own dismissal and deducted 50 per cent from the award. However, the tribunal did not make a deduction from the award under the DDA 1995. The EAT held that this was wrong and confirmed that deductions can be made from awards under the DDA 1995 for contributors conduct.[25] **9.14**

---

[22] *Rooproy v Rollins Elliot & Anor* [2005] All ER (D), UKEAT/0822/04.

[23] See *Way v Crouch* [2005] ICR 1362, [2005] IRLR 603, EAT at para.11; *Fife Council v McPhee* UKEAT/750/00 and *The Blackpool Fylde And Wyre Society For The Blind v Begg* UKEAT/0035/05/ZT.

[24] *Fife Council v McPhee* EAT/750/00 per Johnstone LJ.

[25] See also *Alexander v Home Office* [1998] ICR 685, [1988] IRLR 190, CA.

C. Compensation for Financial Loss

9.15 Most financial losses in discrimination claims arise from discriminatory dismissals which cause a loss of income. However, financial losses can arise in other ways. For instance, where a disabled person is passed over for promotion, he will lose the income that he would otherwise have received in the more senior role.

9.16 Losses arising from a dismissal include past loss of earnings, future loss of earnings and other past and future financial losses such as pension losses. These are dealt with in turn below.

1. Compensation for Past Financial Loss

9.17 The calculation of past loss is, for the most part, a simple exercise in addition and subtraction. Earnings lost as a result of the discrimination and other losses, such as the cost of seeking new employment, should all be added together to give a figure for total loss. Any benefits, such as earnings received from new employment or savings made through not having to pay for childcare,[26] should be deducted from this total loss figure to arrive at an actual loss.

9.18 The claimant's net weekly wage is normally used to make the calculation.[27] This is because tribunal awards are normally low enough not to be subjected to tax and so an award made on a gross basis would overcompensate the claimant. Where tax is payable on an award, then the award should be grossed up to reflect the fact that tax will be paid.[28] Tax will generally be payable where a tribunal awards more than £30,000 for loss of earnings.[29]

2. Compensation for Future Financial Loss

9.19 In discriminatory dismissal cases where the claimant is unemployed at the time of the remedies hearing, compensation is generally calculated by estimating how long the claimant will be unemployed for, and comparing this with what he would have earned had he remained in employment. Even if the claimant has found work, the loss may continue if his new salary is lower than his old one.

---

26 *Cannock v Ministry of Defence* [1994] IRLR 509, EAT at para 103.

27 *Visa International Services Association v Paul* [2004] IRLR 42, EAT.

28 *Shove v Downs Surgical [1984] 1 All ER 7,* and *Jones v Global Crossing (UK) Telecommunications Ltd [2008] All ER (D) 19.*

29 Income Tax (Earnings and Pension) Act 2003 ss 401 to 403. See the HMRC guide EIM12965—Termination payments and benefits: statutory compensation for discrimination and compensation for hurt feelings.

Future Loss of Earnings

The claimant's loss of earnings will be measured by comparing what he would have earned had the discrimination not occurred, with what he is likely to earn in the future. Other financial losses are calculated in a similar way. **9.20**

Claimants who are still unemployed at the date of the remedy hearing present particular difficulties. The tribunal will not only have to predict what would have happened had the claimant remained in employment but will also have to predict when the claimant will actually find work and what he will earn. This is frequently a difficult and speculative exercise.[30] **9.21**

Forecasting what would have happened had the claimant not been unfairly dismissed is a similar exercise. The significant difference between unfair dismissal and discrimination cases is that when making predictions in an unfair dismissal case the tribunal asks whether *a reasonable employer could* have dismissed the claimant in any event whereas in discrimination claims the tribunal asks what *the actual employer would* have done in the absence of discrimination. The approach to the rest of the factual matrix, and in particular to predicting future earnings, are otherwise very similar in unfair dismissal and discrimination claims. The EAT gave useful guidance in *Kingston Upon Hull City Council v Dunnachie (No.3)*.[31] Although this is an unfair dismissal case the principles are clearly relevant to discrimination.[32] **9.22**

Burton J recommended comparing what he described as Old Job Facts (what would have happened) with New Job Facts (what will happen) in order to determine what the claimant's losses are. Burton J gave the following examples of Old Job Facts and New Job Facts: **9.23**

Old Job Facts

Would the claimant have remained in the job anyway?

- if yes, how long would the claimant have remained in the job?
- how long the claimant would have remained in the job may be dependent on personal factors such as:
  - age;
  - qualifications;
  - skills;
  - experience;
  - personal commitments (that is, childcare);
  - health;

30 See the guidance of Sir John Donaldson in *Norton Tool Co Ltd v Tewson* [1972] ICR 501 at 504.

31 [2003] IRLR 843, EAT. (NB – this is not the more celebrated appeal about whether damages for injury to feelings can be claimed as a result of an unfair dismissal).

32 This was recognised in *Birmingham City Council v Jaddoo* UKEAT/0448/04/LA.

- how long they would have remained in the job may be dependent on economic factors such as:
  - – new technology;
  - – fall-off in orders;
  - – redundancies;
- would the claimant have been promoted?
- would the claimant's earnings have remained stable?
- would the claimant have taken retirement (whether early or otherwise) or considered a second career?

New Job Facts

- the type of work that the claimant can be expected to look for;
- the claimant's prospects on the labour market;
- whether the claimant is able to get a new job;
- the steps the claimant should take/have taken to get a new job;
- what new job is the claimant likely to obtain and when will the claimant obtain it?
- if the claimant has a new job:
  - – how does the rate of pay in the new job compare with the old job?
  - – would he stay in that job or change to one that is better paid?
  - – would the claimant have been promoted?
  - – would the earnings in the new job be stable or would they improve?

9.24 Burton J's factors are certainly not intended to be exhaustive, and any other factors that might affect the claimant's predicted earnings in either his new or old job will be relevant. Burton J also recognized[33] the probability that a tribunal may not arrive at one single annual figure for estimated loss: it may consider that there would be a reducing figure or a single figure for a first period of one or two years and then a lower figure in respect of later periods.

9.25 The personal characteristics of the claimant are an essential factor in any attempt to make an accurate forecast of his future losses.[34] Qualifications, immigration status, experience, age and state of health can all influence both how long a person would have remained in employment (Old Job Fact) and how quickly he might find work (New Job Fact). For instance, a highly motivated employee living in London who has outstanding qualifications and who has rarely been out of work will not be able to claim as long a period of loss as a manual worker from a small town whose steel factory has just closed. On the other hand, a claimant

[33] At para 29.

[34] *Fougere v Phoenix Motor Co Ltd* [1976] IRLR 259, EAT.

seeking low paid manual work is generally likely to find employment more quickly than a person seeking work in a particular field or specialism.

Tribunals have recognized the particular difficulties facing older people in the workplace and that some older people may not find work again.[35] **9.26**

Disability discrimination cases have resulted in some of the highest level of awards for future loss of earnings. This reflects the reality that disabled people frequently face difficulties in finding work if they are forced back onto the labour market. This was recognized even before the DDA 1995 was introduced. In *Brittains Aborfield Ltd v Van Uden*[36] the fact that a visually impaired employee was disadvantaged in the job market was taken into account when quantifying the claimant's compensation for unfair dismissal. **9.27**

The state of the job market itself may also affect how easy it is to find work. In *Barrell Plating and Phosphating Co Ltd v Danks*[37] the area where the claimant lived was suffering from 20 per cent unemployment. The claimant received substantial compensation for future loss of earnings to reflect the likelihood that he would be out of work for some time. **9.28**

Tribunals can be reluctant to accept that there will be significant periods of unemployment. If a claimant is likely to be out of the labour market for a considerable period of time, the parties should consider instructing an expert[38] to provide his opinion on how long it might take for a person with the claimant's characteristics to find new work.[39] **9.29**

Once the predicted future earnings are identified, there are essentially two methods of making the calculation. The first method is to use a rough and ready calculation based upon a weekly wage. We will call this first method the Normal Method as it is the most frequently used. The second method is to perform a calculation using the Ogden Tables. The Ogden Tables are actuarial tables used to calculate losses in personal injuries cl aims. **9.30**

---

35 *Isle of Wight Tourist Board v Coombes* [1976] IRLR 413, EAT.

36 [1977] ICR 211, EAT.

37 [1976] IRLR 262, EAT.

38 For instance, a medical expert may be able to comment on whether (or for how long) a claimant's health might affect his ability to work, or an employment expert may be able, using his knowledge of market conditions, to comment on what jobs the claimant could perform and on the prospects of the claimant securing such a job.

39 Where the claimant is as young as 31 or 32, tribunals will exercise great caution before drawing any conclusions that a loss will be lifelong; *Kingston Upon Hull City Council v Dunnachie* (No.3) [2003] IRLR 843, EAT at paras 28 to 34.

Normal Method of Calculation

9.31 Once the tribunal has determined what the claimant would have earned but for the discrimination and predicted what the claimant will actually earn, the calculations are relatively straightforward. The actual earnings are simply subtracted from what the earnings would have been. The comparison of earnings is normally made using weekly pay. Any pay rises, even if not contractual, should be taken into account[40] as should any commissions or bonus payments. As with past loss of earnings, the tribunal will normally award the claimant his loss of earnings on a net basis for the requisite period. If an award of compensation for loss of earnings is greater than £30,000, tax will be payable and so the figures should be grossed up.

9.32 Where it is difficult to identify whether any particular event might have occurred but for the discrimination, the tribunal should *not* make a finding on the balance of probabilities. Instead, the award of damages should reflect the percentage chance that particular events might occur. The tribunal should (a) assess the percentage probability that a particular event might occur, (b) calculate damages in accordance with that event occurring and then (c) reduce the figure by the percentage chance that it might not occur.[41]

Using the Ogden Tables

9.33 The Ogden Tables are actuarial tables that are used to calculate loss of earnings in personal injury claims. They should only be used in the tribunal where it has been established using the Old and New Job facts (see paragraph 9.23 above) that there is a career-long period of loss.[42] In *Kingston Upon Hull City Council v Dunnachie (No.3)*[43] Burton J stated at paragraph 28:

> We are entirely satisfied that the Ogden Tables, and any similar such tables which may be devised, should only be relied upon by employment tribunals in relation to the calculation of future loss . . . .so far as concerns loss of remuneration and benefits, if it is sought to be, and once it is, established that there is a prima-facie career-long loss.

9.34 The use of the Ogden Tables should therefore be limited to the most serious cases. If the tables are used, practitioners should bear in mind that they are a tool for the

---

40 *York Trailer Company v Sparks* [1973] IRLR 348, NIRC.

41 *Ministry of Defence v Cannock* [1995] 2 All ER 449. [1994] ICR 918 at 951, [1994] IRLR 509, EAT paras 133–134. See also *Vento v Chief Constable of West Yorkshire Police (No.2)* 2003 IRLR 102, CA; *Kingston Upon Hull City Council v Dunnachie (No.3)* [2003] IRLR 843, EAT and *Council of City of Sunderland v Newsome* EAT/36/02/ST.

42 In *Ministry of Defence v Cannock* [1995] 2 All ER 449, [1994] ICR 918 at 954, [1994] IRLR 509, EAT at 524, Morison J indicated that it was appropriate to use the Ogden tables in the same way that they are used in the civil courts. See also *Vento v Chief Constable of West Yorkshire Police (No.2)* 2003 IRLR 102, CA at para 32.

43 [2003] IRLR 843, EAT.

accurate calculation of a discount for accelerated payment and for the general risk of mortality.[44] The tables do not reflect risks other than mortality, such as the risk that the claimant might have lost his job anyway. Deductions should be made to reflect these risks.[45]

Accelerated Receipt

In cases where the Ogden Tables are not used, account should be taken of the fact that the claimant is receiving the benefit of compensation immediately for losses forecast to occur in the future. Take, for instance, a claimant who would have earned £50,000 over five years but is awarded £50,000 at the remedy hearing. Rather than having to wait for the money to be paid monthly over the five years, he is able to invest the money straight away. A reduction for accelerated receipt is designed to prevent this betterment by reducing the compensatory award by a figure representing the annual yield of the £50,000 should it be invested. If the compensation is a very small figure then this process is an unnecessary complication and no deduction should be made.[46] **9.35**

In personal injury claims the current deduction rate is provided by the Damages Act 1996 and stands at 2.5 per cent annually. This figure for deduction has frequently been used by tribunals.[47] **9.36**

3. Other Financial Losses

Employees can receive their remuneration in a wide variety of ways. When calculating a claimant's losses, care should be taken to include claims for fringe benefits and other financial remuneration such as bonuses. The list below is a non-exhaustive list of some of the benefits that employers offer: **9.37**

(a) accommodation;
(b) cheap or free canteen meals;
(c) childcare for children aged under 18;
(d) childcare vouchers;
(e) computer equipment;

---

44 Although the explanatory notes to the Ogden Tables discuss contingencies other than mortality, the tables themselves do not. For detailed instructions on how to use the Ogden Tables see P Barrie Personal Injury Law (2nd edn, OUP, 2005).

45 See further the guidance of Sir John Donaldson in *Norton Tool Co Ltd v Tewson* [1972] ICR 501 at 504. See also *Chagger v Abbey National and Hopkins*, UK EAT/0041/08/RN.

46 *Bentwood Bros (Manchester) Ltd v Shepherd* [2003] EWCA Civ 380; [2003] ICR 1000; [2003] IRLR 364.

47 See *Melia v Magna Kansei Ltd* [2005] ICR 874, CA and *Bentwood Bros (Manchester) Ltd v Shepherd* [2003] EWCA Civ 380; [2003] ICR 1000; [2003] IRLR 364. In the context of the Ogden Tables see *Kingston Upon Hull City Council v Dunnachie (No.3)* [2003] IRLR 843, EAT.

(f) contributions into an approved pension scheme;
(g) discounted services such as dry cleaning;
(h) financial planning;
(i) free banking/loan facilities;
(j) charitable contributions;
(k) telephone packages;
(l) in-house sports facilities;
(m) insurance (medical, life, legal etc.);
(n) luncheon vouchers;
(o) private health care;
(p) private medical insurance;
(q) private use of a vehicle;
(r) share schemes;
(s) travel insurance;
(t) parking;
(u) subsidies for transport.

9.38 In addition to losing fringe financial benefits, employees may also have incurred expenses as a result of the discrimination such as the cost of attending an interview for a new job or paying for retraining. In *AON Training Ltd & Anor v Dore*,[48] a claimant with dyslexia who succeeded in a disability discrimination claim took out a bank loan of £48,122 in order to finance a new business. The Court of Appeal held that damages in these circumstances should be calculated as follows:

(a) first, calculate what sum represents the claimant's loss of remuneration;
(b) then consider the costs incurred in mitigating the loss and, if reasonably incurred, add this to the loss;
(c) deduct the earnings from the new business from the total of (a) and (b).

9.39 Although it was permissible when calculating damages to take into account the interest of £10,688 that the claimant had paid on the loan, the court of Appeal held that the tribunal had erred by failing to take into account the remuneration he had lost as a result of the discrimination and the earnings he had received from the new business.

D. Compensation for Injury to Feelings

9.40 DDA 1995, s17A(4) provides that compensation for discrimination may include compensation for injury to feelings. It is impossible to place a financial value on

48 [2005] IRLR 891, CA.

an award for injury to feelings and as a result, tribunals have developed a general approach to the valuation of injury to feelings. They retain a very broad discretion to award the amount that they consider to be appropriate and an appeal court will only interfere with the tribunal's assessments of damages where it has reached a wholly erroneous estimate of the damage suffered.[49]

Even though an award for injury to feelings is almost inevitable in most discrimination cases,[50] claimants must still prove that they have suffered an injury[51] and that the injury was caused by the discrimination.[52] In most cases, once the discrimination is proved, this will simply entail the claimant giving evidence about the hurt he has suffered to his feelings in his witness statement. **9.41**

In *HM Prison Service v Johnson*[53] Smith J summarized the principles relevant to quantifying the injury to feelings award: **9.42**

> **Principles Relevant to Assessing Compensation for Injury to Feelings**
>
> (i) Awards for injury to feelings are compensatory. They should be just to both parties. They should fully compensate without punishing the tortfeasor. Feelings of indignation at the tortfeasor's conduct should not be allowed to inflate the award.
>
> (ii) Awards should not be too low, as that would diminish respect for the policy of the anti-discrimination legislation. Society has condemned discrimination and awards must ensure that it is seen to be wrong. On the other hand, awards should be restrained, as excessive awards could . . . be seen as a way to 'untaxed riches'.[54]
>
> (iii) Awards should bear some broad general similarity to the range of awards in personal injury cases. We do not think this should be done by reference to any particular type of personal injury award; rather to the whole range of such awards.
>
> (iv) In exercising their discretion in assessing a sum, tribunals should remind themselves of the value in everyday life of the sum they have in mind. This may be done by reference to purchasing power or to earnings.
>
> (v) Finally, tribunals should bear in mind Sir Thomas Bingham's reference to the need for public respect for the level of awards made.

This approach has been refined in *Vento v Chief Constable of West Yorkshire Police*[55] which suggests three broad bands of awards, similar to those given for **9.43**

---

49 *Noone v North West Thames Regional Health Authority* [1988] IRLR 195, CA. See also *Martins v Choudhary* [2007] EWCA Civ 1379 per Smith LJ at para 24.

50 See for instance *Murray v Powertech (Scotland) Ltd* [1992] IRLR 257, EAT per Lord Mayfield at para 7.

51 *Ministry of Defence v Cannock* [1994] ICR 918, EAT.

52 *Coleman v Skyrail Oceanic Ltd* [1981] IRLR 398, CA per Lawton LJ at para 13.

53 [1997] ICR 275, [1997] IRLR 162, EAT at para 27.

54 The phrase 'untaxed riches' is taken from Bingham LJ in *Elton John v MGN* [1996] 3 WLR 593.

55 (No.2) [2003] ICR 318, [2003] IRLR 102, CA.

injuries in the JSB Guidelines.[56] These bands have been adopted by both tribunals and practitioners as parameters which should be used to calculate awards for injury to feelings. The bands are:

(a) £15,000 to £25,000 for the most serious cases;
(b) £5,000 to £15,000 for serious cases;
(c) £500 to £5,000 for less serious cases.

9.44 Mummery LJ warned that awards of less than £500 were likely to be regarded as too low to constitute proper recognition of injury to feelings[57] and in *Purves v Joydisc Ltd,* the Scottish Court of Session regarded £750 as the very minimum award for injury to feelings that were not 'de minimis'.[58]

9.45 The decision in *Vento* was handed down on 20 December 2002 so these brackets should be adjusted for inflation.

Of course, these figures are for guidance only. Even in *Vento,* Mummery LJ indicated that in the most exceptional cases an award might exceed the £25,000 that the court had set out.[59] In reality, a tribunal is likely to choose a round figure somewhere in the ballpark of where they think the award should lie.

9.46 In *Vento,* Mummery LJ described the most serious cases as those where there was a lengthy campaign of discrimination. Less serious cases were described as isolated or one-off acts of discrimination, and serious cases as those that fell between the most serious and the less serious brackets.

9.47 There is a wide variety of factors that might assist the tribunal to identify which bracket the award should fall into:

whether or not the incident was an isolated one (*Vento v Chief Constable of West Yorkshire Police (No.2)* [2003] ICR 318, [2003] IRLR 102 and *Crofton v Yeboah* [2002] IRLR 634);

the seriousness of the incident/s and whether it was deliberate (*Voith Turbo Ltd v Stowe* [2005] IRLR 228 and *Moything v Barts NHS Trust* [2006] IRLR 860);

the nature of the employment *(Orlando v Didcot Power Station Sports and Social Club* [1996] IRLR 262);

---

56 The court considered that the JSB Guidelines should be examined alongside its own guidance.

57 See *Ministry of Defence v Anderson* [1996] IRLR 139, EAT in which an award of £250 was found to be perverse.

58 [2003] IRLR 420, Ct of Session.

59 At para 65.

the willingness of the respondent to own up to admit that it has breached the discrimination legislation *(Orlando v Didcot Power Station Sports and Social Club* [1996] IRLR 262);

where the discrimination affected the health of the claimant's unborn child *(Miles v Gillbank* [2006 EWCA Civ 543, [2006] IRLR 538);

the loss of congenial employment (*Ministry of Defence v Cannock* [1994] ICR 918 and *Alexander v Home Office* [1988] IRLR 190);

the manner in which the respondent dealt with the claimant's grievances, discipline or tribunal claim (*Orlando v Didcot Power Station Sports and Social Club* [1996] IRLR 262);

the claimant's personal characteristics (if, for instance, a claimant is particularly vulnerable it is more likely that he would have suffered a greater injury);

whether the discrimination was personally directed at the claimant (*Moyhing v Barts London NHS Trust* [2006] IRLR 860).

Since an award of injury to feelings is an assessment of the injury caused to the claimant, no *Polkey* type deductions should be made. Furthermore, no tax is payable on awards for injury to feelings and so no deductions should be made to take tax into account.[60] **9.48**

Where there are multiple instances of discrimination, the tribunal, while having regard to the overall total, should consider each instance of discrimination separately. Although it is not wrong to award a single sum for injury to feelings, the tribunal must make it clear how it arrived at the total figure and how much each instance of discrimination contributed to it.[61] For instance, in a disability discrimination case the tribunal may award a global figure for injury to feelings but must make it clear what contribution direct discrimination made to it and what contribution a failure to make reasonable adjustments made to it.[62] **9.49**

1. Indirect Discrimination and Injury to Feelings

In other areas of discrimination there is a distinction between an award for damages in cases of indirect discrimination, and damages in cases of direct discrimination. Although the duty to make adjustments is the DDA 1995's equivalent of indirect discrimination, the DDA 1995 makes no distinction between awards of damages for a breach of the duty to make adjustments and awards in direct discrimination cases. **9.50**

60 *Orthet Ltd v Vince-Cain* [2005] ICR 374, EAT.

61 *Al Jumard v Clywd Leisure Ltd & Ors* UKEAT/0334/07/ZT [2008] IRLR 345, EAT.

62 *Al Jumard v Clywd Leisure Ltd & Ors* UKEAT/0334/07/ZT [2008] IRLR 345, EAT per Elias J at para 54.

9.51 In *Instant Muscle v Kharwaja*[63] the claimant, in order to join colleagues during their breaks, was forced to crawl into a communal area and sit on the floor because the employers had not taken the simple expedient of fitting a wheelchair ramp. The tribunal awarded the claimant £6,000 but the EAT held that this was manifestly too high and substituted an award of £2,500! Richardson J stated that it would be rare for an award for injury to feelings in a disability discrimination case to fall within the top band of *Vento* awards.

9.52 By confining significant awards to cases of harassment, Richardson J also appears to suggest in Instant Muscle that there is a link between significant injury to feelings and direct or intentional discrimination.[64] The author's submit that any assumption that a failure to make adjustments is incapable of giving rise to serious injury to feelings is clearly incorrect.[65] While in other areas of discrimination[66] an award of compensation will not generally be made for unintentional indirect discrimination, the DDA 1995 makes no such distinction. This is consistent with the fact that it can be equally hurtful or humiliating for a disabled person to have to struggle with a PCP that puts him at a substantial disadvantage as it is for a disabled person to suffer direct discrimination.

E. Aggravated Damages

9.53 **Principles Relevant to Awarding Aggravated Damages**[67]

(i) Aggravated compensation may be awarded in a discrimination case;
(ii) aggravated damages may only be awarded in a case in which it is established that the discriminator has acted in a high handed, malicious, insulting or oppressive manner;
(iii) while any discrimination is offensive and regrettable and may potentially be very distressing the fact that there has been discrimination and that the victim has been upset or distressed or even injured in his health as a result of the discrimination is not of itself enough;

63 UKEAT/0216/03/ILB.

64 See *Instant Muscle v Kharwaja* UKEAT/0216/03/KB, EAT, at paras 18–20. A similar comment was made by Elias J in *Al Jumard v Clywd Leisure Ltd & Ors* UKEAT/0344/07/ZT, [2008] IRLR 345, EAT at para 50: 'a deliberate act of race discrimination may quite understandably cause greater injury to feelings than, say, a thoughtless failure to make an adjustment under the Disability Discrimination Act.'

65 It is also questionable whether Richardson J's conclusions that disabled people are rarely subjected to lengthy campaigns of harassment is correct. In January 2005 a joint research report, Improving the Life Chances of Disabled People, published by the Prime Minister's Strategy Unit in association with a number of government departments, found that a quarter of all disabled people said that they had experienced a hate crime or harassment (although this figure rose to 47% of people with mental health conditions).

66 SDA 1975 ss65 & 66, RRA 1976 s 57, RBR 2003 reg 30, SOR 2003 reg 30 and the AR 2006 reg 38.

67 *Singh v University Hospital NHS Trust* UKEAT/1409/01 Per Burke J at para 10.

(iv) if, on the facts of the case, the discriminator has acted in a high handed, malicious, insulting or oppressive manner, the case is one in which aggravated compensation should be awarded;
(v) an award of aggravated compensation may, but need not be, included in the award for injury to feelings. It may be included, it may be separate;
(vi) aggravated damages may be awarded even though the injury to feelings award is in the 'lower category' not the 'higher category' of the two very broad categories described in *Tchoula*;[68]
(vii) an award of aggravated compensation should be compensatory not punitive.

Although, as noted above, aggravated damages are awarded according to whether the employer's behaviour has been high-handed, malicious, insulting or oppressive, aggravated damages should still be compensatory in nature.[69] Aggravated damages should only be awarded to the extent that the aggravating features have increased the impact of the discriminatory act or conduct on the claimant and thus the injury to his feelings.[70] Unlike exemplary damages, aggravated damages are not intended to be punitive.

The following are examples of conduct for which aggravated damages have been awarded: **9.54**

repeated and unmeritorious threats of costs during the conduct of tribunal proceedings (*Zaiwalla & Co v Walia* [2002] IRLR 697);

pre-judging disciplinary proceedings (*Scott v Commissioner of Inland Revenue* [2004] IRLR 713);

failing properly to investigate a claim of discrimination and attributing a claimant's complaints about discrimination as due to defects in his personality (*HM Prison Service v Johnson* [1997] ICR 275, [1997] IRLR 162,EAT);

trying to cover up discriminatory conduct and refusing to admit it in the face of strong evidence (*HM Prison Service v Salmon* [2001] IRLR 425);

waiting an unreasonable length of time before disciplining the perpetrator of the discriminatory act (*HM Prison Service v Salmon* [2001] IRLR 425);

minimizing the seriousness of discriminatory conduct (*HM Prison Service v Salmon* [2001] IRLR 425);

unsatisfactory answers to a statutory discrimination questionnaire (*City of Bradford Metropolitan Council v Arora* [1989] IRLR 442);[71]

68 *ICTS (UK) Ltd v Tchoula* [2000] IRLR 632, EAT.

69 *Alexander v Home Office* [1988] IRLR 190, CA.

70 Per Recorder Underhill QC in *HM Prison Service v Salmon* [2001] IRLR 425, EAT at para 23.

71 NB the decision on exemplary damages was appealed to the Court of Appeal. The decision on aggravated damages in the EAT stands.

promoting the perpetrator of discrimination before determining whether that person was guilty of discrimination *(British Telecommunications plc v Reid* [2004] IRLR 327*);*

(*ICTS (UK) Ltd v Tchoula* [2000] IRLR 643);

making remarks that are particularly insulting or humiliating *(Doshoki v Draeger Ltd.* See also *HM Prison Service v Johnson* and *Martins v Choudhary.*

9.55 There has been a good deal of uncertainty about whether an award of aggravated damages should be made separately to an award of injury to feelings. Initially, the Northern Ireland Court of Appeal, in *McConnell v Police Authority for Northern Ireland*,[72] concluded that a single award should be made for aggravated damages and damages for injury to feelings.[73] Then the EAT in *ICTS v Tchoula*[74] held that it was a matter of form rather than substance whether the award for aggravated damages was expressed as being separate. In *Scott v Commissioner of Inland Revenue*[75] the Court of Appeal held that an award of aggravated damages should be made separately to an award for injury to feelings.[76] Finally, Lady Justice Smith in *Martins v Choudhary*[77] stated that there should not be a hard and fast rule that aggravated damages are awarded separately to an injury to feelings award but that the most satisfactory solution, in a discrimination case, was for the aggravated damages to be reflected in the quantum of damage for injury to feelings.[78]

9.56 Any mitigating conduct of the employer should be taken into account when assessing aggravated damages, including conduct after the discrimination has occurred.[79] Respondents facing a complaint of discrimination should, therefore, make every effort to ensure that their equal opportunities processes are in good order and that they are able to present evidence of their efforts/improved efforts to the tribunal in mitigation.

F. Exemplary Damages

9.57 Exemplary damages can be awarded in discrimination claims.[80] The object of damages in the usual sense of the term is to compensate, whereas the object of

---

72 [1997] IRLR 625, CA.

73 At para 20.

74 [2000] IRLR 643, EAT.

75 [2004] IRLR 713, CA.

76 At paras 34 to 37.

77 [2007] EWCA Civ 1379.

78 See paras 18 and 20.

79 See Smith J in *HM Prison Service v Johnson* [1997] ICR 275, [1997] IRLR 162, EAT (at para. 43).

80 *Kuddus v Chief Constable of Leicestershire Constabulary* [2001] UKHL 29, [2002] AC 122; and *Virgo Fidelis Senior School v Boyle* [2004] ICR 1210, HL.

exemplary damages is to punish and deter. Awards of exemplary damages indicate the strength of the law.[81] Exemplary damages are awarded in order to punish the wrongdoer and can be awarded for behaviour that is:

> oppressive, arbitrary or unconstitutional action by servants of the government;
>
> calculated to make a profit for the wrongdoer that may exceed any compensation payable to the claimant;
>
> expressly authorized by statute.[82]

In *Rookes v Barnard*[83] Lord Devlin set out three factors governing the award of exemplary damages: first, the claimant cannot recover exemplary damages unless he is the victim of the punishable behaviour; second, the power to award exemplary damages constitutes a weapon that should be used with restraint; and third, everything which aggravates or mitigates the defendant's conduct is relevant to an assessment of exemplary damages. **9.58**

An award of exemplary damages will be rare, and practitioners should consider very carefully the advice that they give to a claimant about making a claim for such damages so as not to expose the claimant to any suggestion that the claim is misconceived. **9.59**

G. Reductions and Increases in Compensation

Compensation awards for discrimination can be subject to a number of deductions. No deduction should be made from the award for injury to feelings in a discrimination claim but otherwise deductions can be made: **9.60**

(a) because the employee has contributed to his dismissal;[84]
(b) for accelerated receipt;[85]
(c) for the receipt of state benefits;
(d) for the employee's failure to comply with the statutory dismissal or grievance procedures;
(e) for the employee's failure to mitigate his own loss.

The first two deductions above have already been dealt with—the others are dealt with here. **9.61**

---

81 *Rookes v Barnard* [1964] AC 1129, [1964] 2 WLR 269, HL, per Lord Devlin at page 328.
82 *Rookes v Barnard* [1964] AC 1129, [1964] 2 WLR 269, HL.
83 *Rookes v Barnard* [1964] AC 1129, [1964] 2 WLR 269, HL.
84 See para 9.13
85 See para 9.35.

1. State Benefits

9.62 Although the *Employment Protection (Recoupment of Jobseeker's Allowance and Income Support) Regulations 1996* do not apply to awards for discrimination, a claimant who becomes entitled to receive jobseeker's allowance, income support or other state benefit as a result of the discrimination, must give credit for the benefits that he has received when claiming compensation because his loss has been reduced by the receipt of these benefits.[86]

2. Deductions as a Result of the Dispute Resolution Procedures

9.63 Although the statutory procedures will be abolished in April 2009[87] and replaced with a different system, they may affect quantum awards for some time to come.

9.64 The Employment Act 2002 s 31 provides that a tribunal must reduce any award by 10 per cent and may reduce it by 50 per cent where:

(a) the claim concerns a matter to which one of the dispute resolution procedures applies;
(b) the statutory procedure was not completed before the proceedings were begun;

and the non-completion was wholly or mainly attributable to a failure by the employee to comply with a requirement of the procedure or to exercise a right of appeal.

9.65 Conversely, the Employment Act 2002 section 31(3) provides that compensation must be increased where:

> the claim concerns a matter to which one of the statutory procedures applies;
> the statutory procedure was not completed before the proceedings were begun; and

the non-completion was wholly or mainly attributable to failure by the employer to comply with a requirement of the procedure.

9.66 Where either the respondent or the claimant fail to comply with the procedures, unless there are exceptional circumstances, the award must be increased or decreased by at least 10 per cent and may be increased or decreased by as much as 50 per cent.[88] Whether the tribunal will increase or decrease the award by more

---

[86] The reason for this is that the regulations only apply to the payments listed in the schedule to the regulations. Claims of disability discrimination are not included in that schedule.

[87] See para 10.08.

[88] EA 2002 s 31(4) provides that if there are exceptional circumstances the tribunal may exercise its discretion to make an increase or decrease of less than 10%.

than 10 per cent is determined in accordance with what the tribunal thinks is just and equitable and it, therefore, has a very wide discretion.[89]

Although a claimant's failure to follow an appeal procedure will not mean that he has failed to mitigate his loss, it will lead to a reduction in the award of at least 10 per cent and possibly more under EA 2002, s 31(2). **9.67**

3. Mitigation of Loss

Claimants are expected to take reasonable steps to reduce the losses that they have suffered and if they do not, the tribunal may reduce their compensation. This requirement for a claimant to 'mitigate' his loss most often means that the claimant must take steps to look for other work and not simply sit back and wait for compensation. **9.68**

Principles Relevant to Mitigation of Loss[90]

(i) a claimant is required to act in mitigation of his loss as a reasonable man unaffected by the hope of compensation from his former employer;
(ii) the onus is on the wrongdoer to show that the claimant has failed in his duty to mitigate his loss (for example by unreasonably refusing the offer of re-employment);
(iii) the test of unreasonableness is an objective one based on the totality of the evidence;
(iv) in applying that test all the surrounding circumstances should be taken into account including the claimant's state of mind;
(v) the court or tribunal deciding the issue must not be too stringent in its expectations of the injured party.

Although the burden of proof required of claimants is not meant to be too stringent, proving that the claimant has adequately mitigated his or her loss can, in practice, be a real problem. Many claimants do not keep a record of the efforts that they have made to look for work and some make no real attempt to find work, in the expectation that they may receive compensation from the respondent at a later date. **9.69**

The claimant's advisers should remind their clients, at an early stage, that they will need to look for work and to keep a record of all the attempts that they have made. Claimants should keep all the letters that they have sent to, or received from, potential employers. If the claimant has engaged an employment agent to look for work for him, the agent should be asked to provide a list of the employers who **9.70**

[89] See, for instance, *Bainbridge & Ors v Redcar & Cleveland Borough Council (No. 2)* [2007] IRLR 494, CA.

[90] *Wilding v British Telecommunications Plc* [2002] EWCA Civ 349, [2002] ICR 1079, [2002] IRLR 524, CA, at para 37.

have been approached. However, a refusal to take up an offer of re-employment from the respondent is not necessarily unreasonable.[91]

9.71 An employee might, in some circumstances, reasonably mitigate his losses by starting a business on his own account. An employee who does this, may claim not only any loss of earnings resulting from a reduced income, but also the expenses incurred when setting up the business. In *AON Training v Dore*[92] the Court of Appeal accepted a tribunal's finding that a person with a disability such as dyslexia might find it difficult to obtain another appropriate job and that he had, therefore, acted reasonably in starting up his own business.

9.72 A claimant might also reasonably mitigate his loss by undertaking a training course or other further education to assist in a career change or to improve his job prospects.[93] Whether the tribunal will consider this reasonable mitigation will depend on the facts of each individual case. In *Orthet Limited v Vince-Cain*[94] the EAT upheld an award of four years' loss of earnings to a claimant who had reasonably mitigated his loss by electing to attend university and retrain for a different career. Following the reasoning in *AON Training v Dore*,[95] a disabled person having difficulty finding work would have a strong argument that it was reasonable to undertake additional training to improve his prospects.

9.73 It should be noted that a failure to appeal a discriminatory dismissal through the employers' internal appeals procedure cannot, as a matter of law, amount to a failure to mitigate loss.[96]

H. Pension Losses

9.74 Pension losses can be very large, particularly if the claimant is a member of a final salary pension scheme. Calculating the losses can be a difficult process that may require input from a financial expert. A thorough discussion of pension losses is beyond the scope of this work.

9.75 A committee of employment tribunal chairmen and the government actuary have compiled a useful publication, *Compensation for Loss of Pension Rights: Employment tribunals, 3rd Edition* to assist tribunals to calculate pension losses.

---

91 *Wilding v British Telecommunications Plc* [2002] EWCA Civ 349, [2002] ICR 1079, [2002] IRLR 524, CA.

92 [2005] IRLR 835.

93 *Simrad Ltd v Scott* [1997] IRLR 147, EAT (in the context of an unfair dismissal claim). See also *Khanum v IBC Vehicles Ltd* EAT/685/98, *Orthet Limited v Vince-Cain* [2004] IRLR 857, EAT and, EAT *ICTS (UK) Ltd v Tchoula* [2000] ICR 1191, [2000] IRLR 643, EAT.

94 [2004] IRLR 857, EAT.

95 [2005] IRLR 835, CA.

96 *Lock v Connell Estate Agents* [1994] IRLR 444, EAT.

It is not compulsory to use the guidance[97] but it is regarded by most practitioners and tribunals as authoritative. The guidance sets out two approaches that may be adopted. They are called the 'Simplified Approach' and the 'Substantial Loss Approach'.

If a different approach is adopted, the tribunal must explain not only what approach it applied but also why it selected that approach rather than some other approach. The following approach was set out in *Greenhof v Barnsley Metropolitan Borough Council*.[98] **9.76**

Approach to Pensions Calculation set out in Greenhof v Barnsley Metropolitan Borough Council[99]

1. Identify all possible benefits that the employee could obtain under the pension scheme;
2. Set out the terms of the pension relevant to each possible benefit;
3. Consider in respect of each possible benefit first the advantages and disadvantages of applying . . . the 'simplified approach' or the 'the substantial loss approach' and also any other approach that might be considered appropriate by the tribunal or by the parties;
4. Explain why it has adopted a particular approach and rejected any other possible approach;
5. Set out its conclusions and explain the compensation that it has arrived at in respect of each head of claim to allow the parties to identify whether there has been an error.

I. Compensation for Personal Injury

Where a claimant suffers injury to health as a direct consequence of discrimination, he is entitled to be compensated for that injury.[100] This is the equivalent of a general damages award for pain suffering and loss of amenity in the County Court. **9.77**

The vast majority of personal injury claims arising out of discrimination claims are likely to be claims for psychiatric damage. The distinction between injury to feelings and psychiatric damage can sometimes be blurred and in the absence of medical evidence, a tribunal may well make an award for injury to feelings rather than an award for personal injury. **9.78**

---

[97] See *Bingham v Hobourn Engineering Ltd* [1992] IRLR 298, EAT. This booklet can be downloaded from www.employmenttribunal.gov.uk

[98] See *Greenhof v Barnsley Metropolitan Borough Council* UKEAT/0093/06 [2006] IRLR 98, EAT per Silber J at paragraph 19; see also n 55 (NB. there are two unreported cases with this name. This judgment was delivered on 31 May 2006).

[99] *Greenhof v Barnsley Metropolitan Borough Council* UKEAT/0093/06 per Silber J at para 19; see also n 55.

[100] *Sheriff v Klyne Tugs (Lowestoft) Ltd* [1999] ICR 1770, CA.

9.79 The tribunal may make a single award for injury to feelings that includes compensation for psychiatric damage or may make a separate award for psychiatric damage and for injury to feelings. So long as the tribunal makes the basis upon which it is awarding damages clear, it has a considerable discretion to do what it wishes.[101] If tribunals make a separate award for injury to feelings and psychiatric injury they should be careful to avoid double recovery. Since damages are awarded on a tortious basis, the aim is not to improve the claimant's position but to return him to the position that he would have been in but for the tort.

9.80 If the tribunal is awarding compensation for a psychiatric injury, there is no reason to think that the calculation of damages for that injury should be different from that used by county courts dealing with personal injury cases.

9.81 When awarding general damages for psychiatric injury in a personal injury case, regard is normally had to the JSB Guidelines. The eighth edition of the guidelines dealing with psychiatric damage provides:

> **(A) Psychiatric Damage Generally**
>
> The factors to be taken into account in valuing claims of this nature are as follows:
>
> (i) the injured person's ability to cope with life and work;
> (ii) the effect on the injured person's relationships with family, friends and those with whom he or she comes into contact;
> (iii) the extent to which treatment would be successful;
> (iv) future vulnerability;
> (v) prognosis;
> (vi) whether medical help has been sought;
> (vii) (a) whether the injury results from sexual and/or physical abuse and/or breach of trust;
> (b) if so, the nature of the relationship between victim and abuser, the nature of the abuse, its duration and the symptoms caused by it.
>
> (a) ***Severe:*** In these cases the injured person will have marked problems with respect to factors (i) to (iv) above and the prognosis will be very poor.
> £32,000 to £67,200
>
> (b) ***Moderately Severe:*** In these cases there will be significant problems associated with factors (i) to (iv) above but the prognosis will be much more optimistic than in (a) above. While there are awards which support both extremes of this bracket, the majority are somewhere near the middle of the bracket. Cases of work-related stress resulting in a permanent or long-standing disability preventing a return to comparable employment would appear to come within this category.
> £11,200 to £32,000
>
> (c) ***Moderate:*** While there may have been the sort of problems associated with factors (i) to (iv) above there will have been marked improvement by trial and the prognosis will be good.
> £3,450 to £11,200

---

101 *HM Prison Service v Salmon* [2001] IRLR 425, EAT and *Martins v Choudhary* [2007] EWCA Civ 1379, CA, per Smith LJ at paras 18 to 19.

(d) ***Minor:*** The level of the award will take into consideration the length of the period of disability and the extent to which daily activities and sleep were affected. Awards have been made below this bracket in cases of temporary 'anxiety'.
£840 to £3,450

A county court judge would also examine other cases in which comparable injuries have been suffered. Most personal injury practitioners cite their cases from a looseleaf called *Kemp and Kemp.*[102] By comparing the awards made in cases where similar injuries were suffered, and by also having regard to the JSB Guidelines, practitioners should be able to predict what the approximate level of damages should be. **9.82**

If the tribunal considers that the discrimination only caused part of the psychiatric damage, it should award only that percentage of the loss that is attributable to the discrimination.[103] **9.83**

J. Interest

The Employment Tribunals (Interest on Awards in Discrimination Cases) Regulations 1996[104] provides that a tribunal may award interest in discrimination cases. Although there is no automatic right to interest the tribunal must consider awarding of interest even if the claimant does not apply for it.[105] **9.84**

Under Regulation 3, interest is awarded on a simple basis and accrues from day-to-day. The rate at which interest should be awarded is the special account rate.[106] The special account rate from 1 February 2002 has been 6 per cent. **9.85**

No interest can be awarded on future losses.[107] Interest on awards for injury to feelings is awarded from the date of injury.[108] Interest on other awards is frequently calculated from the date halfway between the date of the loss and the date upon which the award is made.[109] **9.86**

---

102 Kemp & Kemp: *The Quantum of Damages* (Sweet & Maxwell, 2005).

103 *HM Prison Service v Salmon* [2001] IRLR 425, EAT.

104 SI 1996 No. 2803.

105 Regulation 2(b).

106 Where the special account rate differs over the period of the loss, the tribunal may, for simplicity, take an average of those rates and use that figure, Regulation 3(2).

107 Reg4(5).

108 Regulation 6(1)(a). See also *Al Jumard v Clwyd Leisure Ltd & Ors* UKEAT/0334/07/ZT, [2008] IRLR 345, EAT in which Elias J remitted the award of interest to the tribunal to reconsider because they appeared to have miscalculated the date from which interest should be awarded (although it should be noted that Elias J stated that he would not have remitted this issue had other more substantial issues not also been remitted).

109 Reg 6(1)(b).

9.87 The tribunal may, if it considers that serious injustice would be caused, award interest on some other basis.[110] It can also make an award of interest at a rate that has been agreed by the parties.[111]

9.88 The tribunal should ignore the fact that interest will be awarded when it is determining the actual size of the award[112] and should, in its statement of reasons, either include a table showing how it has calculated the interest or include a description of the methods it has used.[113]

K. Declarations

9.89 DDA 1995, s 17A(2) provides that if the tribunal considers it just and equitable, it may make an order declaring the rights of the complainant and the respondent in relation to matters to which the complaint relates. Any such declaration will reflect the tribunal's judgment on the issues and the findings of fact.

L. Recommendations

9.90 DDA 1995, s 17A(2) empowers the tribunal to make a recommendation if it considers it just and equitable to do so. The tribunal may recommend that the respondent take, within a specified period, action appearing to the tribunal to be *reasonable*, in all the circumstances of the case, for the purpose of obviating or reducing the adverse affect of any matter to which the complaint relates.

9.91 DDA 1995, s 17A(2) is drafted in a different way to the equivalent provisions contained in the other equal opportunities legislation. SDA 1975, s 65 provides, for instance, that the tribunal may recommend that the respondent take such action as is *practicable* for the purpose of obviating or reducing the adverse affect on the claimant.

9.92 There is little case law on the form that a recommendation may take. In the racial diacrimination case of *British Gas Plc v Sharma* [114] the EAT considered that the tribunal did not have jurisdiction to make a recommendation that the claimant be transferred to the next available open post. The reason the EAT gave was that the RRA 1976 did not allow positive discrimination. Since the duty to make

110 Reg 6(3).

111 Reg 2(2).

112 *Ministry of Defence v Cannock* [1994] ICR 918, [1994] IRLR 509, EAT.

113 Reg 7.

114 [1991] ICR 19, EAT, *Noone v North West Thames Regional Health Authority (No. 2)* [1988] IRLR 530, CA.

reasonable adjustments may, in fact, require the employer to engage in a measure of positive discrimination, this restriction would not appear to apply to the DDA 1995. Indeed, in *Archibald v Fife,*[115] it was held that the DDA 1995 imposed a duty on the employer to transfer the disabled person to a vacant post rather than simply allowing her to apply for it, envisaging exactly the sort of action that *British Gas v Sharma*[116] considered to be unacceptable under the RRA 1976.

The tribunal has a limited power to enforce any recommendations that it makes under DDA 1995, s 17A(5). In the event that a recommendation is not complied with, the tribunal may, if it considers it just and equitable, either increase the compensation required to be paid to the complainant in respect of the complaint or, if an order for compensation could previously have been made but was not, order the respondent to pay compensation. **9.93**

M. Case Management of Remedies Hearings

In *Buxton v Equinox Design Ltd*[117] the EAT indicated that the type of informal hearing on remedies that takes place in unfair dismissal cases is not appropriate in discrimination claims where the compensation is uncapped. **9.94**

Morrison J stated that remedies hearings in discrimination cases should be subject to careful judicial management. The tribunal should provide appropriate direction for disclosure and the exchange of witness statements. **9.95**

115 [2004] UKHL 32, [2004] 4 All ER 303, [2004] ICR 954, [2004] IRLR 651.
116 [1991] ICR 19, EAT.
117 [1999] IRLR 158, EAT.

10

PRACTICE AND PROCEDURE IN THE TRIBUNAL

A. Introduction

10.01 Practice and procedure in the modern employment tribunal is increasingly complex. The rules governing procedure in disability discrimination cases are contained in Schedule 1 of the Procedure Regulations.[1] This chapter provides an introduction to some of the more frequently encountered rules of procedure and to some of the important issues that arise in practice in disability cases. It deals with such topics as the statutory dispute resolution procedures, time limits, expert evidence and the burden of proof. A short introduction to procedure in the Employment Appeal Tribunal is also included.

10.02 Tribunals have an overriding objective to deal with cases justly. This requirement was introduced into tribunal procedure for the first time in July 2001[2] following the introduction of the Civil Procedure Rules 1998. The overriding objective must be taken into account when interpreting the rules of procedure discussed in this chapter and when the tribunal exercises any power under those rules.[3]

B. Statutory Disciplinary, Dismissal, and Grievance Procedures

10.03 From October 2004, the EA 2002 together with the Employment Act 2002 (Dispute Resolution) Regulations 2004[4] have prescribed minimum standards of practice for employers dealing with discipline, dismissals and grievances in the workplace. These statutory dispute resolution procedures have had a significant effect on tribunal procedure. If the procedures are not followed, the tribunal may not have jurisdiction to hear the claim.

10.04 The dispute resolution procedures only apply in respect of employees. Their introduction has greatly increased the complexity of tribunal procedure and they

---

[1] The Employment Tribunals (Constitution and Rules of Procedure) Regulations 2004 SI 2004/1861 replaced the Employment Tribunals (Constitution and Rules of Procedure) Regulations 2001 (SI No 2001/1171) and the Employment Tribunals (Constitution and Rules of Procedure) (Scotland) Regulations 2001. The Procedure Regulations therefore unified the regulations across England, Wales and Scotland.

[2] Employment Tribunals (Constitution and Rules of Procedure) Regulations 2001, SI 2001/1170.

[3] The draft Employment Tribunals (Constitution and Rules of Procedure)(Amendment) Regulations 2009 amend the overriding objective so that it is more prescriptive. For example, the tribunal is required to take into account any apparent disparities in the skills of the representatives where it is relevant to the presentation of the case.

[4] SI 2004/752.

have proved so troublesome that they have, as Lady Smith observed in the EAT,[5] 'provoked a sea of negative comment of Pacific rather than Caspian proportions'. The procedures will be repealed in April 2009 by the Employment Act 2008.[6] Despite this, they will remain relevant to cases started before April 2009 and so a general commentary on the statutory procedures and the consequences of not complying with them is given here.

In short, the procedures require employers to follow the disciplinary and dismissal procedure ("DDP") before dismissing employees or subjecting them to relevant disciplinary action and they require employees to follow the grievance procedures before bringing any disability discrimination claim other than a claim concerning a discriminatory dismissal.[7] Both parties must co-operate in the grievance or disciplinary processes. **10.05**

The requirements of the statutory procedures are minimum standards and an employee may argue, in unfair dismissal proceedings for instance, that the employer should have done more than follow the statutory procedures. However, non-compliance with the minimum standards is not a free-standing cause of action[8] and the statutory procedures are not incorporated into the employee's contract of employment. A failure to follow the statutory procedures can never result in an automatic finding that the dismissal was discriminatory. Instead, a failure to comply with the statutory procedures has a number of consequences, of which the three most important are: **10.06**

(a) the tribunal may not have jurisdiction to deal with a complaint if the employee has failed to comply with Step 1 of the grievance procedure;
(b) the tribunal may, provided that the employee has the requisite length of service, find that the dismissal was automatically unfair if the DDP has not been complied with;
(c) compensation can be increased or decreased if either party has failed to comply with the procedures.

Another significant consequence of the statutory procedures is that they can extend time for the presentation of claims.[9] Following the introduction of the Employment Act 2008, time limits will no longer be extended after **10.07**

---

[5] *Clyde Valley Housing Association Ltd v MacAuley*, UKEATS/0045/07/MT.

[6] See below at para 10.08.

[7] The grievance procedure must be followed before bringing any of the claims listed in Schedule 4 of the EA 2002. In *Lawrence v HM Prison Service* [2007] IRLR 468, EAT, the EAT held that the grievance procedures did not apply to a dismissal under the DDA 1995. See also *Otaiku v Rotherham Primary Care NHS Trúst*, [2007] All ER (D) 134, EAT.

[8] *Scott-Davies v Redgate Medical Services* [2007] ICR 348, EAT.

[9] See para. 10.29.

April 2009 and careful attention will need to be paid to limitation periods during the transitional period.

C. The New ACAS Disciplinary and Grievance Procedures

10.08 The Employment Act 2008 replaces the statutory procedures with a new and simpler system of dispute resolution from April 2009. This new system will give the tribunal power to increase or reduce compensation by up to 25 per cent where a party fails, unreasonably, to comply with any relevant statutory code of practice.[10] The concept of an automatically unfair dismissal because of a failure to follow a procedure is abolished, time limits will no longer be extended and the statutory reversal of *Polkey v AE Dayton Services* will, itself, be reversed.[11] These new procedures will therefore have relatively little impact on tribunal procedure.

10.09 The discretion to increase or reduce compensation will apply to DDA 1995, s 17A.[12] It will, therefore, be important to observe any relevant codes of practice in circumstances which might give rise to a disability discrimination claim.

10.10 A 'relevant code of practice' is defined as one issued under chapter III of TULRA 1992.[13] This definition is intended to refer to the ACAS Code on discipline and grievance, a draft of which was published on 2 May 2008.[14] The ACAS Code will come into effect at the same time as the Employment Act 2008. For the purposes of determining whether to increase or decrease compensation, only those parts of the ACAS Code relating to 'procedures to be followed for the resolution of disputes' qualify as a 'relevant code of practice'.[15]

10.11 The ACAS Code contains a section on discipline, a section on grievance, and a section on a worker's right to be accompanied. It sets out a broad outline of

---

10 Employment Act 2008, s 3 inserts a new s 207A into TULRA 1992. The new s 207A gives tribunals power to increase an award of compensation following an unreasonable failure to comply with a code of practice in respect of any of the jurisdictions listed in sch A2.

11 *Polkey v A E Dayton Services* [1988] AC 344, [1987] IRLR 503, CA. Section 98A provides that a failure to follow a procedure in respect of a dismissal will not, by itself, make a dismissal unfair if the employer can show that he would have dismissed the employee even had he followed the procedure.

12 The discretion to increase or reduce compensation applies to those claims listed in TULRA 1992 sch 2A.

13 See the proposed TULRA 1992, s 207A(4). Practitioners should note that the Code of Practice 2004 was not issued under TULRA 1992, and so does *not* qualify as a 'relevant code of practice'.

14 See <http://www.acas.org.uk>.

15 TULRA 1992, s 207A(1) to (4).

the approach employers should take towards handling disciplinary and grievance procedures and contains 9 core principles of reasonable behaviour that ACAS states are important when dealing with employees fairly:

> Use procedures primarily to help and encourage employees to improve rather than just as a way of imposing a punishment.
>
> Inform the employee of the complaint against them, and provide them with an opportunity to state their case before decisions are reached.
>
> Allow employees to be accompanied at disciplinary meetings.
>
> Make sure that disciplinary action is not taken until the facts of the case have been established and that the action is reasonable in the circumstances.
>
> Never dismiss an employee for a first disciplinary offence, unless it is case of gross misconduct.
>
> Give the employee a written explanation for any disciplinary action taken and make sure they know what improvement is expected.
>
> Give the employee an opportunity to appeal.
>
> Deal with issues as thoroughly and promptly as possible.
>
> Act consistently.

The annex to the ACAS Code sets out a three-stage disciplinary and grievance procedure. The procedures are straightforward and copies of them can be found on the ACAS website.[16] **10.12**

D. Time Limits

1. Introduction

Applications to an employment tribunal must be served within the time limit prescribed by the particular statutory provision under which the application is made. If a claim formc (ET1) is not served within that time limit, the tribunal will not have jurisdiction to hear the claim. Time limits are short and most claims, including disability discrimination and unfair dismissal claims, must be brought within 3 months. **10.13**

Time limits can be enforced with a startling rigour. In one case, a claimant who presented his unfair dismissal claim 9 seconds late was barred from proceeding **10.14**

[16] <http://www.acas.org.uk>.

because it was practicable for him to have filed it on time.[17] One hopes the tribunal clock was very accurate!

10.15 Unlike unfair dismissal claims where time is measured from the effective date of termination, complaints of disability discrimination under Part II of the DDA 1995 must be presented at the tribunal before the end of the period of 3 months from when the act of discrimination occurred.[18] Where the act complained of is a discriminatory dismissal, time starts to run from when the employment ceases after the notice period expires.[19] The date of the act of discrimination is *included* in the calculation of time so, for example, the time limit with respect to a discriminatory act that occurred on 2 April would expire at midnight on 1 July.[20]

10.16 It can sometimes be difficult to identify the date when the act complained of occurred. Where, for instance, the discriminatory act is a decision not to promote a person because he is disabled, time starts to run from the date that the decision was taken and not from the date upon which the claimant became aware of the decision.[21] In some cases, discrimination can continue over a long period of time and in others, such as where there is a discriminatory omission, specific rules govern when time starts to run.

2. Continuing Discrimination

10.17 The question often arises as to whether the client may make a claim in respect of discrimination occurring more than three months before the ET1 was presented. For example, a claimant may have suffered from harassment over a period of years or the employment contract may contain a discriminatory term that has been in force for a long time. In these circumstances DDA 1995, sch 3, Part 1, para 3(3) provides that:

(a) where an unlawful act is attributable to a term in the contract, the act is to be treated as extending throughout the duration of the contract;
(b) any act extending over a period shall be treated as having been done at the end of that period.

---

[17] See the EAT case of *Miller v Community Links Trust Ltd*, UKEAT/0486/07. The test for granting an extension of time in discrimination cases is not as stringent (see para. 10.33).
[18] Sch 3, para 3.
[19] *British Gas Services v McCaull* [2001] IRLR 60, EAT.
[20] *Post Office v Moore* [1981] 1 ICR 623, EAT and *University of Cambridge v Murray* [1993] ICR 460, EAT.
[21] *Virdi v Commissioner of Police of the Metropolis*[2007] IRLR 24, EAT.

Discriminatory Terms in a Contract

Where a term in a contract discriminates against a disabled person, the act of discrimination continues while the contract is in force and so time runs from the point at which the contract *ceases* to have force. It would seem common sense to interpret 'throughout the duration of the contract' as meaning 'while the discriminatory terms were in force' or else one would be allowed to make a claim years after a discriminatory provision of a contract had been removed. However, the authors are not aware of any case determining this particular issue. **10.18**

Acts Extending over a Period

Where there are a series of discrete acts, time starts to run when each act is completed. Where the discrimination can be described as continuing or extending over a period, time starts to run when the last act was completed. The distinction between a series of discrete acts and continuing discrimination can, therefore, be very important since it frequently determines whether or not a claim has been presented in time. Whether the discrimination can be described as a single act extending over a period rather than a series of discrete acts is a difficult question to answer and has given rise to a considerable body of case law.[22] **10.19**

A number of acts, even though discrete, may provide prima facie evidence that there was a continuing act. In *Owusu v London Fire and Civil Defence Authority*,[23] a number of discrete acts demonstrated that the respondent was maintaining a practice which, when followed or applied, excluded Mr Owusu from regrading or promotion.[24] Mummery J drew a distinction between a continuing act and an act with continuing consequences in the following way: **10.20**

> An act does not extend over a period simply because the doing of the act has continuing consequences. A specific decision not to upgrade may be a specific act with continuing consequences. The continuing consequences do not make it a continuing act. On the other hand, an act does extend over a period of time if it takes the form of some policy, rule or practice, in accordance with which decisions are taken

22 *Amies v Inner London Eduation Authority* [1977] ICR 308, EAT; *Calder v James Finlay Corporation* [1989] IRLR 55, EAT; *Barclays Bank Plc v Kapur* [1991] ICR 208, HL; *Clarke v Hampshire Electro-Plating Co Ltd* [1992] ICR 312, EAT; *Owusu v London Fire and Civil Defence Authority* [1995] IRLR 574, EAT; *Sougrin v Haringey Health Authority* [1992] ICR 650, CA; *Littlewoods Organization v Traynor* [1993] IRLR 154, [1993] ICR 154, EAT; *Adekeye v Post Office* [1993] ICR 464, EAT; *Cast v Croydon College* [1998] ICR 500, CA; *Rovenska v General Medical Council* [1998] ICR 85, CA; *Tyagi v BBC World Service* [2001] IRLR 465, CA; *Hendricks v Metropolitan Police Commissioner* [2003] ICR 330, CA; *Relaxion Group Plc v Rhys Harper* [2003] ICR 867, HL; *Lyfar v Brighton and Sussex University Hospitals Trust* [2006] All ER (D) 182, CA; *Tait v Redcar & Cleveland Borough Council* UKEAT/0096/08; *East and North Herefordshire NHS Trust v Fernando* EAT0727/04.

23 [1995] IRLR 574, EAT.

24 See also *Cast v Croydon College* [1998] ICR 500, CA and *Sougrin v Haringey Health Authority* [1992] IRLR 416, CA.

> from time to time. What is continuing is alleged in this case to be a practice which results in consistent decisions discriminatory of Mr Owusu. It would be a matter of evidence for the tribunal as to whether such a practice . . . in fact exists. It may be that, when explanations are given by the respondents, it will be shown that there is no link between one instance and another, no linking practice but a matter of one-off decisions with different explanations which cannot constitute a practice.

10.21 Often, a tribunal will determine that there was a continuing act where a policy, rule, scheme, regime or practice existed. However, it is possible for discrimination to continue in the absence of these factors and so tribunals should not treat their absence as decisive.[25] The tribunal should examine the facts of each case to determine whether a discriminatory policy, rule, scheme, regime or practice existed or whether the incidents were so connected in some other way as to be acts extending over a period.

10.22 Where the continuing consequences arise out of a contractual entitlement, for instance, a lower rate of remuneration, then there may be a continuing act. In *Barclays Bank Plc v Kapur*[26] the House of Lords held that there was a continuing act of discrimination where the bank refused to credit the claimant's service in Africa for the purpose of calculating pensionable service. The pension was part of the employee's overall remuneration and the House of Lords held that where an employee could show that his remuneration was less favourable than that of other employees, the disadvantage would continue throughout the period of employment.

10.23 Discrimination against a job applicant cannot give rise to an act of continuing discrimination[27] because, even if the respondent has a discriminatory policy, there is no actual relationship between the job applicant and the respondent that can be said to be continuing once the application process has been completed.[28]

3. Discriminating Omissions

10.24 DDA 1995, sch 3 s 3(3)(c) provides that a deliberate omission is treated as having been done when the person decided upon it.[29] An omission can only be 'decided upon' if the person has the power to implement the decision. In *Swithland*

---

25 See *Hendricks v Metropolitan Police Commissioner* [2003] ICR 530, [2003] IRLR 95, CA; *Lyfar v Brighton and Sussex University Hospitals Trust* [2006] All ER (D) 182, CA, and *Cast v Croydon College* [1998] ICR 500 [1998] IRLR 318, CA.

26 [1991] ICR 208. Cf. *Sougrin v Haringey Health Authority* [1992] ICR 650 and *Cumbria County Council v Dow & Ors (No. 2)* [2008] IRLR 109.

27 *Tyagi v BBC World Service* [2001] EWCA Civ 549, [2001] IRLR 465, CA.

28 *Tyagi v BBC World Service* [2001] EWCA Civ 549, [2001] IRLR 465, CA.

29 Most other equal opportunities legislation contains identical provisions: for example, SDA 1975 s 76(6), RRA 1976 s 68(7).

Motors Plc v Clarke[30] the claimants were employed by Colmore Depot Ltd which was eventually purchased by the respondent. At the time the respondent decided to purchase Colmore it also decided not to employ the claimants. This was some time before the purchase actually took place and more than three months before the claimants presented their discrimination claims. The claimants claimed that the respondent omitted to offer them employment because it had a policy of discriminating against men. The respondent argued that time started to run from the date when it took the decision not to employ the claimants and that they were, therefore, out of time. The tribunal accepted this argument but the decision was overturned on appeal. The EAT held that an omission could only be decided upon when the person making the decision was in a position actually to implement it. In this case that date was when the respondent assumed control of Colmore's assets after the purchase: this was within three months of the claimants presenting their claims and they were, therefore, within time.

An omission, like an act, can constitute continuing discrimination. In *Littlewoods Organisation Plc v Traynor*[31] the claimant complained about a racist remark made by his supervisor. He raised a grievance at which certain remedial measures were agreed, including transferring his supervisor to a different department. When the claimant returned to work after being sick, the remedial measures had not been implemented and the claimant submitted a complaint of race discrimination. The EAT held that so long as the remedial measures were not actually implemented, the racial discrimination continued and that allowing the situation to continue, amounted to a continuing act. **10.25**

A failure to make an adjustment has been held to be an omission. This can have serious consequences for time limits in reasonable adjustments cases. This issue is discussed in detail at paragraphs 4.64 to 4.72. **10.26**

4. Time Limit for Responding to the ET1

An employer must respond to an ET1 within 28 days. The 28 days is calculated from the date the tribunal sent the form rather than the date the respondent received it[32] and the date the form was sent is excluded from the calculation[33] so, for example, where the respondent receives a blank ET3 from the tribunal, bearing a date stamp of 1 July, it must present the completed ET3 at the tribunal office by midnight 29 July at the latest. **10.27**

30 [1994] ICR 231, EAT.

31 [1993] IRLR 154, EAT.

32 Employment Tribunals (Constitution & Rules etc) Regulations 2004, sch 1, reg 4; see also *Bone v Fabcon Projects Ltd* [2006] 1 ICR 1421, EAT.

33 Employment Tribunals (Constitution & Rules etc) Regulations 2004, reg 15(2).

10.28 A respondent cannot take any part in a case unless it enters a response and the response is accepted.[34]

5. Time Limits and the Dispute Resolution Procedures

10.29 Where either the statutory DDP or Grievance Procedure applies, the time limits may be extended.[35]

10.30 **Where the DDP applies,** time is extended by three months as long as, when the time limit expired without a complaint having been presented, the employee had reasonable grounds for believing that a disciplinary procedure (whether statutory or otherwise) was ongoing.

10.31 **Where the Grievance Procedure applies,** time is extended by three months in the following situations:

(a) where the employee presents the ET1 within time, without having sent a Step 1 grievance letter. The ET1 should be rejected, but time will be extended, one if the employee sends the Step 1 letter within one month of the expiry of the original time limit. The claimant must then resubmit the claim within the extended time limit (Dispute Regulations reg 15(3)(a));
(b) where the employee sent a Step 1 grievance letter within time, the period is extended by three months and the ET1 must be filed within the extended time limit (Dispute Regulations reg 15(3)(b));
(c) where the employee presented his complaint within the normal time limit but did not wait 28 days after sending the Step 1 letter to his employer, time is extended, but the employee must wait the full 28 days before resubmitting the claim (EA 2002 s 32(3));
(d) finally, time is extended where the employee had reasonable grounds for believing, when the time limit expired, that a grievance procedure was being followed in respect of matters that consisted of, or included, the substance of the tribunal complaint (Dispute Regulations reg 15(2)).

10.32 Employees may consequently have up to six months less one day for presenting their claims.[36] So, for example, a person who believes that he has been discriminated against on 2 June, must present his complaint by 1 September to comply with the ordinary time limits. If, however, he has sent a Step 1 grievance letter before the expiry of the normal time limit, the limitation period is automatically extended to 1 December.

---

34 However, see para. 10.103.

35 See reg 15 of the Employment Act 2002 (Dispute Resolution) Regulations 2004.

36 *Joshi v Manchester City Council* UKEAT/0235/07/DA. Time limits in unfair dismissal and discrimination cases are normally calculated as three months minus one day.

6. Extending Time for Filing an ET1

The tribunal may, where either the normal or extended deadline has been missed, extend the time limit for the presentation of claims. The nature of the discretion varies depending on the type of claim being made. 10.33

The tribunal has a broader discretion to extend time in discrimination cases than it does in unfair dismissal cases. Unfair dismissal cases in which a person's disability has made it reasonably impracticable to present a claim on time can, therefore, be relevant to the discretion to extend time in discrimination cases. The 'reasonably practicable' test is discussed here for that reason. 10.34

Extending Time in Unfair Dismissal Claims

In unfair dismissal claims if it was not *reasonably practicable* to present the ET1 on time, the tribunal has a discretion to extend time to allow it to be presented. When exercising its discretion the tribunal will ask two questions: 10.35

(a) was it reasonably practicable to have presented the claim on time and, if not;
(b) by what date would it have been reasonable to have presented the claim?[37]

Although the Court of Appeal has indicated that the discretion to extend time should be given a liberal interpretation in favour of the employee,[38] the reality is that the phrase 'reasonably practicable' provides little room for manoeuvre and time limits are enforced strictly. It is not reasonably practicable to do something only if there is some impediment which reasonably prevents, or interferes with, or inhibits, performance. The impediment may be physical or mental.[39] In *Miller v Community Links Trust Ltd*[40] the claimant's representative pressed the submit button on the tribunal website at 23.59.59 and the ET1 was received 9 seconds late at 00.00.08. The EAT upheld the tribunal's refusal to admit the claim because it had been reasonably practicable for the claim to be presented within time. 10.36

If it was not reasonably practicable for the claimant to have presented his claim on time but he did not bring his claim within a further reasonable period, the tribunal will refuse to grant an extension.[41] A tribunal will only extend time to the date by which it would have been reasonable to have presented the claim. 10.37

---

37 ERA 1996, s 111(2).

38 *Dedman v British Building Engineering Appliances Ltd* [1974] ICR 53, CA.

39 See Brandon LJ in *Wall's Meat Co v Khan* [1979] ICR 52, CA at 60F. In *Palmer and Anor v Southend on Sea Borough Council* (1984) IRLR 119, CA the question whether it was reasonably practicable to present a complaint on time was equated with asking whether it was reasonably feasible to present the claim on time.

40 UKEAT/0486/07.

41 See, for instance, *Cook (James W) & Co (Wivenhoe) Ltd (in liquidation) v Tipper* [1990] IRLR 386, CA.

Reasonable Practicability and Illness and/or Disability

10.38 Where an unfair dismissal claim is presented late on behalf of a claimant who is ill or disabled, consideration should be given to the question whether the illness or disability made it reasonably impracticable to present the claim within time.[42] The cases referred to below are also helpful when applying for, or opposing, an extension of time in discrimination claims.[43]

10.39 A disability is only relevant to the discretion to extend time if it plays a part in making it impracticable for the claimant to present the claim on time. It is up to the person asserting that he is disabled to produce medical evidence of the extent and effect of the disability in order to prove that the disability affected his ability to comply with the time limits.[44]

10.40 Only a serious illness or disability would make it reasonably impracticable to present the claim for a whole three month period.[45] A claimant must be unable to take steps to keep in touch with his representative and be so affected by his illness that he was unable to address his mind to his business affairs or to take the steps that common sense suggested.[46]

10.41 It is unlikely that the person seeking to extend time will be able to prove this degree of incapacity without medical evidence. However, although medical evidence may assume considerable importance, the tribunal is entitled to take into account other matters indicating that the claimant was fit to prepare and present the ET1, such as the way the claimant dealt with an appeal hearing at work during the relevant time[47] or the quality of their correspondence.

10.42 The period during which the disability had its disabling effect can be important. A period of disability towards the beginning of the limitation period is not as

---

[42] The test for extending time in disability discrimination case is discussed below at para 10.33. This passage concerns disabled claimants bringing claims other than disability discrimination, to which the 'reasonably practicable' rule applies such as unfair dismissal.

[43] See also *Mire v Odeon Cinema* [2007] EWCA Civ 979; *Chouafi v London United Busways Ltd* [2006] EWCA Civ 689; *Abbey National Plc v Riddick* EAT 0919/04; *Imperial Tobacco Ltd v Wright* EAT/0369/04; *Shultz v Esso Petroleum Co Ltd* [1999] IRLR 488, CA; *Midland Bank Plc v Samuels* EAT/672/92; *McGee v Perth & Kinross Council* EATS/0046/02.

[44] In *Midlands Bank Plc. v Samuels* EAT 672/92 the claimant was ill with depression and presented her claim one month late in February 1992. She produced evidence to the tribunal from her GP that she was affected by depression in August and September 1991 and that this had affected her memory. The tribunal found that it was reasonably practicable for her to have presented her claim on time. The claimant had failed to produce appropriate medical evidence in support of her application for an extension and the evidence she did produce did not deal with the relevant period of time and was, therefore, inadequate.

[45] See *Midland Bank Plc v Samuels* EAT 672/92 where the EAT expressed the view that it was a 'strong thing' to assert that it was not reasonably practicable to present a claim for an entire three months.

[46] *Midland Bank Plc v Samuels* EAT 672/92.

[47] *Schultz v Esso Petroleum Co Ltd* [1999] IRLR 488, CA.

relevant as an unexpected bout of disability towards the end of the period[48] because the latter is much more likely to prevent the claimant complying with the time limit than the former.

Extending Time in Disability Discrimination Cases

Where the claimant is complaining of disability discrimination but does not present his ET1 in time, the tribunal has a discretion to grant an extension where it is *just and equitable* to do so.[49] This discretion is wider than the discretion to extend time only where it was not reasonably practicable to present the claim on time.[50] **10.43**

The determination of whether it is just and equitable to extend time includes a consideration of the reason for the delay in presenting the claim, the merits of the case[51] and the availability and substance of legal advice. Limitation Act 1980 s 33 provides a useful list of relevant factors[52] and an appropriately amended version of that list was cited in *British Coal Corporation v Keeble*:[53] **10.44**

(a) the length of, and reasons for, the delay;
(b) the extent to which the cogency of the evidence is likely to be affected by the delay;
(c) the extent to which the party sued had co-operated with any requests for information;
(d) the promptness with which the claimant acted once he, or she, knew of the facts giving rise to the cause of action; and
(e) the steps taken by the claimant to obtain appropriate professional advice once he, or she, knew of the possibility of taking action.

These factors are only a guide and it is not mandatory to set them out or even, refer to them.[54] One or other of the factors in the list may be more or less relevant depending on the circumstances of the case and it may be appropriate in some **10.45**

48 *Schultz v Esso Petroleum Co Ltd* [1999] IRLR 488, CA. See also *Agrico v Ireland* EAT 0024/05.

49 DDA 1995, sch 3 para 3(2).

50 The approach to incorrect legal advice provides a good illustration of the difference. A claimant who has missed a deadline in reliance on incorrect legal advice, is unlikely to persuade a tribunal that it was not reasonably practicable to present the claim on time but he may well succeed in arguing that it is just and equitable to extend time: *British Coal Corporation v Keeble* [1997] IRLR 336, EAT and *Chohan v Derby Law Centre* [2004] IRLR 685, EAT. See also *Hutchinson v Westward Television Ltd* [1977] ICR 279, EAT.

51 *Lupetti v Wrens Old House Ltd* [1984] ICR 384, EAT.

52 The list in s 33 Limitation Act 1980 is a list of those factors that a civil court is required to take into account when considering whether to extend time under that Act. See *Chohan v Derby* [2004] IRLR 685, EAT; *British Coal Corporation v Keeble* [1997] IRLR 336, EAT; *Daniel v Homerton Hospital Trust* (9 July 1999, unreported), CA.

53 [1997] IRLR 336, EAT. Confirmed in *Department of Constitutional Affairs v Jones* [2007] EWCA Civ 894, [2008] IRLR 128, CA.

54 *London Borough of Southwark v Afolabi* [2003] EWCA Civ 15 at para. 33.

cases to discount one or more factors if they are irrelevant.[55] The tribunal may also examine the merits of the claim.[56]

10.46 The claimant's reluctance to admit that he has a disability can be a relevant factor when considering the reasons for the delay. In *Department of Constitutional Affairs v Jones*[57] the claimant began to suffer from depression. His evidence to the tribunal was that he had delayed presenting his claim because he was reluctant to acknowledge that he was so mentally ill as to be disabled. The tribunal found that, in the circumstances, it was just and equitable for the time to be extended and the EAT and Court of Appeal rejected the respondent's appeal.

10.47 While taking pains to make it clear that he was not laying down a rule that disabled claimants were entitled to delay as a matter of course, Pill LJ recognized the difficulties time limits pose to disabled claimants. An impairment must generally last for at least 12 months before it qualifies as a disability under the DDA 1995[58] and there may be cases where the 12 month period expires after the claim was brought. Any person with an impairment has, therefore, to predict whether he is likely to come within the definition.[59]

10.48 Claimants who are uncertain about whether they meet the statutory definition of disability should, therefore, seek medical advice as quickly as possible and should make every endeavour to present their claim in time. A claimant who does not seek medical advice may well not be granted an extension of time simply because he was unaware that he was disabled. Even though the DDA 1995 may present particular difficulties, the list of factors set out in the case of *Keeble*[60] should guide the discretion to extend time even if the party's disability has played a role in the time limit being missed.[61]

10.49 A claimant should be wary of applying for an extension on the basis that he did not know whether he was disabled. If he is bringing a reasonable adjustment

---

[55] See *Department of Constitutional Affairs v Jones* [2007] EWCA Civ 894, [2008] IRLR 128 per Pill LJ at para 50.

[56] *Hutchison v Westward Television Ltd* [1977] IRLR 68, EAT, per Phillips J at paragraph 10 and *Anderson v George S Hall Ltd* UKEAT/0631/05/DA per Clarke J at para. 20.

[57] [2008] IRLR 128, CA.

[58] DDA 1995 sch 1 at para 2.

[59] Per Pill L J at para 53.

[60] See para 10.44.

[61] In *Department of Constitutional Affairs v Jones* [2007] EWCA Civ 894, [2008] IRLR 128 the claimant had not sought medical advice but other factors swung the tribunal's decision to extend time in his favour: (a) he was genuinely unwilling to admit that he was disabled, (b) the respondent advanced the date of dismissal and, therefore, the date by which the decision as to his disability had to be made and (c) the respondent disputed that the claimant was disabled (this made it difficult for the respondent to argue that it was unreasonable for the claimant not to acknowledge his disability).

claim, he may find that he has unwittingly bolstered the respondent's knowledge defence.[62]

The authorities referred to above on whether it was reasonably practicable to present an infair dismissal claim in time due to a disability or illness are also highly relevant to the extension of time in disability discrimination cases. If the claimant's disability made it not reasonably practicable to present the claim on time then it will almost certainly be just and equitable to extend time. **10.50**

Extending Time for Filing the ET3

If a response is not presented within the 28 day time limit it will be rejected.[63] A respondent who wishes to make an application to extend time for presenting an ET3 must do so before the time limit expires. Applications to extend time are dealt with under rule 11 of the Procedure Regulations. **10.51**

If the response is presented out of time the judge may enter a default judgment.[64] If the respondent wishes to participate in the proceedings it must seek a review of the default judgment or, if a default judgment has not been entered, of the decision not to accept the ET3. Reviews are dealt with at paragraph 10.103. **10.52**

E. Proving Discrimination

1. Questionnaires

Questionnaires are a statutory procedure by which the claimant can ask the respondent written questions about his treatment and, where relevant, the respondent's treatment of disabled persons generally.[65] Both the questions and responses are admissible as evidence in tribunal proceedings. Questionnaires can be used before lodging an ET1 to help the claimant frame his complaints as accurately as possible. If a respondent does not answer relevant and admissible questions, or the answers are unsatisfactory, the tribunal is entitled to draw, any inference that it considers just and equitable to draw, including an inference that the respondent committed an unlawful act. **10.53**

---

62 A respondent is not under a duty to make a reasonable adjustment if it did not know, and could not reasonably be expected to know, that the claimant was disabled or likely to be disadvantaged by its PCP (see para. 4.139).

63 Procedure Regulations, r 9.

64 Note that when the draft Employment Tribunals (Constitution and Rules of Procedure) (Amendment) Regulations 2009 come into force it will be mandatory to issue default judgments.

65 DDA 1995, s 56(2), (4) and the Disability Discrimination (Questions and Replies) Order 2004.

The Prescribed Forms

10.54 Forms for asking questions are prescribed in the *Disability Discrimination (Questionnaire and Replies) Order 2004*.[66] The standard form for claimants only prescribes two questions: firstly, whether the respondent agrees with the facts outlined in the form and secondly, whether the respondent agrees that he has unlawfully discriminated against the claimant. The form allows the user to insert any additional questions that he wishes to ask. The response form is shorter but mirrors the structure of the claimant's questionnaire.

Time Limits for Serving Questionnaires

10.55 The time limit for serving a questionnaire depends upon whether proceedings have started. If they have not started, the questionnaire must be served within three months of when the act complained of, was done or, if time has been extended under the statutory dispute resolution procedures, within that extended period. If proceedings have started, the questionnaire must be served within 28 days of the date the ET1 was presented. If the questionnaire is not served within 28 days, the claimant must seek the leave of the tribunal and must, if leave is granted, serve it within the period specified by the tribunal.

10.56 Although an inference can be drawn under the questionnaire procedure, whether or not the questions are asked in accordance with the prescribed form,[67] a question is only admissible in evidence if it is served within the prescribed time limit.[68]

Responding to the Questionnaire

Responding to the Questionnaire—S.56(3)

(3) Where the person aggrieved questions the respondent in accordance with forms prescribed by [the Questionnaire Order]—

- (a) the question and any reply by the respondent (whether in accordance with such an order or not), shall be admissible as evidence in any proceedings under Part 2;
- (b) if it appears to the court or tribunal in any such proceedings—
  - (i) that the respondent deliberately, and without reasonable excuse, omitted to reply within the period of eight weeks beginning with the day on which the question was served upon him; or

---

66 This order was enacted under DDA 1995, s 56 which gives the Secretary of State power to devise forms 'by which the person aggrieved may question the respondent on his reasons for doing any relevant act, or on any other matter which is or may be relevant.' Provision is also made for prescribing forms for the response to these questions. DDA 1995, s 56 sets out the consequences of failing to answer the questions contained on the form.

67 DDA 1995, s 56(3).

68 Disability Discrimination (Questionnaire and Replies) Order 2004, reg 4.

(ii) that the respondent's reply is evasive or equivocal,
it may draw any inference which it considers is just and equitable to draw, including an inference that the respondent committed an unlawful act.

The important point to note is that the respondent must reply to the questionnaire within eight weeks of being served the questionnaire. If the respondent fails to reply to the questions or if its answers are evasive or equivocal, then the tribunal may draw any inference from that failure that it considers just and equitable.[69] An inference can be drawn whether, or not, the question was asked on a prescribed form.[70] **10.57**

Although the questionnaire form states that the aggrieved person may ask any questions that they wish, the questions must in fact be relevant. The Secretary of State was only given power to devise a form for questioning the respondent on his reasons for doing any *relevant act* or questions about any other *relevant matter*. In practice, respondents often refuse to answer questions on the grounds that they are irrelevant or oppressive. If the tribunal agrees that the question was irrelevant it should refuse to draw any inference from a lack of response. **10.58**

Questionnaire is not a Statutory Grievance

Regulation 14 of the Employment Act 2002 (Dispute Resolution) Regulations 2004[71] provides that questions to obtain information under DDA 1995, s 56 do not constitute a statement of grievance under the statutory dispute resolution procedures.[72] **10.59**

2. Expert Medical Evidence

Guidance on the procedure to be adopted when using experts was given in *De Keyser Limited v Wilson*[73]. It can be summarized as follows: **10.60**

(a) Expert evidence will not be admitted as a matter of course, and guidance can be drawn from the rules of procedure in civil courts. The evidence should be, and be seen to be, the independent product of the expert, uninfluenced as to form or content by the exigencies of litigation;

---

69 In *Barton v Investec Crosthwaite Securities Ltd* [2003] IRLR 332. The EAT held that the respondent's failure to deal properly with the questionnaire procedure and its unclear and inconsistent replies to the questions that it finally answered, obliged the ET to draw an adverse inference that the respondent had committed an act of discrimination. However, in *D'Silva v NATFHE*, UKEAT/0384/07/LA, the EAT held that such a failiure will not by itself support an inference of discrimination.

70 DDA 1995, s 56(3).

71 SI 2004/752.

72 See also *Horc-Gale v Makers UK Ltd* [2006] ICR 462, IRLR 178, EAT.

73 [2001] IRLR 324, EAT at para 36.

(b) save where one side has already committed itself to the use of its own expert (which is to be avoided in the absence of special circumstances), the joint instruction of a single expert is the preferred course;
(c) if a joint expert is to be instructed, parties should agree who will bear the cost. Although the parties may agree that the tribunal should give an indication at a later date, the tribunal is not bound to do so. The tribunal has no power to award costs beyond the general provisions of Procedure Regulations, r 12;
(d) if a party refuses to share the cost then the other party may instruct its own expert. However, where a party instructs its own expert, the weight of that evidence may be increased by submitting the instructions to the other side for comment;
(e) where a joint expert is used, the tribunal may fix deadlines for the agreement of the identity of the expert and the joint instructions;
(f) any letter of instruction should specify in as much detail as can be given any particular question the expert is to be invited to answer and all more general subjects which he is to be asked to address;
(g) instructions should avoid being partisan or tendentious. Instructions should set out the facts that the expert is being asked to assume, should avoid asking the expert simply to determine the very question being raised and should emphasise the expert's principal and overriding duty to the tribunal rather than the parties;
(h) if the parties fail to agree the identity of the expert or the letter of instruction, the tribunal may relist the matter to assist the parties;
(i) the tribunal may give formal directions that expert evidence be confined to particular issues;
(j) where there is no joint expert, the tribunal should specify a timetable for the disclosure or exchange of expert's reports and for meetings between the experts;
(k) any timetable set by the tribunal may also provide for the parties to ask the experts supplemental questions;
(l) where separate experts are instructed, the tribunal should encourage the experts to meet on a without prejudice basis with a view to their resolving any conflicts between them and where possible, producing a schedule of agreed issues and of points in dispute;
(m) if a party fails without good reason to follow these guidelines and if, in consequence, another party suffers delay or is put to expense which would have been avoided had these guidelines been followed, then the tribunal may wish to consider whether the defaulting party's conduct is so unreasonable that a costs order should be made against him.

10.61 The tribunal's discretion whether to allow expert evidence is broad. The overriding objective is particularly relevant to the decision whether or not to allow expert evidence;[74] it provides that parties must, so far as is practicable, be kept on an equal footing; cases must be dealt with in a way that is proportionate to their complexity or the importance of the issues, must be dealt with expeditiously and fairly, and expense must be saved.

The use of expert evidence in the tribunal should be restricted to that which is reasonably required to resolve the proceedings.[75] In many disability discrimination cases expert evidence is almost inevitably required to resolve the proceedings. Questions, such as whether, but for medical treatment, a disability would affect the claimant's day-to-day activities, can frequently only be answered with the assistance of a medical expert.[76] The EAT has also recognized that disability discrimination cases require careful case management and that if expert evidence cannot be agreed, the tribunal should give consideration to accommodating the medical expert when it is fixing the hearing.[77] **10.62**

Where expert medical evidence is essential to the resolution of a dispute, the claimant can be expected to submit himself for relevant and appropriate medical examination, whether by his own expert, a joint expert or the respondent's expert.[78] A failure to do so may result in his claim being struck out.[79] **10.63**

It is important to remember that the tribunal's function should not be usurped by the expert. In *Vicary v British Telecommunications plc*[80] the EAT warned that it was not for the expert to determine what is a normal day-to-day activity for the purposes of the DDA 1995 or to tell the tribunal whether an impairment was substantial. The medical expert is entitled to provide a relevant prognosis and an opinion on the effect of medication but the tribunal must reserve the legal conclusions to itself. While an expert can, for instance, report his observations of the claimant carrying out activities and comment on the ease with which an activity is performed, the judgment of what constitutes a 'day-to-day' activity or whether the adverse affect identified by the expert is substantial are ultimately matters for the tribunal.[81] **10.64**

---

74 See *De Keyser Limited v Wilson* [2001] IRLR 324, EAT at para 36.

75 This principle is taken from Part 35.1 of the CPR which, although not directly applicable to employment tribunals, provides valuable guidance (see Burke J in *Mid-Devon District Council v Stevenson* [2007] All ER (D) 277, EAT at para. 27) and the guidelines given in *De Keyser Limited v Wilson*[2001] IRLR 324, EAT(see para 10.60).

76 *Woodrup v Southwark LBC* [2002] EWCA Civ 1716, [2003] IRLR 111 CA.

77 *Buxton v Equinox Design Ltd* [1999] IRLR 158, EAT.

78 See *De Keyser Limited v Wilson* [2001] IRLR 324, EAT at para 27.

79 *Hanlon Kirklees Metropolitan Council & Ors* [2004] All ER D 154, EAT. See para 10.72.

80 [1999] IRLR 680. See also *Dunham v Ashford Windows* UKEAT/0915/04/DM, [2005] IRLR 608, EAT.

81 *Vicary v British Telecommunications plc* [1999] IRLR 680, EAT; *De Keyser Limited v Wilson* [2001] IRLR 324, EAT and *Dunham v Ashford Windows* UKEAT/0915/04/DM, [2005] IRLR 608, EAT.

3. Disclosure

10.65 There is no general duty of disclosure in the tribunal. Disclosure normally arises as a result of a direction or order of the tribunal, by request of a party or by agreement.

10.66 A party giving voluntary disclosure is not obliged to disclose all his documents but where voluntary disclosure is provided, the party providing it is under an obligation to ensure that the disclosure is not unfairly selective. The party must be careful not to convey a false or misleading impression to the tribunal or the other party as to the true nature, purport or effect of any disclosed document.[82]

10.67 In addition, tribunals have power to make orders for disclosure. The power extends to ordering any person in Great Britain to disclose, such documents or information to a party as might be ordered by a county court.[83] Disclosure in the county court is governed by Rule 31 of the Civil Procedure Rules and the associated practice direction at CPR 31PD. There are two types of disclosure under the CPR, standard disclosure and specific disclosure. For standard disclosure CPR 31.6 provides that a party must disclose only those documents:

(a) on which he relies; and
(b) which:
    (i) adversely affect his own case; or
    (ii) adversely affect another party's case; or
    (iii) support another party's case; or
(c) which he is required to disclose by a relevant practice direction.

10.68 A document which would lead a person on a train of inquiry which in turn might lead to him discovering material or information that undermines or supports a party's case should also be disclosed.[84] A 'document'[85] includes anything in which information of any description is recorded. A 'copy', in relation to a document, means anything onto which information recorded in a document has been copied, by whatever means and whether directly or indirectly; thereby including electronic copies of documents, e-mails and other electronic forms of storage including mobile telephones.[86] So long as a document or a copy is relevant[87] to the proceedings, it is susceptible to an order for disclosure.

---

82 *Birds Eye Walls Ltd v Harrison* [1985] IRLR 47, EAT.

83 Employment tribunals (Constitution and Rules of Procedure Regulations 2004), reg 10(2)(d).

84 *Compagnie Financière v Peruvian Guano Co* (1882) LR 11 QBD 55, CA per Brett LJ at page 63.

85 See CPR 31.4.

86 In *Derby & Co. Ltd v Weldon (No.9)* [1991] 1 WLR 652 document was construed to include a computer database.

87 *Ministry of Defence v Meredith* [1995] IRLR 539, EAT.

There are a number of possible exceptions to when disclosure may be ordered: **10.69**

(a) confidentiality;
(b) without prejudice privilege;
(c) public interest immunity;
(d) legal professional privilege.

Claimants often wish for their medical records to remain private or for the personnel files of other employees, who may be relevant comparators, to be disclosed. The principles governing the disclosure of confidential documents are, therefore, discussed here. Without prejudice privilege, legal privilege and public interest immunity are beyond the scope of this work. **10.70**

Confidentiality

Documents that may be confidential include medical records and the personnel files of other employees. These documents are not immune from disclosure[88] but the tribunal should not order them to be disclosed unless it is necessary for disposing fairly of the proceedings or for saving costs. The tribunal should have regard to (a) the fact that the documents were confidential and the strength and value of the interest in preserving that confidentiality (b) the damage which may be caused by breaking the confidentiality. If disclosure is necessary for fairly disposing of the proceedings then disclosure must be ordered notwithstanding the documents' confidentiality.[89] **10.71**

Claimants can frequently be concerned about being examined by the respondent's medical expert or producing their medical records, but the claimant's co-operation is fundamental to the respondent's right to a fair trial. In *Hanlon v Kirklees Metropolitan Council & Ors*[90] the EAT upheld a tribunal's decision to strike out a claimant's case for failing to disclose his medical records. The claimant's right to respect for his private life under article 8 of the EHRC was not absolute and had to be balanced against the respondent's right to a fair trial. Since a fair trial was impossible without the claimant's medical records, the tribunal was entitled to strike out the claimant's claim if he did not disclose them. **10.72**

Claimants are effectively presented with a choice between keeping their medical records private or pursuing the claim. If the person chooses to pursue the claim **10.73**

---

88 *Alfred Compton Amusement Machines Ltd v Customs and Excise Commissioners (No.2)* [1974] AC 405, [1973] 2 All ER 1169.

89 See *Science Research Council v Nassé* [1979] IRLR 465, HL, *Perera v Civil Service Commission* [1980] ICR 699, CA, *Selvarajan v Inner London Education Authority* [1980] IRLR 313, EAT, and *Arquiva Ltd v Sagoo* UKEAT/0135/07.

90 [2004] All ER D 154.

then the public interest of ensuring equality of arms will normally override the claimant's right to privacy.[91]

10.74 Before ordering the disclosure of a confidential document, a tribunal should inspect the document and consider whether any special measures could be taken such as covering up confidential but irrelevant parts of the document or substituting anonymous references for specific names.[92]

4. The Burden of Proof

The Burden of Proof: DDA 1995 s 17A(1C)

17A(1C) Where, on the hearing of a complaint under subsection (1) [a complaint of discrimination], the complainant proves facts from which the tribunal could, apart from this subsection, conclude in the absence of an adequate explanation that the respondent has acted in a way which is unlawful under this Part, the tribunal shall uphold the complaint unless the respondent proves that he did not so act.

10.75 In the county court the claimant is required to prove his case on the balance of probabilities. Disability discrimination cases in the employment tribunal are different because DDA 1995, s 17A(1C) provides that the burden of proof shifts to the respondent once the claimant has proved facts which show a prima facie case. The shifting burden of proof provisions in DDA 1995, s 17A(1C) implement the Framework Directive[93] and mirror the provisions contained in other equality legislation dealing with discrimination in employment.[94] Discrimination is often disguised and is rarely overt and so there are difficulties inherent in proving that discrimination exists. The shifting burden of proof recognizes this and aims to ensure the effective enforcement of the principle of equal treatment by requiring respondents to prove that it did not breach the principle where the claimant proves a prima facie case.

10.76 The correct approach to applying the shifting burden of proof was set out by the Court of Appeal in *Igen v Wong*[95] and is now well established.[96] Although *Igen* was a sex discrimination case, the DRC intervened because of the ramifications that

---

[91] See also *De Keyser Limited v Wilson* [2001] IRLR 324, EAT at paras 27 to 28 and *Khudados v Hayden & Others* [2007] EWCA Civ 1316.

[92] *Science Research Council v Nassé* [1979] IRLR 465, HL.

[93] Article 10 of the Framework Directive required EU Member States to implement a shifting burden of proof.

[94] SDA 1975, s 63A, RRA 1976, s 54A, Religion or Belief Regulations, reg 29, Sexual Orientation Regulations, reg 29, Age Regulations, reg 37.

[95] [2005] EWCA Civ 142, [2005] IRLR 258. Cf further *Barton v Investec Henderson Crosthwaite Securities Ltd* [2003] ICR 1205, *EAT and Madarasy v Nomura* [2007] IRLR 246, CA.

[96] See the comments of Mummery LJ at para 5 in *Madarasy v Nomura* [2007] IRLR 246, CA.

the decision had on the interpretation of the DDA 1995.[97] The guidance in *Igen* is as follows:[98]

Guidance on the Burden of Proof given in Igen

(1) Pursuant to section 63A of the SDA 1975, it is for the claimant who complains of sex discrimination to prove on the balance of probabilities facts from which the tribunal could conclude, in the absence of an adequate explanation, that the respondent has committed an act of discrimination against the claimant which is unlawful by virtue of Part II or which by virtue of s 41 or s 42 of the SDA 1975 is to be treated as having been committed against the claimant. These are referred to below as 'such facts'.

(2) If the claimant does not prove such facts he or she will fail.

(3) It is important to bear in mind in deciding whether the claimant has proved such facts that it is unusual to find direct evidence of sex discrimination. Few employers would be prepared to admit such discrimination, even to themselves. In some cases the discrimination will not be an intention but merely based on the assumption that 'he or she would not have fitted in'.

(4) In deciding whether the claimant has proved such facts, it is important to remember that the outcome at this stage of the analysis by the tribunal will therefore usually depend on what inferences it is proper to draw from the primary facts found by the tribunal.

(5) It is important to note the word 'could' in SDA 1975, s 63A(2). At this stage the tribunal does not have to reach a definitive determination that such facts would lead it to the conclusion that there was an act of unlawful discrimination. At this stage a tribunal is looking at the primary facts before it to see what inferences of secondary fact could be drawn from them.

(6) In considering what inferences or conclusions can be drawn from the primary facts, the tribunal must assume that there is no adequate explanation for those facts.

(7) These inferences can include, in appropriate cases, any inferences that it is just and equitable to draw in accordance with SDA 1975, 74(2)(b) from an evasive or equivocal reply to a questionnaire or any other questions that fall within SDA 1975, s 74(2).

(8) Likewise, the tribunal must decide whether any provision of any relevant code of practice is relevant and if so, take it into account in determining such facts pursuant to SDA 1975, s 56A(10). This means that inferences may also be drawn from any failure to comply with any relevant code of practice.

(9) Where the claimant has proved facts from which conclusions could be drawn that the respondent has treated the claimant less favourably on the ground of sex, then the burden of proof moves to the respondent.

(10) It is then for the respondent to prove that he did not commit, or as the case may be, is not to be treated as having committed, that act.

(11) To discharge that burden it is necessary for the respondent to prove, on the balance of probabilities, that the treatment was in no sense whatsoever on the grounds of sex, since 'no discrimination whatsoever' is compatible with the Burden of Proof Directive.

---

[97] See Gibson LJ at para 15.

[98] This guidance was initially provided with some slight differences in *Barton v Investec Henderson Crosthwaite Securities Ltd* [2003] ICR 1205, EAT.

(12) That requires a tribunal to assess not merely whether the respondent has proved an explanation for the facts from which such inferences can be drawn, but further that it is adequate to discharge the burden of proof on the balance of probabilities that sex was not a ground for the treatment in question.

(13) Since the facts necessary to prove an explanation would normally be in the possession of the respondent, a tribunal would normally expect cogent evidence to discharge that burden of proof. In particular, the tribunal will need to examine carefully explanations for failure to deal with the questionnaire procedure and/or code of practice.

10.77 The *Igen* approach to the burden of proof is, therefore, a two-stage test. The first stage requires the claimant to prove primary facts from which the tribunal *could conclude* that the employer had committed an act of discrimination. If the claimant does this, the employer is then required, in the second stage, to prove on the balance of probabilities that he did not act unlawfully.[99]

10.78 The burden does not shift once a claimant proves facts that show an employer *could have committed an act of discrimination*.[100] The term 'could' in DDA 1995, s 17A (1C) refers to the conclusions that can properly be drawn from the primary facts and not to whether or not there *might* have been an act of discrimination. Before a tribunal *could conclude* that a respondent was guilty of discrimination the claimant must prove the facts that are necessary to prove each element of the discriminatory conduct. The claimant must prove, on the balance of probabilities, facts from which the tribunal could conclude that the respondent had committed an act of discrimination.[101] At the first stage, when the tribunal is determining these primary facts, it must have regard to all the evidence tending to establish or undermine the facts including evidence presented by the respondent. The tribunal must however, when considering the first stage, disregard the respondent's explanation for its behaviour.

10.79 While it is important to keep a mental separation between the stages, the Court of Appeal indicated in *Igen*[102] that it did not consider that tribunals should separate hearings into two parts to correspond to the two stages. The expectation was that the tribunals would generally wish to hear all the evidence, including the respondent's explanation, before deciding whether the requirements at the first stage were satisfied and, if so, whether the respondent has discharged the onus shifted to him.

99 *EB v BA* [2006] IRLR 471, EAT.

100 *Madarassy v Nomura International Plc* [2007] ICR 867, CA.

101 *Madarassy v Nomura International Plc* [2007] ICR 867, CA at para 56. Note Mummery J's comments at para 52 where he states that the claimant does not have to prove a 'conclusive case' of unlawful discrimination, he only has to set up a 'prima facie' case.

102 Per Gibson LJ at para 19.

Example of the Burden of Proof in a Reasonable Adjustments Claim

The following is an example of how the burden of proof might shift in a reasonable adjustments case.[103] A claimant who is vision impaired is complaining of a respondent's failure to make a reasonable adjustment. He is employed as a computer programmer. The respondent requires all computer programmers to maintain their competence by sitting examinations every year on a computer. In order to use a computer efficiently, the claimant normally uses a special computer program. This program translates text into speech via a synthesizer and is specifically designed to help people with a visual impairment to use a computer. The respondent refuses to allow the claimant to use the program when taking the examination but provides him instead with a person to read out the questions and gives him extra time to complete the examination. **10.80**

Stage One—The claimant must prove such facts from which the tribunal could conclude, in the absence of an adequate explanation, that the respondent committed an act of discrimination. In a reasonable adjustments case the claimant must prove:[104] **10.81**

(a) that he is a disabled employee;
(b) that he is placed at a substantial disadvantage compared to non-disabled persons by the employer's PCP;
(c) that the employer did not take such steps, as were reasonable in the circumstances, to mitigate the substantial disadvantage.

The burden remains on the claimant throughout to prove the facts showing that the duty to make adjustments has arisen.[105] In this example the claimant must prove that he was disabled and placed at a substantial disadvantage by the respondent's practice of not providing the special program or allowing it to be used. **10.82**

After this the claimant must prove such facts from which the tribunal could conclude that the respondent breached the duty by not making a reasonable adjustment that would have been effective to prevent the respondent's PCP causing the disadvantage. The tribunal must, therefore ,be able to identify the proposed adjustment and to make the kind of assessment of reasonableness envisaged by the DDA 1995 and in particular DDA 1995, s 18B.[106] **10.83**

---

[103] *Project Management v Latif* [2007] IRLR 579, EAT and *HM Prison Service v Johnson* [2007] IRLR 951, EAT provide a helpful discussion of the application of the burden of proof in reasonable adjustments cases.

[104] See the summary at the beginning of chapter 4 for a quick guide to the reasonable adjustments duty.

[105] See *Project Management Institute v Latif* [2007] IRLR 579, EAT, per Elias J at para 45.

[106] In other words, factors such as the cost, the practicability of implementing it, the nature and size of the employers' undertaking and the other factors mentioned in s 18B. For a more detailed

10.84 The degree of detail required from the claimant to prove a prima facie case will vary depending on the type of adjustment suggested. The claimant will not, in every case, have to provide comprehensive details of an adjustment before a tribunal could conclude that a reasonable adjustment was not made.[107] In some cases a mere suggestion might be sufficient, on its own, to shift the burden of proof. For example, a suggestion that the respondent should have installed a wheelchair ramp in a large factory to enable the claimant to enter with his wheelchair may well be sufficient. A tribunal could conclude, from this suggestion, that the adjustment was reasonable, should have been made and would have prevented the disadvantage.

10.85 Where the required adjustment is more complex, a mere suggestion may not suffice to enable a conclusion to be so easily drawn. In these circumstances the burden would not shift unless other facts were proved such as the fact that outside help from a registered charity was available or that the size of the respondent's organization meant that it had a sufficiently large budget to deal easily with the proposed adjustment.

10.86 The tribunal should consider all the evidence when determining the primary facts upon which its decision is based. The tribunal is, for example, entitled to accept the respondent's evidence of the cost of the software and to reject the claimant's evidence of the cost. This finding of primary fact can then be used as a factor to determine whether or not the proposed adjustment could be reasonable. Obviously, cost and other factors such as the size of the respondent's resources will determine what inferences *could* be drawn. The tribunal must not have regard to the respondent's arguments on reasonableness at the first stage.[108]

10.87 In this example the claimant is able to prove that the program software was readily available, easy to install, did not cost (on the face of it) an unreasonable amount, and was an effective adjustment that prevented the disadvantage. The claimant must, of course, show that the adjustment was not actually made but in this case that is admitted. The respondent's arguments in support of its assertion that the program is too expensive are disregarded. The tribunal certainly *could* conclude from these facts that the respondent had breached the duty to make adjustments and so the burden shifts to the respondent.

10.88 Stage Two—Once the onus shifts to the respondent, it must show, on the balance of probabilities, that it did not act unlawfully. In this example the respondent

---

discussion of s18B see para 4.74 See also *HM Prison Service v Johnson* [2007] IRLR 951, EAT, paras 89 to 90.

107 Per Elias J at para 55.

108 *Laing v Manchester City Council* [2006] IRLR 748, EAT.

would have to prove that it was unreasonable to provide the program or that it would not have been effective. The respondent would have to provide detailed evidence and cannot simply rely upon assertion. For instance, an argument that the program was too expensive may be given short shrift if the respondent fails to produce either its own financial accounts, quotes for the cost of the software and/or other documentary evidence to support its case. The consequences of a failure to produce the relevant information must, once the burden is reversed, be adverse to the respondent rather than the claimant.[109]

F. Compromise Agreements

Most employment disputes are settled before they reach the tribunal. The vast majority of settlements involve the respondent paying money to the claimant in return for the claimant withdrawing his claim and promising not to sue it for anything else. **10.89**

Most statutory employment rights are protected by restrictions that prevent a party contracting out of them.[110] DDA 1995, s 17C contains such a restriction in respect of a right to bring a disability discrimination claim. Since a compromise agreement is a contract purporting to exclude or limit the operation of the DDA 1995, it would be void unless the DDA 1995 provided a mechanism by which a valid compromise agreement could be made. DDA 1995, sch 3A and s 17C(2(1) together provide that the prohibition on contracting out does not apply to: **10.90**

(a) a contract made with the assistance of a conciliation officer designated by ACAS;[111]
(b) a contract settling a complaint (compromise agreement) where certain conditions are met.

---

[109] *EB v BA* [2006] IRLR 471, EAT.

[110] SDA 1975, s 7; RRA 1976, s 73; National Minimum Wage Act 1988, s 49; Trade Union and Labour Relations (Consolidation) Act 1992, s 288; ERA 1996, s 203; Working Time Regulations 1998, SI 1998/1833 reg 35; Part-Time Workers (Prevention of Less Favourable Treatment) Regulations 2000 SI 2000/1551, reg 9; Fixed Term Employees (Prevention of Less Favourable Treatment) Regulations 2002, SI 2002/2034 reg 10; Employment Equality (Religion or Belief) Regulations 2003 SI 2003/1660, reg 35, sch 4; Employment Equality (Sexual Orientation) Regulations 2003 SI 2003/1661 reg 35, sch 4; Employment Equality (Age) Regulations 2006 SI 2006/1031 reg 43, sch 5; Transfer of Undertakings (Protection of Employment) Regulations 2006 SI 2006/246, reg 8.

[111] For the definition of Conciliation Officer see of the Trade Union and Labour Relations (Consolidation) Act 1992, s 211.

In addition to these two methods a tribunal may also make an order disposing of the proceedings with the consent of the parties.[112]

1. ACAS Conciliated Settlements

10.91 ACAS plays a major role in conciliating tribunal claims. Where a settlement under the DDA 1995 is made 'with the assistance' of an ACAS conciliation officer, the restrictions on contracting out contained in DDA 1995, sch 3A and s 17C(1)(3) do not apply.

10.92 The Employment Tribunals Act 1996, s 18 requires the ACAS conciliation officer to endeavour to promote a settlement between the parties (a) where he is requested to do so by a party or (b) where he considers that there are reasonable prospects of successfully promoting a settlement.[113]

10.93 Most agreements made with the assistance of the ACAS officer are recorded on a form called a COT3 but there is no requirement for the agreement to be recorded in writing and even an oral agreement will be sufficient.[114]

10.94 The ACAS officer's actions must correspond to the functions which a conciliation officer is under a duty to perform or has a power to discharge. However, it is sufficient that the officer intended and purported to act under his duties and the tribunal will not enquire whether the officer correctly interpreted his duties.[115] In practice, where an ACAS officer has been involved in the settlement negotiations between the parties and an agreement is subsequently reached, the agreement will almost always have been made with the 'assistance' of the ACAS officer.[116] This is the case whether or not a claim has been presented to a tribunal so long as there is a possibility that a claim *might* be presented.[117]

---

[112] See para 10.100.

[113] Procedure Regulations, Sched 1, r 22 sets out fixed periods of conciliation in respect of some claims (not DDA 1995 claims). However, ACAS indicated in a press release dated 3 April 2008, that it would extend the conciliation period beyond any fixed period where a party requests it or, alternatively, where the ACAS conciliator considers that there is a reasonable prospect that it may assist in resolving the case without the need for determination by the tribunal. This effectively abolishes the fixed conciliation periods.

[114] *Gilbert v Kembridge Fibres Ltd* [1984] IRLR 52, EAT.

[115] The duties and powers of a conciliation officer are very broad and are not confined to those powers in of the Employment Tribunals Act 1996, s 18. See for instance *Clarke v Redcar & Cleveland Borough Council* [2006] ICR 897, EAT per McMullen J at para 36.

[116] *Clarke v Redcar & Cleveland Borough Council* [2006] ICR 897 at para 36. See also *Slack v Greenham (Plant Hire)* [1983] ICR 617.

[117] *Moore v Duport Funiture Products Ltd & Anor* [1982] ICR 84 HL.

2. Compromise Agreements

DDA 1995, sch 3A and s 17C(2)(2) set out the conditions that a contract must meet in order to escape the prohibition on contracting out of the obligations imposed by the DDA 1995. An agreement compromising a DDA 1995 claim that is not made with the assistance of ACAS must meet these requirements. If it does not it will be void and the claimant will be free to pursue the claim that was purportedly compromised. The conditions in DDA 1995, sch 3A and s 17C are that: **10.95**

(a) the contract must be in writing;
(b) the contract must relate to the particular complaint;
(c) the complainant must have received advice from a relevant independent adviser[118] as to the terms and effect of the proposed contract and in particular its effect on his ability to pursue a complaint before an employment tribunal;
(d) there must be in force, when the adviser gives the advice, a contract of insurance, or an indemnity provided for members of a profession or professional body, covering the risk of a claim by the complainant in respect of loss arising in consequence of the advice;
(e) the contract must identify the adviser; and
(f) the contract must state that the conditions regulating compromise contracts under this schedule are satisfied.

The above conditions must all be complied with in order to compromise a claim under the DDA 1995. If they are, the employee will be prevented from pursuing the claim that has been compromised. **10.96**

In *Lunt v Merseyside TEC Ltd*[119] the EAT held that a compromise agreement must relate to the particular complaint. Although a 'blanket' agreement compromising claims which had never been indicated in the past is not permitted, a single compromise agreement can cover claims under more than one statute.[120] This does not mean that only complaints that have been presented to an employment tribunal can be compromised, but there must be some indication that the employee has a complaint of some description before the compromise agreement was executed. **10.97**

118 Relevant independent advisers are qualified lawyers, legal executives, certified trade union members and certified advice centre workers.

119 [1999] IRLR 458, EAT.

120 See, however, *Hilton UK Hotels Ltd v McNaughton* [2006] All ER (D) 327, EAT, in which Lady Smith stated that, as a matter of general law, a party could contractually compromise a future claim of which he had no knowledge. It is not clear whether Lady Smith's reference to 'general law' was a reference to there being no restriction on compromising future claims in circumstances where the contract was not subject to any statutory restrictions.

10.98 It is also worth remembering that a compromise agreement is a contract like any other and is subject to the normal rules of contractual formation and interpretation. *Investors Compensation Scheme Ltd v West Bromwich Building Society*[121] provides a useful reminder of the correct approach:

(a) interpretation is the ascertainment of the meaning which the document would convey to a reasonable person having all the background knowledge which would reasonably be available to the parties in the situation which they were in at the time of the contract;
(b) the background includes absolutely anything which would have affected the way in which the language of the document would have been understood by a reasonable man;
(c) the law excludes from the background the previous negotiations of the parties and their declarations of subjective intent;
(d) the meaning which a document would convey to a reasonable man is not the same thing as the meaning of its words. The meaning of the document is what the parties, using the words against the relevant background, would reasonably understand the document to mean;
(e) the rule that words should be given their ordinary and natural meaning reflects the proposition that courts do not easily accept that people have made linguistic mistakes, particularly in formal documents.

10.99 Since many cases settle at the doorstep of the tribunal, and to save having to re-invent the wheel each time a claim settles, it is worthwhile taking a draft compromise agreement each time one attends the tribunal. The agreement should however be tailored, in so far as is possible, to the case being compromised.

3. Consent Orders

10.100 The Procedure Regulations give the tribunal power, if it thinks fit, to make an order in terms that have been agreed between the parties.[122] Consent orders can be a useful way of compromising a claim. Once a claim is dismissed pursuant to a consent order, the claimant is prevented from bringing the same claim to the tribunal again in the absence of fraud or misrepresentation.[123]

10.101 A consent order is a valid way of compromising a claim if ACAS are unable to offer assistance or if the claimant is unrepresented and cannot sign a valid compromise agreement under DDA 1995, s 17C. It cannot be used for

121 [1998] 1 WLR 896 per Lord Hoffman at pages 112H to 113F.
122 Procedure Regulations, r 28(2).
123 See *Times Newspapers v Fitt* [1981] ICR 637, EAT.

compromising claims other than the claim that has been brought, since the dismissal of a claim only affects the claim that has actually been dismissed.

G. Reviews and Appeals

There are two principle ways to challenge a tribunal's decision: by requesting the tribunal to review its decision or by appealing the decision to the EAT. **10.102**

1. Applying for a Review

A review may be sought of decisions not to accept a claim, response or counterclaim and of judgments.[124] A review must be sought within 14 days of the date on which the decision was sent to the parties.[125] The application must be in writing and must identify the grounds of the application under the Procedure Regulations.[126] The 14 day time limit can be extended if it is just and equitable to do so.[127] A judge may also initiate a review of a judgment (other than a default judgment) or a decision of his own motion.[128] A party may seek a review under rules 33 to 36 of Schedule 1 of the Procedure Regulations. A judgment in default is reviewed under r 33. Other judgments and decisions are reviewed under rules 34 to 36. Where a respondent has failed to submit an ET3 in time and has not applied, prior to time expiring, for an extension, the respondent should apply for a review of either the default judgment under r 33 or the decision to reject the ET3 under r 6(6) and r 34.[129] **10.103**

Grounds of Review

The grounds for reviewing judgments and decisions under r 34 are: **10.104**

a) the decision was wrongly made as a result of an administrative error;
b) a party did not receive notice of the proceedings leading to the decision;
c) the decision was made in the absence of a party;

124 A judgment is defined in Procedure Regulations, r 28 as a final determination of the proceedings or of a particular issue. A judgment can include an award of compensation, a declaration or recommendation and awards for costs or preparation time.

125 Procedure Regulations r 35(1).

126 Procedure Regulations r 33(1) and (2) for default judgments and r 35(2) for other judgments and decisions.

127 Procedure Regulations r 33(1) for default judgments and r 35(1) for other judgments and decisions.

128 Procedure Regulations r 34(5). The judgment or decision must be the judge's own decision and the review must be carried out by him unless it is not reasonably practicable (r 36(1)).

129 *Moroak (trading as Blake Envelopes) v Cromie* [2005] IRLR 353, EAT.

d) new evidence has become available since the conclusion of the hearing to which the decision relates, provided that its existence could not have been reasonably known or foreseen at that time;
e) the interests of justice require such a review.

A decision not to accept a claim or response form may only be reviewed on the grounds that the decision was wrongly made as a result of an administrative error or if the interests of justice require such a review.[130]

10.105 For reviews under both rules 33 and 34 the respondent should apply for an extension of time when he makes his application for a review. The tests for whether to revoke the default judgment or refusal to accept the ET1 or ET3 are the same under both rules: whether it is just and equitable to do so.[131] The factors relevant to the exercise of the tribunal's discretion whether to extend time were described by HHJ Clark in *The Pestle & Mortar v Turner*:[132]

> In short, in exercising the discretion, a chairman should take account of all relevant factors including the explanation or lack of explanation for the delay and merits of the defence, weighing and balancing them one against the other, and reach a conclusion which was objectively justified on the grounds of reason and justice and, in doing so, to balance the possible prejudice to each party.[133]

The Sift and the Review

10.106 Applications for review undergo a sifting procedure. The judge who made the decision (or another prescribed judge)[134] may refuse the application for review if he determines either that there are no grounds for the decision to be reviewed or that there are no reasonable prospects of the decision being varied or revoked.[135]

10.107 If the application for review is not rejected in the sift, the decision or judgment in question is then reviewed by the judge who made it.[136] The judge may confirm, vary or revoke the decision that he made. If the decision is revoked, the judge must order the decision to be taken again.

---

130 Procedure Regulations r 34(4).

131 See *Moroak (trading as Blake Envelopes) v Cromie* [2005] ICR 1226, EAT at 1233C–E. See also *Pendragon Plc (trading as CD Bramall Bradford) v Copus* [2005] ICR 671, EAT; *Bone v Fabcon Projects* [2006] IRLR 908, EAT; and *The Pestle & Mortar v Turner* UKEAT/0652/05; *Barrosso & Ors v Fahy* UKEAT/0558/06/DA.

132 UKEAT/0652/05.

133 The factors originated from the judgment of Mummery J in *Kwik Save Stores Ltd v Swain* [1997] ICR 49, EAT.

134 The judges who may conduct a sift for a review are described in r 35(1).

135 Procedure Regulations, r 35(3).

136 In some circumstances, Procedure Regulations, r 36 allows other judges to conduct the review.

2. Appealing to the EAT

The procedural rules governing an appeal to the EAT are set out in the Employment Appeal Tribunal Rules 1993 (EAT Rules), the Practice Direction (Employment Appeal Tribunal—Procedure) (2008) and the EAT Practice Statement (2005). These documents are all relatively short and it is worth reading them in full, particularly the Practice Direction. **10.108**

Both the EAT Practice Direction and the EAT Rules 1993 require the EAT to apply the overriding objective when exercising its powers under the rules or practice direction.[137] The overriding objective is expressed in the same terms as the overriding objective in the Procedure Regulations. **10.109**

The Notice of Appeal

The Notice of Appeal must be substantially in accordance with Form 1 of the Practice Direction which can be downloaded from the EAT website.[138] **10.110**

The Notice of Appeal must be filed at the EAT, 42 days from when the written *judgment* was sent to the parties. If the parties requested written reasons or the tribunal reserved its judgment, the appellant has 42 days from the date that the written *reasons* were sent to the parties.[139] If the appeal is in respect of a decision rather than a judgment, the appeal must be instituted within 42 days of the date of the decision. Unlike the tribunal where documents can be served until midnight on the relevant day, documents served at the EAT must arrive by 4pm.[140] **10.111**

Copies of the judgment, decision or order appealed against should be attached to the Notice of Appeal together with a copy of the tribunal's written reasons and the ET1 and ET3. If the judgment, decision or order being appealed is not attached, a written explanation must be given.[141] **10.112**

The Sift

Once the appeal has been instituted, it is sifted by a judge or the registrar to determine how the appeal will proceed. The EAT Practice Direction sets out 4 tracks but most appeals are dealt with by what is known as the rule 3(7) procedure.[142] **10.113**

137 EAT Rules 1993, r 2A and EAT Practice Direction 1.4.

138 <http://www.employmentappeals.gov.uk>. Follow the link to forms and guidance.

139 EAT Rules 1993, r 3(3).

140 EAT Practice Direction 1.8.2.

141 EAT Rules 1993, r 3(1) and EAT Practice Direction 2.1.

142 EAT Rules 2003, r 3(7). On other tracks the case is sent either to a preliminary hearing, a full hearing, or a fast track full hearing. See EAT Practice Direction 9.5.

10.114 In Rule 3(7) cases a judge or registrar considers the notice of appeal and if he decides that it discloses no reasonable grounds for bringing the appeal,[143] the appellant is informed of the judge's decision and no further action is taken on the appeal unless the appellant either serves a fresh notice of appeal or requests an oral hearing before a judge (commonly called a rule 3(10) hearing). Normally, only the appellant attends the rule 3(10) hearing. The appellant must convince the judge presiding over the hearing that the notice of appeal raises a point of law with a reasonable prospect of success.

10.115 If the appeal is allowed to proceed, the EAT will send the notice of appeal and any submissions or skeleton arguments to the parties who are respondents to the appeal. The respondent must send its answer within 14 days of the date of the order allowing the appeal to proceed.

Grounds of Appeal

10.116 The tribunal at first instance is the supreme arbiter of fact. It is only possible to appeal a decision where the tribunal has made an error of law. The EAT will only normally hear new evidence in exceptional circumstances[144] and is also unlikely to permit a new point of law to be raised for the first time on appeal. The following are the most common categories of appeals on questions of law:

(a) misapplication of law;
(b) perversity;
(c) inadequate reasons;
(d) bias, improper conduct or procedural irregularity.

Misapplication of Law

10.117 The notice of appeal must clearly identify the points of law which form the grounds of appeal. Allegations that the tribunal has misapplied the law are generally allegations that the tribunal has either failed to consider, misconstrued or misapplied a relevant authority or statute. The appellant must show, from the tribunal's judgement, what test it was that the tribunal misconstrued and what the consequences were. The appeal should not be an academic appeal. The EAT is not interested in debating the law for the sake of it. The tribunal's error must have made a real difference to the outcome of the case.

---

143 The judge may also consider that the notice of appeal is an abuse of process or is otherwise likely to obstruct the just disposal of proceedings.

144 See EAT Practice Direction 8.2 and *Ladd v Marshall* [1954] 1 WLR 1489, CA. The EAT will have regard to the overriding objective and whether (i) the evidence could have been obtained with reasonable diligence for use at the tribunal hearing, (ii) the evidence is relevant and would probably have had an important influence on the hearing, (iii) the evidence is apparently credible.

Perversity

The only time that the EAT will disturb a finding of fact will be if the finding was perverse. The most frequently cited case giving guidance on the approach to perversity appeals is *Yeboah v Crofton*.[145] In that case the Court of Appeal warned that perversity appeals ought only to succeed where an overwhelming case is made out that the tribunal reached a conclusion that no reasonable tribunal would have reached. This is obviously an extremely difficult ground of appeal to succeed on. **10.118**

The Practice Direction sets out specific requirements for any notice of appeal containing an allegation of perversity. PD 2.6 provides that: **10.119**

> *Perversity Appeals:* An appellant may not state as a ground of appeal simply words to the effect that 'the judgment or order was contrary to the evidence,' or that 'there was no evidence to support the judgment or order', or that 'the judgment or order was one which no reasonable tribunal could have reached and was perverse' unless the Notice of Appeal also sets out full particulars of the matters relied on in support of those general grounds.

One example of a perversity appeal is where the tribunal makes a finding of fact that is unsupported by the evidence. In order for a perversity appeal to succeed on this basis, there must be no evidence upon which the tribunal could have based its factual findings. The tribunal's finding of fact will be unimpeachable even if it is contrary to the weight of the evidence.[146] A misunderstanding or misapplication of the facts is insufficient. **10.120**

Inadequate Reasons

A tribunal is obliged to give reasons for the decision or judgment that it has made. Tribunals are not required to produce refined legal draftsmanship but the decision should contain an account of the basic facts and the parties should be able to tell why they have won or lost.[147] There should be a sufficient account of the facts and of the reasoning to enable the appeal tribunal to see whether any question of law arises. If the judgment is inadequate even on a broad brush approach, the EAT will not rake through a patently deficient decision for signs of the missing elements to amplify them into an adequate set of reasons.[148] **10.121**

145 [2002] EWCA Civ 794, [2002] IRLR 634, CA.

146 *Eclipse Blinds Ltd v Wright* [1992] ICR 723, Ct of Session, CA.

147 See *English v Emery Reimbold and Strick Ltd* [2002] EWCA Civ 605, [2002] 1 WLR 2409.

148 *Anya v University of Oxford* [2001] IRLR 377, *CA, and Meek v City of Birmingham District Council* [1987] IRLR 250, CA.

Bias, Improper Conduct, or Procedural Irregularity

10.122 Practice Direction 11 sets out a special procedure to be followed in respect of an appeal involving a complaint about the conduct of the tribunal judge. Any appeal alleging bias, improper conduct or procedural irregularity[149] is required to follow this procedure. The appellant must provide full particulars of the alleged bias in the notice of appeal, and the judge, upon receiving the notice, may require the appellant or any person present at the hearing to file an affidavit or witness statement giving this account of events.

10.123 An allegation of bias or an allegation that there was the appearance of bias is essentially an allegation that the judge either unfairly favoured, or disfavoured, one party over another. The circumstances in which a judge could properly be said to be biased are well set out in *Locabail (UK) Ltd v Bayfield Properties Ltd*[150] and can be summarized as follows:

there is no definitive list of factors which may, or may not, give rise to a risk of bias, each case depends on its facts;

allegations of bias based on the following grounds are unlikely to succeed:

- religion, ethnic or national origin, gender, age, class, means or sexual orientation;
- the judge's social background, employment history, previous political associations, membership of social or sporting or charitable bodies, Masonic associations;
- previous judicial decisions or extra curricular utterances (whether in textbooks, lectures, speeches, articles, interviews, reports or responses to consultation papers);
- previous receipt of instructions to act for or against any party, solicitor or advocate engaged in a case before him;
- membership of the same Inn, circuit, local law society or chambers.

By contrast, a real danger of bias might be thought to arise:

- if there was any personal friendship or animosity between the judge and any member of the public involved in the case;
- if the judge was closely acquainted with any member of the public involved in the case (particularly if the credibility of the individual could be significant to the decision in the case);

149 In order to be a valid ground of appeal the procedural irregularity must be a serious one which caused an unjust decision: *Tanfern Ltd v Cameron-MacDonald* [2000] 1 WLR 1311, CA.

150 [2000] IRLR 96, CA.

- if, in any case, the credibility of any individual was an issue to be decided by the judge and he had in a previous case rejected the evidence of the person in such outspoken terms as to throw doubt on his ability to approach the person's evidence with an open mind on a later occasion;
- if the judge has expressed views, particularly during the course of the hearing, in such extreme and unbalanced terms as to throw doubt on his ability to try the issue with an objective judicial mind;
- for any other reason that casts doubt on the judge's ability to ignore extraneous considerations, prejudices, predilections, and bring an objective judgment to bear on the issues before him.

The EAT will examine all the circumstances of the case to determine whether a fair-minded and informed observer would conclude that there was a real possibility that the tribunal was biased.[151] **10.124**

H. Restriction on Publicity in Disability Cases

Where evidence of a personal nature is likely to be heard in the case, the employee may apply to the tribunal or the EAT for a restricted reporting order.[152] The tribunal hearing the complaint may also make an order of its own motion.[153] **10.125**

Evidence is of a personal nature if it is medical evidence or other evidence of an intimate nature which might reasonably be assumed to cause significant embarrassment to the employee if it were reported. **10.126**

Once in place, a restricted reporting order prevents the publication in Great Britain of any matter that is likely to lead members of the public to identify the employee or any other persons who are named in the order. **10.127**

---

151 *Re Medicaments and Related Classes of Goods (No 2)*, sub nom *Director General of Fair Trading v Proprietary Association for Great Britain* [2001] ICR 564, CA at para 85.

152 See Procedure Regulations, r 50 for the tribunal and EAT Rules 1993, r 23A for the EAT.

153 Procedure Regulations, r 50(2) and EAT Rules 1993, r 23A (2).

APPENDIX 1

Disability Discrimination Act 1995

1995 CHAPTER 50

An Act to make it unlawful to discriminate against disabled persons in connection with employment, the provision of goods, facilities and services or the disposal or management of premises; to make provision about the employment of disabled persons; and to establish a National Disability Council

[8th November 1995]

BE IT ENACTED by the Queen's most Excellent Majesty, by and with the advice and consent of the Lords Spiritual and Temporal, and Commons, in this present Parliament assembled, and by the authority of the same, as follows:—

NOTES

Miscellaneous

The Disability Rights Commission Act 1999, s 1, provides for the abolition of the National Disability Council and its replacement by a body known as the Disability Rights Commission.

Part I

Disability

1 Meaning of "disability" and "disabled person"

(1) Subject to the provisions of Schedule 1, a person has a disability for the purposes of this Act [and Part III of the 2005 Order] if he has a physical or mental impairment which has a substantial and long-term adverse effect on his ability to carry out normal day-to-day activities.

(2) In this Act [and Part III of the 2005 Order] "disabled person" means a person who has a disability.

NOTES

Initial Commencement

To be appointed

To be appointed: see s 70(3).

Appointment

Appointment (in relation to England, Wales and Scotland): 17 May 1996: see SI 1996/1336, arts 2, 3(a).

Appointment (in relation to Northern Ireland): 30 May 1996: see the Disability Discrimination Act 1995 (Commencement No 2) Order (Northern Ireland) 1996, SR 1996/219, arts 2, 3(a).

Amendment

Sub-s (1): words "and Part III of the 2005 Order" in square brackets inserted, in relation to Northern Ireland, by the Special Educational Needs and Disability (Northern Ireland) Order 2005, SI 2005/1117, art 48(1), (2).

> Date in force: 1 September 2005: see the Special Educational Needs and Disability (2005 Order) (Commencement No 1) Order (Northern Ireland) 2005, SR 2005/336, art 2, Schedule (as amended by the Special Educational Needs and Disability (2005 Order) (Commencement No 1) (Amendment) Order (Northern Ireland) 2007, SR 2007/25, art 2) and the Special Educational Needs and Disability (2005 Order) (Commencement No 2) Order (Northern Ireland) 2005, SR 2005/337, art 2, Schedule.

Sub-s (2): words "and Part III of the 2005 Order" in square brackets inserted, in relation to Northern Ireland, by the Special Educational Needs and Disability (Northern Ireland) Order 2005, SI 2005/1117, art 48(1), (2).

> Date in force: 1 September 2005: see the Special Educational Needs and Disability (2005 Order) (Commencement No 1) Order (Northern Ireland) 2005, SR 2005/336, art 2, Schedule (as amended by the Special Educational Needs and Disability (2005 Order) (Commencement No 1) (Amendment) Order (Northern Ireland) 2007, SR 2007/25, art 2) and the Special Educational Needs and Disability (2005 Order) (Commencement No 2) Order (Northern Ireland) 2005, SR 2005/337, art 2, Schedule.

2 Past disabilities

(1) The provisions of this Part and Parts II [to 4] [and 5A] [and Part III of the 2005 Order] apply in relation to a person who has had a disability as they apply in relation to a person who has that disability.

(2) Those provisions are subject to the modifications made by Schedule 2.

(3) Any regulations or order made under this Act [by the Secretary of State, the Scottish Ministers or the] [Welsh Ministers] [or Part III of the 2005 Order] may include provision with respect to persons who have had a disability.

(4) In any proceedings under Part [2, 3, 4 or 5A] of this Act [or Part III of the 2005 Order], the question whether a person had a disability at a particular time ("the relevant time") shall be determined, for the purposes of this section, as if the provisions of, or made under, this Act [or Part III of the 2005 Order] in force when the act complained of was done had been in force at the relevant time.

(5) The relevant time may be a time before the passing of this Act [or (as the case may be) the making of the 2005 Order].

NOTES

Initial Commencement

To be appointed

To be appointed: see s 70(3).

Appointment

Appointment (in relation to England, Wales and Scotland): 17 May 1996: see SI 1996/1336, arts 2, 3(b).

Appointment (in relation to Northern Ireland): 30 May 1996: see the Disability Discrimination Act 1995 (Commencement No 2) Order (Northern Ireland) 1996, SR 1996/219, arts 2, 3(b).

Amendment

Sub-s (1): words "to 4" in square brackets substituted by the Special Educational Needs and Disability Act 2001, s 38(1), (2)(a).

Date in force: 1 September 2002: see SI 2002/2217, art 3, Sch 1, Pt 1.

Sub-s (1): words "and 5A" in square brackets inserted by the Disability Discrimination Act 2005, s 19(1), Sch 1, Pt 1, paras 1, 2(1), (2).

Date in force: 5 December 2005: see SI 2005/2774, art 3(j).

Sub-s (1): words "and Part III of the 2005 Order" in square brackets inserted, in relation to Northern Ireland, by the Special Educational Needs and Disability (Northern Ireland) Order 2005, SI 2005/1117, art 48(1), (3)(a).

Date in force: 1 September 2005: see the Special Educational Needs and Disability (2005 Order) (Commencement No 1) Order (Northern Ireland) 2005, SR 2005/336, art 2, Schedule (as amended by the Special Educational Needs and Disability (2005 Order) (Commencement No 1) (Amendment) Order (Northern Ireland) 2007, SR 2007/25, art 2) and the Special Educational Needs and Disability (2005 Order) (Commencement No 2) Order (Northern Ireland) 2005, SR 2005/337, art 2, Schedule.

Sub-s (3): words "by the Secretary of State, the Scottish Ministers or the National Assembly for Wales" in square brackets inserted by the Disability Discrimination Act 2005, s 19(1), Sch 1, Pt 1, paras 1, 2(1), (3).

Date in force: 30 June 2005: see SI 2005/1676, art 2(1)(c).

Sub-s (3): words "Welsh Ministers" in square brackets substituted by SI 2007/1388, art 3, Sch 1, paras 47, 48.

Date in force: this amendment came into force on 25 May 2007 being the date on which the initial period ended (following the appointment of the First Minister): see SI 2007/1388, art 1(2) and the Government of Wales Act 2006, ss 46, 161(5).

Sub-s (3): words "or Part III of the 2005 Order" in square brackets inserted, in relation to Northern Ireland, by the Special Educational Needs and Disability (Northern Ireland) Order 2005, SI 2005/1117, art 48(1), (3)(b).

Date in force: 1 September 2005: see the Special Educational Needs and Disability (2005 Order) (Commencement No 1) Order (Northern Ireland) 2005, SR 2005/336, art 2,

Schedule (as amended by the Special Educational Needs and Disability (2005 Order) (Commencement No 1) (Amendment) Order (Northern Ireland) 2007, SR 2007/25, art 2) and the Special Educational Needs and Disability (2005 Order) (Commencement No 2) Order (Northern Ireland) 2005, SR 2005/337, art 2, Schedule.

Sub-s (4): words "2, 3, 4 or 5A" in square brackets substituted by the Disability Discrimination Act 2005, s 19(1), Sch 1, Pt 1, paras 1, 2(1), (4).

Date in force: 4 December 2006: see SI 2005/2774, art 4(f).

Sub-s (4): words "or Part III of the 2005 Order" in square brackets in both places they occur inserted, in relation to Northern Ireland, by the Special Educational Needs and Disability (Northern Ireland) Order 2005, SI 2005/1117, art 48(1), (3)(c).

Date in force: 1 September 2005: see the Special Educational Needs and Disability (2005 Order) (Commencement No 1) Order (Northern Ireland) 2005, SR 2005/336, art 2, Schedule (as amended by the Special Educational Needs and Disability (2005 Order) (Commencement No 1) (Amendment) Order (Northern Ireland) 2007, SR 2007/25, art 2) and the Special Educational Needs and Disability (2005 Order) (Commencement No 2) Order (Northern Ireland) 2005, SR 2005/337, art 2, Schedule.

Sub-s (5): words "or (as the case may be) the making of the 2005 Order" in square brackets inserted, in relation to Northern Ireland, by the Special Educational Needs and Disability (Northern Ireland) Order 2005, SI 2005/1117, art 48(1), (3)(d).

Date in force: 1 September 2005: see the Special Educational Needs and Disability (2005 Order) (Commencement No 1) Order (Northern Ireland) 2005, SR 2005/336, art 2, Schedule (as amended by the Special Educational Needs and Disability (2005 Order) (Commencement No 1) (Amendment) Order (Northern Ireland) 2007, SR 2007/25, art 2) and the Special Educational Needs and Disability (2005 Order) (Commencement No 2) Order (Northern Ireland) 2005, SR 2005/337, art 2(1), Schedule.

See Further

See further: corresponding amendments to those made to sub-ss (1), (4) above by the Disability Discrimination Act 2005 have been made in relation to Northern Ireland: the Disability Discrimination (Northern Ireland) Order 2006, SI 2006/312, art 19(1), Sch 1.

3 Guidance

[(A1) The Secretary of State may issue guidance about matters to be taken into account in determining whether a person is a disabled person.]

(1) [Without prejudice to the generality of subsection (A1),] the Secretary of State may[, in particular,] issue guidance about the matters to be taken into account in determining—
  - (a) whether an impairment has a substantial adverse effect on a person's ability to carry out normal day-to-day activities; or
  - (b) whether such an impairment has a long-term effect.

(2) [Without prejudice to the generality of subsection (A1), guidance about the matters mentioned in subsection (1)] may, among other things, give examples of—
  - (a) effects which it would be reasonable, in relation to particular activities, to regard for purposes of this Act as substantial adverse effects;

(b) effects which it would not be reasonable, in relation to particular activities, to regard for such purposes as substantial adverse effects;
(c) substantial adverse effects which it would be reasonable to regard, for such purposes, as long-term;
(d) substantial adverse effects which it would not be reasonable to regard, for such purposes, as long-term.

(3) [An adjudicating body] determining, for any purpose of this Act [or Part III of the 2005 Order], whether [a person is a disabled person], shall take into account any guidance which appears to it to be relevant.

[(3A) "Adjudicating body" means—
(a) a court;
(b) a tribunal; and
(c) any other person who, or body which, may decide a claim under Part 4.]

(4) In preparing a draft of any guidance, the Secretary of State shall consult such persons as he considers appropriate.

(5) Where the Secretary of State proposes to issue any guidance, he shall publish a draft of it, consider any representations that are made to him about the draft and, if he thinks it appropriate, modify his proposals in the light of any of those representations.

(6) If the Secretary of State decides to proceed with any proposed guidance, he shall lay a draft of it before each House of Parliament.

(7) If, within the 40-day period, either House resolves not to approve the draft, the Secretary of State shall take no further steps in relation to the proposed guidance.

(8) If no such resolution is made within the 40-day period, the Secretary of State shall issue the guidance in the form of his draft.

(9) The guidance shall come into force on such date as the Secretary of State may appoint by order.

(10) Subsection (7) does not prevent a new draft of the proposed guidance from being laid before Parliament.

(11) The Secretary of State may—
(a) from time to time revise the whole or part of any guidance and re-issue it;
(b) by order revoke any guidance.

(12) In this section—
"40-day period", in relation to the draft of any proposed guidance, means—
(a) if the draft is laid before one House on a day later than the day on which it is laid before the other House, the period of 40 days beginning with the later of the two days, and
(b) in any other case, the period of 40 days beginning with the day on which the draft is laid before each House,

no account being taken of any period during which Parliament is dissolved or prorogued or during which both Houses are adjourned for more than 4 days; and

"guidance" means guidance issued by the Secretary of State under this section and includes guidance which has been revised and re-issued.

NOTES

Initial Commencement

To be appointed

To be appointed: see s 70(3).

Appointment

Appointment (in relation to England, Wales and Scotland): 17 May 1996: see SI 1996/1336, arts 2, 3(c).

Appointment (in relation to Northern Ireland): 30 May 1996: see the Disability Discrimination Act 1995 (Commencement No 2) Order (Northern Ireland) 1996, SR 1996/219, arts 2, 3(c).

Appointed Day

Appointed day, for the purposes of sub-s (9): 31 July 1996: see SI 1996/1996.

Amendment

Sub-s (A1): inserted by the Disability Discrimination Act 2005, s 19(1), Sch 1, Pt 1, paras 1, 3(1), (2).

Date in force: 30 June 2005: see SI 2005/1676, art 2(1)(c).

Sub-s (1): words "Without prejudice to the generality of subsection (A1)," in square brackets inserted by the Disability Discrimination Act 2005, s 19(1), Sch 1, Pt 1, paras 1, 3(1), (3)(a).

Date in force: 30 June 2005: see SI 2005/1676, art 2(1)(c).

Sub-s (1): words ", in particular," in square brackets inserted by the Disability Discrimination Act 2005, s 19(1), Sch 1, Pt 1, paras 1, 3(1), (3)(b).

Date in force: 30 June 2005: see SI 2005/1676, art 2(1)(c).

Sub-s (2): words from "Without prejudice to" to "mentioned in subsection (1)" in square brackets substituted by the Disability Discrimination Act 2005, s 19(1), Sch 1, Pt 1, paras 1, 3(1), (4).

Date in force: 30 June 2005: see SI 2005/1676, art 2(1)(c).

Sub-s (3): words "An adjudicating body" in square brackets substituted by the Special Educational Needs and Disability Act 2001, s 38(1), (3).

Date in force: 1 September 2002: see SI 2002/2217, art 3, Sch 1, Pt 1.

Sub-s (3): words "or Part III of the 2005 Order" in square brackets inserted, in relation to Northern Ireland, by the Special Educational Needs and Disability (Northern Ireland) Order 2005, SI 2005/1117, art 48(1), (4).

Date in force: 1 September 2005: see the Special Educational Needs and Disability (2005 Order) (Commencement No 1) Order (Northern Ireland) 2005, SR 2005/336, art 2, Schedule (as amended by the Special Educational Needs and Disability (2005 Order) (Commencement No 1) (Amendment) Order (Northern Ireland) 2007, SR 2007/25, art 2) and the Special Educational Needs and Disability (2005 Order) (Commencement No 2) Order (Northern Ireland) 2005, SR 2005/337, art 2, Schedule.

Sub-s (3): words "a person is a disabled person" in square brackets substituted by the Disability Discrimination Act 2005, s 19(1), Sch 1, Pt 1, paras 1, 3(1), (5).

Date in force: 5 December 2005: see SI 2005/2774, art 3(j).

Sub-s (3A): inserted by the Special Educational Needs and Disability Act 2001, s 38(1), (4).

Date in force: 1 September 2002: see SI 2002/2217, art 3, Sch 1, Pt 1.

See Further

See further: corresponding amendments to those made to sub-ss (A1), (1)-(3) above by the Disability Discrimination Act 2005 have been made in relation to Northern Ireland: the Disability Discrimination (Northern Ireland) Order 2006, SI 2006/312, art 19(1), Sch 1, paras 1, 3.

Subordinate Legislation

Disability Discrimination (Guidance on the Definition of Disability) Appointed Day Order 2006, SI 2006/1005 (made under sub-s (9)).

Disability Discrimination (Guidance on the Definition of Disability) Revocation Order 2006, SI 2006/1007 (made under sub-s (11)(b)).

Part II

[The Employment Field] [and Members of Locally-Electable Authorities]

NOTES

Amendment

Part heading: words "The Employment Field" in square brackets substituted by SI 2003/1673, regs 3(1), 4(1).

Date in force (for certain purposes): 3 July 2003: see SI 2003/1673, reg 1(2).

Date in force (for remaining purposes): 1 October 2004: see SI 2003/1673, reg 1(3).

Part heading: words "and Members of Locally-Electable Authorities" in square brackets inserted by the Disability Discrimination Act 2005, s 19(1), Sch 1, Pt 1, paras 1, 4.

Date in force: 5 December 2005: see SI 2005/2774, art 3(j).

[Meaning of "discrimination" and "harassment"]

NOTES

Amendment

Inserted by SI 2003/1673, regs 3(1), 4(2).

Date in force (for certain purposes): 3 July 2003: see SI 2003/1673, reg 1(2).

Date in force (for remaining purposes): 1 October 2004: see SI 2003/1673, reg 1(3).

[3A Meaning of "discrimination"]

[(1) For the purposes of this Part, a person discriminates against a disabled person if—
  (a) for a reason which relates to the disabled person's disability, he treats him less favourably than he treats or would treat others to whom that reason does not or would not apply, and
  (b) he cannot show that the treatment in question is justified.
(2) For the purposes of this Part, a person also discriminates against a disabled person if he fails to comply with a duty to make reasonable adjustments imposed on him in relation to the disabled person.
(3) Treatment is justified for the purposes of subsection (1)(b) if, but only if, the reason for it is both material to the circumstances of the particular case and substantial.
(4) But treatment of a disabled person cannot be justified under subsection (3) if it amounts to direct discrimination falling within subsection (5).
(5) A person directly discriminates against a disabled person if, on the ground of the disabled person's disability, he treats the disabled person less favourably than he treats or would treat a person not having that particular disability whose relevant circumstances, including his abilities, are the same as, or not materially different from, those of the disabled person.
(6) If, in a case falling within subsection (1), a person is under a duty to make reasonable adjustments in relation to a disabled person but fails to comply with that duty, his treatment of that person cannot be justified under subsection (3) unless it would have been justified even if he had complied with that duty.]

NOTES

Amendment

Inserted by SI 2003/1673, regs 3(1), 4(2).

Date in force (for certain purposes): 3 July 2003: see SI 2003/1673, reg 1(2).

Date in force (for remaining purposes): 1 October 2004: see SI 2003/1673, reg 1(3).

[3B Meaning of "harassment"]

[(1) For the purposes of this Part, a person subjects a disabled person to harassment where, for a reason which relates to the disabled person's disability, he engages in unwanted conduct which has the purpose or effect of—
  (a) violating the disabled person's dignity, or
  (b) creating an intimidating, hostile, degrading, humiliating or offensive environment for him.
(2) Conduct shall be regarded as having the effect referred to in paragraph (a) or (b) of subsection (1) only if, having regard to all the circumstances, including in particular the perception of the disabled person, it should reasonably be considered as having that effect.]

NOTES

Amendment

Inserted by SI 2003/1673, regs 3(1), 4(2).

Date in force (for certain purposes): 3 July 2003: see SI 2003/1673, reg 1(2).

Date in force (for remaining purposes): 1 October 2004: see SI 2003/1673, reg 1(3).

[EMPLOYMENT]

NOTES

Amendment

Cross-heading: substituted by SI 2003/1673, regs 3(1), 5.

Date in force (for certain purposes): 3 July 2003: see SI 2003/1673, reg 1(2).

Date in force (for remaining purposes): 1 October 2004: see SI 2003/1673, reg 1(3).

[4 Employers: discrimination and harassment]

[(1) It is unlawful for an employer to discriminate against a disabled person—
  (a) in the arrangements which he makes for the purpose of determining to whom he should offer employment;
  (b) in the terms on which he offers that person employment; or
  (c) by refusing to offer, or deliberately not offering, him employment.

(2) It is unlawful for an employer to discriminate against a disabled person whom he employs—
  (a) in the terms of employment which he affords him;
  (b) in the opportunities which he affords him for promotion, a transfer, training or receiving any other benefit;
  (c) by refusing to afford him, or deliberately not affording him, any such oppor tunity; or
  (d) by dismissing him, or subjecting him to any other detriment.

(3) It is also unlawful for an employer, in relation to employment by him, to subject to harassment—
  (a) a disabled person whom he employs; or
  (b) a disabled person who has applied to him for employment.

(4) Subsection (2) does not apply to benefits of any description if the employer is concerned with the provision (whether or not for payment) of benefits of that description to the public, or to a section of the public which includes the employee in question, unless—
  (a) that provision differs in a material respect from the provision of the benefits by the employer to his employees;
  (b) the provision of the benefits to the employee in question is regulated by his contract of employment; or
  (c) the benefits relate to training.

(5) The reference in subsection (2)(d) to the dismissal of a person includes a reference—
  (a) to the termination of that person's employment by the expiration of any period (including a period expiring by reference to an event or circumstance), not being a termination immediately after which the employment is renewed on the same terms; and

(b) to the termination of that person's employment by any act of his (including the giving of notice) in circumstances such that he is entitled to terminate it without notice by reason of the conduct of the employer.

(6) This section applies only in relation to employment at an establishment in Great Britain.]

NOTES

Appointment

Appointment (in relation to Northern Ireland): 2 December 1996: see the Disability Discrimination Act 1995 (Commencement No 3 and Saving and Transitional Provisions) Order (Northern Ireland) 1996, SR 1996/280, art 2(2), Schedule, Pt II.

Appointment (in relation to England, Wales and Scotland): 2 December 1996: see SI 1996/1474, art 2(3), Schedule, Pt III.

Amendment

Substituted, together with ss 4A-4F, for ss 4-6 as originally enacted, by SI 2003/1673, regs 3(1), 5.

Date in force (for certain purposes): 3 July 2003: see SI 2003/1673, reg 1(2).

Date in force (for remaining purposes): 1 October 2004: see SI 2003/1673, reg 1(3).

Modification

Modified, in its application to employment by the governing body of a school having a right to a delegated budget, by the Education (Modification of Enactments Relating to Employment) (England) Order 2003, SI 2003/1964, art 3, Schedule.

Modified, in its application to employment by the governing body of a school having a right to a delegated budget, by the Education (Modification of Enactments Relating to Employment) (Wales) Order 2006, SI 2006/1073, art 3, Schedule.

[4A Employers: duty to make adjustments]

[(1) Where—

(a) a provision, criterion or practice applied by or on behalf of an employer, or

(b) any physical feature of premises occupied by the employer,

places the disabled person concerned at a substantial disadvantage in comparison with persons who are not disabled, it is the duty of the employer to take such steps as it is reasonable, in all the circumstances of the case, for him to have to take in order to prevent the provision, criterion or practice, or feature, having that effect.

(2) In subsection (1), "the disabled person concerned" means—

(a) in the case of a provision, criterion or practice for determining to whom employment should be offered, any disabled person who is, or has notified the employer that he may be, an applicant for that employment;

(b) in any other case, a disabled person who is—

(i) an applicant for the employment concerned, or

(ii) an employee of the employer concerned.

(3) Nothing in this section imposes any duty on an employer in relation to a disabled person if the employer does not know, and could not reasonably be expected to know—

(a) in the case of an applicant or potential applicant, that the disabled person concerned is, or may be, an applicant for the employment; or

(b) in any case, that that person has a disability and is likely to be affected in the way mentioned in subsection (1).]

NOTES

Amendment

Substituted, together with ss 4, 4B-4F, for ss 4-6 as originally enacted, by SI 2003/1673, regs 3(1), 5.

Date in force (for certain purposes): 3 July 2003: see SI 2003/1673, reg 1(2).

Date in force (for remaining purposes): 1 October 2004: see SI 2003/1673, reg 1(3).

Modification

Modified, in its application to employment by the governing body of a school having a right to a delegated budget, by the Education (Modification of Enactments Relating to Employment) (England) Order 2003, SI 2003/1964, art 3, Schedule.

Modified, in its application to employment by the governing body of a school having a right to a delegated budget, by the Education (Modification of Enactments Relating to Employment) (Wales) Order 2006, SI 2006/1073, art 3, Schedule.

[CONTRACT WORKERS]

NOTES

Amendment

Substituted, together with ss 4, 4A-4F, for ss 4-6 as originally enacted, by SI 2003/1673, regs 3(1), 5.

Date in force (for certain purposes): 3 July 2003: see SI 2003/1673, reg 1(2).

Date in force (for remaining purposes): 1 October 2004: see SI 2003/1673, reg 1(3).

[4B Contract workers]

[(1) It is unlawful for a principal, in relation to contract work, to discriminate against a disabled person who is a contract worker (a "disabled contract worker")—

(a) in the terms on which he allows him to do that work;

(b) by not allowing him to do it or continue to do it;

(c) in the way he affords him access to any benefits or by refusing or deliberately omitting to afford him access to them; or

(d) by subjecting him to any other detriment.

(2) It is also unlawful for a principal, in relation to contract work, to subject a disabled contract worker to harassment.

(3) Subsection (1) does not apply to benefits of any description if the principal is concerned with the provision (whether or not for payment) of benefits of that description to the public, or to a section of the public which includes the contract worker in question, unless that provision differs in a material respect from the provision of the benefits by the principal to contract workers.

(4) This subsection applies to a disabled contract worker where, by virtue of—

(a) a provision, criterion or practice applied by or on behalf of all or most of the principals to whom he is or might be supplied, or

(b) a physical feature of premises occupied by such persons,

he is likely, on each occasion when he is supplied to a principal to do contract work, to be placed at a substantial disadvantage in comparison with persons who are not disabled which is the same or similar in each case.

(5) Where subsection (4) applies to a disabled contract worker, his employer must take such steps as he would have to take under section 4A if the provision, criterion or practice were applied by him or on his behalf or (as the case may be) if the premises were occupied by him.

(6) Section 4A applies to any principal, in relation to contract work, as if he were, or would be, the employer of the disabled contract worker and as if any contract worker supplied to do work for him were an employee of his.

(7) However, for the purposes of section 4A as applied by subsection (6), a principal is not required to take a step in relation to a disabled contract worker if under that section the disabled contract worker's employer is required to take the step in relation to him.

(8) This section applies only in relation to contract work done at an establishment in Great Britain (the provisions of section 68 about the meaning of "employment at an establishment in Great Britain" applying for the purposes of this subsection with the appropriate modifications).

(9) In this section—

"principal" means a person ("A") who makes work available for doing by individuals who are employed by another person who supplies them under a contract made with A;

"contract work" means work so made available; and

"contract worker" means any individual who is supplied to the principal under such a contract.]

NOTES

Amendment

Substituted, together with ss 4, 4A, 4C-4F, for ss 4-6 as originally enacted, by SI 2003/1673, regs 3(1), 5.

Date in force (for certain purposes): 3 July 2003: see SI 2003/1673, reg 1(2).

Date in force (for remaining purposes): 1 October 2004: see SI 2003/1673, reg 1(3).

Modification

Modified, in its application to employment by the governing body of a school having a right to a delegated budget, by the Education (Modification of Enactments Relating to Employment) (England) Order 2003, SI 2003/1964, art 3, Schedule.

Modified, in its application to employment by the governing body of a school having a right to a delegated budget, by the Education (Modification of Enactments Relating to Employment) (Wales) Order 2006, SI 2006/1073, art 3, Schedule.

[Office-holders]

NOTES

Amendment

Substituted, together with ss 4, 4A-4F, for ss 4-6 as originally enacted, by SI 2003/1673, regs 3(1), 5.

Date in force (for certain purposes): 3 July 2003: see SI 2003/1673, reg 1(2).

Date in force (for remaining purposes): 1 October 2004: see SI 2003/1673, reg 1(3).

[4C Office-holders: introductory]

[(1) Subject to subsection (5), sections 4D and 4E apply to an office or post if—
   (a) no relevant provision of this Part applies in relation to an appointment to the office or post; and
   (b) one or more of the conditions specified in subsection (3) is satisfied.
(2) The following are relevant provisions of this Part for the purposes of subsection (1)(a): section 4, section 4B, section 6A, section 7A, section 7C[, section 14C and section 15B(3)(b)].
(3) The conditions specified in this subsection are that—
   (a) the office or post is one to which persons are appointed to discharge functions personally under the direction of another person, and in respect of which they are entitled to remuneration;
   (b) the office or post is one to which appointments are made by a Minister of the Crown, a government department, the [Welsh Ministers, the First Minister for Wales, the Counsel General to the Welsh Assembly Government] or any part of the Scottish Administration;
   (c) the office or post is one to which appointments are made on the recommendation of, or subject to the approval of, a person referred to in paragraph (b).
(4) For the purposes of subsection (3)(a) the holder of an office or post—
   (a) is to be regarded as discharging his functions under the direction of another person if that other person is entitled to direct him as to when and where he discharges those functions;
   (b) is not to be regarded as entitled to remuneration merely because he is entitled to payments—
      (i) in respect of expenses incurred by him in carrying out the functions of the office or post, or
      (ii) by way of compensation for the loss of income or benefits he would or might have received from any person had he not been carrying out the functions of the office or post.
(5) Sections 4D and 4E do not apply to—
   (a) any office of the House of Commons held by a member of it,
   (b) a life peerage within the meaning of the Life Peerages Act 1958, or any office of the House of Lords held by a member of it,

(c) any office mentioned in Schedule 2 (Ministerial offices) to the House of Commons Disqualification Act 1975,
(d) the offices of Leader of the Opposition, Chief Opposition Whip or Assistant Opposition Whip within the meaning of the Ministerial and other Salaries Act 1975,
(e) any office of the Scottish Parliament held by a member of it,
(f) a member of the Scottish Executive within the meaning of section 44 of the Scotland Act 1998, or a junior Scottish Minister within the meaning of section 49 of that Act,
(g) any office of the National Assembly for Wales held by a member of it,
[(ga) a member of the Welsh Assembly Government,]
(h) in England, any office of a county council, a London borough council, a district council or a parish council held by a member of it,
(i) in Wales, any office of a county council, a county borough council or a community council held by a member of it,
(j) in relation to a council constituted under section 2 of the Local Government etc (Scotland) Act 1994 or a community council established under section 51 of the Local Government (Scotland) Act 1973, any office of such a council held by a member of it,
(k) any office of the Greater London Authority held by a member of it,
(l) any office of the Common Council of the City of London held by a member of it,
(m) any office of the Council of the Isles of Scilly held by a member of it, or
(n) any office of a political party.]

NOTES

Amendment

Substituted, together with ss 4, 4A, 4B, 4D-4F, for ss 4-6 as originally enacted, by SI 2003/1673, regs 3(1), 5.

Date in force (for certain purposes): 3 July 2003: see SI 2003/1673, reg 1(2).

Date in force (for remaining purposes): 1 October 2004: see SI 2003/1673, reg 1(3).

Sub-s (2): words ", section 14C and section 15B(3)(b)" in square brackets substituted by the Disability Discrimination Act 2005, s 19(1), Sch 1, Pt 1, paras 1, 5.

Date in force: 5 December 2005: see SI 2005/2774, art 3(j).

Sub-s (3): in para (b) words "Welsh Ministers, the First Minister for Wales, the Counsel General to the Welsh Assembly Government" in square brackets substituted by SI 2007/1388, art 3, Sch 1, paras 47, 49(1), (2).

Date in force: this amendment came into force on 25 May 2007 being the date on which the initial period ended (following the appointment of the First Minister): see SI 2007/1388, art 1(2) and the Government of Wales Act 2006, ss 46, 161(5).

Sub-s (5): para (ga) inserted by SI 2007/1388, art 3, Sch 1, paras 47, 49(1), (3).

Date in force: this amendment came into force on 25 May 2007 being the date on which the initial period ended (following the appointment of the First Minister): see SI 2007/1388, art 1(2) and the Government of Wales Act 2006, ss 46, 161(5).

Modification

Modified, in its application to employment by the governing body of a school having a right to a delegated budget, by the Education (Modification of Enactments Relating to Employment) (England) Order 2003, SI 2003/1964, art 3, Schedule.

Modified, in its application to employment by the governing body of a school having a right to a delegated budget, by the Education (Modification of Enactments Relating to Employment) (Wales) Order 2006, SI 2006/1073, art 3, Schedule.

See Further

See further: corresponding amendments to those made to sub-s (2) above by the Disability Discrimination Act 2005, have been made in relation to Northern Ireland: the Disability Discrimination (Northern Ireland) Order 2006, SI 2006/312, art 19(1), Sch 1, paras 1, 5.

[4D Office-holders: discrimination and harassment]

[(1) It is unlawful for a relevant person, in relation to an appointment to an office or post to which this section applies, to discriminate against a disabled person—
   (a) in the arrangements which he makes for the purpose of determining who should be offered the appointment;
   (b) in the terms on which he offers him the appointment; or
   (c) by refusing to offer him the appointment.

(2) It is unlawful for a relevant person, in relation to an appointment to an office or post to which this section applies and which satisfies the condition set out in section 4C(3)(c), to discriminate against a disabled person—
   (a) in the arrangements which he makes for the purpose of determining who should be recommended or approved in relation to the appointment; or
   (b) in making or refusing to make a recommendation, or giving or refusing to give an approval, in relation to the appointment.

(3) It is unlawful for a relevant person, in relation to a disabled person who has been appointed to an office or post to which this section applies, to discriminate against him—
   (a) in the terms of the appointment;
   (b) in the opportunities which he affords him for promotion, a transfer, training or receiving any other benefit, or by refusing to afford him any such opportunity;
   (c) by terminating the appointment; or
   (d) by subjecting him to any other detriment in relation to the appointment.

(4) It is also unlawful for a relevant person, in relation to an office or post to which this section applies, to subject to harassment a disabled person—
   (a) who has been appointed to the office or post;
   (b) who is seeking or being considered for appointment to the office or post; or
   (c) who is seeking or being considered for a recommendation or approval in relation to an appointment to an office or post satisfying the condition set out in section 4C(3)(c).

(5) Subsection (3) does not apply to benefits of any description if the relevant person is concerned with the provision (for payment or not) of benefits of that description to the public, or a section of the public to which the disabled person belongs, unless—
   (a) that provision differs in a material respect from the provision of the benefits to persons appointed to offices or posts which are the same as, or not materially different from, that to which the disabled person has been appointed;

(b) the provision of the benefits to the person appointed is regulated by the terms and conditions of his appointment; or

(c) the benefits relate to training.

(6) In subsection (3)(c) the reference to the termination of the appointment includes a reference—

(a) to the termination of the appointment by the expiration of any period (including a period expiring by reference to an event or circumstance), not being a termination immediately after which the appointment is renewed on the same terms and conditions; and

(b) to the termination of the appointment by any act of the person appointed (including the giving of notice) in circumstances such that he is entitled to terminate the appointment by reason of the conduct of the relevant person.

(7) In this section—

(a) references to making a recommendation include references to making a negative recommendation; and

(b) references to refusal include references to deliberate omission.]

NOTES

Amendment

Substituted, together with ss 4, 4A-4C, 4E, 4F, for ss 4-6 as originally enacted, by SI 2003/1673, regs 3(1), 5.

Date in force (for certain purposes): 3 July 2003: see SI 2003/1673, reg 1(2).

Date in force (for remaining purposes): 1 October 2004: see SI 2003/1673, reg 1(3).

Modification

Modified, in its application to employment by the governing body of a school having a right to a delegated budget, by the Education (Modification of Enactments Relating to Employment) (England) Order 2003, SI 2003/1964, art 3, Schedule.

Modified, in its application to employment by the governing body of a school having a right to a delegated budget, by the Education (Modification of Enactments Relating to Employment) (Wales) Order 2006, SI 2006/1073, art 3, Schedule.

[4E Office-holders: duty to make adjustments]

[(1) Where—

(a) a provision, criterion or practice applied by or on behalf of a relevant person, or

(b) any physical feature of premises—

(i) under the control of a relevant person, and

(ii) at or from which the functions of an office or post to which this section applies are performed,

places the disabled person concerned at a substantial disadvantage in comparison with persons who are not disabled, it is the duty of the relevant person to take such steps as it is reasonable, in all the circumstances of the case, for him to have to take in order to prevent the provision, criterion or practice, or feature, having that effect.

(2) In this section, "the disabled person concerned" means—
(a) in the case of a provision, criterion or practice for determining who should be appointed to, or recommended or approved in relation to, an office or post to which this section applies, any disabled person who—
(i) is, or has notified the relevant person that he may be, seeking appointment to, or (as the case may be) seeking a recommendation or approval in relation to, that office or post, or
(ii) is being considered for appointment to, or (as the case may be) for a recommendation or approval in relation to, that office or post;
(b) in any other case, a disabled person—
(i) who is seeking or being considered for appointment to, or a recommendation or approval in relation to, the office or post concerned, or
(ii) who has been appointed to the office or post concerned.

(3) Nothing in this section imposes any duty on the relevant person in relation to a disabled person if the relevant person does not know, and could not reasonably be expected to know—
(a) in the case of a person who is being considered for, or is or may be seeking, appointment to, or a recommendation or approval in relation to, an office or post, that the disabled person concerned—
(i) is, or may be, seeking appointment to, or (as the case may be) seeking a recommendation or approval in relation to, that office or post, or
(ii) is being considered for appointment to, or (as the case may be) for a recommendation or approval in relation to, that office or post; or
(b) in any case, that that person has a disability and is likely to be affected in the way mentioned in subsection (1).]

NOTES

Amendment

Substituted, together with ss 4, 4A-4D, 4F, for ss 4-6 as originally enacted, by SI 2003/1673, regs 3(1), 5.

Date in force (for certain purposes): 3 July 2003: see SI 2003/1673, reg 1(2).

Date in force (for remaining purposes): 1 October 2004: see SI 2003/1673, reg 1(3).

Modification

Modified, in its application to employment by the governing body of a school having a right to a delegated budget, by the Education (Modification of Enactments Relating to Employment) (England) Order 2003, SI 2003/1964, art 3, Schedule.

Modified, in its application to employment by the governing body of a school having a right to a delegated budget, by the Education (Modification of Enactments Relating to Employment) (Wales) Order 2006, SI 2006/1073, art 3, Schedule.

[4F Office-holders: supplementary]

[(1) In sections 4C to 4E, appointment to an office or post does not include election to an office or post.

(2) In sections 4D and 4E, "relevant person" means—
   (a) in a case relating to an appointment to an office or post, the person with power to make that appointment;
   (b) in a case relating to the making of a recommendation or the giving of an approval in relation to an appointment, a person or body referred to in section 4C(3)(b) with power to make that recommendation or (as the case may be) to give that approval;
   (c) in a case relating to a term of an appointment, the person with power to determine that term;
   (d) in a case relating to a working condition afforded in relation to an appointment—
      (i) the person with power to determine that working condition; or
      (ii) where there is no such person, the person with power to make the appointment;
   (e) in a case relating to the termination of an appointment, the person with power to terminate the appointment;
   (f) in a case relating to the subjection of a disabled person to any other detriment or to harassment, any person or body falling within one or more of paragraphs (a) to (e) in relation to such cases as are there mentioned.

(3) In subsection (2)(d), "working condition" includes—
   (a) any opportunity for promotion, a transfer, training or receiving any other benefit; and
   (b) any physical feature of premises at or from which the functions of an office or post are performed.]

NOTES

Amendment

Substituted, together with ss 4, 4A-4E, for ss 4-6 as originally enacted, by SI 2003/1673, regs 3(1), 5.

Date in force (for certain purposes): 3 July 2003: see SI 2003/1673, reg 1(2).

Date in force (for remaining purposes): 1 October 2004: see SI 2003/1673, reg 1(3).

Modification

Modified, in its application to employment by the governing body of a school having a right to a delegated budget, by the Education (Modification of Enactments Relating to Employment) (England) Order 2003, SI 2003/1964, art 3, Schedule.

Modified, in its application to employment by the governing body of a school having a right to a delegated budget, by the Education (Modification of Enactments Relating to Employment) (Wales) Order 2006, SI 2006/1073, art 3, Schedule.

[Occupational pension schemes]

NOTES

Amendment

Inserted by SI 2003/2770, regs 2, 3.

Date in force (for certain purposes): 1 December 2003: see SI 2003/2770, reg 1(2).

Date in force (for remaining purposes): 1 October 2004: see SI 2003/2770, reg 1(3).

[4G Occupational pension schemes: non-discrimination rule]

[(1) Every occupational pension scheme shall be taken to include a provision ("the non-discrimination rule") containing the following requirements—

(a) a requirement that the trustees or managers of the scheme refrain from discriminating against a relevant disabled person in carrying out any of their functions in relation to the scheme (including in particular their functions relating to the admission of members to the scheme and the treatment of members of the scheme);

(b) a requirement that the trustees or managers of the scheme do not subject a relevant disabled person to harassment in relation to the scheme.

(2) The other provisions of the scheme are to have effect subject to the non-discrimination rule.

(3) It is unlawful for the trustees or managers of an occupational pension scheme—

(a) to discriminate against a relevant disabled person contrary to requirement (a) of the non-discrimination rule; or

(b) to subject a relevant disabled person to harassment contrary to requirement (b) of the non-discrimination rule.

(4) The non-discrimination rule does not apply in relation to rights accrued, or benefits payable, in respect of periods of service prior to the coming into force of this section (but it does apply to communications with members or prospective members of the scheme in relation to such rights or benefits).

(5) The trustees or managers of an occupational pension scheme may, if—

(a) they do not (apart from this subsection) have power to make such alterations to the scheme as may be required to secure conformity with the non-discrimination rule, or

(b) they have such power but the procedure for doing so—

(i) is liable to be unduly complex or protracted, or

(ii) involves the obtaining of consents which cannot be obtained, or can only be obtained with undue delay or difficulty,

by resolution make such alterations to the scheme.

(6) The alterations referred to in subsection (5) may have effect in relation to a period before the alterations are made (but may not have effect in relation to a period before the coming into force of this section).]

NOTES

Amendment

Inserted by SI 2003/2770, regs 2, 3.

Date in force (for certain purposes): 1 December 2003: see SI 2003/2770, reg 1(2).

Date in force (for remaining purposes): 1 October 2004: see SI 2003/2770, reg 1(3).

Modification

Modified, in its application to employment by the governing body of a school having a right to a delegated budget, by the Education (Modification of Enactments Relating to Employment) (England) Order 2003, SI 2003/1964, art 3, Schedule.

Modified, in its application to employment by the governing body of a school having a right to a delegated budget, by the Education (Modification of Enactments Relating to Employment) (Wales) Order 2006, SI 2006/1073, art 3, Schedule.

[4H Occupational pension schemes: duty to make adjustments]

[(1) Where—

(a) a provision, criterion or practice (including a scheme rule) applied by or on behalf of the trustees or managers of an occupational pension scheme, or

(b) any physical feature of premises occupied by the trustees or managers,

places a relevant disabled person at a substantial disadvantage in comparison with persons who are not disabled, it is the duty of the trustees or managers to take such steps as it is reasonable, in all the circumstances of the case, for them to have to take in order to prevent the provision, criterion or practice, or feature, having that effect.

(2) The making of alterations to scheme rules is (in addition to the examples set out in section 18B(2)) an example of a step which trustees or managers may have to take in order to comply with the duty set out in subsection (1).

(3) Nothing in subsection (1) imposes any duty on trustees or managers in relation to a disabled person if they do not know, and could not reasonably be expected to know—

(a) that the disabled person is a relevant disabled person; or

(b) that that person has a disability and is likely to be affected in the way mentioned in subsection (1).]

NOTES

Amendment

Inserted by SI 2003/2770, regs 2, 3.

Date in force (for certain purposes): 1 December 2003: see SI 2003/2770, reg 1(2).

Date in force (for remaining purposes): 1 October 2004: see SI 2003/2770, reg 1(3).

Modification

Modified, in its application to employment by the governing body of a school having a right to a delegated budget, by the Education (Modification of Enactments Relating to Employment) (England) Order 2003, SI 2003/1964, art 3, Schedule.

Modified, in its application to employment by the governing body of a school having a right to a delegated budget, by the Education (Modification of Enactments Relating to Employment) (Wales) Order 2006, SI 2006/1073, art 3, Schedule.

[4I Occupational pension schemes: procedure]

[(1) Where under section 17A a relevant disabled person presents a complaint to an employment tribunal that the trustees or managers of an occupational pension scheme have acted in relation to him in a way which is unlawful under this Part, the employer in relation to that scheme shall, for the purposes of the rules governing procedure, be treated as a party and be entitled to appear and be heard in accordance with those rules.

(2) In this section, "employer", in relation to an occupational pension scheme, has the meaning given by section 124(1) of the Pensions Act 1995 as at the date of coming into force of this section.]

NOTES

Amendment

Inserted by SI 2003/2770, regs 2, 3.

Date in force (for certain purposes): 1 December 2003: see SI 2003/2770, reg 1(2).

Date in force (for remaining purposes): 1 October 2004: see SI 2003/2770, reg 1(3).

Modification

Modified, in its application to employment by the governing body of a school having a right to a delegated budget, by the Education (Modification of Enactments Relating to Employment) (England) Order 2003, SI 2003/1964, art 3, Schedule.

Modified, in its application to employment by the governing body of a school having a right to a delegated budget, by the Education (Modification of Enactments Relating to Employment) (Wales) Order 2006, SI 2006/1073, art 3, Schedule.

[4J Occupational pension schemes: remedies]

[(1) This section applies where—
- (a) under section 17A a relevant disabled person presents to an employment tribunal a complaint that—
  - (i) the trustees or managers of an occupational pension scheme have acted in relation to him in a way which is unlawful under this Part; or
  - (ii) an employer has so acted in relation to him;
- (b) the complaint relates to—
  - (i) the terms on which persons become members of an occupational pension scheme, or
  - (ii) the terms on which members of the scheme are treated;
- (c) the disabled person is not a pensioner member of the scheme; and
- (d) the tribunal finds that the complaint is well-founded.

(2) The tribunal may, without prejudice to the generality of its power under section 17A(2)(a), make a declaration that the complainant has a right—
- (a) (where subsection (1)(b)(i) applies) to be admitted to the scheme in question; or
- (b) (where subsection (1)(b)(ii) applies) to membership of the scheme without discrimination.

(3) A declaration under subsection (2)—
- (a) may be made in respect of such period as the declaration may specify (but may not be made in respect of any period before the coming into force of this section);
- (b) may make such provision as the tribunal considers appropriate as to the terms upon which, or the capacity in which, the disabled person is to enjoy such admission or membership.

(4) The tribunal may not award the disabled person any compensation under section 17A(2)(b) (whether in relation to arrears of benefits or otherwise) other than—
- (a) compensation for injury to feelings;
- (b) compensation pursuant to section 17A(5).]

NOTES

Amendment

Inserted by SI 2003/2770, regs 2, 3.

Date in force (for certain purposes): 1 December 2003: see SI 2003/2770, reg 1(2).

Date in force (for remaining purposes): 1 October 2004: see SI 2003/2770, reg 1(3).

Modification

Modified, in its application to employment by the governing body of a school having a right to a delegated budget, by the Education (Modification of Enactments Relating to Employment) (England) Order 2003, SI 2003/1964, art 3, Schedule.

Modified, in its application to employment by the governing body of a school having a right to a delegated budget, by the Education (Modification of Enactments Relating to Employment) (Wales) Order 2006, SI 2006/1073, art 3, Schedule.

[4K Occupational pension schemes: supplementary]

[(1) In their application to communications, sections 4G to 4J apply in relation to a disabled person who is—

(a) entitled to the present payment of dependants' or survivors' benefits under an occupational pension scheme; or

(b) a pension credit member of such a scheme,

as they apply in relation to a disabled person who is a pensioner member of the scheme.

(2) In sections 4G to 4J and in this section—

"active member", "deferred member", "managers", "pension credit member", "pensioner member" and "trustees or managers" have the meanings given by section 124(1) of the Pensions Act 1995 as at the date of coming into force of this section;

"communications" includes—

(i) the provision of information, and

(ii) the operation of a dispute resolution procedure;

"member", in relation to an occupational pension scheme, means any active, deferred or pensioner member;

"non-discrimination rule" means the rule in section 4G(1);

"relevant disabled person", in relation to an occupational pension scheme, means a disabled person who is a member or prospective member of the scheme; and

"prospective member" means any person who, under the terms of his contract of employment or the scheme rules or both—

(i) is able, at his own option, to become a member of the scheme,

(ii) will become so able if he continues in the same employment for a sufficiently long period,

(iii) will be admitted to it automatically unless he makes an election not to become a member, or

(iv) may be admitted to it subject to the consent of his employer.]

NOTES

Amendment

Inserted by SI 2003/2770, regs 2, 3.

Date in force (for certain purposes): 1 December 2003: see SI 2003/2770, reg 1(2).

Date in force (for remaining purposes): 1 October 2004: see SI 2003/2770, reg 1(3).

Modification

Modified, in its application to employment by the governing body of a school having a right to a delegated budget, by the Education (Modification of Enactments Relating to Employment) (England) Order 2003, SI 2003/1964, art 3, Schedule.

Modified, in its application to employment by the governing body of a school having a right to a delegated budget, by the Education (Modification of Enactments Relating to Employment) (Wales) Order 2006, SI 2006/1073, art 3, Schedule.

5 . . .

. . .

NOTES

Amendment

Substituted, together with ss 4, 6, by new ss 4, 4A-4F, by SI 2003/1673, regs 3(1), 5.

Date in force (for certain purposes): 3 July 2003: see SI 2003/1673, reg 1(2).

Date in force (for remaining purposes): 1 October 2004: see SI 2003/1673, reg 1(3).

6 . . .

. . .

NOTES

Amendment

Substituted, together with ss 4, 5, by new ss 4, 4A-4F, by SI 2003/1673, regs 3(1), 5.

Date in force (for certain purposes): 3 July 2003: see SI 2003/1673, reg 1(2).

Date in force (for remaining purposes): 1 October 2004: see SI 2003/1673, reg 1(3).

[Partnerships]

NOTES

Amendment

Inserted by SI 2003/1673, regs 3(1), 6.

Date in force (for certain purposes): 3 July 2003: see SI 2003/1673, reg 1(2).

Date in force (for remaining purposes): 1 October 2004: see SI 2003/1673, reg 1(3).

[6A Partnerships: discrimination and harassment]

[(1) It is unlawful for a firm, in relation to a position as partner in the firm, to discriminate against a disabled person—
- (a) in the arrangements which they make for the purpose of determining who should be offered that position;
- (b) in the terms on which they offer him that position;
- (c) by refusing or deliberately omitting to offer him that position; or
- (d) in a case where the person already holds that position—
  - (i) in the way they afford him access to any benefits or by refusing or deliberately omitting to afford him access to them; or
  - (ii) by expelling him from that position, or subjecting him to any other detriment.

(2) It is also unlawful for a firm, in relation to a position as partner in the firm, to subject to harassment a disabled person who holds or has applied for that position.

(3) Subsection (1) does not apply to benefits of any description if the firm are concerned with the provision (whether or not for payment) of benefits of that description to the public, or to a section of the public which includes the partner in question, unless that provision differs in a material respect from the provision of the benefits to other partners.

(4) The reference in subsection (1)(d)(ii) to the expulsion of a person from a position as partner includes a reference—
- (a) to the termination of that person's partnership by the expiration of any period (including a period expiring by reference to an event or circumstance), not being a termination immediately after which the partnership is renewed on the same terms; and
- (b) to the termination of that person's partnership by any act of his (including the giving of notice) in circumstances such that he is entitled to terminate it without notice by reason of the conduct of the other partners.]

NOTES

Amendment

Inserted by SI 2003/1673, regs 3(1), 6.

Date in force (for certain purposes): 3 July 2003: see SI 2003/1673, reg 1(2).

Date in force (for remaining purposes): 1 October 2004: see SI 2003/1673, reg 1(3).

[6B Partnerships: duty to make adjustments]

[(1) Where—
- (a) a provision, criterion or practice applied by or on behalf of a firm, or
- (b) any physical feature of premises occupied by the firm,

places the disabled person concerned at a substantial disadvantage in comparison with persons who are not disabled, it is the duty of the firm to take such steps as it is reasonable, in all the circumstances of the case, for them to have to take in order to prevent the provision, criterion or practice, or feature, having that effect.

"pupil", "pupillage" and "set of chambers" have the meanings commonly associated with their use in the context of barristers practising in independent practice; and

"tenancy" and "tenant" have the meanings commonly associated with their use in the context of barristers practising in independent practice, but they also include reference to any barrister permitted to practise from a set of chambers.]

NOTES

Extent

This section applies to England and Wales only: see s 70(5A).

Amendment

Inserted by SI 2003/1673, regs 3(1), 8.

Date in force (for certain purposes): 3 July 2003: see SI 2003/1673, reg 1(2).

Date in force (for remaining purposes): 1 October 2004: see SI 2003/1673, reg 1(3).

[7B Barristers: duty to make adjustments]

[(1) Where—

(a) a provision, criterion or practice applied by or on behalf of a barrister or barrister's clerk, or

(b) any physical feature of premises occupied by a barrister or a barrister's clerk,

places the disabled person concerned at a substantial disadvantage in comparison with persons who are not disabled, it is the duty of the barrister or barrister's clerk to take such steps as it is reasonable, in all the circumstances of the case, for him to have to take in order to prevent the provision, criterion or practice, or feature, having that effect.

(2) In a case where subsection (1) applies in relation to two or more barristers in a set of chambers, the duty in that subsection is a duty on each of them to take such steps as it is reasonable, in all of the circumstances of the case, for him to have to take.

(3) In this section, "the disabled person concerned" means—

(a) in the case of a provision, criterion or practice for determining to whom a pupillage or tenancy should be offered, any disabled person who is, or has notified the barrister or the barrister's clerk concerned that he may be, an applicant for a pupillage or tenancy;

(b) in any other case, a disabled person who is—

(i) a tenant;

(ii) a pupil; or

(iii) an applicant for a pupillage or tenancy.

(4) Nothing in this section imposes any duty on a barrister or a barrister's clerk in relation to a disabled person if he does not know, and could not reasonably be expected to know—

(a) in the case of an applicant or potential applicant, that the disabled person concerned is, or may be, an applicant for a pupillage or tenancy; or

(b) in any case, that that person has a disability and is likely to be affected in the way mentioned in subsection (1).]

NOTES

Extent

This section applies to England and Wales only: see s 70(5A).

Amendment

Inserted by SI 2003/1673, regs 3(1), 8.

Date in force (for certain purposes): 3 July 2003: see SI 2003/1673, reg 1(2).

Date in force (for remaining purposes): 1 October 2004: see SI 2003/1673, reg 1(3).

[7C Advocates: discrimination and harassment]

[(1) It is unlawful for an advocate, in relation to taking any person as his pupil, to discriminate against a disabled person—

(a) in the arrangements which he makes for the purpose of determining whom he will take as his pupil;

(b) in respect of any terms on which he offers to take the disabled person as his pupil; or

(c) by refusing, or deliberately omitting, to take the disabled person as his pupil.

(2) It is unlawful for an advocate, in relation to a disabled person who is a pupil, to discriminate against him—

(a) in respect of any terms applicable to him as a pupil;

(b) in the opportunities for training, or gaining experience, which are afforded or denied to him;

(c) in the benefits which are afforded or denied to him;

(d) by terminating the relationship or by subjecting him to any pressure to leave; or

(e) by subjecting him to any other detriment.

(3) It is unlawful for an advocate, in relation to taking any person as his pupil, to subject to harassment a disabled person who is, or has applied to be taken as, his pupil.

(4) It is also unlawful for any person, in relation to the giving, withholding or acceptance of instructions to an advocate, to discriminate against a disabled person or to subject him to harassment.

(5) In this section and section 7D—

"advocate" means a member of the Faculty of Advocates practising as such; and

"pupil" has the meaning commonly associated with its use in the context of a person training to be an advocate.]

NOTES

Extent

This section applies to Scotland only: see s 70(5B).

Amendment

Inserted by SI 2003/1673, regs 3(1), 8.

Date in force (for certain purposes): 3 July 2003: see SI 2003/1673, reg 1(2).

Date in force (for remaining purposes): 1 October 2004: see SI 2003/1673, reg 1(3).

[7D Advocates: duty to make adjustments]

[(1) Where—

(a) a provision, criterion or practice applied by or on behalf of an advocate, or

(b) any physical feature of premises occupied by, and under the control of, an advocate, places the disabled person concerned at a substantial disadvantage in comparison with persons who are not disabled, it is the duty of the advocate to take such steps as it is reasonable, in all the circumstances of the case, for him to have to take in order to prevent the provision, criterion or practice, or feature, having that effect.

(2) In this section, "the disabled person concerned" means—
   (a) in the case of a provision, criterion or practice for determining whom he will take as his pupil, any disabled person who has applied, or has notified the advocate that he may apply, to be taken as a pupil;
   (b) in any other case, a disabled person who is—
      (i) an applicant to be taken as the advocate's pupil, or
      (ii) a pupil.

(3) Nothing in this section imposes any duty on an advocate in relation to a disabled person if he does not know, and could not reasonably be expected to know—
   (a) in the case of an applicant or potential applicant, that the disabled person concerned is, or may be, applying to be taken as his pupil; or
   (b) in any case, that that person has a disability and is likely to be affected in the way mentioned in subsection (1).]

NOTES

Extent

This section applies to Scotland only: see s 70(5B).

Amendment

Inserted by SI 2003/1673, regs 3(1), 8.

Date in force (for certain purposes): 3 July 2003: see SI 2003/1673, reg 1(2).

Date in force (for remaining purposes): 1 October 2004: see SI 2003/1673, reg 1(3).

. . .

NOTES

Amendment

Repealed by virtue of SI 2003/1673, regs 3(1), 9(1).

Date in force (for certain purposes): 3 July 2003: see SI 2003/1673, reg 1(2).

Date in force (for remaining purposes): 1 October 2004: see SI 2003/1673, reg 1(3).

8 . . .

. . .

NOTES

Amendment

Repealed by virtue of SI 2003/1673, regs 3(1), 9(1).

Date in force (for certain purposes): 3 July 2003: see SI 2003/1673, reg 1(2).

Date in force (for remaining purposes): 1 October 2004: see SI 2003/1673, reg 1(3).

9 . . .

. . .

NOTES

Amendment

Repealed by SI 2003/1673, regs 3(1), 10.

Date in force (for certain purposes): 3 July 2003: see SI 2003/1673, reg 1(2).

Date in force (for remaining purposes): 1 October 2004: see SI 2003/1673, reg 1(3).

Subordinate Legislation

Compromise Agreements (Description of Person) Order 2004, SI 2004/754 (made under sub-s (4)(d)).

Compromise Agreements (Description of Person) Order 2004 (Amendment) Order 2004, SI 2004/2515 (made under sub-s (4)(d)).

10 . . .

. . .

NOTES

Amendment

Repealed by virtue of SI 2003/1673, regs 3(1), 11.

Date in force (for certain purposes): 3 July 2003: see SI 2003/1673, reg 1(2).

Date in force (for remaining purposes): 1 October 2004: see SI 2003/1673, reg 1(3).

11 . . .

. . .

NOTES

Amendment

Repealed by SI 2003/1673, regs 3(1), 12.

Date in force (for certain purposes): 3 July 2003: see SI 2003/1673, reg 1(2).

Date in force (for remaining purposes): 1 October 2004: see SI 2003/1673, reg 1(3).

. . .

NOTES

Amendment

Repealed by SI 2003/1673, regs 3(1), 12.

Date in force (for certain purposes): 3 July 2003: see SI 2003/1673, reg 1(2).

Date in force (for remaining purposes): 1 October 2004: see SI 2003/1673, reg 1(3).

12 . . .

. . .

NOTES

Amendment

Repealed by SI 2003/1673, regs 3(1), 12.

Date in force (for certain purposes): 3 July 2003: see SI 2003/1673, reg 1(2).

Date in force (for remaining purposes): 1 October 2004: see SI 2003/1673, reg 1(3).

[Trade and professional bodies]

NOTES

Amendment

Substituted, together with ss 13, 14, 14A-14D, for ss 13-15 as originally enacted, by SI 2003/1673, regs 3(1), 13.

Date in force (for certain purposes): 3 July 2003: see SI 2003/1673, reg 1(2).

Date in force (for remaining purposes): 1 October 2004: see SI 2003/1673, reg 1(3).

[13 Trade organisations: discrimination and harassment]

[(1) It is unlawful for a trade organisation to discriminate against a disabled person—
- (a) in the arrangements which it makes for the purpose of determining who should be offered membership of the organisation;
- (b) in the terms on which it is prepared to admit him to membership of the organisation; or
- (c) by refusing to accept, or deliberately not accepting, his application for membership.

(2) It is unlawful for a trade organisation, in the case of a disabled person who is a member of the organisation, to discriminate against him—
- (a) in the way it affords him access to any benefits or by refusing or deliberately omitting to afford him access to them;
- (b) by depriving him of membership, or varying the terms on which he is a member; or
- (c) by subjecting him to any other detriment.

(3) It is also unlawful for a trade organisation, in relation to membership of that organisation, to subject to harassment a disabled person who—
- (a) is a member of the organisation; or
- (b) has applied for membership of the organisation.

(4) In this section and section 14 "trade organisation" means—
- (a) an organisation of workers;
- (b) an organisation of employers; or
- (c) any other organisation whose members carry on a particular profession or trade for the purposes of which the organisation exists.]

NOTES

Amendment

Substituted, together with ss 14, 14A-14D, for ss 13-15 as originally enacted, by SI 2003/1673, regs 3(1), 13.

Date in force (for certain purposes): 3 July 2003: see SI 2003/1673, reg 1(2).

Date in force (for remaining purposes): 1 October 2004: see SI 2003/1673, reg 1(3).

[14 Trade organisations: duty to make adjustments]

[(1) Where—

(a) a provision, criterion or practice applied by or on behalf of a trade organisation, or

(b) any physical feature of premises occupied by the organisation,

places the disabled person concerned at a substantial disadvantage in comparison with persons who are not disabled, it is the duty of the organisation to take such steps as it is reasonable, in all the circumstances of the case, for it to have to take in order to prevent the provision, criterion or practice, or feature, having that effect.

(2) In this section "the disabled person concerned" means—

(a) in the case of a provision, criterion or practice for determining to whom membership should be offered, any disabled person who is, or has notified the organisation that he may be, an applicant for membership;

(b) in any other case, a disabled person who is—

(i) a member of the organisation, or

(ii) an applicant for membership of the organisation.

(3) Nothing in this section imposes any duty on an organisation in relation to a disabled person if the organisation does not know, and could not reasonably be expected to know—

(a) in the case of an applicant or potential applicant, that the disabled person concerned is, or may be, an applicant for membership of the organisation; or

(b) in any case, that that person has a disability and is likely to be affected in the way mentioned in subsection (1).]

NOTES

Amendment

Substituted, together with ss 13, 14A-14D, for ss 13-15 as originally enacted, by SI 2003/1673, regs 3(1), 13.

Date in force (for certain purposes): 3 July 2003: see SI 2003/1673, reg 1(2).

Date in force (for remaining purposes): 1 October 2004: see SI 2003/1673, reg 1(3).

[14A Qualifications bodies: discrimination and harassment]

[(1) It is unlawful for a qualifications body to discriminate against a disabled person—

(a) in the arrangements which it makes for the purpose of determining upon whom to confer a professional or trade qualification;

(b) in the terms on which it is prepared to confer a professional or trade qualification on him;

(c) by refusing or deliberately omitting to grant any application by him for such a qualification; or

(d) by withdrawing such a qualification from him or varying the terms on which he holds it.

(2) It is also unlawful for a qualifications body, in relation to a professional or trade qualification conferred by it, to subject to harassment a disabled person who holds or applies for such a qualification.

(3) In determining for the purposes of subsection (1) whether the application by a qualifications body of a competence standard to a disabled person constitutes discrimination within the meaning of section 3A, the application of the standard is justified for the purposes of section 3A(1)(b) if, but only if, the qualifications body can show that—

(a) the standard is, or would be, applied equally to persons who do not have his particular disability; and

(b) its application is a proportionate means of achieving a legitimate aim.

(4) For the purposes of subsection (3)—

(a) section 3A(2) (and (6)) does not apply; and

(b) section 3A(4) has effect as if the reference to section 3A(3) were a reference to subsection (3) of this section.

(5) In this section and section 14B—

"qualifications body" means any authority or body which can confer a professional or trade qualification, but it does not include—

(a) a responsible body (within the meaning of Chapter 1 or 2 of Part 4),

(b) a local education authority in England or Wales, or

(c) an education authority (within the meaning of section 135(1) of the Education (Scotland) Act 1980);

"confer" includes renew or extend;

"professional or trade qualification" means an authorisation, qualification, recognition, registration, enrolment, approval or certification which is needed for, or facilitates engagement in, a particular profession or trade;

"competence standard" means an academic, medical or other standard applied by or on behalf of a qualifications body for the purpose of determining whether or not a person has a particular level of competence or ability.]

NOTES

Amendment

Substituted, together with ss 13, 14, 14B-14D, for ss 13-15 as originally enacted, by SI 2003/1673, regs 3(1), 13.

Date in force (for certain purposes): 3 July 2003: see SI 2003/1673, reg 1(2).

Date in force (for remaining purposes): 1 October 2004: see SI 2003/1673, reg 1(3).

[14B Qualifications bodies: duty to make adjustments]

[(1) Where—

(a) a provision, criterion or practice, other than a competence standard, applied by or on behalf of a qualifications body; or

(b) any physical feature of premises occupied by a qualifications body,

places the disabled person concerned at a substantial disadvantage in comparison with persons who are not disabled, it is the duty of the qualifications body to take such steps as it is reasonable, in all the circumstances of the case, for it to have to take in order to prevent the provision, criterion or practice, or feature, having that effect.

(2) In this section "the disabled person concerned" means—

(a) in the case of a provision, criterion or practice for determining on whom a professional or trade qualification is to be conferred, any disabled person who is, or has notified the qualifications body that he may be, an applicant for the conferment of that qualification;

(b) in any other case, a disabled person who—

(i) holds a professional or trade qualification conferred by the qualifications body, or

(ii) applies for a professional or trade qualification which it confers.

(3) Nothing in this section imposes a duty on a qualifications body in relation to a disabled person if the body does not know, and could not reasonably be expected to know—

(a) in the case of an applicant or potential applicant, that the disabled person con cerned is, or may be, an applicant for the conferment of a professional or trade qualification; or

(b) in any case, that that person has a disability and is likely to be affected in the way mentioned in subsection (1).]

NOTES

Amendment

Substituted, together with ss 13, 14, 14A, 14C, 14D, for ss 13-15 as originally enacted, by SI 2003/1673, regs 3(1), 13.

Date in force (for certain purposes): 3 July 2003: see SI 2003/1673, reg 1(2).

Date in force (for remaining purposes): 1 October 2004: see SI 2003/1673, reg 1(3).

[PRACTICAL WORK EXPERIENCE]

NOTES

Amendment

Substituted, together with ss 13, 14, 14A-14D, for ss 13-15 as originally enacted, by SI 2003/1673, regs 3(1), 13.

Date in force (for certain purposes): 3 July 2003: see SI 2003/1673, reg 1(2).

Date in force (for remaining purposes): 1 October 2004: see SI 2003/1673, reg 1(3).

[14C Practical work experience: discrimination and harassment]

[(1) It is unlawful, in the case of a disabled person seeking or undertaking a work placement, for a placement provider to discriminate against him—

(a) in the arrangements which he makes for the purpose of determining who should be offered a work placement;

(b) in the terms on which he affords him access to any work placement or any facilities concerned with such a placement;

(c) by refusing or deliberately omitting to afford him such access;

(d) by terminating the placement; or

(e) by subjecting him to any other detriment in relation to the placement.

(2) It is also unlawful for a placement provider, in relation to a work placement, to subject to harassment—
(a) a disabled person to whom he is providing a placement; or
(b) a disabled person who has applied to him for a placement.

[(3) This section and section 14D do not apply—
(a) to anything which is unlawful under any provision of section 4, sections 19 to 21A, sections 21F to 21J or Part 4; or
(b) to anything which would be unlawful under any such provision but for the operation of any provision in or made under this Act.]

(4) In this section and section 14D—
"work placement" means practical work experience undertaken for a limited period for the purposes of a person's vocational training;
"placement provider" means any person who provides a work placement to a person whom he does not employ.

(5) This section and section 14D do not apply to a work placement undertaken in any of the naval, military and air forces of the Crown.]

NOTES

Amendment

Substituted, together with ss 13, 14, 14A, 14B, 14D, for ss 13-15 as originally enacted, by SI 2003/1673, regs 3(1), 13.

Date in force (for certain purposes): 3 July 2003: see SI 2003/1673, reg 1(2).

Date in force (for remaining purposes): 1 October 2004: see SI 2003/1673, reg 1(3).

Sub-s (3): substituted by the Disability Discrimination Act 2005, s 19(1), Sch 1, Pt 1, paras 1, 6.

Date in force: 5 December 2005: see SI 2005/2774, art 3(j).

See Further

See further: a corresponding amendment has been made to that made to sub-s (3) above by the Disability Discrimination Act 2005, in relation to Northern Ireland: the Disability Discrimination (Northern Ireland) Order 2006, SI 2006/312, art 19(1), Sch 1, paras 1, 6.

[14D Practical work experience: duty to make adjustments]

[(1) Where—
(a) a provision, criterion or practice applied by or on behalf of a placement provider, or
(b) any physical feature of premises occupied by the placement provider,

places the disabled person concerned at a substantial disadvantage in comparison with persons who are not disabled, it is the duty of the placement provider to take such steps as it is reasonable, in all the circumstances of the case, for him to have to take in order to prevent the provision, criterion or practice, or feature, having that effect.

(2) In this section, "the disabled person concerned" means—
(a) in the case of a provision, criterion or practice for determining to whom a work placement should be offered, any disabled person who is, or has notified the placement provider that he may be, an applicant for that work placement;

(b) in any other case, a disabled person who is—
  (i) an applicant for the work placement concerned, or
  (ii) undertaking a work placement with the placement provider.

(3) Nothing in this section imposes any duty on a placement provider in relation to the disabled person concerned if he does not know, and could not reasonably be expected to know—
  (a) in the case of an applicant or potential applicant, that the disabled person concerned is, or may be, an applicant for the work placement; or
  (b) in any case, that that person has a disability and is likely to be affected in the way mentioned in subsection (1).]

NOTES

Amendment

Substituted, together with ss 13, 14, 14A-14C, for ss 13-15 as originally enacted, by SI 2003/1673, regs 3(1), 13.

Date in force (for certain purposes): 3 July 2003: see SI 2003/1673, reg 1(2).

Date in force (for remaining purposes): 1 October 2004: see SI 2003/1673, reg 1(3).

15 . . .

. . .

NOTES

Amendment

Substituted, together with ss 13, 14, 14A-14D, for ss 13-15 as originally enacted, by SI 2003/1673, regs 3(1), 13.

Date in force (for certain purposes): 3 July 2003: see SI 2003/1673, reg 1(2).

Date in force (for remaining purposes): 1 October 2004: see SI 2003/1673, reg 1(3).

[RELATIONSHIPS BETWEEN LOCALLY-ELECTABLE AUTHORITIES AND THEIR MEMBERS]

NOTES

Amendment

Inserted by the Disability Discrimination Act 2005, s 1.

Date in force (for certain purposes): 5 December 2005: see SI 2005/2774, art 3(a).

Date in force (for remaining purposes): 4 December 2006: see SI 2005/2774, art 4(a).

[15A Interpretation of sections 15B and 15C]

[(1) Sections 15B and 15C apply to the following authorities—
  (a) the Greater London Authority;
  (b) a county council (in England or Wales);
  (c) a county borough council (in Wales);

(d) a district council (in England);
(e) a London borough council;
(f) the Common Council of the City of London;
(g) the Council of the Isles of Scilly;
(h) a council constituted under section 2 of the Local Government etc (Scotland) Act 1994;
(i) a parish council (in England); and
(j) a community council (in Wales or Scotland).

(2) In relation to a member of an authority to which sections 15B and 15C apply, a reference in those sections to his carrying-out of official business is to his doing of anything—
(a) as member of the authority;
(b) as member of any body to which he is appointed by, or is appointed following nomination by, the authority or a group of bodies that includes the authority; or
(c) as member of any other body if it is a public body.

(3) In this section and sections 15B and 15C "member", in relation to the Greater London Authority, means Mayor of London or member of the London Assembly.]

NOTES

Amendment

Inserted by the Disability Discrimination Act 2005, s 1.

Date in force (for certain purposes): 5 December 2005: see SI 2005/2774, art 3(a).

Date in force (for remaining purposes): 4 December 2006: see SI 2005/2774, art 4(a).

See Further

See further: a corresponding amendment has been made in relation to Northern Ireland: the Disability Discrimination (Northern Ireland) Order 2006, SI 2006/312, art 3.

[15B Authorities and their members: discrimination and harassment]

[(1) It is unlawful for an authority to which this section applies to discriminate against a disabled person who is a member of the authority—
(a) in the opportunities which it affords the disabled person to receive training, or any other facility, for his carrying-out of official business;
(b) by refusing to afford, or deliberately not affording, the disabled person any such opportunities; or
(c) by subjecting the disabled person to any other detriment in connection with his carrying-out of official business.

(2) It is unlawful for an authority to which this section applies to subject a disabled person who is a member of the authority to harassment in connection with his carrying-out of official business.

(3) A member of an authority to which this section applies is not subjected to a detriment for the purposes of subsection (1)(c) by reason of—
(a) his not being appointed or elected to an office of the authority;
(b) his not being appointed or elected to, or to an office of, a committee or sub-committee of the authority; or
(c) his not being appointed or nominated in exercise of any power of the authority, or of a group of bodies that includes the authority, to appoint, or nominate for appointment, to any body.

(4) Regulations may make provision as to the circumstances in which treatment is to be taken to be justified, or is to be taken not to be justified, for the purposes of section 3A(1)(b) as it has effect for the interpretation of "discriminate" in subsection (1).

(5) Regulations under subsection (4) may (in particular) provide for section 3A(3) to apply with prescribed modifications, or not to apply, for those purposes; but treatment of a disabled person cannot be justified under subsection (4) if it amounts to direct discrimination falling within section 3A(5).

(6) If, in a case falling within section 3A(1) as it has effect for the interpretation of "discriminate" in subsection (1), an authority to which this section applies is under a duty imposed by section 15C in relation to a disabled person but fails to comply with that duty, its treatment of that person cannot be justified under subsection (4) unless it would have been justified even if it had complied with that duty.]

NOTES

Amendment

Inserted by the Disability Discrimination Act 2005, s 1.

Date in force: 5 December 2005: see SI 2005/2774, art 3(a).

See Further

See further: a corresponding amendment has been made in relation to Northern Ireland: the Disability Discrimination (Northern Ireland) Order 2006, SI 2006/312, art 3.

[15C Authorities and their members: duty to make adjustments]

[(1) Subsection (2) applies where—

(a) a provision, criterion or practice applied by or on behalf of an authority to which this section applies, or

(b) any physical feature of premises occupied by, or under the control of, such an authority,

places a disabled person who is a member of the authority at a substantial disadvantage, in comparison with members of the authority who are not disabled persons, in connection with his carrying-out of official business.

(2) It is the duty of the authority to take such steps as it is reasonable, in all the circumstances of the case, for it to have to take in order to prevent the provision, criterion or practice, or feature, having that effect.

(3) Subsection (2) does not impose any duty on an authority to which this section applies in relation to a member of the authority who is a disabled person if the authority does not know, and could not reasonably be expected to know, that the member—

(a) has a disability; and

(b) is likely to be affected in the way mentioned in subsection (1).

(4) Regulations may make provision, for purposes of this section—

(a) as to circumstances in which a provision, criterion or practice, or physical feature, is to be taken to have the effect mentioned in subsection (1);

(b) as to circumstances in which a provision, criterion or practice, or physical feature, is to be taken not to have the effect mentioned in subsection (1);

(c) as to circumstances in which it is, or as to circumstances in which it is not, reasonable for an authority to have to take steps of a prescribed description;

(d) as to steps which it is always, or as to steps which it is never, reasonable for an authority to have to take;

(e) as to things which are, or as to things which are not, to be treated as physical features.]

NOTES

Amendment

Inserted by the Disability Discrimination Act 2005, s 1.

Date in force: 4 December 2006: see SI 2005/2774, art 4(a).

See Further

See further: a corresponding amendment has been made in relation to Northern Ireland: the Disability Discrimination (Northern Ireland) Order 2006, SI 2006/312, art 3.

. . .

NOTES

Amendment

Cross-heading: repealed by SI 2003/1673, regs 3(1), 14(1).

Date in force (for certain purposes): 3 July 2003: see SI 2003/1673, reg 1(2).

Date in force (for remaining purposes): 1 October 2004: see SI 2003/1673, reg 1(3).

16 . . .

. . .

NOTES

Amendment

Repealed by virtue of SI 2003/1673, regs 3(1), 14(2).

Date in force (for certain purposes): 3 July 2003: see SI 2003/1673, reg 1(2).

Date in force (for remaining purposes): 1 October 2004: see SI 2003/1673, reg 1(3).

[Other unlawful acts]

NOTES

Amendment

Inserted by SI 2003/1673, regs 3(1), 15(1).

Date in force (for certain purposes): 3 July 2003: see SI 2003/1673, reg 1(2).

Date in force (for remaining purposes): 1 October 2004: see SI 2003/1673, reg 1(3).

[16A Relationships which have come to an end]

[(1) This section applies where—
(a) there has been a relevant relationship between a disabled person and another person ("the relevant person"), and
(b) the relationship has come to an end.
(2) In this section a "relevant relationship" is—
(a) a relationship during the course of which an act of discrimination against, or harassment of, one party to the relationship by the other party to it is unlawful under any preceding provision of this Part[, other than sections 15B and 15C]; or
(b) a relationship between a person providing employment services . . . and a person receiving such services.
(3) It is unlawful for the relevant person—
(a) to discriminate against the disabled person by subjecting him to a detriment, or
(b) to subject the disabled person to harassment,
where the discrimination or harassment arises out of and is closely connected to the relevant relationship.
(4) This subsection applies where—
(a) a provision, criterion or practice applied by the relevant person to the disabled person in relation to any matter arising out of the relevant relationship, or
(b) a physical feature of premises which are occupied by the relevant person,
places the disabled person at a substantial disadvantage in comparison with persons who are not disabled, but are in the same position as the disabled person in relation to the relevant person.
(5) Where subsection (4) applies, it is the duty of the relevant person to take such steps as it is reasonable, in all the circumstances of the case, for him to have to take in order to prevent the provision, practice or criterion, or feature, having that effect.
(6) Nothing in subsection (5) imposes any duty on the relevant person if he does not know, and could not reasonably be expected to know, that the disabled person has a disability and is likely to be affected in the way mentioned in that subsection.
(7) In subsection (2), reference to an act of discrimination or harassment which is unlawful includes, in the case of a relationship which has come to an end before the commencement of this section, reference to such an act which would, after the commencement of this section, be unlawful.]

NOTES

Amendment

Inserted by SI 2003/1673, regs 3(1), 15(1).

Date in force (for certain purposes): 3 July 2003: see SI 2003/1673, reg 1(2).

Date in force (for remaining purposes): 1 October 2004: see SI 2003/1673, reg 1(3).

Sub-s (2): in para (a) words ", other than sections 15B and 15C" in square brackets inserted by the Disability Discrimination Act 2005, s 19(1), Sch 1, Pt 1, paras 1, 7(a).

Date in force (for certain purposes): 5 December 2005: see SI 2005/2774, art 3(j).

Date in force (for remaining purposes): 4 December 2006: see SI 2005/2774, art 4(f).

Sub-s (2): in para (b) words omitted repealed by the Disability Discrimination Act 2005, s 19, Sch 1, Pt 1, paras 1, 7(b), Sch 2.

Date in force: 5 December 2005: see SI 2005/2774, art 3(j), (k)(i).

See Further

See further: a corresponding amendment and repeal to those made to sub-s (2) above by the Disability Discrimination Act 205 have been made in relation to Northern Ireland: the Disability Discrimination (Northern Ireland) Order 2006, SI 2006/312, art 19, Sch 1, paras 1, 7, Sch 2.

[16B Discriminatory advertisements]

[[(1) It is unlawful for a person to publish or cause to be published an advertisement which—

(a) invites applications for a relevant appointment or benefit; and

(b) indicates, or might reasonably be understood to indicate, that an application will or may be determined to any extent by reference to—

(i) the applicant not having any disability, or any particular disability,

(ii) the applicant not having had any disability, or any particular disability, or

(iii) any reluctance of the person determining the application to comply with a duty to make reasonable adjustments or (in relation to employment services) with the duty imposed by section 21(1) as modified by section 21A(6).]

(2) Subsection (1) does not apply where it would not in fact be unlawful under this Part or, to the extent that it relates to the provision of employment services, Part 3 for an application to be determined in the manner indicated (or understood to be indicated) in the advertisement.

[(2A) A person who publishes an advertisement of the kind described in subsection (1) shall not be subject to any liability under subsection (1) in respect of the publication of the advertisement if he proves—

(a) that the advertisement was published in reliance on a statement made to him by the person who caused it to be published to the effect that, by reason of the operation of subsection (2), the publication would not be unlawful; and

(b) that it was reasonable for him to rely on the statement.

(2B) A person who knowingly or recklessly makes a statement such as is mentioned in subsection (2A)(a) which in a material respect is false or misleading commits an offence, and shall be liable on summary conviction to a fine not exceeding level 5 on the standard scale.]

[(2C) Subsection (1) does not apply in relation to an advertisement so far as it invites persons to apply, in their capacity as members of an authority to which sections 15B and 15C apply, for a relevant appointment or benefit which the authority is intending to make or confer.]

(3) In [this section], "relevant appointment or benefit" means—

(a) any employment, promotion or transfer of employment;

(b) membership of, or a benefit under, an occupational pension scheme;

(c) an appointment to any office or post to which section 4D applies;

(d) any partnership in a firm (within the meaning of section 6A);

(e) any tenancy or pupillage (within the meaning of section 7A or 7C);

(f) any membership of a trade organisation (within the meaning of section 13);

(g) any professional or trade qualification (within the meaning of section 14A);
(h) any work placement (within the meaning of section 14C);
(i) any employment services . . ..

(4) In this section, "advertisement" includes every form of advertisement or notice, whether to the public or not.

[(5) Proceedings in respect of a contravention of subsection (1) may be brought only—
(a) by the Commission for Equality and Human Rights, and
(b) in accordance with section 25 of the Equality Act 2006.]]

NOTES

Amendment

Inserted by SI 2003/1673, regs 3(1), 15(1).

Date in force (for certain purposes): 3 July 2003: see SI 2003/1673, reg 1(2).

Date in force (for remaining purposes): 1 October 2004: see SI 2003/1673, reg 1(3).

Sub-s (1): substituted by the Disability Discrimination Act 2005, s 10(1), (2).

Date in force: 5 December 2005: see SI 2005/2774, art 3(e).

Sub-ss (2A), (2B): inserted by the Disability Discrimination Act 2005, s 10(1), (3).

Date in force: 5 December 2005: see SI 2005/2774, art 3(e).

Sub-s (2C): inserted by the Disability Discrimination Act 2005, s 19(1), Sch 1, Pt 1, paras 1, 8(1), (2).

Date in force (for certain purposes): 5 December 2005: see SI 2005/2774, art 3(j).

Date in force (for remaining purposes): 4 December 2006: see SI 2005/2774, art 4(f).

Sub-s (3): words "this section" in square brackets substituted by the Disability Discrimination Act 2005, s 10(1), (4).

Date in force: 5 December 2005: see SI 2005/2774, art 3(e).

Sub-s (3): in para (i) words omitted repealed by the Disability Discrimination Act 2005, s 19, Sch 1, Pt 1, paras 1, 8(1), (3), Sch 2.

Date in force: 5 December 2005: see SI 2005/2774, art 3(j), (k)(i).

Sub-s (5): inserted by the Equality Act 2006, s 40, Sch 3, paras 41, 42.

Date in force: 1 October 2007: see SI 2007/2603, art 2(b), (d).

See Further

See further: corresponding amendments and a repeal to those made to sub-ss (1), (2A)-(2C), (3) above by the Disability Discrimination Act 2005, have been made in relation to Northern Ireland: the Disability Discrimination (Northern Ireland) Order 2006, SI 2006/312, arts 11, 19, Sch 1, paras 1, 8, Sch 2.

[16C Instructions and pressure to discriminate]

[(1) It is unlawful for a person—
(a) who has authority over another person, or
(b) in accordance with whose wishes that other person is accustomed to act,

to instruct him to do any act which is unlawful under this Part or, to the extent that it relates to the provision of employment services, Part 3, or to procure or attempt to procure the doing by him of any such act.

(2) It is also unlawful to induce, or attempt to induce, a person to do any act which contravenes this Part or, to the extent that it relates to the provision of employment services, Part 3 by—

(a) providing or offering to provide him with any benefit, or

(b) subjecting or threatening to subject him to any detriment.

(3) An attempted inducement is not prevented from falling within subsection (2) because it is not made directly to the person in question, if it is made in such a way that he is likely to hear of it.

[(4) Proceedings in respect of a contravention of this section may be brought only—

(a) by the Commission for Equality and Human Rights, and

(b) in accordance with section 25 of the Equality Act 2006.]]

NOTES

Amendment

Inserted by SI 2003/1673, regs 3(1), 15(1).

Date in force (for certain purposes): 3 July 2003: see SI 2003/1673, reg 1(2).

Date in force (for remaining purposes): 1 October 2004: see SI 2003/1673, reg 1(3).

Sub-s (4): inserted by the Equality Act 2006, s 40, Sch 3, paras 41, 43.

Date in force: 1 October 2007: see SI 2007/2603, art 2(b), (d).

. . .

NOTES

Amendment

Cross-heading: repealed by SI 2003/2770, regs 2, 4(1).

Date in force (for certain purposes): 1 December 2003: see SI 2003/2770, reg 1(2).

Date in force (for remaining purposes): 1 October 2004: see SI 2003/2770, reg 1(3).

17 . . .

. . .

NOTES

Amendment

Repealed by SI 2003/2770, regs 2, 4(1).

Date in force (for certain purposes): 1 December 2003: see SI 2003/2770, reg 1(2).

Date in force (for remaining purposes): 1 October 2004: see SI 2003/2770, reg 1(3).

[Enforcement etc]

NOTES

Amendment

Inserted by virtue of SI 2003/1673, regs 3(1), 9(1) (this cross-heading was originally enacted as the cross-heading which preceded s 8 hereof).

Date in force (for certain purposes): 3 July 2003: see SI 2003/1673, reg 1(2).

Date in force (for remaining purposes): 1 October 2004: see SI 2003/1673, reg 1(3).

[17A Enforcement, remedies and procedure]

[(1) A complaint by any person that another person—

(a) has discriminated against him[, or subjected him to harassment,] in a way which is unlawful under this Part, or

(b) is, by virtue of section 57 or 58, to be treated as having [done so],

may be presented to an [employment tribunal].

[(1A) Subsection (1) does not apply to a complaint under section 14A(1) or (2) of an act in respect of which an appeal, or proceedings in the nature of an appeal, may be brought under any enactment.

(1B) . . .

(1C) Where, on the hearing of a complaint under subsection (1), the complainant proves facts from which the tribunal could, apart from this subsection, conclude in the absence of an adequate explanation that the respondent has acted in a way which is unlawful under this Part, the tribunal shall uphold the complaint unless the respondent proves that he did not so act.]

(2) Where an [employment tribunal] finds that a complaint presented to it under this section is well-founded, it shall take such of the following steps as it considers just and equitable—

(a) making a declaration as to the rights of the complainant and the respondent in relation to the matters to which the complaint relates;

(b) ordering the respondent to pay compensation to the complainant;

(c) recommending that the respondent take, within a specified period, action appearing to the tribunal to be reasonable, in all the circumstances of the case, for the purpose of obviating or reducing the adverse effect on the complainant of any matter to which the complaint relates.

(3) Where a tribunal orders compensation under subsection (2)(b), the amount of the compensation shall be calculated by applying the principles applicable to the calculation of damages in claims in tort or (in Scotland) in reparation for breach of statutory duty.

(4) For the avoidance of doubt it is hereby declared that compensation in respect of discrimination in a way which is unlawful under this Part may include compensation for injury to feelings whether or not it includes compensation under any other head.

(5) If the respondent to a complaint fails, without reasonable justification, to comply with a recommendation made by an [employment tribunal] under subsection (2)(c) the tribunal may, if it thinks it just and equitable to do so—

(a) increase the amount of compensation required to be paid to the complainant in respect of the complaint, where an order was made under subsection (2)(b); or

(b) make an order under subsection (2)(b).

(6) Regulations may make provision—
  (a) for enabling a tribunal, where an amount of compensation falls to be awarded under subsection (2)(b), to include in the award interest on that amount; and
  (b) specifying, for cases where a tribunal decides that an award is to include an amount in respect of interest, the manner in which and the periods and rate by reference to which the interest is to be determined.

(7) Regulations may modify the operation of any order made under [section 14 of [the Employment Tribunals Act 1996]] (power to make provision as to interest on sums payable in pursuance of [employment tribunal] decisions) to the extent that it relates to an award of compensation under subsection (2)(b).

(8) Part I of Schedule 3 makes further provision about the enforcement of this Part and about procedure.]

NOTES

Amendment

Inserted by virtue of SI 2003/1673, regs 3(1), 9(1) (this section was originally enacted as s 8 hereof).

Date in force (for certain purposes): 3 July 2003: see SI 2003/1673, reg 1(2).

Date in force (for remaining purposes): 1 October 2004: see SI 2003/1673, reg 1(3).

Sub-s (1): in para (a) words ", or subjected him to harassment," in square brackets inserted by SI 2003/1673, regs 3(1), 9(2)(a).

Date in force (for certain purposes): 3 July 2003: see SI 2003/1673, reg 1(2).

Date in force (for remaining purposes): 1 October 2004: see SI 2003/1673, reg 1(3).

Sub-s (1): in para (b) words "done so" in square brackets substituted by SI 2003/1673, regs 3(1), 9(2)(b).

Date in force (for certain purposes): 3 July 2003: see SI 2003/1673, reg 1(2).

Date in force (for remaining purposes): 1 October 2004: see SI 2003/1673, reg 1(3).

Sub-s (1): words "employment tribunal" in square brackets substituted by the Employment Rights (Dispute Resolution) Act 1998, s 1(2)(a).

Date in force: 1 August 1998: see SI 1998/1658, art 2(1), Sch 1.

Sub-ss (1A)-(1C): inserted by SI 2003/1673, regs 3(1), 9(2)(c); for transitional provisions in relation to sub-s (1C) see reg 2(1), (4) thereof.

Date in force (for certain purposes): 3 July 2003: see SI 2003/1673, reg 1(2).

Date in force (for remaining purposes): 1 October 2004: see SI 2003/1673, reg 1(3).

Sub-s (1B): repealed by the Disability Discrimination Act 2005, s 19, Sch 1, Pt 1, paras 1, 9, Sch 2.

Date in force: 30 June 2005: see SI 2005/1676, art 2(1)(c), (d).

Sub-s (2): words "employment tribunal" in square brackets substituted by the Employment Rights (Dispute Resolution) Act 1998, s 1(2)(a).

Date in force: 1 August 1998: see SI 1998/1658, art 2(1), Sch 1.

Sub-s (5): words "employment tribunal" in square brackets substituted by the Employment Rights (Dispute Resolution) Act 1998, s 1(2)(a).

Date in force: 1 August 1998: see SI 1998/1658, art 2(1), Sch 1.

Sub-s (7): words in square brackets beginning with the words "section 14" substituted by the Employment Tribunals Act 1996, s 43, Sch 1, para 12(1), (2).

Sub-s (7): words "the Employment Tribunals Act 1996" in square brackets substituted by the Employment Rights (Dispute Resolution) Act 1998, s 1(2)(c).

Date in force: 1 August 1998: see SI 1998/1658, art 2(1), Sch 1.

Sub-s (7): words "employment tribunal" in square brackets substituted by the Employment Rights (Dispute Resolution) Act 1998, s 1(2)(a).

Date in force: 1 August 1998: see SI 1998/1658, art 2(1), Sch 1.

[17B . . .]

[. . .]

NOTES

Amendment

Inserted by SI 2003/1673, regs 3(1), 16(1).

Date in force (for certain purposes): 3 July 2003: see SI 2003/1673, reg 1(2).

Date in force (for remaining purposes): 1 October 2004: see SI 2003/1673, reg 1(3).

Repealed by the Equality Act 2006, ss 40, 91, Sch 3, paras 41, 44, Sch 4.

Date in force: 1 October 2007: see SI 2007/2603, art 2(b)-(d).

[17C Validity of contracts, collective agreements and rules of undertakings]

[Schedule 3A shall have effect.]

NOTES

Amendment

Inserted by SI 2003/1673, regs 3(1), 16(1).

Date in force (for certain purposes): 3 July 2003: see SI 2003/1673, reg 1(2).

Date in force (for remaining purposes): 1 October 2004: see SI 2003/1673, reg 1(3).

[Supplementary and general]

NOTES

Amendment

Cross-heading: inserted by SI 2003/1673, regs 3(1), 17(1).

Date in force (for certain purposes): 3 July 2003: see SI 2003/1673, reg 1(2).

Date in force (for remaining purposes): 1 October 2004: see SI 2003/1673, reg 1(3).

18 . . .

. . .

NOTES

Amendment

Repealed by the Disability Discrimination Act 2005, ss 11(1), 19(2), Sch 2.

Date in force: 5 December 2005: see SI 2005/2774, art 3(f), (k)(i).

See Further

See further: a corresponding repeal has been made in relation to Northern Ireland: the Disability Discrimination (Northern Ireland) Order 2006, SI 2006/312, art 19(2), Sch 2.

[18A Alterations to premises occupied under leases]

[(1) This section applies where—
  (a) [a person to whom a duty to make reasonable adjustments applies] ("the occupier") occupies premises under a lease;
  (b) but for this section, the occupier would not be entitled to make a particular alteration to the premises; and
  (c) the alteration is one which the occupier proposes to make in order to comply with [that duty].
(2) Except to the extent to which it expressly so provides, the lease shall have effect by virtue of this subsection as if it provided—
  (a) for the occupier to be entitled to make the alteration with the written consent of the lessor;
  (b) for the occupier to have to make a written application to the lessor for consent if he wishes to make the alteration;
  (c) if such an application is made, for the lessor not to withhold his consent unreasonably; and
  (d) for the lessor to be entitled to make his consent subject to reasonable conditions.
3) In this section—
  "lease" includes a tenancy, sub-lease or sub-tenancy and an agreement for a lease, tenancy, sub-lease or sub-tenancy; and
  "sub-lease" and "sub-tenancy" have such meaning as may be prescribed.
(4) If the terms and conditions of a lease—
  (a) impose conditions which are to apply if the occupier alters the premises, or
  (b) entitle the lessor to impose conditions when consenting to the occupier's altering the premises,
  the occupier is to be treated for the purposes of subsection (1) as not being entitled to make the alteration.
(5) Part I of Schedule 4 supplements the provisions of this section.]

NOTES

Amendment

Inserted by virtue of SI 2003/1673, regs 3(1), 14(2) (this section was originally enacted as s 16 hereof).

Date in force (for certain purposes): 3 July 2003: see SI 2003/1673, reg 1(2).

Date in force (for remaining purposes): 1 October 2004: see SI 2003/1673, reg 1(3).

Sub-s (1): in para (a) words "a person to whom a duty to make reasonable adjustments applies" in square brackets substituted by SI 2003/1673, regs 3(1), 14(3)(a).

Date in force (for certain purposes): 3 July 2003: see SI 2003/1673, reg 1(2).

Date in force (for remaining purposes): 1 October 2004: see SI 2003/1673, reg 1(3).

Sub-s (1): in para (c) words "that duty" in square brackets substituted by SI 2003/1673, regs 3(1), 14(3)(b).

Date in force (for certain purposes): 3 July 2003: see SI 2003/1673, reg 1(2).

Date in force (for remaining purposes): 1 October 2004: see SI 2003/1673, reg 1(3).

Modification

Modified, in its application to employment by the governing body of a school having a right to a delegated budget, by virtue of the Education (Modification of Enactments Relating to Employment) (England) Order 2003, SI 2003/1964, art 3, Schedule.

Modified, in relation to any case where the occupier occupies premises under a sub-lease or sub-tenancy, by the Disability Discrimination (Employment Field) (Leasehold Premises) Regulations 2004, SI 2004/153, regs 8, 9(a), (b).

Modified, in its application to employment by the governing body of a school having a right to a delegated budget, by virtue of the Education (Modification of Enactments Relating to Employment) (Wales) Order 2006, SI 2006/1073, art 3, Schedule.

Subordinate Legislation

Disability Discrimination (Employment Field) (Leasehold Premises) Regulations 2004, SI 2004/153 (made under sub-s (3)).

[18B Reasonable adjustments: supplementary]

[(1) In determining whether it is reasonable for a person to have to take a particular step in order to comply with a duty to make reasonable adjustments, regard shall be had, in particular, to—

(a) the extent to which taking the step would prevent the effect in relation to which the duty is imposed;

(b) the extent to which it is practicable for him to take the step;

(c) the financial and other costs which would be incurred by him in taking the step and the extent to which taking it would disrupt any of his activities;

(d) the extent of his financial and other resources;

(e) the availability to him of financial or other assistance with respect to taking the step;

(f) the nature of his activities and the size of his undertaking;

(g) where the step would be taken in relation to a private household, the extent to which taking it would—

(i) disrupt that household, or

(ii) disturb any person residing there.

(2) The following are examples of steps which a person may need to take in relation to a disabled person in order to comply with a duty to make reasonable adjustments—
(a) making adjustments to premises;
(b) allocating some of the disabled person's duties to another person;
(c) transferring him to fill an existing vacancy;
(d) altering his hours of working or training;
(e) assigning him to a different place of work or training;
(f) allowing him to be absent during working or training hours for rehabilitation, assessment or treatment;
(g) giving, or arranging for, training or mentoring (whether for the disabled person or any other person);
(h) acquiring or modifying equipment;
(i) modifying instructions or reference manuals;
(j) modifying procedures for testing or assessment;
(k) providing a reader or interpreter;
(l) providing supervision or other support.

(3) For the purposes of a duty to make reasonable adjustments, where under any binding obligation a person is required to obtain the consent of another person to any alteration of the premises occupied by him—
(a) it is always reasonable for him to have to take steps to obtain that consent; and
(b) it is never reasonable for him to have to make that alteration before that consent is obtained.

(4) The steps referred to in subsection (3)(a) shall not be taken to include an application to a court or tribunal.

(5) In subsection (3), "binding obligation" means a legally binding obligation (not contained in a lease (within the meaning of section 18A(3)) in relation to the premises, whether arising from an agreement or otherwise.

(6) A provision of this Part imposing a duty to make reasonable adjustments applies only for the purpose of determining whether a person has discriminated against a disabled person; and accordingly a breach of any such duty is not actionable as such.]

NOTES

Amendment

Inserted by SI 2003/1673, regs 3(1), 17(2).

Date in force (for certain purposes): 3 July 2003: see SI 2003/1673, reg 1(2).

Date in force (for remaining purposes): 1 October 2004: see SI 2003/1673, reg 1(3).

[18C Charities and support for particular groups of persons]

[(1) Nothing in this Part—
(a) affects any charitable instrument which provides for conferring benefits on one or more categories of person determined by reference to any physical or mental capacity; or
(b) makes unlawful any act done by a charity or recognised body in pursuance of any of its charitable purposes, so far as those purposes are connected with persons so determined.

(2) Nothing in this Part prevents—
  (a) a person who provides supported employment from treating members of a particular group of disabled persons more favourably than other persons in providing such employment; or
  (b) the Secretary of State from agreeing to arrangements for the provision of supported employment which will, or may, have that effect.

(3) In this section—

"charitable instrument" means an enactment or other instrument (whenever taking effect) so far as it relates to charitable purposes;

"charity" has the same meaning as in the Charities Act 1993;

"recognised body" means a body which is a recognised body for the purposes of Part I of the Law Reform (Miscellaneous Provisions) (Scotland) Act 1990; and

"supported employment" means facilities provided, or in respect of which payments are made, under section 15 of the Disabled Persons (Employment) Act 1944.

(4) In the application of this section to England and Wales, "charitable purposes" means purposes which are exclusively charitable according to the law of England and Wales.

(5) In the application of this section to Scotland, "charitable purposes" shall be construed in the same way as if it were contained in the Income Tax Acts.]

NOTES

Amendment

Inserted by virtue of SI 2003/1673, regs 3(1), 11 (this section was originally enacted as s 10 hereof).

Date in force (for certain purposes): 3 July 2003: see SI 2003/1673, reg 1(2).

Date in force (for remaining purposes): 1 October 2004: see SI 2003/1673, reg 1(3).

[18D Interpretation of Part 2]

[(1) Subject to any duty to make reasonable adjustments, nothing in this Part is to be taken to require a person to treat a disabled person more favourably than he treats or would treat others.

(2) In this Part—

"benefits"[, except in sections 4G to 4K,] includes facilities and services;

"detriment", except in section 16C(2)(b), does not include conduct of the nature referred to in section 3B (harassment);

"discriminate", "discrimination" and other related expressions are to be construed in accordance with section 3A;

"duty to make reasonable adjustments" means a duty imposed by or under section 4A, 4B(5) or (6), 4E, [4H,] 6B, 7B, 7D, 14, 14B, 14D[, 15C] or 16A(5);

"employer" includes a person who has no employees but is seeking to employ another person;

"harassment" is to be construed in accordance with section 3B;

"physical feature", in relation to any premises, includes [(subject to any provision under section 15C(4)(e))] any of the following (whether permanent or temporary)—

(a) any feature arising from the design or construction of a building on the premises,

(b) any feature on the premises of any approach to, exit from or access to such a building,

(c) any fixtures, fittings, furnishings, furniture, equipment or material in or on the premises,

(d) any other physical element or quality of any land comprised in the premises;

"provision, criterion or practice" includes any arrangements.]

NOTES

Amendment

Inserted by SI 2003/1673, regs 3(1), 18.

Date in force (for certain purposes): 3 July 2003: see SI 2003/1673, reg 1(2).

Date in force (for remaining purposes): 1 October 2004: see SI 2003/1673, reg 1(3).

Sub-s (2): in definition "benefits" words ", except in sections 4G to 4K," in square brackets inserted by SI 2003/2770, regs 2, 4(2)(a).

Date in force (for certain purposes): 1 December 2003: see SI 2003/2770, reg 1(2).

Date in force (for remaining purposes): 1 October 2004: see SI 2003/2770, reg 1(3).

Sub-s (2): in definition "duty to make reasonable adjustments" reference to "4H," in square brackets inserted by SI 2003/2770, regs 2, 4(2)(b).

Date in force (for certain purposes): 1 December 2003: see SI 2003/2770, reg 1(2).

Date in force (for remaining purposes): 1 October 2004: see SI 2003/2770, reg 1(3).

Sub-s (2): in definition "duty to make reasonable adjustments" reference to ", 15C" in square brackets inserted by the Disability Discrimination Act 2005, s 19(1), Sch 1, Pt 1, paras 1, 11(a).

Date in force: 4 December 2006: see SI 2005/2774, art 4(f).

Sub-s (2): in definition "physical feature" words "(subject to any provision under section 15C(4)(e))" in square brackets inserted by the Disability Discrimination Act 2005, s 19(1), Sch 1, Pt 1, paras 1, 11(b).

Date in force: 4 December 2006: see SI 2005/2774, art 4(f).

See Further

See further: a corresponding amendment to that made to sub-s (2) above by the Disability Discrimination Act 2005, has been made in relation to Northern Ireland: the Disability Discrimination (Northern Ireland) Order 2006, SI 2006/312, art 19(1), Sch 1, paras 1, 10.

[18E Premises provided otherwise than in course of a Part 2 relationship]

[(1) This Part does not apply in relation to the provision, otherwise than in the course of a Part 2 relationship, of premises by the regulated party to the other party.

(2) For the purposes of subsection (1)—
   (a) "Part 2 relationship" means a relationship during the course of which an act of discrimination against, or harassment of, one party to the relationship by the other party to it is unlawful under sections 4 to 15C; and
   (b) in relation to a Part 2 relationship, "regulated party" means the party whose acts of discrimination, or harassment, are made unlawful by sections 4 to 15C.]

NOTES

Amendment

Inserted by the Disability Discrimination Act 2005, s 19(1), Sch 1, Pt 1, paras 1, 12.

Date in force: 4 December 2006: see SI 2005/2774, art 4(f).

See Further

See further: a corresponding amendment has been made in relation to Northern Ireland: the Disability Discrimination (Northern Ireland) Order 2006, SI 2006/312, art 19(1), Sch 1, paras 1, 11.

Part VII

Supplemental

[53A . . .]

[. . .]

NOTES

Amendment

Inserted by the Disability Rights Commission Act 1999, s 9.

Date in force: 25 April 2000: see SI 2000/880, art 2, Sch 2.

Repealed by the Equality Act 2006, ss 40, 91, Sch 3, paras 41, 52, Sch 4.

Date in force: 1 October 2007: see SI 2007/2603, art 2(b)-(d).

53 . . .

. . .

NOTES

Amendment

Repealed by the Disability Rights Commission Act 1999, s 14(2), Sch 5.

Date in force (in relation to sub-ss (1-(3), (8), (9)): 25 April 2000: see SI 2000/880, art 2, Sch 2, Appendix.

Date in force (for remaining purposes): 4 December 2006: see SI 2006/3189, art 2.

UK Parliament Acts/D/DH-DN/Disability Discrimination Act 1995 (1995 c 50)/Part VII Supplemental/55 Victimisation

55 Victimisation

(1) For the purposes of [Part 2 or Part 4, or Part 3 other than sections 24A to 24L,] a person ("A") discriminates against another person ("B") if—

(a) he treats B less favourably than he treats or would treat other persons whose circumstances are the same as B's; and

(b) he does so for a reason mentioned in subsection (2).

(2) The reasons are that—

(a) B has—

(i) brought proceedings against A or any other person under this Act [or Part III of the 2005 Order]; or

(ii) given evidence or information in connection with such proceedings brought by any person; or

(iii) otherwise done anything under[, or by reference to,] this Act [or Part III of the 2005 Order] in relation to A or any other person; or

(iv) alleged that A or any other person has (whether or not the allegation so states) contravened this Act; or

(b) A believes or suspects that B has done or intends to do any of those things.

(3) Where B is a disabled person, or a person who has had a disability, the disability in question shall be disregarded in comparing his circumstances with those of any other person for the purposes of subsection (1)(a).

[(3A) For the purposes of Chapter 1 of Part 4—

(a) references in subsection (2) to B include references to—

(i) a person who is, for the purposes of that Chapter, B's parent; and

(ii) a sibling of B; and

(b) references in that subsection to this Act are, as respects a person mentioned in sub-paragraph (i) or (ii) of paragraph (a), restricted to that Chapter.]

(4) Subsection (1) does not apply to treatment of a person because of an allegation made by him if the allegation was false and not made in good faith.

[(5) In the case of an act which constitutes discrimination by virtue of this section, sections 4, 4B, 4D, [4G,] 6A, 7A, 7C, 13, 14A, 14C[, 15B] and 16A also apply to discrimination against a person who is not disabled.

(6) . . .]

NOTES

Initial Commencement

To be appointed

To be appointed: see s 70(3).

Appointment

Appointment (in relation to England, Wales and Scotland): 2 December 1996: see SI 1996/1474, art 2(3), Schedule, Pt III.

Appointment (in relation to Northern Ireland): 2 December 1996: see the Disability Discrimination Act 1995 (Commencement No 3 and Saving and Transitional Provisions) Order (Northern Ireland) 1996, SR 1996/280, art 2(2), Schedule, Pt II.

Amendment

Sub-s (1): words "Part 2 or Part 4, or Part 3 other than sections 24A to 24L," in square brackets substituted by the Disability Discrimination Act 2005, s 19(1), Sch 1, Pt 1, paras 1, 29(1), (2).

Date in force: 4 December 2006: see SI 2005/2774, art 4(f).

Sub-s (2): in para (a)(i), (iii) words "or Part III of the 2005 Order" in square brackets inserted, in relation to Northern Ireland, by the Special Educational Needs and Disability (Northern Ireland) Order 2005, SI 2005/1117, art 48(1), (7).

Date in force: 1 September 2005: see the Special Educational Needs and Disability (2005 Order) (Commencement No 1) Order (Northern Ireland) 2005, SR 2005/336, art 2, Schedule (as amended by the Special Educational Needs and Disability (2005 Order) (Commencement No 1) (Amendment) Order (Northern Ireland) 2007, SR 2007/25, art 2) and the Special Educational Needs and Disability (2005 Order) (Commencement No 2) Order (Northern Ireland) 2005, SR 2005/337, art 2, Schedule.

Sub-s (2): in para (a)(iii) words ", or by reference to," in square brackets inserted by the Disability Discrimination Act 2005, s 19(1), Sch 1, Pt 1, paras 1, 29(1), (3).

Date in force: 5 December 2005: see SI 2005/2774, art 3(j).

Sub-s (3A): inserted by the Special Educational Needs and Disability Act 2001, s 38(1), (8); a corresponding amendment has been made in relation to Northern Ireland by the Special Educational Needs and Disability (Northern Ireland) Order 2005, SI 2005/1117, art 48(1), (8).

Date in force (in relation to England, Wales and Scotland): 1 September 2002: see SI 2002/2217, art 3, Sch 1, Pt 1.

Date in force (in relation to Northern Ireland): 1 September 2005: see the Special Educational Needs and Disability (2005 Order) (Commencement No 1) Order (Northern Ireland) 2005, SR 2005/336, art 2, Schedule (as amended by the Special Educational Needs and Disability (2005 Order) (Commencement No 1) (Amendment) Order (Northern Ireland) 2007, SR 2007/25, art 2) and the Special Educational Needs and Disability (2005 Order) (Commencement No 2) Order (Northern Ireland) 2005, SR 2005/337, art 2, Schedule.

Sub-ss (5), (6): inserted by SI 2003/1673, regs 3(1), 21.

Date in force (for certain purposes): 3 July 2003: see SI 2003/1673, reg 1(2).

Date in force (for remaining purposes): 1 October 2004: see SI 2003/1673, reg 1(3).

Sub-s (5): reference to "4G," in square brackets inserted by SI 2003/2770, regs 2, 4(3).

Date in force (for certain purposes): 1 December 2003: see SI 2003/2770, reg 1(2).

Date in force (for remaining purposes): 1 October 2004: see SI 2003/2770, reg 1(3).

Sub-s (5): reference to ", 15B" in square brackets inserted by the Disability Discrimination Act 2005, s 19(1), Sch 1, Pt 1, paras 1, 29(1), (4).

Date in force: 5 December 2005: see SI 2005/2774, art 3(j).

Sub-s (6): repealed by the Disability Discrimination Act 2005, s 19, Sch 1, Pt 1, paras 1, 29(1), (5), Sch 2.

Date in force: 5 December 2005: see SI 2005/2774, art 3(j), (k)(i).

Modification

Modified, in its application to employment by the governing body of a school having a right to a delegated budget, by the Education (Modification of Enactments Relating to Employment) (England) Order 2003, SI 2003/1964, art 3, Schedule.

Modified, in its application to employment by the governing body of a school having a right to a delegated budget, by the Education (Modification of Enactments Relating to Employment) (Wales) Order 2006, SI 2006/1073, art 3, Schedule.

See Further

See further: corresponding amendments and a repeal to those made to sub-ss (1), (2)(a)(iii), (5), (6) above by the Disability Discrimination Act 2005, have been made in relation to Northern Ireland: the Disability Discrimination (Northern Ireland) Order 2006, SI 2006/312, art 19, Sch 1, paras 1, 23(1)-(5), Sch 2.

57 Aiding unlawful acts

(1) A person who knowingly aids another person to do an [unlawful act] is to be treated for the purposes of this Act as himself doing the same kind of unlawful act.

(2) For the purposes of subsection (1), an employee or agent for whose act the employer or principal is liable under section 58 (or would be so liable but for section 58(5)) shall be taken to have aided the employer or principal to do the act.

(3) For the purposes of this section, a person does not knowingly aid another to do an unlawful act if—

- (a) he acts in reliance on a statement made to him by that other person that, because of any provision of this Act, the act would not be unlawful; and
- (b) it is reasonable for him to rely on the statement.

(4) A person who knowingly or recklessly makes such a statement which is false or misleading in a material respect is guilty of an offence.

(5) Any person guilty of an offence under subsection (4) shall be liable on summary conviction to a fine not exceeding level 5 on the standard scale.

[(6) "Unlawful act" means an act made unlawful by any provision of this Act other than a provision contained in Chapter 1 of Part 4.]

NOTES

Initial Commencement

To be appointed

To be appointed: see s 70(3).

Appointment

Appointment (in relation to England, Wales and Scotland): 2 December 1996: see SI 1996/1474, art 2(3), Schedule, Pt III.

Appointment (in relation to Northern Ireland): 2 December 1996: see the Disability Discrimination Act 1995 (Commencement No 3 and Saving and Transitional Provisions) Order (Northern Ireland) 1996, SR 1996/280, art 2(2), Schedule, Pt II.

Amendment

Sub-s (1): words "unlawful act" in square brackets substituted by the Special Educational Needs and Disability Act 2001, s 38(1), (9).

Date in force: 1 September 2002: see SI 2002/2217, art 3, Sch 1, Pt 1.

Sub-s (6): inserted by the Special Educational Needs and Disability Act 2001, s 38(1), (10).

Date in force: 1 September 2002: see SI 2002/2217, art 3, Sch 1, Pt 1.

Modification

Modified, in its application to employment by the governing body of a school having a right to a delegated budget, by the Education (Modification of Enactments Relating to Employment) (England) Order 2003, SI 2003/1964, art 3, Schedule.

Modified, in its application to employment by the governing body of a school having a right to a delegated budget, by the Education (Modification of Enactments Relating to Employment) (Wales) Order 2006, SI 2006/1073, art 3, Schedule.

58 Liability of employers and principals

(1) Anything done by a person in the course of his employment shall be treated for the purposes of this Act as also done by his employer, whether or not it was done with the employer's knowledge or approval.

(2) Anything done by a person as agent for another person with the authority of that other person shall be treated for the purposes of this Act as also done by that other person.

(3) Subsection (2) applies whether the authority was—
  (a) express or implied; or
  (b) given before or after the act in question was done.

(4) Subsections (1) and (2) do not apply in relation to an offence under section 57(4).

(5) In proceedings under this Act against any person in respect of an act alleged to have been done by an employee of his, it shall be a defence for that person to prove that he took such steps as were reasonably practicable to prevent the employee from—
  (a) doing that act; or
  (b) doing, in the course of his employment, acts of that description.

NOTES

Initial Commencement

To be appointed

To be appointed: see s 70(3).

Appointment

Appointment (in relation to England, Wales and Scotland): 2 December 1996: see SI 1996/1474, art 2(3), Schedule, Pt III.

Appointment (in relation to Northern Ireland): 2 December 1996: see the Disability Discrimination Act 1995 (Commencement No 3 and Saving and Transitional Provisions) Order (Northern Ireland) 1996, SR 1996/280, art 2(2), Schedule, Pt II.

Modification

Modified, in its application to employment by the governing body of a school having a right to a delegated budget, by the Education (Modification of Enactments Relating to Employment) (England) Order 2003, SI 2003/1964, art 3, Schedule.

Modified, in its application to employment by the governing body of a school having a right to a delegated budget, by the Education (Modification of Enactments Relating to Employment) (Wales) Order 2006, SI 2006/1073, art 3, Schedule.

59 Statutory authority and national security etc

(1) Nothing in this Act makes unlawful any act done—

(a) in pursuance of any enactment; or

[(b) in pursuance of any instrument made under any enactment by—

(i) a Minister of the Crown,

(ii) a member of the Scottish Executive, . . .

(iii) the National Assembly for Wales [constituted by the Government of Wales Act 1998, or

(iv) the Welsh Ministers, the First Minister for Wales or the Counsel General to the Welsh Assembly Government]; or

(c) to comply with any condition or requirement—

(i) imposed by a Minister of the Crown (whether before or after the passing of this Act) by virtue of any enactment,

(ii) imposed by a member of the Scottish Executive (whether before or after the coming into force of this sub-paragraph) by virtue of any enactment, . . .

(iii) imposed by the National Assembly for Wales [constituted by the Government of Wales Act 1998] (whether before or after the coming into force of this sub-paragraph) by virtue of any enactment][, or

(iv) imposed by the Welsh Ministers, the First Minister for Wales or the Counsel General to the Welsh Assembly Government].

(2) In subsection (1) "enactment" includes one passed or made after the date on which this Act is passed and "instrument" includes one made after that date.

[(2A) Nothing in—

(a) Part 2 of this Act, or

(b) Part 3 of this Act to the extent that it relates to the provision of employment services,

makes unlawful any act done for the purpose of safeguarding national security if the doing of the act was justified by that purpose.]

(3) Nothing in [any other provision of] this Act makes unlawful any act done for the purpose of safeguarding national security.

NOTES

Initial Commencement

To be appointed

To be appointed: see s 70(3).

Appointment

Appointment (in relation to England, Wales and Scotland): 17 May 1996: see SI 1996/1336, arts 2, 3(f).

Appointment (in relation to Northern Ireland): 30 May 1996: see the Disability Discrimination Act 1995 (Commencement No 2) Order (Northern Ireland) 1996, SR 996/219, arts 2, 3(f).

Amendment

Sub-s (1): paras (b), (c) substituted by the Disability Discrimination Act 2005, s 19(1), Sch 1, Pt 1, paras 1, 30.

Date in force: 30 June 2005: see SI 2005/1676, art 2(1)(c).

Sub-s (1): in para (b)(ii) word omitted repealed by SI 2007/1388, art 3, Sch 1, paras 47, 61(1), (2).

Date in force: this repeal came into force on 25 May 2007 being the date on which the initial period ended (following the appointment of the First Minister): see SI 2007/1388, art 1(2) and the Government of Wales Act 2006, ss 46, 161(5).

Sub-s (1): in para (b) words from "constituted by the" to "Welsh Assembly Government" in square brackets inserted by SI 2007/1388, art 3, Sch 1, paras 47, 61(1), (3).

Date in force: this amendment came into force on 25 May 2007 being the date on which the initial period ended (following the appointment of the First Minister): see SI 2007/1388, art 1(2) and the Government of Wales Act 2006, ss 46, 161(5).

Sub-s (1): in para (c)(ii) word omitted repealed by SI 2007/1388, art 3, Sch 1, paras 47, 61(1), (4).

Date in force: this repeal came into force on 25 May 2007 being the date on which the initial period ended (following the appointment of the First Minister): see SI 2007/1388, art 1(2) and the Government of Wales Act 2006, ss 46, 161(5).

Sub-s (1): in para (c)(iii) words "constituted by the Government of Wales Act 1998" in square brackets inserted by SI 2007/1388, art 3, Sch 1, paras 47, 61(1), (5).

Date in force: this amendment came into force on 25 May 2007 being the date on which the initial period ended (following the appointment of the First Minister): see SI 2007/1388, art 1(2) and the Government of Wales Act 2006, ss 46, 161(5).

Sub-s (1): para (c)(iv) and word "or" immediately preceding it inserted by SI 2007/1388, art 3, Sch 1, paras 47, 61(1), (6).

Date in force: this amendment came into force on 25 May 2007 being the date on which the initial period ended (following the appointment of the First Minister): see SI 2007/1388, art 1(2) and the Government of Wales Act 2006, ss 46, 161(5).

Sub-s (2A): inserted by SI 2003/1673, regs 3(1), 23(a).

Date in force (for certain purposes): 3 July 2003: see SI 2003/1673, reg 1(2).

Date in force (for remaining purposes): 1 October 2004: see SI 2003/1673, reg 1(3).

Sub-s (3): words "any other provision of" in square brackets inserted by SI 2003/1673, regs 3(1), 23(b).

Date in force (for certain purposes): 3 July 2003: see SI 2003/1673, reg 1(2).

Date in force (for remaining purposes): 1 October 2004: see SI 2003/1673, reg 1(3).

UK Parliament Acts/D/DH-DN/Disability Discrimination Act 1995 (1995 c 50)/Part VII Supplemental/[59A National security]

[59A National security]

[(1) Rules of court may make provision for enabling a county court or sheriff court in which a claim is brought in respect of alleged discrimination contrary to this Act (including anything treated by virtue of this Act as amounting to discrimination contrary to this Act), where the court considers it expedient in the interests of national security—

(a) to exclude from all or part of the proceedings—

(i) the claimant;

(ii) the claimant's representatives;

(iii) any assessors;

(b) to permit a claimant or representative who has been excluded to make a statement to the court before the commencement of the proceedings, or the part of the proceedings, from which he is excluded;

(c) to take steps to keep secret all or part of the reasons for the court's decision in the proceedings.

(2) The Attorney General or, in Scotland, the Advocate General for Scotland, may appoint a person to represent the interests of a claimant in, or in any part of, proceedings from which the claimant or his representatives are excluded by virtue of sub section (1).

(3) A person may be appointed under subsection (2) only—

(a) in relation to proceedings in England and Wales, if he has a general qualification (within the meaning of section 71 of the Courts and Legal Services Act 1990 (c 41)), or

(b) in relation to proceedings in Scotland, if he is—

(i) an advocate, or

(ii) qualified to practice as a solicitor in Scotland.

(4) A person appointed under subsection (2) shall not be responsible to the person whose interests he is appointed to represent.]

NOTES

Amendment

Inserted by the Equality Act 2006, s 89.

Date in force: 18 April 2006: see SI 2006/1082, art 2(j).

Subordinate Legislation

Act of Sederunt (Ordinary Cause, Summary Application, Summary Cause and Small Claim Rules) Amendment (Equality Act 2006 etc) 2006, SSI 2006/509.

Part VIII

Miscellaneous

60 Appointment by Secretary of State of advisers

(1) The Secretary of State may appoint such persons as he thinks fit to advise or assist him in connection with matters relating to the employment of disabled persons and persons who have had a disability.

(2) Persons may be appointed by the Secretary of State to act generally or in relation to a particular area or locality.

(3) The Secretary of State may pay to any person appointed under this section such allowances and compensation for loss of earnings as he considers appropriate.

(4) The approval of the Treasury is required for any payment under this section.

(5) In subsection (1) "employment" includes self-employment.

(6) The Secretary of State may by order—

(a) provide for section 17 of, and Schedule 2 to, the Disabled Persons (Employment) Act 1944 (national advisory council and district advisory committees) to cease to have effect—

(i) so far as concerns the national advisory council; or

(ii) so far as concerns district advisory committees; or

(b) repeal that section and Schedule.

(7) At any time before the coming into force of an order under paragraph (b) of subsection (6), section 17 of the Act of 1944 shall have effect as if in subsection (1), after "disabled persons" in each case there were inserted ", and persons who have had a disability," and as if at the end of the section there were added—

"(3) For the purposes of this section—

(a) a person is a disabled person if he is a disabled person for the purposes of the Disability Discrimination Act 1995; and

(b) "disability" has the same meaning as in that Act."

(8) At any time before the coming into force of an order under paragraph (a)(i) or (b) of subsection (6), section 16 of the Chronically Sick and Disabled Persons Act 1970 (which extends the functions of the national advisory council) shall have effect as if after "disabled persons" in each case there were inserted ", and persons who have had a disability," and as if at the end of the section there were added—

"(2) For the purposes of this section—

(a) a person is a disabled person if he is a disabled person for the purposes of the Disability Discrimination Act 1995; and

(b) "disability" has the same meaning as in that Act."

NOTES

Initial Commencement

To be appointed

To be appointed: see s 70(3).

Appointment

Appointment (in relation to England, Wales and Scotland): 2 December 1996: see SI 1996/1474, art 2(3), Schedule, Pt III.

Appointment (in relation to Northern Ireland): 2 December 1996: see the Disability Discrimination Act 1995 (Commencement No 3 and Saving and Transitional Provisions) Order (Northern Ireland) 1996, SR 1996/280, art 2(2), Schedule, Pt II.

Subordinate Legislation

Disability Discrimination (Abolition of District Advisory Committees) Order 1997, SI 1997/536 (made under sub-s (6)).

Disability Discrimination (Repeal of section 17 of, and Schedule 2 to, the Disabled Persons (Employment) Act, 1944) Order 1998, SI 1998/565 (made under sub-s (6)(b)).

61 Amendment of Disabled Persons (Employment) Act 1944

(1)-(7) . . .

(8) Any provision of subordinate legislation in which "disabled person" is defined by reference to the Act of 1944 shall be construed as if that expression had the same meaning as in this Act.

(9) Subsection (8) does not prevent the further amendment of any such provision by subordinate legislation.

NOTES

Initial Commencement

To be appointed

To be appointed: see s 70(3).

Appointment

Appointment (in relation to England, Wales and Scotland): 2 December 1996: see SI 1996/1474, art 2(3), Schedule, Pt III.

Appointment (in relation to Northern Ireland): 2 December 1996: see the Disability Discrimination Act 1995 (Commencement No 3 and Saving and Transitional Provisions) Order (Northern Ireland) 1996, SR 1996/280, art 2(2), Schedule, Pt II; for savings and transitional provisions see arts 2(2), 3 thereof.

Amendment

Sub-ss (1)-(7): amend the Disabled Persons (Employment) Act 1944, ss 15, 16 and repeal ss 1, 6-14, 19, 21.

62 . . .

. . .

NOTES

Amendment

Repealed in relation to England, Wales and Scotland by the Employment Tribunals Act 1996, s 45, Sch 3, Pt I, and in relation to Northern Ireland by SI 1996/1921 (NI 18), art 28(1), Sch 3.

63 Restriction of publicity: Employment Appeal Tribunal

. . .

NOTES

Amendment

Repealed in relation to England, Wales and Scotland by the Employment Tribunals Act 1996, s 45, Sch 3, Pt I.

64 Application to Crown etc

[(A1) The following provisions bind the Crown—

(a) sections 21B to 21E and Part 5A, and

(b) the other provisions of this Act so far as applying for the purposes of provisions mentioned in paragraph (a);

and sections 57 and 58 shall apply for purposes of provisions mentioned in paragraph (a) as if service as a Crown servant were employment by the Crown.]

(1) This Act[, other than the provisions mentioned in paragraphs (a) and (b) of subsection (A1),] applies—

(a) to an act done by or for purposes of a Minister of the Crown or government department, or

(b) to an act done on behalf of the Crown by a statutory body, or a person holding a statutory office,

as it applies to an act done by a private person.

(2) . . . Part II applies to service—

(a) for purposes of a Minister of the Crown or government department, other than service of a person holding a statutory office, or

(b) on behalf of the Crown for purposes of a person holding a statutory office or purposes of a statutory body,

as it applies to employment by a private person.

[(2A) Subsections [(A1) to] (2) have effect subject to section 64A.]

(3) The provisions of Parts II to IV of the 1947 Act apply to proceedings against the Crown under this Act as they apply to Crown proceedings in England and Wales; . . ..

(4) The provisions of Part V of the 1947 Act apply to proceedings against the Crown under this Act as they apply to proceedings in Scotland which by virtue of that Part are treated as civil proceedings by or against the Crown; but the proviso to

section 44 of that Act (removal of proceedings from the sheriff court to the Court of Session) does not apply.

(5) . . .

(6) . . .

(7) . . . Part II does not apply to service in any of the naval, military or air forces of the Crown.

(8) In this section—

"the 1947 Act" means the Crown Proceedings Act 1947;

. . .

"Crown proceedings" means proceedings which, by virtue of section 23 of the 1947 Act, are treated for the purposes of Part II of that Act as civil proceedings by or against the Crown;

. . .

. . .

. . .

. . .

"service for purposes of a Minister of the Crown or government department" does not include service in any office for the time being mentioned in Schedule 2 (Ministerial offices) to the House of Commons Disqualification Act 1975;

"statutory body" means a body set up by or under an enactment;

"statutory office" means an office so set up; . . .

. . ..

NOTES

Initial Commencement

To be appointed

To be appointed: see s 70(3).

Appointment

Appointment (in relation to England, Wales and Scotland): 2 December 1996: see SI 1996/1474, art 2(3), Schedule, Pt III.

Appointment (in relation to Northern Ireland): 2 December 1996: see the Disability Discrimination Act 1995 (Commencement No 3 and Saving and Transitional Provisions) Order (Northern Ireland) 1996, SR 1996/280, art 2(2), Schedule, Pt II.

Amendment

Sub-s (A1): inserted by the Disability Discrimination Act 2005, s 19(1), Sch 1, Pt 1, paras 1, 31(1), (2).

Date in force (for certain purposes): 5 December 2005: see SI 2005/2774, art 3(j).

Date in force (for remaining purposes): 4 December 2006: see SI 2005/2774, art 4(f).

Sub-s (1): words ", other than the provisions mentioned in paragraphs (a) and (b) of subsection (A1)," in square brackets inserted by the Disability Discrimination Act 2005, s 19(1), Sch 1, Pt 1, paras 1, 31(1), (3).

Date in force (for certain purposes): 5 December 2005: see SI 2005/2774, art 3(j).

Date in force (for remaining purposes): 4 December 2006: see SI 2005/2774, art 4(f).

Sub-s (2): words omitted repealed by SI 2003/1673, regs 3(1), 24(a).

Date in force (for certain purposes): 3 July 2003: see SI 2003/1673, reg 1(2).

Date in force (for remaining purposes): 1 October 2004: see SI 2003/1673, reg 1(3).

Sub-s (2A): inserted by SI 2003/1673, regs 3(1), 24(b).

Date in force (for certain purposes): 3 July 2003: see SI 2003/1673, reg 1(2).

Date in force (for remaining purposes): 1 October 2004: see SI 2003/1673, reg 1(3).

Sub-s (2A): words "(A1) to" in square brackets substituted by the Disability Discrimination Act 2005, s 19(1), Sch 1, Pt 1, paras 1, 31(1), (4).

Date in force (for certain purposes): 5 December 2005: see SI 2005/2774, art 3(j).

Date in force (for remaining purposes): 4 December 2006: see SI 2005/2774, art 4(f).

Sub-s (3): words omitted repealed by SI 2005/2712, art 3, Sch 2, para 3.

Date in force: 1 October 2005: see SI 2005/2712, art 1(1).

Sub-ss (5), (6): repealed by SI 2003/1673, regs 3(1), 24(c).

Date in force (for certain purposes): 3 July 2003: see SI 2003/1673, reg 1(2).

Date in force (for remaining purposes): 1 October 2004: see SI 2003/1673, reg 1(3).

Sub-s (7): words omitted repealed by SI 2003/1673, regs 3(1), 24(d).

Date in force (for certain purposes): 3 July 2003: see SI 2003/1673, reg 1(2).

Date in force (for remaining purposes): 1 October 2004: see SI 2003/1673, reg 1(3).

Sub-s (8): definition "British Transport Police" (omitted) repealed by SI 2003/1673, regs 3(1), 24(e).

Date in force (for certain purposes): 3 July 2003: see SI 2003/1673, reg 1(2).

Date in force (for remaining purposes): 1 October 2004: see SI 2003/1673, reg 1(3).

Sub-s (8): definition "fire brigade" (omitted) repealed by SI 2003/1673, regs 3(1), 24(e).

Date in force (for certain purposes): 3 July 2003: see SI 2003/1673, reg 1(2).

Date in force (for remaining purposes): 1 October 2004: see SI 2003/1673, reg 1(3).

Sub-s (8): definition "Ministry of Defence Police" (omitted) repealed by SI 2003/1673, regs 3(1), 24(e).

Date in force (for certain purposes): 3 July 2003: see SI 2003/1673, reg 1(2).

Date in force (for remaining purposes): 1 October 2004: see SI 2003/1673, reg 1(3).

Sub-s (8): definition "prison officer" (omitted) repealed by SI 2003/1673, regs 3(1), 24(e).

Date in force (for certain purposes): 3 July 2003: see SI 2003/1673, reg 1(2).

Date in force (for remaining purposes): 1 October 2004: see SI 2003/1673, reg 1(3).

Sub-s (8): definition "Royal Parks Constabulary" (omitted) repealed by SI 2003/1673, regs 3(1), 24(e).

Date in force (for certain purposes): 3 July 2003: see SI 2003/1673, reg 1(2).

Date in force (for remaining purposes): 1 October 2004: see SI 2003/1673, reg 1(3).

Sub-s (8): definition "United Kingdom Atomic Energy Authority Constabulary" (omitted) and word omitted immediately preceding it repealed by SI 2003/1673, regs 3(1), 24(e).

Date in force (for certain purposes): 3 July 2003: see SI 2003/1673, reg 1(2).

Date in force (for remaining purposes): 1 October 2004: see SI 2003/1673, reg 1(3).

See Further

See further, in relation to references to the British Transport Police: the Railways and Transport Safety Act 2003, s 73(1), Sch 5, para 4(1), (2)(g).

See further: corresponding amendments to those made to sub-ss (A1), (1), (2A) above by the Disability Discrimination Act 2005, have been made in relation to Northern Ireland: the Disability Discrimination (Northern Ireland) Order 2006, SI 2006/312, art 19(1), Sch 1, paras 1, 24.

[64A Police]

[(1) For the purposes of Part 2, the holding of the office of constable shall be treated as employment—
(a) by the chief officer of police as respects any act done by him in relation to a constable or that office;
(b) by the police authority as respects any act done by them in relation to a constable or that office.

(2) For the purposes of section 58—
(a) the holding of the office of constable shall be treated as employment by the chief officer of police (and as not being employment by any other person); and
(b) anything done by a person holding such an office in the performance, or purported performance, of his functions shall be treated as done in the course of that employment.

(3) There shall be paid out of the police fund—
(a) any compensation, costs or expenses awarded against a chief officer of police in any proceedings brought against him under Part 2 [or 3], and any costs or expenses incurred by him in any such proceedings so far as not recovered by him in the proceedings; and
(b) any sum required by a chief officer of police for the settlement of any claim made against him under Part 2 [or 3] if the settlement is approved by the police authority.

(4) Any proceedings under Part 2 [or 3] which, by virtue of [this section], would lie against a chief officer of police shall be brought against—
(a) the chief officer of police for the time being, or
(b) in the case of a vacancy in that office, against the person for the time being performing the functions of that office;

and references in subsection (3) to the chief officer of police shall be construed accordingly.

(5) A police authority may, in such cases and to such extent as appear to it to be appropriate, pay out of the police fund—
(a) any compensation, costs or expenses awarded in proceedings under Part 2 [or 3] of this Act against a person under the direction and control of the chief officer of police;

(b) any costs or expenses incurred and not recovered by such a person in such proceedings; and
(c) any sum required in connection with the settlement of a claim that has or might have given rise to such proceedings.

(6) Subsections (1) and (2) apply to a police cadet and appointment as a police cadet as they apply to a constable and the office of constable.

(7) Subject to subsection (8), in this section—
"chief officer of police"—
(a) in relation to a person appointed, or an appointment falling to be made, under a specified Act, has the same meaning as in the Police Act 1996,
(b) . . .
(c) in relation to a person appointed, or an appointment falling to be made, under the Police (Scotland) Act 1967, means the chief constable of the relevant police force,
(d) in relation to any other person or appointment means the officer or other person who has the direction and control of the body of constables or cadets in question;
"police authority"—
(a) in relation to a person appointed, or an appointment falling to be made, under a specified Act, has the same meaning as in the Police Act 1996,
(b) . . .
(c) in relation to a person appointed, or an appointment falling to be made, under the Police (Scotland) Act 1967, has the meaning given in that Act,
(d) in relation to any other person or appointment, means the authority by whom the person in question is or on appointment would be paid;
"police cadet" means any person appointed to undergo training with a view to becoming a constable;
"police fund"—
(a) in relation to a chief officer of police within paragraph (a) of the above definition of that term, has the same meaning as in the Police Act 1996,
(b) . . . and
(c) in any other case means money provided by the police authority;
"specified Act" means the Metropolitan Police Act 1829, the City of London Police Act 1839 or the Police Act 1996.

(8) In relation to a constable of a force who is not under the direction and control of the chief officer of police for that force, references in this section to the chief officer of police are references to the chief officer of the force under whose direction and control he is, and references in this section to the police authority are references to the relevant police authority for that force.]

NOTES

Amendment

Inserted by SI 2003/1673, regs 3(1), 25.

Date in force (for certain purposes): 3 July 2003: see SI 2003/1673, reg 1(2).

Date in force (for remaining purposes): 1 October 2004: see SI 2003/1673, reg 1(3).

Sub-s (3): words "or 3" in square brackets in both places they occur inserted by the Disability Discrimination Act 2005, s 4(1), (2).

Date in force: 5 December 2005: see SI 2005/2774, art 3(c).

Sub-s (4): words "or 3" in square brackets inserted by the Disability Discrimination Act 2005, s 4(1), (2).

Date in force: 5 December 2005: see SI 2005/2774, art 3(c).

Sub-s (4): words "this section" in square brackets substituted by the Disability Discrimination Act 2005, s 4(1), (3).

Date in force: 5 December 2005: see SI 2005/2774, art 3(c).

Sub-s (5): in para (a) words "or 3" in square brackets inserted by the Disability Discrimination Act 2005, s 4(1), (2).

Date in force: 5 December 2005: see SI 2005/2774, art 3(c).

Sub-s (7): in definition "chief officer of police" para (b) repealed by the Serious Organised Crime and Police Act 2005, ss 59, 174(2), Sch 4, paras 64, 65(1), (2)(a), Sch 17, Pt 2.

Date in force: 1 April 2006: see SI 2006/378, art 4(1), Schedule, para 10.

Sub-s (7): in definition "police authority" para (b) repealed by the Serious Organised Crime and Police Act 2005, ss 59, 174(2), Sch 4, paras 64, 65(1), (2)(b), Sch 17, Pt 2.

Date in force: 1 April 2006: see SI 2006/378, art 4(1), Schedule, para 10.

Sub-s (7): in definition "police fund" para (b) repealed by the Serious Organised Crime and Police Act 2005, ss 59, 174(2), Sch 4, paras 64, 65(1), (2)(c), Sch 17, Pt 2.

Date in force: 1 April 2006: see SI 2006/378, art 4(1), Schedule, para 10.

See Further

See further: corresponding amendments to those made to sub-ss (3), (4) above by the Disability Discrimination Act 2005 have been made in relation to Northern Ireland: the Disability Discrimination (Northern Ireland) Order 2006, SI 2006/312, art 6.

65 Application to Parliament

(1) This Act applies to an act done by or for purposes of the House of Lords or the House of Commons as it applies to an act done by a private person.

(2) For the purposes of the application of Part II in relation to the House of Commons, the Corporate Officer of that House shall be treated as the employer of a person who is (or would be) a relevant member of the House of Commons staff for the purposes of [section 195 of the Employment Rights Act 1996].

(3) Except as provided in subsection (4), for the purposes of the application of sections 19 to 21, the provider of services is—

(a) as respects the House of Lords, the Corporate Officer of that House; and

(b) as respects the House of Commons, the Corporate Officer of that House.

(4) Where the service in question is access to and use of any place in the Palace of Westminster which members of the public are permitted to enter, the Corporate Officers of both Houses jointly are the provider of that service.

(5) Nothing in any rule of law or the law or practice of Parliament prevents proceedings being instituted before an [employment tribunal] under [Part 2 or 3] or before any court under Part III.

NOTES

Initial Commencement

To be appointed

To be appointed: see s 70(3).

Appointment

Appointment (in relation to England, Wales and Scotland): 2 December 1996: see SI 1996/1474, art 2(3), Schedule, Pt III.

Amendment

Sub-s (2): words in square brackets substituted by the Employment Rights Act 1996, s 240, Sch 1, para 69(1), (3).

Sub-s (5): words "employment tribunal" in square brackets substituted by the Employment Rights (Dispute Resolution) Act 1998, s 1(2)(a).

Date in force: 1 August 1998: see SI 1998/1658, art 2(1), Sch 1.

Sub-s (5): words "Part 2 or 3" in square brackets substituted by the Disability Discrimination Act 2005, s 19(1), Sch 1, Pt 1, paras 1, 32.

Date in force: 5 December 2005: see SI 2005/2774, art 3(j).

66 . . .

. . .

NOTES

Amendment

Repealed by SI 2003/1673, regs 3(1), 26.

Date in force (for certain purposes): 3 July 2003: see SI 2003/1673, reg 1(2).

Date in force (for remaining purposes): 1 October 2004: see SI 2003/1673, reg 1(3).

SCHEDULE 1

Provisions Supplementing Section 1

Section 1(1)

IMPAIRMENT

1

(1) . . .

(2) Regulations may make provision, for the purposes of this Act—

(a) for conditions of a prescribed description to be treated as amounting to impairments;

(b) for conditions of a prescribed description to be treated as not amounting to impairments.

(3) Regulations made under sub-paragraph (2) may make provision as to the meaning of "condition" for the purposes of those regulations.

Long-term effects

2

(1) The effect of an impairment is a long-term effect if—
 (a) it has lasted at least 12 months;
 (b) the period for which it lasts is likely to be at least 12 months; or
 (c) it is likely to last for the rest of the life of the person affected.

(2) Where an impairment ceases to have a substantial adverse effect on a person's ability to carry out normal day-to-day activities, it is to be treated as continuing to have that effect if that effect is likely to recur.

(3) For the purposes of sub-paragraph (2), the likelihood of an effect recurring shall be disregarded in prescribed circumstances.

(4) Regulations may prescribe circumstances in which, for the purposes of this Act—
 (a) an effect which would not otherwise be a long-term effect is to be treated as such an effect; or
 (b) an effect which would otherwise be a long-term effect is to be treated as not being such an effect.

Severe disfigurement

3

(1) An impairment which consists of a severe disfigurement is to be treated as having a substantial adverse effect on the ability of the person concerned to carry out normal day-to-day activities.

(2) Regulations may provide that in prescribed circumstances a severe disfigurement is not to be treated as having that effect.

(3) Regulations under sub-paragraph (2) may, in particular, make provision with respect to deliberately acquired disfigurements.

Normal day-to-day activities

4

(1) An impairment is to be taken to affect the ability of the person concerned to carry out normal day-to-day activities only if it affects one of the following—
 (a) mobility;
 (b) manual dexterity;
 (c) physical co-ordination;
 (d) continence;
 (e) ability to lift, carry or otherwise move everyday objects;
 (f) speech, hearing or eyesight;
 (g) memory or ability to concentrate, learn or understand; or
 (h) perception of the risk of physical danger.

(2) Regulations may prescribe—
   (a) circumstances in which an impairment which does not have an effect falling within sub-paragraph (1) is to be taken to affect the ability of the person concerned to carry out normal day-to-day activities;
   (b) circumstances in which an impairment which has an effect falling within sub-paragraph (1) is to be taken not to affect the ability of the person concerned to carry out normal day-to-day activities.

Substantial adverse effects

5

Regulations may make provision for the purposes of this Act—
   (a) for an effect of a prescribed kind on the ability of a person to carry out normal day-to-day activities to be treated as a substantial adverse effect;
   (b) for an effect of a prescribed kind on the ability of a person to carry out normal day-to-day activities to be treated as not being a substantial adverse effect.

Effect of medical treatment

6

(1) An impairment which would be likely to have a substantial adverse effect on the ability of the person concerned to carry out normal day-to-day activities, but for the fact that measures are being taken to treat or correct it, is to be treated as having that effect.
(2) In sub-paragraph (1) "measures" includes, in particular, medical treatment and the use of a prosthesis or other aid.
(3) Sub-paragraph (1) does not apply—
   (a) in relation to the impairment of a person's sight, to the extent that the impairment is, in his case, correctable by spectacles or contact lenses or in such other ways as may be prescribed; or
   (b) in relation to such other impairments as may be prescribed, in such circumstances as may be prescribed.

[6A

(1) Subject to sub-paragraph (2), a person who has cancer, HIV infection or multiple sclerosis is to be deemed to have a disability, and hence to be a disabled person.
(2) Regulations may provide for sub-paragraph (1) not to apply in the case of a person who has cancer if he has cancer of a prescribed description.
(3) A description of cancer prescribed under sub-paragraph (2) may (in particular) be framed by reference to consequences for a person of his having it.]

Persons deemed to be disabled

7

(1) Sub-paragraph (2) applies to any person whose name is, both on 12th January 1995 and on the date when this paragraph comes into force, in the register of disabled persons maintained under section 6 of the Disabled Persons (Employment) Act 1944.

(2) That person is to be deemed—

(a) during the initial period, to have a disability, and hence to be a disabled person; and

(b) afterwards, to have had a disability and hence to have been a disabled person during that period.

(3) A certificate of registration shall be conclusive evidence, in relation to the person with respect to whom it was issued, of the matters certified.

(4) Unless the contrary is shown, any document purporting to be a certificate of registration shall be taken to be such a certificate and to have been validly issued.

(5) Regulations may provide for prescribed descriptions of person to be deemed to have disabilities, and hence to be disabled persons, for the purposes of this Act.

[(5A) The generality of sub-paragraph (5) shall not be taken to be prejudiced by the other provisions of this Schedule.]

(6) Regulations may prescribe circumstances in which a person who has been deemed to be a disabled person by the provisions of sub-paragraph (1) or regulations made under sub-paragraph (5) is to be treated as no longer being deemed to be such a person.

(7) In this paragraph—

"certificate of registration" means a certificate issued under regulations made under section 6 of the Act of 1944; and

"initial period" means the period of three years beginning with the date on which this paragraph comes into force.

Progressive conditions

8

(1) Where—

(a) a person has a progressive condition (such as cancer, multiple sclerosis or muscular dystrophy or [HIV infection]),

(b) as a result of that condition, he has an impairment which has (or had) an effect on his ability to carry out normal day-to-day activities, but

(c) that-effect is not (or was not) a substantial adverse effect,

he shall be taken to have an impairment which has such a substantial adverse effect if the condition is likely to result in his having such an impairment.

(2) Regulations may make provision, for the purposes of this paragraph—

(a) for conditions of a prescribed description to be treated as being progressive;

(b) for conditions of a prescribed description to be treated as not being progressive.

[INTERPRETATION

9

In this Schedule "HIV infection" means infection by a virus capable of causing the Acquired Immune Deficiency Syndrome.]

NOTES

Initial Commencement

To be appointed

To be appointed: see s 70(3).

Appointment

Paras 1-6, 8: Appointment (in relation to England, Wales and Scotland): 17 May 1996: see SI 1996/1336, arts 2, 3(m).

Paras 1-6, 8: Appointment (in relation to Northern Ireland): 30 May 1996: see the Disability Discrimination Act 1995 (Commencement No 2) 1996 (Northern Ireland) 1996, SR 1996/219, arts 2, 3(l).

Para 7: Appointment (in relation to England, Wales and Scotland): 2 December 1996: see SI 1996/1474, art 2(3), Schedule, Pt III.

Para 7: Appointment (in relation to Northern Ireland): 2 December 1996: see the Disability Discrimination Act 1995 (Commencement No 3 and Saving and Transitional Provisions) Order (Northern Ireland) 1996, SR 1996/280, art 2(2), Schedule, Pt II.

Amendment

Para 1: sub-para (1) repealed by the Disability Discrimination Act 2005, ss 18(1), (2), 19(2), Sch 2.

Date in force (for certain purposes): 30 June 2005: see SI 2005/1676, art 2(2)(f).

Date in force (for remaining purposes): 5 December 2005: see SI 2005/2774, art 3(i), (k)(i).

Para 6A: inserted by the Disability Discrimination Act 2005, s 18(1), (3).

Date in force (for the purpose of exercising any power to make regulations): 30 June 2005: see SI 2005/1676, art 2(2)(f).

Date in force (for remaining purposes): 5 December 2005: see SI 2005/2774, art 3(i).

Para 7: sub-para (5A) inserted by the Disability Discrimination Act 2005, s 18(1), (4).

Date in force (for the purpose of exercising any power to make regulations): 30 June 2005: see SI 2005/1676, art 2(2)(f).

Date in force (for remaining purposes): 5 December 2005: see SI 2005/2774, art 3(i).

Para 8: in sub-para (1)(a) words "HIV infection" in square brackets substituted by the Disability Discrimination Act 2005, s 19(1), Sch 1, Pt 1, paras 1, 36.

Date in force: 5 December 2005: see SI 2005/2774, art 3(j).

Para 9: inserted by the Disability Discrimination Act 2005, s 18(1), (5).

Date in force (for the purpose of exercising any power to make regulations): 30 June 2005: see SI 2005/1676, art 2(2)(f).

Date in force (for remaining purposes): 5 December 2005: see SI 2005/2774, art 3(i).

See Further

See further: corresponding amendments and a repeal to those made to paras 1, 7-9 above by the Disability Discrimination Act 2005, have been made in relation to Northern Ireland: the Disability Discrimination (Northern Ireland) Order 2006, SI 2006/312, arts 18, 19, Sch 1, paras 1, 27, Sch 2.

Subordinate Legislation

Disability Discrimination (Meaning of Disability) Regulations 1996, SI 1996/1455 (made under paras 1(2), 2(3), 3(2), (3), 4(2)(a), 5(a)).

Disability Discrimination (Blind and Partially Sighted Persons) Regulations 2003, SI 2003/712 (made under para 7(5)).

SCHEDULE 2

Past Disabilities

Section 2(2)

1

The modifications referred to in section 2 are as follows.

2

References in Parts II [to 4] [and 5A] [and Part III of the 2005 Order] to a disabled person are to be read as references to a person who has had a disability.

[2A

References in Chapter 1 of Part 4 to a disabled pupil are to be read as references to a pupil who has had a disability.

2B

References in Chapter 2 of Part 4 to a disabled student are to be read as references to a student who has had a disability.]

[2C

In [sections 3A(5) and 31AB(8)], after "not having that particular disability" insert "and who has not had that particular disability".]

[3

In sections 4A(1), 4B(4), 4E(1), [4H(1),] 6B(1), 7B(1), 7D(1), 14(1), 14B(1), 14D(1)[, 15C(1)] and 16A(4), section 21A(4)(a) (in the words to be read as section 19(1)(aa)) and section 21A(6)(a) (in the words to be substituted in section 21(1)), [and section 31AD(1)(d), (2)(c) and (3),] after "not disabled" (in each place it occurs) insert "and who have not had a disability".]

[4

In sections 4A(3)(b), 4E(3)(b), [4H(3)(b),] 6B(3)(b), 7B(4)(b), 7D(3)(b), 14(3)(b), 14B(3)(b), 14D(3)(b)[, 15C(3)(a)][, 16A(6) and 31AD(4)(b),] for "has" (in each place it occurs) substitute "has had".]

[4ZA

In section 24(3)(e)(i) and (f)(i), after "having" insert "had".

4ZB

In sections 24D(2)(a) and 24J(3)(b), for "did not have" substitute "had not had".]

[4A

In section 28B(3)(a) and (4), after "disabled" insert "or that he had had a disability".

4B

In section 28C(1), in paragraphs (a) and (b), after "not disabled" insert "and who have not had a disability".

[4C

In section 28S

(a) in subsection (3)(a), after "disabled" insert "or that he had had a disability",
(b) in subsection (6)(a), after "who do not have" insert "and have not had", and
(c) in subsection (10), for "that particular disability" substitute "and who has not had that particular disability and".]

4D

In [subsections (1), (1A), (1B), (1C) and (1D)] of section 28T, after "not disabled" insert "and who have not had a disability".

4E

In [subsection (1) of that section] as substituted by paragraphs 2 [9, 14 and 21] of Schedule 4C, after "not disabled" insert "and who have not had a disability".]

5

For paragraph 2(1) to (3) of Schedule 1, substitute—

"(1) The effect of an impairment is a long-term effect if it has lasted for at least 12 months.

(2) Where an impairment ceases to have a substantial adverse effect on a person's ability to carry out normal day-to-day activities, it is to be treated as continuing to have that effect if that effect recurs.

(3) For the purposes of sub-paragraph (2), the recurrence of an effect shall be disregarded in prescribed circumstances."

[6

References in Chapter I of Part III of the 2005 Order to a disabled pupil are to be read as references to a pupil who has had a disability.

7

References in Chapter II of Part III of the 2005 Order to a disabled student are to be read as references to a student who has had a disability.

8

In Article 15(3)(a) and (4) of the 2005 Order, after "disabled" insert "or that he had had a disability".

9

In Article 16(1) of the 2005 Order, in sub-paragraphs (a) and (b), after "not disabled" insert "and who have not had a disability".

10

In Article 29(3)(a) and (4) of the 2005 Order, after "disabled" insert "or that he had had a disability".

11

In Articles 30(1)(a) and (b) and 37(1)(d), (2)(c) and (3) of the 2005 Order, after "not disabled" insert "and who have not had a disability".

12

In Article 35(8) of the 2005 Order after "not having that particular disability" insert "and who has not had that particular disability".

13

In Article 37(4)(b) of the 2005 Order for "has" substitute "has had".]

NOTES

Initial Commencement

To be appointed

To be appointed: see s 70(3).

Appointment

Appointment (in relation to England, Wales and Scotland): 17 May 1996: see SI 1996/1336, arts 2, 3(n).

Appointment (in relation to Northern Ireland): 30 May 1996: see the Disability Discrimination Act 1995 (Commencement No 2) Order (Northern Ireland) 1996, SR 1996/219, arts 2, 3(m).

Amendment

Para 2: words "to 4" in square brackets substituted by the Special Educational Needs and Disability Act 2001, s 38(1), (11).

Date in force: 1 September 2002: see SI 2002/2217, art 3, Sch 1, Pt 1.

Para 2: words "and 5A" in square brackets inserted by the Disability Discrimination Act 2005, s 19(1), Sch 1, Pt 1, paras 1, 37(1), (2).

Date in force: 5 December 2005: see SI 2005/2774, art 3(j).

Para 2: words "and Part III of the 2005 Order" in square brackets inserted, in relation to Northern Ireland, by the Special Educational Needs and Disability (Northern Ireland) Order 2005, SI 2005/1117, art 48(1), (9).

Date in force: 1 September 2005: see the Special Educational Needs and Disability (2005 Order) (Commencement No 1) Order (Northern Ireland) 2005, SR 2005/336, art 2, Schedule (as amended by the Special Educational Needs and Disability (2005 Order) (Commencement No 1) (Amendment) Order (Northern Ireland) 2007, SR 2007/25, art 2) and the Special Educational Needs and Disability (2005 Order) (Commencement No 2) Order (Northern Ireland) 2005, SR 2005/337, art 2, Schedule.

Paras 2A, 2B: inserted by the Special Educational Needs and Disability Act 2001, s 38(1), (12).

Date in force: 1 September 2002: see SI 2002/2217, art 3, Sch 1, Pt 1.

Para 2C: inserted by SI 2003/1673, regs 3(1), 29(1)(a).

Date in force (for certain purposes): 3 July 2003: see SI 2003/1673, reg 1(2).

Date in force (for remaining purposes): 1 October 2004: see SI 2003/1673, reg 1(3).

Para 2C: words "sections 3A(5) and 31AB(8)" in square brackets substituted by the Disability Discrimination Act 2005, s 19(1), Sch 1, Pt 1, paras 1, 37(1), (3).

Date in force: 1 September 2007: see SI 2007/1555, art 3(b).

Para 3: substituted by SI 2003/1673, regs 3(1), 29(1)(b).

Date in force (for certain purposes): 3 July 2003: see SI 2003/1673, reg 1(2).

Date in force (for remaining purposes): 1 October 2004: see SI 2003/1673, reg 1(3).

Para 3: reference to "4H(1)," in square brackets inserted by SI 2003/2770, regs 2, 4(4)(a).

Date in force (for certain purposes): 1 December 2003: see SI 2003/2770, reg 1(2).

Date in force (for remaining purposes): 1 October 2004: see SI 2003/2770, reg 1(3).

Para 3: reference to ", 15C(1)" in square brackets inserted by the Disability Discrimination Act 2005, s 19(1), Sch 1, Pt 1, paras 1, 37(1), (4)(a).

Date in force: 4 December 2006: see SI 2005/2774, art 4(f).

Para 3: words "and section 31AD(1)(d), (2)(c) and (3)," in square brackets inserted by the Disability Discrimination Act 2005, s 19(1), Sch 1, Pt 1, paras 1, 37(1), (4)(b).

Date in force: 1 September 2007: see SI 2007/1555, art 3(b).

Para 4: substituted by SI 2003/1673, regs 3(1), 29(1)(c).

Date in force (for certain purposes): 3 July 2003: see SI 2003/1673, reg 1(2).

Date in force (for remaining purposes): 1 October 2004: see SI 2003/1673, reg 1(3).

Para 4: reference to "4H(3)(b)," in square brackets inserted by SI 2003/2770, regs 2, 4(4)(b).

Date in force (for certain purposes): 1 December 2003: see SI 2003/2770, reg 1(2).

Date in force (for remaining purposes): 1 October 2004: see SI 2003/2770, reg 1(3).

Para 4: reference to ", 15C(3)(a)" in square brackets inserted by the Disability Discrimination Act 2005, s 19(1), Sch 1, Pt 1, paras 1, 37(1), (5)(a).

Date in force: 4 December 2006: see SI 2005/2774, art 4(f).

Para 4: words ", 16A(6) and 31AD(4)(b)," in square brackets substituted by the Disability Discrimination Act 2005, s 19(1), Sch 1, Pt 1, paras 37(1), (5)(b).

Date in force: 1 September 2007: see SI 2007/1555, art 3(b).

Paras 4ZA, 4ZB: inserted by the Disability Discrimination Act 2005, s 19(1), Sch 1, Pt 1, paras 1, 37(1), (6).

Date in force: 4 December 2006: see SI 2005/2774, art 4(f).

Paras 4A-4E: inserted by the Special Educational Needs and Disability Act 2001, s 38(1), (13).

Date in force: 1 September 2002: see SI 2002/2217, art 3, Sch 1, Pt 1.

Para 4C: substituted by SI 2006/1721, regs 4(1), 18(1), (2).

Date in force (for certain purposes): 30 June 2006: see SI 2006/1721, reg 1(2).

Date in force (for remaining purposes): 1 September 2006: see SI 2006/1721, reg 1(3).

Para 4D: words "subsections (1), (1A), (1B), (1C) and (1D)" in square brackets substituted by SI 2006/1721, regs 4(1), 18(1), (3).

Date in force (for certain purposes): 30 June 2006: see SI 2006/1721, reg 1(2).

Date in force (for remaining purposes): 1 September 2006: see SI 2006/1721, reg 1(3).

Para 4E: words "subsection (1) of that section" in square brackets substituted by SI 2006/1721, regs 4(1), 18(1), (4)(a).

Date in force (for certain purposes): 30 June 2006: see SI 2006/1721, reg 1(2).

Date in force (for remaining purposes): 1 September 2006: see SI 2006/1721, reg 1(3).

Para 4E: words "9, 14 and 21" in square brackets substituted by SI 2006/1721, regs 4(1), 18(1), (4)(b).

Date in force (for certain purposes): 30 June 2006: see SI 2006/1721, reg 1(2).

Date in force (for remaining purposes): 1 September 2006: see SI 2006/1721, reg 1(3).

Paras 6-13: inserted, in relation to Northern Ireland, by the Special Educational Needs and Disability (Northern Ireland) Order 2005, SI 2005/1117, art 48(1), (10).

Date in force: 1 September 2005: see the Special Educational Needs and Disability (2005 Order) (Commencement No 1) Order (Northern Ireland) 2005, SR 2005/336, art 2, Schedule (as amended by the Special Educational Needs and Disability (2005 Order) (Commencement No 1) (Amendment) Order (Northern Ireland) 2007, SR 2007/25, art 2) and the Special Educational Needs and Disability (2005 Order) (Commencement No 2) Order (Northern Ireland) 2005, SR 2005/337, art 2, Schedule.

See Further

See further: corresponding amendments to those made to paras 2-4, 4ZA, 4ZB above by the Disability Discrimination Act 2005, have been made in relation to Northern Ireland: the Disability Discrimination (Northern Ireland) Order 2006, SI 2006/312, art 19(1), Sch 1, paras 1, 28.

SCHEDULE 3

Enforcement and Procedure

Sections [17A(8)], 25(6)[, 31ADA]

NOTES

Amendment

Schedule heading: reference to "17A(8)" in square brackets substituted by SI 2003/1673, regs 3(1), 29(2)(a).

Date in force (for certain purposes): 3 July 2003: see SI 2003/1673, reg 1(2).

Date in force (for remaining purposes): 1 October 2004: see SI 2003/1673, reg 1(3).

Schedule heading: reference to ", 31ADA" in square brackets inserted by SI 2007/2405, regs 2(1), 4(1), (2).

Date in force: 1 September 2007: see SI 2007/2405, reg 1(2).

Part I

Employment

Conciliation

1

. . .

Restriction on proceedings for breach of Part II

2

[(1) Except as provided by Part 2, no civil or criminal proceedings may be brought against any person in respect of an act merely because the act is unlawful under that Part.]

(2) Sub-paragraph (1) does not prevent the making of an application for judicial review [or the investigation or determination of any matter in accordance with Part 10 (investigations) of the Pension Schemes Act 1993 by the Pensions Ombudsman].

[(3) Sub-paragraph (1) does not prevent the bringing of proceedings in respect of an offence under section 16B(2B).]

Period within which proceedings must be brought

3

(1) An [employment tribunal] shall not consider a complaint under [section 17A or 25(8)] unless it is presented before the end of the period of three months beginning when the act complained of was done.

(2) A tribunal may consider any such complaint which is out of time if, in all the circumstances of the case, it considers that it is just and equitable to do so.

(3) For the purposes of sub-paragraph (1)—

- (a) where an unlawful act . . . is attributable to a term in a contract, that act is to be treated as extending throughout the duration of the contract;
- (b) any act extending over a period shall be treated as done at the end of that period; and
- (c) a deliberate omission shall be treated as done when the person in question decided upon it.

(4) In the absence of evidence establishing the contrary, a person shall be taken for the purposes of this paragraph to decide upon an omission—

- (a) when he does an act inconsistent with doing the omitted act; or
- (b) if he has done no such inconsistent act, when the period expires within which he might reasonably have been expected to do the omitted act if it was to be done.

Evidence

4

(1) In any proceedings under [section 17A or 25(8)], a certificate signed by or on behalf of a Minister of the Crown and certifying—

(a) that any conditions or requirements specified in the certificate were imposed by a Minister of the Crown and were in operation at a time or throughout a time so specified, . . .

(b) . . .

shall be conclusive evidence of the matters certified.

[(1A) In any proceedings under section 17A or 25(8), a certificate signed by or on behalf of the Scottish Ministers and certifying that any conditions or requirements specified in the certificate—

(a) were imposed by a member of the Scottish Executive, and

(b) were in operation at a time or throughout a time so specified,

shall be conclusive evidence of the matters certified.

(1B) In any proceedings under section 17A or 25(8), a certificate signed by or on behalf of the [Welsh Ministers] and certifying that any conditions or requirements specified in the certificate—

(a) were imposed by the [National Assembly for Wales constituted by the Government of Wales Act 1998, the Welsh Ministers, the First Minister for Wales or the Counsel General to the Welsh Assembly Government], and

(b) were in operation at a time or throughout a time so specified,

shall be conclusive evidence of the matters certified.]

(2) A document purporting to be such a certificate [as is mentioned in sub-paragraph (1), (1A) or (1B)] shall be received in evidence and, unless the contrary is proved, be deemed to be such a certificate.

NOTES

Initial Commencement

To be appointed

To be appointed: see s 70(3).

Appointment

Appointment (in relation to England, Wales and Scotland): 2 December 1996: see SI 1996/1474, art 2(3), Schedule, Pt III.

Appointment (in relation to Northern Ireland): 2 December 1996: see the Disability Discrimination Act 1995 (Commencement No 3 and Saving and Transitional Provisions) Order (Northern Ireland) 1996, SR 1996/280, art 2(2), Schedule, Pt II.

Amendment

Para 1: repealed by the Employment Tribunals Act 1996, s 45, Sch 3, Pt I.

Para 2: sub-para (1) substituted by SI 2003/1673, regs 3(1), 29(2)(b).

Date in force (for certain purposes): 3 July 2003: see SI 2003/1673, reg 1(2).

Date in force (for remaining purposes): 1 October 2004: see SI 2003/1673, reg 1(3).

Para 2: in sub-para (2) words from "or the investigation" to "the Pensions Ombudsman" in square brackets inserted by SI 2003/2770, regs 2, 4(5).

Date in force (for certain purposes): 1 December 2003: see SI 2003/2770, reg 1(2).

Date in force (for remaining purposes): 1 October 2004: see SI 2003/2770, reg 1(3).

Para 2: sub-para (3) inserted by the Disability Discrimination Act 2005, s 19(1), Sch 1, Pt 1, paras 1, 38(1), (2).

Date in force: 5 December 2005: see SI 2005/2774, art 3(j).

Para 3: in sub-para (1) words "employment tribunal" in square brackets substituted by the Employment Rights (Dispute Resolution) Act 1998, s 1(2)(a).

Date in force: 1 August 1998: see SI 1998/1658, art 2(1), Sch 1.

Para 3: in sub-para (1) words "section 17A or 25(8)" in square brackets substituted by SI 2003/1673, regs 3(1), 29(2)(c).

Date in force (for certain purposes): 3 July 2003: see SI 2003/1673, reg 1(2).

Date in force (for remaining purposes): 1 October 2004: see SI 2003/1673, reg 1(3).

Para 3: in sub-para (3)(a) words omitted repealed by SI 2003/1673, regs 3(1), 29(2)(d).

Date in force (for certain purposes): 3 July 2003: see SI 2003/1673, reg 1(2).

Date in force (for remaining purposes): 1 October 2004: see SI 2003/1673, reg 1(3).

Para 4: in sub-para (1) words "section 17A or 25(8)" in square brackets substituted by SI 2003/1673, regs 3(1), 29(2)(e).

Date in force (for certain purposes): 3 July 2003: see SI 2003/1673, reg 1(2).

Date in force (for remaining purposes): 1 October 2004: see SI 2003/1673, reg 1(3).

Para 4: word omitted from the end of sub-para (1)(a) repealed by the Employment Relations Act 1999, s 44, Sch 9, Table 12.

Date in force: 16 July 2001: see SI 2001/1187, art 3 (as amended by SI 2001/1461).

Para 4: sub-para (1)(b) repealed by the Employment Relations Act 1999, ss 41, 44, Sch 8, para 7, Sch 9, Table 12.

Date in force: 16 July 2001: see SI 2001/1187, art 3 (as amended by SI 2001/1461).

Para 4: sub-paras (1A), (1B) inserted by the Disability Discrimination Act 2005, s 19(1), Sch 1, Pt 1, paras 1, 38(1), (3).

Date in force: 30 June 2005: see SI 2005/1676, art 2(1)(c).

Para 4: in sub-para (1B) words "Welsh Ministers" in square brackets substituted by SI 2007/1388, art 3, Sch 1, paras 47, 63(1), (2)(a).

Date in force: this amendment came into force on 25 May 2007 being the date on which the initial period ended (following the appointment of the First Minister): see SI 2007/1388, art 1(2) and the Government of Wales Act 2006, ss 46, 161(5).

Para 4: in sub-para (1B)(a) words from "National Assembly for Wales" to "Welsh Assembly Government" in square brackets substituted by SI 2007/1388, art 3, Sch 1, paras 47, 63(1), (2)(b).

Date in force: this amendment came into force on 25 May 2007 being the date on which the initial period ended (following the appointment of the First Minister): see SI 2007/1388, art 1(2) and the Government of Wales Act 2006, ss 46, 161(5).

Para 4: in sub-para (2) words "as is mentioned in sub-paragraph (1), (1A) or (1B)" in square brackets inserted by the Disability Discrimination Act 2005, s 19(1), Sch 1, Pt 1, paras 1, 38(1), (4).

Date in force: 30 June 2005: see SI 2005/1676, art 2(1)(c).

See Further

See further: a corresponding amendment to that made to para 2(3) above by the Disability Discrimination Act 2005, has been made in relation to Northern Ireland: the Disability Discrimination (Northern Ireland) Order 2006, SI 2006/312, art 19(1), Sch 1, paras 1, 29(1), (2).

Miscellaneous

By virtue of the Employment Rights (Dispute Resolution) Act 1998, s 1(2), the Industrial Tribunals Act 1996 shall be cited as the Employment Tribunals Act 1996; references to the Industrial Tribunals Act 1996 have been changed accordingly.

[. . .]

APPENDIX 2

1996 NO. 1455

DISABLED PERSONS

THE DISABILITY DISCRIMINATION (MEANING OF DISABILITY) REGULATIONS 1996

In exercise of the powers conferred on the Secretary of State by paragraphs 1(2), 2(4), 3(2) and (3), 4(2)(a) and 5(a) of Schedule 1 to the Disability Discrimination Act 1995, the Secretary of State for Social Security hereby makes the following Regulations:

Citation and commencement

1. These Regulations may be cited as the Disability Discrimination (Meaning of Disability) Regulations 1996 and shall come into force on 30th July 1996.

Interpretation

2. In these Regulations—

"the Act" means the Disability Discrimination Act 1995; and

"addiction" includes a dependency.

Addictions

3.—(1) Subject to paragraph (2) below, addiction to alcohol, nicotine or any other substance is to be treated as not amounting to an impairment for the purposes of the Act.

(2) Paragraph (1) above does not apply to addiction which was originally the result of administration of medically prescribed drugs or other medical treatment.

Other conditions not to be treated as impairments

4.—(1) For the purposes of the Act the following conditions are to be treated as not amounting to impairments:—

(a) a tendency to set fires,
(b) a tendency to steal,
(c) a tendency to physical or sexual abuse of other persons,
(d) exhibitionism, and
(e) voyeurism.

(2) Subject to paragraph (3) below for the purposes of the Act the condition known as seasonal allergic rhinitis shall be treated as not amounting to an impairment.

(3) Paragraph (2) above shall not prevent that condition from being taken into account for the purposes of the Act where it aggravates the effect of another condition.

Tattoos and piercings

5. For the purposes of paragraph 3 of Schedule 1 to the Act a severe disfigurement is not to be treated as having a substantial adverse effect on the ability of the person concerned to carry out normal day-to-day activities if it consists of—

(a) a tattoo (which has not been removed), or

(b) a piercing of the body for decorative or other non-medical purposes, including any object attached through the piercing for such purposes.

Babies and young children

6. For the purposes of the Act where a child under six years of age has an impairment which does not have an effect falling within paragraph 4(1) of Schedule 1 to the Act that impairment is to be taken to have a substantial and long-term adverse effect on the ability of that child to carry out normal day-to-day activities where it would normally have a substantial and long-term adverse effect on the ability of a person aged 6 years or over to carry out normal day-to-day activities.

Alistair Burt

Minister of State, Department of Social Security

4th June 1996

APPENDIX 3

Employers' Forum on Disability

Employers' Forum on Disability is the world's leading employers' organisation working to the mutual benefit of business and people with disabilities.

We make it easier to employ disabled people, welcome disabled customers and develop partnerships with disabled people as stakeholders in the wider community.

Employers' Forum on Disability,

Nutmeg House, 60 Gainsford Street,

London, SE1 2NY

Tel: 020 7403 3020

Minicom: 020 7403 0040

Fax: 020 7403 0404

Email: enquiries@efd.org.uk

Website: www.efd.org.uk

Company limited by guarantee

Registered Charity No: 1018463

Registered in England No: 2603700

Disability communication guide

Employers' Forum on Disability is the world's leading employers' organisation working to the mutual benefit of business and people with disabilities.

We make it easier to employ disabled people, welcome disabled customers and develop partnerships with disabled people as stakeholders in the wider community.

Produced in association with Barclays

Contents

Who should read this?

This guide is for human resources managers, line managers and all other staff for use in their everyday working lives.

The guide will help:

Smooth the process of meeting and working with people who have specific impairments

Recognise and avoid the attitudes and behaviours that create barriers and misunderstandings

Develop a greater understanding of the views and preferences of disabled people.

The basics

The overriding rule is not to be daunted by lists of rights and wrongs. If in doubt, ask yourself how you would want to be treated and always be willing to adapt to a person's individual preference.

The majority of difficulties faced by disabled people are caused by other people's misunderstanding of their capabilities

Improving access means removing barriers; it is not just about spending money on structural alterations. It also involves adjusting policies, procedures and outdated attitudes towards disabled people

The word 'access' should be applied in its broadest sense to all forms of communication and opportunity

'Disability' is not 'sickness'. The general health of most disabled people is as good as that of anyone else.

Communication skills

Communication skills are vital in developing relationships with disabled and non-disabled customers and employees alike.

Common sense and common courtesy tells us:

Be patient and listen attentively

Use a normal tone of voice when extending a verbal welcome

Exercise patience when listening

Do not attempt to speak, or finish a sentence, for the person you are speaking to

Never ask, "What happened to you?". Restrain your curiosity

Address a disabled person by their first name only if addressing everyone with the same familiarity

Speak directly to a disabled person, even if accompanied by an interpreter or companion

Never make assumptions about what anyone can do.

Words and phrases

Certain words and phrases may give offence. Although there are no concrete rules, it is helpful to understand why some terms are preferred to others. And preferences vary, so be prepared to ask the individual.

People are increasingly sensitive to the way in which the 'language of disability' can inadvertently reinforce negative stereotypes.

General guidance

Most people who see disability as an equality issue strongly prefer the term 'disabled people' as they regard themselves as people with impairments or medical conditions who are 'disabled' by a society that fails to remove unnecessary obstacles.

Some prefer the term 'people with disabilities' because it puts the person first, while others, such as many who are pre-lingually deaf (i.e. deaf from birth or an early age) and use British Sign Language; those that have a long-term medical condition; or who have experienced medical illness, may not see themselves as disabled at all, even though the Disability Discrimination Act may define them as such.

A disabled person is not defined by their impairment. Nobody wants to be given a medical label

Labels say nothing about the person, they simply reinforce the stereotype that disabled people are 'sick' and dependent on the medical profession

References such as 'an epileptic' or 'a diabetic' are dehumanising. If you need to refer to a person's condition, say a person who has epilepsy or a person who has diabetes. (Exceptions do, however, exist. The Dyslexia Association advocates the use of the phrase 'dyslexic people' as opposed to 'people with dyslexia'.)

Do not be embarrassed about using common expressions that could relate to someone's impairment, for example, "See you later" or, "I'll be running along then"

Avoid using language that suggests disabled people are always frail or dependent on others, or which could make disabled people objects of pity, such as 'sufferers from' or 'a victim of'

Do not use collective nouns such as 'the disabled', 'the blind', 'the disfigured'. These terms imply people are part of a uniform group which is somehow separate from the rest of society. However, there is one exception and that is 'the Deaf', with a capital 'D'. This is the preferred term for many pre-lingually deaf people who use British Sign Language and see themselves as a cultural minority rather than part of a disabled community.

Specific guidance

Instead of	Use
Mental, mental patient, schizophrenic, lunatic, psycho, etc.	A person with a mental health problem or difficulty.
Cripple, or invalid.	Disabled person, or person with a disability or, if appropriate, a person with a mobility impairment.
Deaf and dumb, or deaf mute.	A person who is deaf without speech, or a Deaf person (see above). Please note that British Sign Language is a recognised form of language.
Midget, or dwarf.	A person of short stature, or a person of restricted growth. (Although some individuals do prefer to be called a dwarf.)
Fits, spells, attacks.	Seizures.
Mentally handicapped, subnormal.	A person with a learning disability or difficulty.
Spastic.	A person with cerebral palsy.
Wheelchair-bound.	A wheelchair user.

When meeting a disabled person

Disability etiquette

The one universal rule is never to assume you know what assistance, if any, a disabled person requires. Ask if, and what, assistance may be needed.

However, here are a few more general pointers that may be useful.

Treat a disabled person in the same manner and with the same respect and courtesy you would anyone else

Treat adults as adults

Do not make assumptions about the existence or absence of a disability; many people have disabilities that are not visible or immediately apparent

Use appropriate physical contact, such as a handshake, as you would with anyone else

A disabled individual may not introduce a personal assistant or human aid to communications (for example an interpreter). Take your lead from the person using their services

Assistance dogs (with a visually or hearing impaired person, a wheelchair user, or someone with epilepsy) are working dogs. They should not be treated as pets. They will, however, need water and somewhere outside to relieve themselves if it is a long meeting

Know where accessible (and other) toilets, drinking fountains, water coolers, and telephones are located.

Meeting people: with a visual impairment

Identify yourself clearly and introduce any other people present. Clearly indicate where people are located

If speaking in a group it is helpful to identify the name of the person you are speaking to. People should introduce themselves before speaking

To shake hands, say, "Shall we shake hands?"

Before offering assistance, ask the individual how you may help. If the person asks for assistance, ask, "May I offer you an arm?" rather than taking their arm. This enables you to guide, rather than 'propel' the person

Remember that most people with impaired vision do have some residual sight

If you are guiding someone, tell them when steps, stairs, ramps or other obstacles occur. And, in the case of steps, stairs and ramps, whether they are up or down

When you are offering a seat, guide the person's hand to the back or the arm of the seat, and say this is what you are going to do

If leaving someone with a visual impairment in an area unfamiliar to them, inform the person you are leaving and connect them with someone else

When entering an unfamiliar area, give a brief description of the layout

Where someone might normally take notes, ask if they would like to tape the meeting or conversation

Provide written communication in an accessible format and, if possible, in the person's preferred format, such as floppy disk, in large print, on audio-cassette or in Braille

Papers for meetings should be available in advance, including minutes and any papers to be tabled.

Meeting people: who are deaf or hard of hearing

There are many different degrees and types of deafness, and different ways for deaf people or those who are hard-of-hearing to communicate. It is estimated that 689,000 people are profoundly deaf and 50,000 people use British Sign Language (BSL) as their first language.

Try not to feel uncomfortable about communicating with a deaf or hard of hearing person, even if the communication feels awkward at first

If you do not understand what someone has said, ask him or her to repeat the sentence. Do not pretend you have understood when you have not

Ask the person to tell you how they prefer to communicate

Speak one at a time in meetings or gatherings. This enables lip-reading or interpreter communication

Written notes may help you present complicated information

Make sure a deaf person is looking at you before you begin speaking as he or she may need to lip-read. A gentle touch on the shoulder or arm will capture their attention

Keep background noise as low as possible

Check regularly that you have been understood

Stick to the agenda

Book interpreters or other support in advance

For interviews and meetings use a qualified British Sign Language interpreter. Qualified interpreters are either CACDP (Council for the Advancement of Communication with Deaf People), registered interpreters or registered trainee interpreters

If a sign language interpreter is present, speak to the individual, not the interpreter

Use an induction loop, enabling hard of hearing people to tune-in their hearing aids directly to speakers and minimise background noise.

Many people reinforce what they hear with lip-reading. A few deaf people with no hearing at all use this alone. This is a demanding and tiring skill.

Look directly at the person you are speaking to

Do not speak with your back to a light source as this will put your lips in shadow

Make sure you are visible and in good lighting when talking

Speak clearly and at an even pace, but do not distort or exaggerate your lip movements

Stop talking if you must turn away

Do not use exaggerated gestures

Do not block your mouth with your hands, cigarettes or food.

Meeting people: who are deafblind

While deafblindness is a combination of hearing and sight impairments, remember that deafblind people are not always completely deaf and blind. In fact, most deafblind people do have some residual hearing or sight or both. The advice provided in the sections on people with impaired vision or hearing may, therefore, also apply.

A deafblind person may speak to you but may not hear your voice. Let the person know you are there. Approach from the front and touch the person lightly on the arm or shoulder to attract their attention

Many deafblind people need to be guided. Individuals will have their particular preference as to how they wish to be guided. Some deafblind people experience poor balance

A deafblind person may be supported by a communicator-guide or interpreter. Remember to speak to the individual rather than their assistant

Do not grab or 'propel' a person. Let them know you are offering to escort them by guiding their hand to your elbow.

Meeting people: with speech difficulties

Be attentive, encouraging and patient, but not patronising

Slowness or impaired speech does not reflect a person's intelligence

Refrain from correcting or speaking for the person. Wait quietly while the person speaks and resist the temptation to finish sentences for them

If you need more information, break down your questions to deal with individual points that require short answers

If you do not understand what someone has said, ask the individual to say it again. Never pretend to understand when you do not.

Meeting people: who use a wheelchair, cane, walking frame or crutches

Leaning on a wheelchair is the equivalent of leaning or hanging onto a person. A wheelchair is a user's personal space

If you are talking for more than a few moments to someone in a wheelchair, try to position yourself so you are at the same level, or at least ask the person if they would like you to sit down

Be aware of your manner when you kneel or crouch to speak with the person. Do not alter your treatment of the individual. Treat adults as adults

If there is a high desk or counter, move to the front

Never touch or move crutches, canes or walking frames, or push a wheelchair without the user's consent

Offer a seat to someone who does not bring their own

Speak directly to a wheelchair user, not their companion

Unless you know it is easy to move around your building in a wheelchair, offer to help. Heavy doors or deep-pile carpets are just some of the hazards to watch for. Do not assume ramps solve everything; they may be too steep or too slippery

Do not be offended if your offer of help is refused. Many wheelchair users prefer to travel independently whenever possible.

Meeting people: with learning disabilities

Many people born with learning disabilities, those in the early stages of dementia or people who acquire a brain injury, live full and independent lives in the community. Most can make their own choices, with varying levels of support.

The following may apply to any of these individuals:

Begin by assuming the person will understand you

Speak to the person as you would anyone else. Do not assume you can predict from your initial impression what the person will or will not understand

Keep all communication simple. Avoid jargon

Consider putting information in writing, including your name and phone number

Provide straightforward summaries of written information

Perhaps offer the person an appropriate record of a conversation (for example, tape, an electronic version, or 'easy read' notes) so they can consider it again later and keep a record.

Meeting people: with mental health problems

Someone experiencing the emotional distress and confusion associated with mental health problems may find everyday activities very hard. Often the most significant disability people with mental health problems experience is created by the attitudes of others

Be patient and non-judgmental

Give the person time to make decisions

Provide clear and timely information with the aim of ensuring people arrive at a meeting as unstressed as possible

Remove any sources of stress and confusion, for example, noise, flashing lights

A person may require an advocate to help access information, or attend meetings or interviews.

Meeting people: with facial disfigurement

Some people are born with a disfigurement and others acquire it through accident or illness. Disfigurement is usually only skin deep, but it can be associated with facial paralysis and other impairment such as speech difficulties.

Like any disability, it does not mean the person is any different and certainly does not affect his or her intelligence.

Most of the difficulties, indeed discrimination, people with facial disfigurement experience, stem from other people's behaviour.

Make eye contact, as you would with anyone else. Do not stare. Smile if you would for someone else

Listen carefully, and do not let the person's appearance distract you.

Interviews

When preparing to interview a disabled person, you may need to adjust your usual arrangements. Do not assume you know what will be needed. Ask the individual.

Every candidate should be asked if they have any particular requirements in connection with the interview, if they are to do well

Although you should be prepared to make adjustments, do not make assumptions about what a person can or cannot do. Disabled people often develop their own creative solutions to work-based challenges

Focus on the main tasks and requirements of the job and the person's skills

Do not be distracted by issues which are not related to work, such as gender, age, disability or ethnic origin

Restrict questions about the effect of the person's disability to those that potentially affect their ability to do the job

One might be, "How can we help you be successful in this job?"

Only ask about the person's life outside work if you would ask such questions of every other candidate

Do not ask, "What happened to you?"

Examples of adjustments include:

Changing the venue to a more accessible interview room for a wheelchair user

Re-arranging the seating or lighting so that a deaf person can lip-read more easily

Arranging for an appropriate person to help you communicate, such as a sign language interpreter

Allowing the individual to bring an assistant or companion to the interview. They might not want them to come in, so a waiting place nearby may be needed.

Meetings and events

When planning a meeting or event remember that 'access' refers to facilities as well as buildings. It covers approaches, entrances, floor surfaces, lifts, speaker platforms, lecterns, catering and toilets, as well as providing extra time, interpreters and communications support, notes in Braille or on audio cassette, large print programmes and auxiliary aids such as portable hearing loops.

If you think there may be access problems, either give advance warning of the problem or, preferably, find a better venue

Advertise that the venue is fully accessible, providing relevant detail, or disabled people may not risk coming

Make sure reception staff know you are expecting disabled people. Make sure they have read this guide and tell them about any particular requests

Ensure there is room for people with visual or mobility impairments to move about easily, both at the meeting and when taking refreshments

Make sure help, and some seats and tables, are available. It is difficult to sign with a glass of champagne in your hand!

Reduce or remove any background noise

Offer clipboards to wheelchair users

Make sure parking arrangements are adequate. Provide directions and, if necessary, valet parking

Clearly sign accessible toilet facilities, and ensure staff are aware of their location

Staff should be aware of the evacuation plan, including refuge point and evacuation procedure

Ideally, the building should be equipped with a 'deaf-alert' (i.e. visual) fire alarm.

Invitations

On papers that go out before the meeting, ask people to let you know what adjustments they need

Rather than referring to, 'special needs', ask if people have 'particular requirements'

Use a phrase such as, "Please let us know what we can do to make our reception fully accessible to you?" or, "Do you need us to change anything to make sure you play a full part in this meeting?"

Further information

Employers' Forum on Disability: Publications

As Employers' Forum on Disability's best seller, more than one million copies of the 'Disability communication guide' have been circulated among UK businesses since its launch in 1999.

Like all EFD publications the 'Disability communication guide' provides a unique source of up-to-date information, giving practical guidance for employers and service providers alike.

For further information on EFD's activities, including publications, events, research, information helpline and membership benefits log on to our website: www.efd.org.uk

For a publications list, a quote for customising our publications to your individual needs and incorporating your company logo and equal opportunities statement, or simply to place an order, please phone 020 7089 2410.

Disability Discrimination Act

The Disability Discrimination Act protects people with a wide range of mental and physical impairments. People with, for example, dyslexia, epilepsy, severe disfigurements, angina, or mental health problems, may be covered by the Act.

Since October 2004, the part of the DDA that relates to employment applies to virtually every organisation. Further provisions apply to service providers and education establishments, and make it unlawful to discriminate.

NB: The DDA is described in more detail in other publications available from Employers' Forum on Disability.

Contact information

Employers' Forum on Disability,

Nutmeg House, 60 Gainsford Street, London, SE1 2NY

Tel: 020 7403 3020 Minicom: 020 7403 0040 Fax: 020 7403 0404

Email: enquiries@efd.org.uk

Website: www.efd.org.uk

Produced in association with Barclays

APPENDIX 4

COUNCIL DIRECTIVE 2000/78/EC

of 27 November 2000

establishing a general framework for equal treatment in employment and occupation

The Council of the European Union

Having regard to the Treaty establishing the European Community, and in particular Article 13 thereof,

Having regard to the proposal from the Commission,[1]

Having regard to the Opinion of the European Parliament,[2]

Having regard to the Opinion of the Economic and Social Committee,[3]

Having regard to the Opinion of the Committee of the Regions,[4]

Whereas:

(1) In accordance with Article 6 of the Treaty on European Union, the European Union is founded on the principles of liberty, democracy, respect for human rights and fundamental freedoms, and the rule of law, principles which are common to all Member States and it respects fundamental rights, as guaranteed by the European Convention for the Protection of Human Rights and Fundamental Freedoms and as they result from the constitutional traditions common to the Member States, as general principles of Community law.

(2) The principle of equal treatment between women and men is well established by an important body of Community law, in particular in Council Directive 76/ 207/EEC of 9 February 1976 on the implementation of the principle of equal treatment for men and women as regards access to employment, vocational training and promotion, and working conditions.[5]

(3) In implementing the principle of equal treatment, the Community should, in accordance with Article 3(2) of the EC Treaty, aim to eliminate inequalities, and to promote equality between men and women, especially since women are often the victims of multiple discrimination.

---

1 OJ C 177 E, 27.6.2000, p. 42.

2 Opinion delivered on 12 October 2000 (not yet published in the Official Journal).

3 OJ C 204, 18.7.2000, p. 82.

4 OJ C 226, 8.8.2000, p. 1.

5 OJ L 39, 14.2.1976, p. 40.

(4) The right of all persons to equality before the law and protection against discrimination constitutes a universal right recognised by the Universal Declaration of Human Rights, the United Nations Convention on the Elimination of All Forms of Discrimination against Women, United Nations Covenants on Civil and Political Rights and on Economic, Social and Cultural Rights and by the European Convention for the Protection of Human Rights and Fundamental Freedoms, to which all Member States are signatories. Convention No 111 of the International Labour Organisation (ILO) prohibits discrimination in the field of employment and occupation.

(5) It is important to respect such fundamental rights and freedoms. This Directive does not prejudice freedom of association, including the right to establish unions with others and to join unions to defend one's interests.

(6) The Community Charter of the Fundamental Social Rights of Workers recognises the importance of combating every form of discrimination, including the need to take appropriate action for the social and economic integration of elderly and disabled people.

(7) The EC Treaty includes among its objectives the promotion of coordination between employment policies of the Member States. To this end, a new employment chapter was incorporated in the EC Treaty as a means of developing a coordinated European strategy for employment to promote a skilled, trained and adaptable workforce.

(8) The Employment Guidelines for 2000 agreed by the European Council at Helsinki on 10 and 11 December 1999 stress the need to foster a labour market favourable to social integration by formulating a coherent set of policies aimed at combating discrimination against groups such as persons with disability. They also emphasise the need to pay particular attention to supporting older workers, in order to increase their participation in the labour force.

(9) Employment and occupation are key elements in guaranteeing equal opportunities for all and contribute strongly to the full participation of citizens in economic, cultural and social life and to realising their potential.

(10) On 29 June 2000 the Council adopted Directive 2000/ 43/EC[6] implementing the principle of equal treatment between persons irrespective of racial or ethnic origin. That Directive already provides protection against such discrimination in the field of employment and occupation.

(11) Discrimination based on religion or belief, disability, age or sexual orientation may undermine the achievement of the objectives of the EC Treaty, in particular the attainment of a high level of employment and social protection, raising the standard of living and the quality of life, economic and social cohesion and solidarity, and the free movement of persons.

(12) To this end, any direct or indirect discrimination based on religion or belief, disability, age or sexual orientation as regards the areas covered by this Directive should be prohibited throughout the Community. This prohibition of discrimination should also apply to nationals of third countries but does not cover differences of treatment based on nationality and is without prejudice to provisions governing the entry and residence of third-country nationals and their access to employment and occupation.

[6] OJ L 180, 19.7.2000, p. 22.

(13) This Directive does not apply to social security and social protection schemes whose benefits are not treated as income within the meaning given to that term for the purpose of applying Article 141 of the EC Treaty, nor to any kind of payment by the State aimed at providing access to employment or maintaining employment.

(14) This Directive shall be without prejudice to national provisions laying down retirement ages.

(15) The appreciation of the facts from which it may be inferred that there has been direct or indirect discrimination is a matter for national judicial or other competent bodies, in accordance with rules of national law or practice. Such rules may provide, in particular, for indirect discrimination to be established by any means including on the basis of statistical evidence.

(16) The provision of measures to accommodate the needs of disabled people at the workplace plays an important role in combating discrimination on grounds of disability.

(17) This Directive does not require the recruitment, promotion, maintenance in employment or training of an individual who is not competent, capable and available to perform the essential functions of the post concerned or to undergo the relevant training, without prejudice to the obligation to provide reasonable accommodation for people with disabilities.

(18) This Directive does not require, in particular, the armed forces and the police, prison or emergency services to recruit or maintain in employment persons who do not have the required capacity to carry out the range of functions that they may be called upon to perform with regard to the legitimate objective of preserving the operational capacity of those services.

(19) Moreover, in order that the Member States may continue to safeguard the combat effectiveness of their armed forces, they may choose not to apply the provisions of this Directive concerning disability and age to all or part of their armed forces. The Member States which make that choice must define the scope of that derogation.

(20) Appropriate measures should be provided, i.e. effective and practical measures to adapt the workplace to the disability, for example adapting premises and equipment, patterns of working time, the distribution of tasks or the provision of training or integration resources.

(21) To determine whether the measures in question give rise to a disproportionate burden, account should be taken in particular of the financial and other costs entailed, the scale and financial resources of the organization or undertaking and the possibility of obtaining public funding or any other assistance.

(22) This Directive is without prejudice to national laws on marital status and the benefits dependent thereon.

(23) In very limited circumstances, a difference of treatment may be justified where a characteristic related to religion or belief, disability, age or sexual orientation constitutes a genuine and determining occupational requirement, when the objective is legitimate and the requirement is proportionate. Such circumstances should be included in the information provided by the Member States to the Commission.

(24) The European Union in its Declaration No 11 on the status of churches and non-confessional organisations, annexed to the Final Act of the Amsterdam Treaty, has explicitly recognised that it respects and does not prejudice the status under national law of churches and religious associations or communities in the Member States and that it equally respects the status of philosophical and non-confessional organisations. With this in view, Member States may maintain or lay down specific provisions on

genuine, legitimate and justified occupational requirements which might be required forcarrying out an occupational activity.

(25) The prohibition of age discrimination is an essential part of meeting the aims set out in the Employment Guidelines and encouraging diversity in the workforce. However, differences in treatment in connection with age may be justified under certain circumstances and therefore require specific provisions which may vary in accordance with the situation in Member States. It is therefore essential to distinguish between differences in treatment which are justified, in particular by legitimate employment policy, labour market and vocational training objectives, and discrimination which must be prohibited.

(26) The prohibition of discrimination should be without prejudice to the maintenance or adoption of measures intended to prevent or compensate for disadvantages suffered by a group of persons of a particular religion or belief, disability, age or sexual orientation, and such measures may permit organisations of persons of a particular religion or belief, disability, age or sexual orientation where their main object is the promotion of the special needs of those persons.

(27) In its Recommendation 86/379/EEC of 24 July 1986 on the employment of disabled people in the Community,[7] the Council established a guideline framework setting out examples of positive action to promote the employment and training of disabled people, and in its Resolution of 17 June 1999 on equal employment opportunities for people with disabilities,[8] affirmed the importance of giving specific attention inter alia to recruitment, retention, training and lifelong learning with regard to disabled persons.

(28) This Directive lays down minimum requirements, thus giving the Member States the option of introducing or maintaining more favourable provisions. The implementation of this Directive should not serve to justify any regression in relation to the situation which already prevails in each Member State.

(29) Persons who have been subject to discrimination based on religion or belief, disability, age or sexual orientation should have adequate means of legal protection. To provide a more effective level of protection, associations or legal entities should also be empowered to engage in proceedings, as the Member States so determine, either on behalf or in support of any victim, without prejudice to national rules of procedure concerning representation and defence before the courts.

(30) The effective implementation of the principle of equality requires adequate judicial protection against victimisation.

(31) The rules on the burden of proof must be adapted when there is a prima facie case of discrimination and, for the principle of equal treatment to be applied effectively, the burden of proof must shift back to the respondent when evidence of such discrimination is brought. However, it is not for the respondent to prove that the plaintiff adheres to a particular religion or belief, has a particular disability, is of a particular age or has a particular sexual orientation.

(32) Member States need not apply the rules on the burden of proof to proceedings in which it is for the court or other competent body to investigate the facts of the case. The procedures thus referred to are those in which the plaintiff is not required to prove the facts, which it is for the court or competent body to investigate.

---

[7] OJ L 225, 12.8.1986, p. 43.

[8] OJ C 186, 2.7.1999, p. 3.

(33) Member States should promote dialogue between the social partners and, within the framework of national practice, with non-governmental organisations to address different forms of discrimination at the workplace and to combat them.
(34) The need to promote peace and reconciliation between the major communities in Northern Ireland necessitates the incorporation of particular provisions into this Directive.
(35) Member States should provide for effective, proportionate and dissuasive sanctions in case of breaches of the obligations under this Directive.
(36) Member States may entrust the social partners, at their joint request, with the implementation of this Directive, as regards the provisions concerning collective agreements, provided they take any necessary steps to ensure that they are at all times able to guarantee the results required by this Directive.
(37) In accordance with the principle of subsidiarity set out in Article 5 of the EC Treaty, the objective of this Directive, namely the creation within the Community of a level playing field as regards equality in employment and occupation, cannot be sufficiently achieved by the Member States and can therefore, by reason of the scale and impact of the action, be better achieved at Community level. In accordance with the principle of proportionality, as set out in that Article, this Directive does not go beyond what is necessary in order to achieve that objective.

Has adopted this Directive:

Chapter I

General Provisions

Article 1

Purpose

The purpose of this Directive is to lay down a general framework for combating discrimination on the grounds of religion or belief, disability, age or sexual orientation as regards employment and occupation, with a view to putting into effect in the Member States the principle of equal treatment.

Article 2

Concept of discrimination

1. For the purposes of this Directive, the 'principle of equal treatment' shall mean that there shall be no direct or indirect discrimination whatsoever on any of the grounds referred to in Article 1.
2. For the purposes of paragraph 1:
   (a) direct discrimination shall be taken to occur where one person is treated less favourably than another is, has been or would be treated in a comparable situation, on any of the grounds referred to in Article 1;
   (b) indirect discrimination shall be taken to occur where an apparently neutral provision, criterion or practice would put persons having a particular religion or belief, a

particular disability, a particular age, or a particular sexual orientation at a particular disadvantage compared with other persons unless:

(i) that provision, criterion or practice is objectively justified by a legitimate aim and the means of achieving that aim are appropriate and necessary, or

(ii) as regards persons with a particular disability, the employer or any person or organisation to whom this Directive applies, is obliged, under national legislation, to take appropriate measures in line with the principles contained in Article 5 in order to eliminate disadvantages entailed by such provision, criterion or practice.

3. Harassment shall be deemed to be a form of discrimination within the meaning of paragraph 1, when unwanted conduct related to any of the grounds referred to in Article 1 takes place with the purpose or effect of violating the dignity of a person and of creating an intimidating, hostile, degrading, humiliating or offensive environment. In this context, the concept of harassment may be defined in accordance with the national laws and practice of the Member States.
4. An instruction to discriminate against persons on any of the grounds referred to in Article 1 shall be deemed to be discrimination within the meaning of paragraph 1.
5. This Directive shall be without prejudice to measures laid down by national law which, in a democratic society, are necessary for public security, for the maintenance of public order and the prevention of criminal offences, for the protection of health and for the protection of the rights and freedoms of others.

Article 3

Scope

1. Within the limits of the areas of competence conferred on the Community, this Directive shall apply to all persons, as regards both the public and private sectors, including public bodies, in relation to:

   (a) conditions for access to employment, to self-employment or to occupation, including selection criteria and recruitment conditions, whatever the branch of activity and at all levels of the professional hierarchy, including promotion;

   (b) access to all types and to all levels of vocational guidance, vocational training, advanced vocational training and retraining, including practical work experience;

   (c) employment and working conditions, including dismissals and pay;

   (d) membership of, and involvement in, an organisation of workers or employers, or any organisation whose members carry on a particular profession, including the benefits provided for by such organisations.
2. This Directive does not cover differences of treatment based on nationality and is without prejudice to provisions and conditions relating to the entry into and residence of third-country nationals and stateless persons in the territory of Member States, and to any treatment which arises from the legal status of the third-country nationals and stateless persons concerned.
3. This Directive does not apply to payments of any kind made by state schemes or similar, including state social security or social protection schemes.
4. Member States may provide that this Directive, in so far as it relates to discrimination on the grounds of disability and age, shall not apply to the armed forces.

Article 4

Occupational requirements

1. Notwithstanding Article 2(1) and (2), Member States may provide that a difference of treatment which is based on a characteristic related to any of the grounds referred to in Article 1 shall not constitute discrimination where, by reason of the nature of the particular occupational activities concerned or of the context in which they are carried out, such a characteristic constitutes a genuine and determining occupational requirement, provided that the objective is legitimate and the requirement is proportionate.
2. Member States may maintain national legislation in force at the date of adoption of this Directive or provide for future legislation incorporating national practices existing at the date of adoption of this Directive pursuant to which, in the case of occupational activities within churches and other public or private organisations the ethos of which is based on religion or belief, a difference of treatment based on a person's religion or belief shall not constitute discrimination where, by reason of the nature of these activities or of the context in which they are carried out, a person's religion or belief constitute a genuine, legitimate and justified occupational requirement, having regard to the organisation's ethos. This difference of treatment shall be implemented taking account of Member States' constitutional provisions and principles, as well as the general principles of Community law, and should not justify discrimination on another ground.

Provided that its provisions are otherwise complied with, this Directive shall thus not prejudice the right of churches and other public or private organisations, the ethos of which is based on religion or belief, acting in conformity with national constitutions and laws, to require individuals working for them to act in good faith and with loyalty to the organisation's ethos.

Article 5

Reasonable accommodation for disabled persons

In order to guarantee compliance with the principle of equal treatment in relation to persons with disabilities, reasonable accommodation shall be provided. This means that employers shall take appropriate measures, where needed in a particular case, to enable a person with a disability to have access to, participate in, or advance in employment, or to undergo training, unless such measures would impose a disproportionate burden on the employer. This burden shall not be disproportionate when it is sufficiently remedied by measures existing within the framework of the disability policy of the Member State concerned.

Article 6

Justification of differences of treatment on grounds of age

1. Notwithstanding Article 2(2), Member States may provide that differences of treatment on grounds of age shall not constitute discrimination, if, within the context of national law, they are objectively and reasonably justified by a legitimate aim, including legitimate employment policy, labour market and vocational training objectives, and if the means of achieving that aim are appropriate and necessary.

Such differences of treatment may include, among others:

(a) the setting of special conditions on access to employment and vocational training, employment and occupation, including dismissal and remuneration conditions, for

young people, older workers and persons with caring responsibilities in order to promote their vocational integration or ensure their protection;
(b) the fixing of minimum conditions of age, professional experience or seniority in service for access to employment or to certain advantages linked to employment;
(c) the fixing of a maximum age for recruitment which is based on the training requirements of the post in question or the need for a reasonable period of employment before retirement.

2. Notwithstanding Article 2(2), Member States may provide that the fixing for occupational social security schemes of ages for admission or entitlement to retirement or invalidity benefits, including the fixing under those schemes of different ages for employees or groups or categories of employees, and the use, in the context of such schemes, of age criteria in actuarial calculations, does not constitute discrimination on the grounds of age, provided this does not result in discrimination on the grounds of sex.

Article 7

Positive action

1. With a view to ensuring full equality in practice, the principle of equal treatment shall not prevent any Member State from maintaining or adopting specific measures to prevent or compensate for disadvantages linked to any of the grounds referred to in Article 1.
2. With regard to disabled persons, the principle of equal treatment shall be without prejudice to the right of Member States to maintain or adopt provisions on the protection of health and safety at work or to measures aimed at creating or maintaining provisions or facilities for safeguarding or promoting their integration into the working environment.

Article 8

Minimum requirements

1. Member States may introduce or maintain provisions which are more favourable to the protection of the principle of equal treatment than those laid down in this Directive.
2. The implementation of this Directive shall under no circumstances constitute grounds for a reduction in the level of protection against discrimination already afforded by Member States in the fields covered by this Directive.

Chapter II

Remedies and Enforcement

Article 9

Defence of rights

1. Member States shall ensure that judicial and/or administrative procedures, including where they deem it appropriate conciliation procedures, for the enforcement of obligations under this Directive are available to all persons who consider themselves wronged by failure to apply the principle of equal treatment to them, even after the relationship in which the discrimination is alleged to have occurred has ended.

2. Member States shall ensure that associations, organisations or other legal entities which have, in accordance with the criteria laid down by their national law, a legitimate interest in ensuring that the provisions of this Directive are complied with, may engage, either on behalf or in support of the complainant, with his or her approval, in any judicial and/or administrative procedure provided for the enforcement of obligations under this Directive.
3. Paragraphs 1 and 2 are without prejudice to national rules relating to time limits for bringing actions as regards the principle of equality of treatment.

Article 10

Burden of proof

1. Member States shall take such measures as are necessary, in accordance with their national judicial systems, to ensure that, when persons who consider themselves wronged because the principle of equal treatment has not been applied to them establish, before a court or other competent authority, facts from which it may be presumed that there has been direct or indirect discrimination, it shall be for the respondent to prove that there has been no breach of the principle of equal treatment.
2. Paragraph 1 shall not prevent Member States from introducing rules of evidence which are more favourable to plaintiffs.
3. Paragraph 1 shall not apply to criminal procedures.
4. Paragraphs 1, 2 and 3 shall also apply to any legal proceedings commenced in accordance with Article 9(2).
5. Member States need not apply paragraph 1 to proceedings in which it is for the court or competent body to investigate the facts of the case.

Article 11

Victimisation

Member States shall introduce into their national legal systems such measures as are necessary to protect employees against dismissal or other adverse treatment by the employer as a reaction to a complaint within the undertaking or to any legal proceedings aimed at enforcing compliance with the principle of equal treatment.

Article 12

Dissemination of information

Member States shall take care that the provisions adopted pursuant to this Directive, together with the relevant provisions already in force in this field, are brought to the attention of the persons concerned by all appropriate means, for example at the workplace, throughout their territory.

Article 13

Social dialogue

1. Member States shall, in accordance with their national traditions and practice, take adequate measures to promote dialogue between the social partners with a view to fostering equal treatment, including through the monitoring of workplace practices, collective agreements, codes of conduct and through research or exchange of experiences and good practices.

2. Where consistent with their national traditions and practice, Member States shall encourage the social partners, without prejudice to their autonomy, to conclude at the appropriate level agreements laying down anti-discrimination rules in the fields referred to in Article 3 which fall within the scope of collective bargaining. These agreements shall respect the minimum requirements laid down by this Directive and by the relevant national implementing measures.

Article 14

Dialogue with non-governmental organisations

Member States shall encourage dialogue with appropriate non-governmental organisations which have, in accordance with their national law and practice, a legitimate interest in contributing to the fight against discrimination on any of the grounds referred to in Article 1 with a view to promoting the principle of equal treatment.

Chapter III

PARTICULAR PROVISIONS

Article 15

Northern Ireland

1. In order to tackle the under-representation of one of the major religious communities in the police service of Northern Ireland, differences in treatment regarding recruitment into that service, including its support staff, shall not constitute discrimination in so far as those differences in treatment are expressly authorised by national legislation.
2. In order to maintain a balance of opportunity in employment for teachers in Northern Ireland while furthering the reconciliation of historical divisions between the major religious communities there, the provisions on religion or belief in this Directive shall not apply to the recruitment of teachers in schools in Northern Ireland in so far as this is expressly authorised by national legislation.

Chapter IV

FINAL PROVISIONS

Article 16

Compliance

Member States shall take the necessary measures to ensure that:

(a) any laws, regulations and administrative provisions contrary to the principle of equal treatment are abolished;

(b) any provisions contrary to the principle of equal treatment which are included in contracts or collective agreements, internal rules of undertakings or rules governing the independent occupations and professions and workers' and employers' organisations are, or may be, declared null and void or are amended.

Article 17

Sanctions

Member States shall lay down the rules on sanctions applicable to infringements of the national provisions adopted pursuant to this Directive and shall take all measures necessary to ensure that they are applied. The sanctions, which may comprise the payment of compensation to the victim, must be effective, proportionate and dissuasive. Member States shall notify those provisions to the Commission by 2 December 2003 at the latest and shall notify it without delay of any subsequent amendment affecting them.

Article 18

Implementation

Member States shall adopt the laws, regulations and administrative provisions necessary to comply with this Directive by 2 December 2003 at the latest or may entrust the social partners, at their joint request, with the implementation of this Directive as regards provisions concerning collective agreements. In such cases, Member States shall ensure that, no later than 2 December 2003, the social partners introduce the necessary measures by agreement, the Member States concerned being required to take any necessary measures to enable them at any time to be in a position to guarantee the results imposed by this Directive. They shall forthwith inform the Commission thereof.

In order to take account of particular conditions, Member States may, if necessary, have an additional period of 3 years from 2 December 2003, that is to say a total of 6 years, to implement the provisions of this Directive on age and disability discrimination. In that event they shall inform the Commission forthwith. Any Member State which chooses to use this additional period shall report annually to the Commission on the steps it is taking to tackle age and disability discrimination and on the progress it is making towards implementation. The Commission shall report annually to the Council.

When Member States adopt these measures, they shall contain a reference to this Directive or be accompanied by such reference on the occasion of their official publication. The methods of making such reference shall be laid down by Member States.

Article 19

Report

1. Member States shall communicate to the Commission, by 2 December 2005 at the latest and every five years thereafter, all the information necessary for the Commission to draw up a report to the European Parliament and the Council on the application of this Directive.
2. The Commission's report shall take into account, as appropriate, the viewpoints of the social partners and relevant non-governmental organisations. In accordance with the principle of gender mainstreaming, this report shall, inter alia, provide an assessment of the impact of the measures taken on women and men. In the light of the information received, this report shall include, if necessary, proposals to revise and update this Directive.

Article 20

Entry into force

This Directive shall enter into force on the day of its publication in the *Official Journal of the European Communities.*

Article 21

Addressees

This Directive is addressed to the Member States.

Done at Brussels, 27 November 2000.

For the Council
The President
É. GUIGOU

APPENDIX 5

Disability Discrimination Act Cases

The cases listed below are a selection of disability discrimination cases from the Employment Appeal Tribunal, Court of Appeal and House of Lords. Disability was not in dispute in all of the cases and not all of the cases concern discrimination in the context of employment.

Adjustment disorder

HM Prison Service v Johnson [2007] IRLR 951.
Swift v Chief Constable of Wiltshire Constabulary [2004] IRLR 540.

Anxiety and stress

HM Prison Service v Johnson [2007] IRLR 951.
Woodrup v London Borough of Southwark [2003] IRLR 111, CA.
Morgan v Staffordshire University [2002] IRLR 190, EAT.
Edwards v Mid Suffolk District Council [2001] IRLR 190, EAT.
Callagan v Glasgow City Council [2001] IRLR 724, EAT.

Asthma

Canary Wharf Management Ltd v Edebi [2006] IRLR 416, EAT.
Cruickshank v Vaw Motorcast Ltd [2002] IRLR 24, EAT.

Attention deficit hyperactivity disorder

Governing Body of X School v SP and Another [2008] EWHC 389.
R (on the application of N by her mother and litigation friend SP) v Independent Appeal Panel and Dagenham London Borough Council [2008] EWHC 390.

Autistic spectrum disorder (autism)

Hewett v Motorola Ltd [2004] IRLR 545, EAT.

Back-related problems

Butt v Children and Family Court Advisory and Support Services [2008] All ER (D) 239, EAT.

Environment Agency v Rowan [2008] IRLR 20, EAT.

Hart v Chief Constable of Derbyshire Constabulary [2007] All ER (D) 78, EAT.

Hospice of St Mary of Furness v Howard [2007] IRLR 944, EAT.

Smith v Churchill Stairlifts plc [2006] IRLR 41, CA.

Bond v Hackney Citizens Advice Bureau [2003] IRLR 484, HL.

Wilding v British Telecommunications plc [2002] IRLR 524, CA.

Law Hospitals NHS Trust v Rush [2001] IRLR 611, CS.

Kent County Council v Mingo [2000] IRLR 90, EAT.

Clark v TDG Ltd t/a Novacold [1999] IRLR 318, CA.

Harvey v Port of Tilbury London Ltd [1999] IRLR 693, EAT.

Bipolar affective disorder

Surrey Police v Marshall [2002] IRLR 843, EAT.

Blackouts

Morse v Wiltshire County Council [1998] IRLR 352, EAT.

Bulimia nervosa

Commissioner of Police of the Metropolis v Harley [2001] IRLR 263, EAT.

Cancer

Kirton v Tetrosyl Ltd [2003] IRLR 353, CA.

Cerebral palsy

Kenny v Hampshire Constabulary [1999] IRLR 76, EAT.

Charcot-Marie-Tooth disease

Weaver v Chief Constable of Lincolnshire Police [2008] All ER (D) 291, EAT.

Deafness

Taylor v OCS Group Ltd [2006] IRLR 613, CA.

Abadeh v British Telecommunications plc [2001] IRLR 23, EAT.

Canniffe v East Riding of Yorkshire Council [2000] IRLR 555, EAT.

Depression (see also Bipolar affective disorder above)

Heggie v Secretary of State for Work and Pensions [2008] All ER (D) 67.

Dolan v Chief Constable of Avon & Somerset Constabulary [2008] All ER (D)309, EAT.

Department for Constitutional Affairs v Jones [2008] IRLR 128, CA.

Pavlou v Governors of the Lord Grey School [2007] All ER (D) 249, EAT.

O'Hanlon v Commissioners for HM Revenue & Customs [IRLR] 404, CA.

Greenhof v Barnsley Metropolitan Borough Council [2006] IRLR 98, EAT.

Royal Liverpool Children's NHS Trust v Dunsby [2006] IRLR 351, EAT.

Tarbuck v Sainsbury's Supermarkets Ltd [2006] IRLR 664, EAT.

Atos Origin IT Services UK Ltd v Haddock [2005] IRLR 20, EAT.

HM Prison Service v Beart [2005] IRLR 171, *HM Prison Service v Beart (No. 2)* [2005] IRLR 568, CA, *Beart v HM Prison Service* [2003] IRLR 238, CA.

Edmund Nuttall Ltd v Butterfield [2005] IRLR 751, EAT.

Power v Panasonic UK Ltd [2003] IRLR 151, EAT.

Relaxion Group plc v Rhys-Harper; D'Souza v Lambeth London Borough Council; Jones v 3M Healthcare Ltd and other appeals [2003] IRLR 484, HL.

Leonard v Southern Derbyshire Chamber of Commerce [2001] IRLR 19, EAT.

Cosgrove v Caesar & Howie [2001] IRLR 653, EAT.

Kapadia v London Borough of Lambeth [2000] IRLR 699, CA.

London Borough of Hammersmith & Fulham v Farnsworth [2000] IRLR 691, EAT.

Greenwood v British Airways plc. [1999] IRLR 600, EAT.

Diabetes

Wright v Croydon London Borough Council [2007] All ER (D).

Macklin v Secretary of State for Work and Pensions [2008] All ER(D) 413, EAT.

Jones v Post Office [2001] IRLR 384, CA.

Abbey Life Assurance Co Ltd v Tansell [2000] IRLR 387, CA.

Dyslexia

Rawson v Doncaster NHS Primary Care Trust [2008] All ER (D) 106, EAT.

Paterson v Commission of Police of the Metropolis [2007] IRLR 763, EAT.

Wright v Croydon London Borough Council [2007] All ER (D).

Aon Training Ltd (formerly Totalamber plc) v Dore [2005] IRLR 891, CA.

Eczema

Lawrence v HM Prison Service [2007] IRLR 468, EAT.

Exhibitionism

Edmund Nuttall Ltd v Butterfield [2005] IRLR 751.

Epilepsy

British Gas Services Ltd v McCaull [2001] IRLR 60, EAT.

Ridout v TC Group [1998] IRLR 628, EAT.

Functional overlay

McNicol v Balfour Bty Rail Maintenance Ltd [2002] IRLR 711, CA.

Rugamer v Sony Music Entertainment UK Ltd [2001] IRLR 644, EAT.

Functional dysphonia

Southampton City College v Randall [2006] IRLR 18, EAT.

Gynaecological problems

Royal Liverpool Children's NHS Trust v Dunsby [2006] IRLR 351, EAT.

Hand-related disabilities

Collins v Royal National Thre Board Ltd [2004] IRLR 395, CA.

Ekpe v Commissioner of Police of the Metropolis [2001] IRLR 605, EAT.

Baynton v Saurus General Engineers Ltd [1999] IRLR 604, EAT.

Morse v Wiltshire County Council [1998] IRLR 352, EAT.

Headaches/migraines

Royal Liverpool Children's NHS Trust v Dunsby [2006] IRLR 351, EAT.

London Clubs Management Ltd v Hood [2001] IRLR 719, EAT.

Heart problems

Murphy v Slough Borough Council [2005] IRLR 382, CA.

Leg/lower limb-related problems

Scott v British Gas Trading Ltd [2008] All ER (D) 135, EAT.

Gichura v Home Office [2008] All ER (D) 257, CA.

Al Jumard v Clwyd Leisure Ltd & Ors [2008] IRLR 345, EAT.

Carden v Pickerings Europe Ltd [2005] IRLR 720, EAT.

Archibald v Fife Council [2004] IRLR 651, HL.

Fu v London Borough of Camden [2001] IRLR 186, EAT.

Morse v Wiltshire County Council [1998] IRLR 352, EAT.

Learning difficulties

Dunham v Ashford Windows [2005] IRLR 608, EAT.

Lupus

Price-Job v Camden London Borough Council [2007] All ER (D) 259, EAT.
Robinson v Post Office [2000] IRLR 804, EAT.

ME/chronic fatigue syndrome

O'Neill v Symm & Co Ltd [1998] IRLR 233, EAT.

Miscellaneous mental impairments

Richmond Adult Community College v McDougall [2008] IRLR 227, CA, EAT.

Multiple sclerosis

Mowat-Brown v University of Surrey [2002] IRLR 235, EAT.
Buxton v Equinox Design Ltd [1999] IRLR 158, EAT.

Muscle fasciculation

College of Ripon & York St John v Hobbs [2002] IRLR 185, EAT.

Obsessive compulsive personality disorder

Floyd v S [2008] 1 WLR 1274, CA.
Abbey National Plc v Fairbrother [2007] IRLR 320, EAT.

Osteoarthritis

Burton v Higham t/a Ace Appointments [2003] IRLR 257, EAT.

Parkinson's disease

Rothwell v Pelikan Hardcopy Scotland Ltd [2006] IRLR 24, EAT.

Personality disorder

Stages v Jackson & Canter [2008] All ER (D), EAT.

Photophobia

Millar v Inland Revenue Commissioners [2006] IRLR 112, CS.

Ptosis

Millar v Inland Revenue Commissioners [2006] IRLR 112, CS.

Post-traumatic stress disorder

Abadeh v British Telecommunications plc [2001] IRLR 23, EAT.

Post-viral fatigue syndrome

Edwards v Mid Suffolk District Council [2001] IRLR 190, EAT.

Rheumatoid arthritis

South East Sheffield Citizens Advice Bureau v Grayson [2004] IRLR 353, EAT.

Catherall v Michelin Tyre plc [2003] IRLR 61, EAT.

Quinn v Schwarzkopf Ltd [2002] IRLR 602, CS.

Schizophrenia

Lewisham London Borough Council v Malcolm UKHL 43, [2008] 4 All ER525, [2008] 3 WLR 194 [2008] IRLR 700 HL.

Murray v Newham Citizens Advice Bureau Ltd [2003] IRLR 340, EAT.

Goodwin v The Patent Office [1999] IRLR 4, EAT.

Shoulder-related problems

Croal v Network Rail Infrastructure [2008] All ER (D) 411, EAT.

Skin condition

Cosgrove v Caesar Howie [2007] IRLR 397, EAT.

Speech difficulties

Mid Staffordshire General Hospitals NHS Trust v Cambridge [2003] IRLR 566, EAT.

Stammer

Spillett v Tesco Stores Ltd [2006] IRLR 248, (jointly reported with *BUPA Care Homes (BNH) Ltd v Cann* [2006] IRLR 248), EAT.

Tinnitus

Abadeh v British Telecommunications plc [2001] IRLR 23, EAT.

Upper arm condition

Vicary v British Telecommunications plc [1999] IRLR 680, EAT.

Urinary incontinence

Kirton v Tetrosyl Ltd [2003] IRLR 353, CA.

Visual impairment

Project Management Institute v Latif [2007] IRLR 579, EAT.

Virdi v Commissioner of Police of the Metropolis [2007] IRLR 24, EAT.

Williams v J Walter Thompson Group Ltd [2005] IRLR 376, CA.

Nottinghamshire County Council v Meikle [2004] IRLR 703, CA.

Purves v Joydisc Ltd [2003] IRLR 420, Sh Ct.

Kirker v British Sugar plc, [1998] IRLR 624, EAT.

Rose v Bouchet [1999] IRLR 463, Sh Ct.

INDEX